Re-authoring Teaching

Re-authoring Teaching

Creating a Collaboratory

Peggy Sax
Middlebury, Vermont, USA

SENSE PUBLISHERS
ROTTERDAM / TAIPEI

A C.I.P. record for this book is available from the Library of Congress.

ISBN 978-90-8790-448-7 (paperback)
ISBN 978-90-8790-449-4 (hardback)
ISBN 978-90-8790-450-0 (e-book)

Published by: Sense Publishers,
P.O. Box 21858, 3001 AW
Rotterdam, The Netherlands
http://www.sensepublishers.com

Printed on acid-free paper

This book is dedicated to Michael White, whose death just as this book was going to press was a terrible shock to me. His wisdom and counsel over the years reverberate throughout my writing. When I turned to Michael as I was struggling with an earlier draft, he advised me to write in my own voice. I hope that I have been true to these words. Thank you, Michael, for everything.

ABOUT THE AUTHOR

Peggy Sax, PhD, is in independent practice in Middlebury, Vermont, USA, as a licensed psychologist, consultant, workshop presenter and university instructor. An enthusiastic teacher, Peggy feels privileged for opportunities to share powerful stories of learnings from over 30 years of work with families and their children, teens, adults, couples, communities and students of all ages.

TABLE OF CONTENTS

ACKNOWLEDGEMENTS

I began writing these acknowledgements while eagerly awaiting the birth of my first grandchild. It seems that not so long ago, I was the one in labor. And I was the practitioner-in-training, beginning my apprenticeship to human services. With a blink of the eyes, I have skipped into an older generation. Writing this book marks a new step on this journey. Many people and fortuitous events have paved the way. It is with a heart of gratefulness that I write these acknowledgements.

Over 100 people contributed to this book, traversing roles of teacher, student, client, guest visitor and manuscript reviewer. I strived to write a book reflective of the values that guide my work as a practitioner and teacher – to convey how much I learn from the people who consult with me and who are my students. Together, we illustrate how the designated roles of teacher, student and client all take turns learning from each other. I believe these multiple perspectives are at the heart of what makes this book special.

I cannot imagine having written this book without the help of my friend and mentor, David Epston. Through email communication, David has made himself completely available to me. He found me a publisher, reviewed my drafts and wrote the foreword. Through his enthusiasm for the manuscript, he connected me with people in various parts of the world. At my request, he shared draft chapters with his partner, Ann, and together they conveyed their enthusiastic support. I am deeply grateful to both of them.

I had always heard that writing is a lonely endeavor. While I certainly experienced some isolation, I also found a powerfully sustaining sense of connection with the people that joined me in this effort. Often I acted as a facilitator within a web of connection – bringing together contributors' unique voices with guiding principles parallel to the construction of a "learning collaboratory," (I explain the word "collaboratory" in Chapter One). I then worked to shape a structure that would allow people to speak for themselves. Incredible energy and generosity of spirit carried this labor of love through multiple revisions.

I spent many weekends writing in indoor solitude, withdrawing from companionship and outdoor splendors. I lost close touch with dear friends, family and my community. I am especially grateful to my husband, Shel Sax, for sticking by me through this project. He has been most impacted by my myopic illusion that this book is the Center of the Universe. Now, as I aim to return to a more balanced life, I hope my friends will welcome me back, and forgive me for my absence.

I once heard the author Isabel Allende respond to a question about how she got so much done. "I have the gift of insomnia" was her reply. I too have this "gift"; I relied heavily on early morning risings and stolen evening hours to get this project done. While writing and revising, I have watched sunrises over the Green Mountains from my home office window, early mists rising on the St. Lawrence

ACKNOWLEDGEMENTS

River from Monica Behan and Deron Johnson's island retreat, ocean views from across the harbor on the coast of Maine, and sunsets from the porch of friend Alex Wylie's Lake Champlain cottage. While traveling with my laptop, I also worked in airports, anonymous hotel rooms and coffee shops.

I am a fan of Helen Keller, who said, "Alone we can do so little; together we can do so much." I could not have completed this book without the people who lent their voices to this project. I strived to do justice to what students, clients and guest visitors have shared with me. So many people have generously contributed that I fear I will either forget to acknowledge someone or incorrectly convey their words or their meaning. If I have in any way misrepresented anyone's voice, please let me know.

Helen Keller also said, "Although the world is full of suffering, it is also full of the overcoming of it." The people in this book shared intimate tales of their efforts to overcome suffering so we can learn from their experiences. I am particularly grateful to Alan, Josie, Mylo, Kate, Nicole, Chava, Ruth, Leah, and Meghan. I have also borrowed voices from my dissertation research project – those of Pamela, Isabelle, Lori, Pru, and Pam – mothers of children with special needs, who generously share some hard-earned wisdom in the search for "finding common ground" with human service providers and planners. There is no way I could put into words what I have learned from all of you and how you inspire me in my daily life.

I greatly appreciate the students who graciously allowed me to include their work in this book. Tracking down students was no small feat, and I was aided by several students and alumni offices. Mohammad Arefina (Smith) and Ellen Williams (University of Vermont) truly extended themselves to help me email addresses, as did Ken Bechtel from the UVM Social Work Department, Pat Gilbert from the Smith Alumni Office, and Tim Etchells from the Middlebury College Alumni Office. With former students' permission, I borrowed archived material from course websites from the UVM Social Work Department (WebCT), Smith College School of Social Work (Blackboard) and Middlebury College Psychology Department (Seque). Getting back in touch with these students was so invigorating for me. I hope that seeing their words in published form will deepen their understanding as to why I (and others) learn so much from them. This book is a celebration of what we have created together.

As I describe in Chapter Six, "Peopling the Course," a number of invited guests have generously contributed to my courses at Smith, University of Vermont and Middlebury College. People drove long distances to come to my classes; their presence has invaluably informed this book's teaching and learning experiences. Other guests have engaged with students online. Guest visitors have included: Chris Beels, Chris Behan, Stephen Bradley, Betsy Buckley, Pam Doyle, Phil Decter, Jonathan Diamond, Lynn Hoffman, Peter Lebenbaum, Lee Monro, David Paré, Prudence Peace, Beth Prullage, Marc Werner-Gavrin and Jo Viljoen.

Throughout, I cite skillful teachers for ideas and practices in this book. Yet something falls short when my name becomes associated with collectively created material. As teachers, I greatly appreciate the spirit of generosity with which many colleagues share our teaching practices with each other. For me, this exchange began in 2002 with the formation of the Northern New England teaching group – Chris Behan, Betsy Buckley, Phil Decter and Steven Gilbert. I knew I could rely on anyone of them whenever I needed inspiration, problem solving or test piloting a new exercise. Behind the scenes, David Epston has given me invaluable guidance and support through teaching dilemmas.

I am particularly grateful to Dean Lobovits, Rick Maisel and Jenny Freeman for their article "Public Practices: An ethic of circulation" (Lobovits, 1995) that greatly informed my approach to therapy and teaching. The teaching faculty of the Dulwich Centre – Maggie Carey, Sue Mann, Shona Russell and Michael White— have given me many ideas for teaching narrative therapy. I have also been inspired by Cheryl White and David Denborough's creative talents, their organization of exceptional international gatherings, and their commitment to community practice. Others – Aileen Cheshire, Gene Combs, Jill Freedman, Dorothea Lewis, Bill Madsen, Wally McKenzie, Marilyn O'Neill, Sallyann Roth and Gaye Stockell – have influenced the development of specific exercises in this book.

David Epston likened my writing process to that of a carpenter building a piece of furniture – "sanding" through multiple drafts until the grain of the writing appears. I greatly admire Lynn Hoffman's writing, and was relieved when she told me she always does multiple drafts. My uncle and cousin, Lou and Roger Lowenstein are both authors. When I was immersed in redrafts, my Uncle Lou reminded me, "A book gets finished many times." And Roger attributed to Hemmingway, "An author publishes to stop rewriting."

Anne Lezak deserves a heartfelt thank you for her skillful editing, which has hugely contributed to this manuscript. Her specific suggestions and our ensuing conversations sustained me through the multiple revisions. She challenged me to write more clearly and without jargon. When I needed additional editing help, Ikey Spear, Anne Geroski and Anne Wallace immediately came to my aid. Peter de Liefde, publisher and general manager of Sense Publishers, stuck with me through many email exchanges, until the quality of all aspects of the book matched my high standards for excellence.

Each reviewer respectfully gave suggestions from a different angle. Several students reviewed earlier drafts of this manuscript. I want to especially thank Mohammad Arefina, Piper Clyborne, Emma Gibbs, Sarah Marx, Elizabeth Parker, Bobbi Rood and Kerry Ann Shearman for their thoughtful review of draft chapters. I hope all see their influence on this final draft.

What a better world this would be if everyone had a friend like Chris Behan! Throughout several years of writing, Chris stayed in close touch with me – checking in to hear how the book was progressing, listening to details of recent developments and reviewing draft chapters. He lifted my spirits during writing retreats in Massachusetts, New York, New Hampshire and Maine.

I deeply appreciate additional colleagues, friends and family who generously extended themselves to thoughtfully review various drafts of this manuscript. Mary Brevda, Marta Campillo, Aileen Cheshire, Lynn Hoffman, Charley Lang, Bill Lax, Beth Prullage, and John Winslade all read the entire manuscript, despite competing pressures for their time. Others read and positively reviewed specific draft chapters: Lyndall Bass, Betsy Buckley, Phil Decter, Edith Fierst, Sonya Fierst, André Grégoire, Sarah Hughes, Devon Jersild, Penny Leikin, Rick Maisel, Jack Mayer, Margaret Olson, Shel Sax, Margarita Tarragona, Penny Tims, Jo Vilgoen, Alex Wylie, and Robin Young. Still others – Laura Basili, Frances Hancock, Sara Hirst, Thomas Jackson, Chip Mayer, Bill Madsen, David Paré and Michael White – gave moral support by periodically checking in with me for progress reports.

Fortuitous events regularly conspired to help me shape the manuscript into what it became. For example, Shel Sax kept me supplied with current literature on educational technology, and through our conversations, rather serendipitously introduced me to the word "Collaboratory"; Shel also came up with "Reauthoring Teaching" for the book title, a clever twist to narrative therapy's "reauthoring conversations." During phone conversations, Charley Lang offered the chapter headings, "Opening the Online Lens" and "Intentional Witnessing." Bill Lax guided me to use the most up-to-date language for my "blended learning" approach to teaching with an interactive website. On an autumn walk, Devon Jersild gave me invaluable writing tips to make room for multiple voices including dissent. Lynn Hoffman continually reminded me to be careful about my language, move away from jargon and edit down my verbosity.

Aileen Cheshire's enthusiasm for the manuscript carried me through long hours of writing – if she found it useful, I knew it was good. My understanding of the relevance of the apprenticeship metaphor for training practitioners was jumpstarted by correspondence several years ago with David Espton, Frances Hancock and Jo Vilgoen. As an independent reviewer for SensePublishing, John Winslade gave both supportive comments, and the kind of insider tips that only another writer could give. Jack Mayer, a pediatrician, encouraged me to share several chapters with physicians, medical students and psychiatric residents. Ongoing conversations with my son Jordan Sax about his medical school training gave me an insider view of pressures on health care and human service practitioners in the 21st Century, and the complex ethical dilemmas that require attention in all practitioners' training.

What is it about New Zealand and New Zealanders that so moves me? While collecting "blurbs" for the back cover, I suddenly realized that I had asked several people from New Zealand – Aileen Cheshire, David Epston and John Winslade. When I asked David if he thought that might be a problem, he responded, "Actually, I believe the world doesn't have enough New Zealand influence. Maybe that is the problem." I wholeheartedly agree. In addition to these New Zealanders, I am grateful to Dorothea Lewis for organizing my workshop at Unitec, which infused me with delight; Ann Epston for her warm hospitality and inquisitive interest in my work; Frances Hancock for her gracious hospitality, and for inspiring me with her fighting spirit and keen intellect; Jill Kelly for her warmhearted approach to technological assistance to David Epston and the Family Therapy Centre; Kathie Crochet for welcoming me into her home and introducing me to her colleagues at University of Waikato; and Wally and Bev McKenzie for living by example, reminding me to remain true to my values.

Acts of generosity have touched me again and again while working on this manuscript. My attorney brothers, Fred and David Fierst, reviewed my book contract. Heidi Ploof directed me to a song, "Unwritten," by Natasha Beddingfield, to listen to while working, reminding me that we are the authors of our own stories and that every day brings the possibility to write a new chapter. Jordan Sax took my photograph for the back cover. My two best friends from high school, Lyndall Bass and Robin Young, were steadfast cheerleaders.

Others might be surprised to hear of their influence on this book. Over the years, I have been mentored by remarkable people whose ongoing presence in my inner life inspires my approach to my work. Each is like a beacon of light, guiding me in a particular direction. I am especially grateful to Dana Brynelsen, the Provincial Advisor to British Columbia Infant Development Programmes, for living by example, a fierce, steadfast commitment to children and families. As co-director of the Addison County Parent-Child Center, Cheryl Mitchell embodied innovative ways of working with families in challenging situations; she continues to inspire me with her steadfast commitment to eradicating poverty in Vermont, and especially in our local community. Both Carolyn Carey and Naomi Tannen shepherded me into the wonderfully vibrant world of community mental health. Peter Lebenbaum, my clinical supervisor at The Counseling Service of Addison County, further demonstrated respectful ways of working with families. Tom Andersen and Dario Lussardi introduced me to the reflecting team and colla- borative approaches to family therapy. I learned a great deal about facilitation, community building, prevention and state government from my work in the 1990s with The Vermont Prevention Consultation Team – in particular, Bill Lofquist, Jack Pransky, Peter Perkins and Jane Vella. Through my work with the Learning Team for "Children Upstream Services" (CUPS) project, I experienced firsthand the creative energy and mutual respect that can emerge when a group of dedicated people (in this instance, all women) share leadership to design services consistent with a shared commitment to Vermont children, families and communities.

Through contact spanning 20 years, Lynn Hoffman's intellectual curiosity, intrigue with language, and feisty irreverence continue to inspire me. Two faculty at The Fielding Institute – Barnett Pearce and Peter Park – helped expand my understandings of collaborative approaches into work with communities and participatory research. I am very grateful to Michael White and David Epston, the co-founders of narrative therapy, for being continual sources of inspiration. Discovering their ideas and practices has had a pivotal influence on my thinking and work as a practitioner. What I learn watching each of their interviews with families is akin to what artists learn studying under a master painter. I am also grateful for our friendships, which have deepened my understandings of what is possible, and buoyed my self confidence.

I have always been drawn to strong women, and I would like to honor several women who may not realize their influence on me and my work. My mother, Edith Fierst, taught me to cultivate a passion for both family and work. I cherish my memories of enlightening and enlivening conversations with the Vermont-based group "The Venerable Mothers" – Mary Brevda, Hope Cannon, Darden Carr,

Randye Cohen, Sydney Crystal, Judy Davidson, Christine Dumont and Lee Monro – about bridging our personal and professional lives. I have been deeply inspired by my experiences of Melissa Elliott – as a presenter and humanitarian; seeing her in action has reinforced my commitment to living intentionally with lovingkindness, and taught me to honor and include the spiritual in my work. Sallyann Roth has shown me the power of conversation when coupling collaborative inquiry with thoughtful precision. I am inspired by Corky Becker's fierce commitment to her friendships, intellectual stimulation and to pursing her passions. My conversations with Shoshana Simons linger, reminding me to live life like an action research project with constant inquiry, on an edge of wonder. Through her embodiment of humility and astute intelligence, Brenda Bean inspires me to remember our shared commitment to improving systems of care for young children and their families in Vermont. Most recently, Leenah Joy inspires me daily with her wise, loving, and adventurous commitment to her spiritual life, despite daunting physical obstacles.

I would like to acknowledge additional copyrighted material in this book. Random House gave me permission to include in Chapter Fourteen, a favorite poem "To be of use" by Marge Piercy." Portions of Chapter Two, "Opening the Online Lens," originally appeared in Sax, P. (2003), "It takes an audience to solve a problem: Teaching narrative therapy online." New Zealand Social Work Review, XV(4), 21-29. An earlier version of Chapter Seven, "Stories of Identity," originally appeared in Sax, P. (2006) "Developing stories of identity as reflective practitioners," Journal of Systemic Therapies, Vol. 25, Issue 4, p. 59-72. Portions of Chapter Twelve, "Remember to ask," originally appeared in Sax, P. (2007) the Journal of Systemic Therapies, Finding Common Ground: Parents Speak out about Family Centered Practices. Vol. 26, Issue 3, p. 72-90.

For the photo on the book cover, I wanted to showcase the exquisite outdoor beauty of Vermont, my adopted home state. The landscape of changing seasons infuses our lives here with indescribable splendor, and creates a balance to the indoor world of educational technology. I envisioned a welcoming photo that takes the reader on a winding road into the colorful and mysterious open air. While spending a heavenly weekend cross-country skiing with friends Margaret Olson and Alex Wylie, we photographed every possible pose of winding Vermont roads in a winter landscape. When I later realized that not everyone finds inspiration in winter scenes, my attention turned to Vermont's deservedly famous fall foliage.

My artist friend, Lyndall Bass, encouraged me to find just the right photo for the cover. Searching the Internet, I fell in love with a photo by George Robinson. On his website, www.georgerobinson.com, George described how he took the photograph in Underhill, Vermont on an autumn morning, just as the fog was lifting. The original photograph was overexposed and of poor quality. However, he saved the chrome, and eventually computer technology (Photoshop) made it possible to capture the beauty of scene – the white birch tree offsetting the trees' true colors in a rising mist. I feel like this photo was made for this book. Every time I look at it, I find new meaning. With careful attention, it is indeed possible to use technology to enhance our quality of life. Even the raised flag on the mailbox reminds me of the now universal symbol for online communication "You've got mail!"

I am in awe of Kathy Milillo's talents as a graphic designer. Kathy's ability to express the tone of teaching experiences described in this book – warm, welcoming colors with room for multiple voices – has infused the book cover, marketing flyer and website.

While writing these acknowledgements, I learned of the death of a dear friend and cycling buddy, Mike Searle. A gifted therapist, conversationalist and philosopher of life, Mike spread wisdom and love everywhere and touched many lives. I would like to think that this book honors his spirit. Within the same 48 hours, my grandson, Nathan Michael Sax was born; he and his parents, Peter and Molly Sax, bring such indescribable joy to my life. I want to acknowledge the joy and sorrow in all of our lives.

Completing this book completes a circle. I am reminded of yet another Helen Keller quote, "When one door of happiness closes, another opens." Indeed, in completing this book project, I am already experiencing some new doors opening. I have started a website, www.reauthoringteaching.com, for readers to send reflections to any of the people who lent their stories to this book. I am talking with Dean Lobovits, David Epston and Suzanne Pregerson about linking this new website with www.narrativeapproaches. If there is sufficient interest, we envision developing a place in cyberspace for continuing this conversation – to learn from people who have been "to hell and back" about their experiences in overcoming serious problems and their tips for practitioners; to exchange ideas and practices about teaching collaborative therapies; to learn from each other about contributions of the online medium. If none of this yet makes sense (or even if it does), I think it's time to read the book. Enjoy!

FOREWORD

HOW I AM GOING TO RE-READ PEGGY'S BOOK

David Epston

As hard as I tried the first time to read this manuscript as an overseer, I found myself swept along with it. It was as if I were being carried along by a gentle current or outgoing tide. Where this was taking me, I did not entirely know, but I had no fear. Somehow or other I knew that I had boon travelling companions, even if we were very different ages or at different stages of our professional lives. Against my better judgment, I found myself falling in love with the people in this book. I was reminded of the mediaeval "scholares vagantes" (wandering scholars), with Peggy like a modern day tour guide whose itinerary was to have us travel from place to place, teacher to teacher, seeking wisdoms.

This had to do, in retrospect, with something so companionable about what was unfolding in my reading of the text. How often did I regret that many of the conversations had ended? How often did I find myself with an almost irresistible desire to join them by butting in? And how often did I anticipate what my companions would have come up with by way of their responses? In fact, I felt as if I had returned to the world of that young student appealing to Rainier Maria Rilke for instructions on how to become a poet like himself (Rilke, 1993):

You are so young, so much before all beginning, and I would like to beg you, dear sir, as well as I can, to have patience with everything unresolved in your heart and to try to love the questions themselves as if they were locked rooms or books written in very foreign language. Do not search for the answers, which could not be given to you now, because you would not be able to live them. And the point is, to live everything, live the questions now.

Rainer Maria Rilke, Letters to a Young Poet,
From letter four, July 16, 1903

I think I was falling in love again with the questions that I have lived and loved for so long. I suspect what Rilke may have been referring to here was that love associated with the amateur. I am thinking here of the original meaning of amateur – a lover of a subject who takes pleasure in what he or she is learning and not the more contemporary meaning of "lack of professional skill or expertise." Here many of the speakers seemed on the verge of invention or of thinking well beyond anything they might have considered before. They seemed gifted amateurs to me, and their commentaries, I observed, continually referred back to that which mattered to them in living their professional lives.

I have been pursuing Peggy's experimenting with teaching narrative therapy by the means she details in this text for several years now, as have several of my colleagues (Dorothea Lewis, Aileen Cheshire and Kay Ingamells) at the School of

Community Development, UNITEC Institute of Technology here in Auckland, New Zealand). Like them, I have been intrigued by the obvious results of her pedagogy, blending classroom teaching with Internet "conversations." I have been continually asking myself, "How is it possible for such a community of students to engage in such profound considerations of the ethics, politics and practice of narrative therapy in a matter of weeks or months? Why were they seemingly able to integrate what they were learning into the missions for their professional lives and the problematics of their internships and former or future workplaces? What has the blending of classroom and Internet conversations got to do with this?"

I was reminded of many academic conversations over my years that by comparison had been so formulaic, so tendentious and even tedious that I would have been reluctant to join even if I were invited to do so. This led to me taking the *Selected Dialogues of Plato* (Plato, 2001) down from my bookshelf. I wondered if much of the genre of western philosophical inquiry and subsequent pedagogy could perhaps be traced back to those "dialogues" Plato told of between Socrates and his fellow conversationalists in which:

> "..both parties must be willing to accept at any given moment that they are wrong, to find that their positions have reversed, or simply that they are left with no tenable position at all. What counts is the underlying loyalty and devotion to the quest for truth: this quest constitutes the closest approximation to truth or knowledge we can hope for."

"Introduction," *Selected Dialogues of Plato* (Pelliccia, 2001), p. xvii

I know on my second reading of Peggy's book, I will want to scrutinize the very means by which she co-evolved something so different than that. How had she shepherded such amiable conversations? I, nor doubtless any of the students involved, would suggest that such animated conversations came to pass merely by chance. Like any diligent shepherd, Peggy seemed to ensure that the conversations didn't stray so far as to risk getting lost as well as keeping the "flock" of conversations on the move, always seeking fresh pasture to avoid overgrazing. You may notice, reader, once you get carried away – and I certainly recommend you surrender to this your first reading through of this text – an insistent momentum, increasing week by week, meeting after meeting, and even one post after another. Once again, you may feel a strong sense of heading somewhere even if no final destination is known. Again, I doubt if this was accidental. Surely Peggy had something to do with this! But how was this sustained throughout each of her courses?

When I tried to find analogous conversations to those that were enthralling me on Peggy's various masters/bachelors courses, I was reminded of some, by now, almost lost arts: the scholar's diary and those correspondences undertaken by letter between life-long colleagues. Both of these genres had an intimacy, immediacy and humility about them, one written to oneself and the other to a like-minded person recording the journeys of their thinking, including of course that which troubled them. It seemed to me these genres privileged the inquiry itself over the conclusion that it finally reached in that they allowed the authors to show how they were making up their minds – a kind of thinking out loud – about the matters that concerned them. In each instance, they left traces of the history of their thought in these texts and made little attempt at final conclusions or grand schemes. Many of those who went on to publish texts out of such conversations would expunge this record, almost as if to admit to the vicissitudes of their thinking was a sign of intellectual weakness. Their final texts were written almost as if its conclusion came first.

If I had the chance, I would ask Peggy, students and visitors, "In your studies so far, had you aspired to the Platonic quest for the truth? If so, at what point in this course did you abandon seeking such a truth for 'truths'? When did you start referencing your inquiries to what mattered to you in the living of your professional life? Can you name an actual point – 'X' – when you replaced the Platonic quest for what might prove to do justice to your moral and ethical commitments? Was there some sort of template underwriting how you went about this course?" If so, might my next reading scrutinize how the genre of "outsider witnessing" practices (White, 1995) flows into almost everything that followed, yielding some form of resolution? It seemed to me that so many of the conversationalists would reference their moral commitments as a significant vantage point for their considerations.

I recall my horror at reading one of the best studies undertaken so far on becoming a professional practitioner in one of the healing arts – *Of Two Minds: An Anthropologist Looks At American Psychiatry* by Tanya Luhrmann, Professor of Social Thought at the University of Chicago (Luhrmann, 2000). Reading this book helps us consider how various pedagogies have us come to "see" those whom we intend to serve. It is important to note that Luhrmann is not in any way a critic of psychiatry but an avowed sympathizer. During her ethnographic studies, she went through seven years herself of pseudo-training as a psychiatrist. She tells how she "knew I was coming to see people in a different way (p. 4)." She relates the circumstances that contrived to result in such a specific kind of "seeing" of the other. To quote: "Young psychiatrists leave an internship with a clear sense of the difference between patient and doctor – that patients are the source of physical exhaustion, danger and humiliation and that doctors are superior and authoritative by virtue of their role (p. 93)."

I would guess that the experiences of Peggy's students couldn't have been more dissimilar than those reported by Luhrmann. For that reason, I resolve in my next reading to query how these students came not only to see themselves as professional practitioners but even more significantly, how did they come to "see" those who will seek their service? Did the fact that so-called "patients/clients" and their voices made very strong and at times unforgettable appearances, either in person or in their texts (eg., through videotapes, writings, and responses in the outsider witnessing protocol) make them super-real? Unlike the disembodied and frequently de-grading accounts common to many professional descriptions, these "patients" stand on their dignity, "knowledged"[1] and justifiably acknowledged by those of us who are privy to their accounts of themselves.

Luhrmann's ethnography gave me pause to reflect: Under what conditions in which we "train" and work would our respect for those who petition for help be inevitable? How could we develop intentional practices that might create and sustain mutual regard and the sense of community and solidarity that flows on from that?

Michael White, having accepted such an inspiration, makes a very good point:

And what of solidarity? I am thinking of a solidarity that is constructed by therapists who refuse to draw a sharp distinction between their lives and the lives of others, who refuse to marginalize those persons who seek help; by therapists who constantly confront the fact that if faced with the troubles of others, they just might not be doing nearly as well. (White, 1993, p. 132).

My next set of enquiries has to do with what the Internet, and what it allows for, and has got to do with this. After all, I admit to a prejudice I had held against web-based learning of something as intimate and skill-based as any therapy practice. Perhaps this was based on what I knew of the manualization of courses so typical of the first generation of attempts at Internet pedagogies, some of which were abandoned as both unsuccessful and unsatisfactory.

However, is the Internet as a genre for pedagogies evolving through trial and error? After all, I have known for a long time that my most rewarding university conversations were after a class with a colleague over coffee or a beer when we both were at our ease, could speak without much concern for getting it right or wrong and could admit to our confusions. But such conversations are often ephemeral, lost to the ravages of time, and even if they remain, except for the very exceptional, they are not stored verbatim. What if a verbatim text could be electronically stored and retrieved at will? According to Alex Ross, writing in the *New Yorker* (Ross, 2007), "this is a voice that effectively could never have been heard before the advent of the Internet...it is sophisticated on the one hand, informal on the other, and immediate in impact." Could such a medium of Internet-based conversations yield a distinctive message?

I believe this could be so in some circumstances by allowing for the seemingly contradictory – scholarly rigor commingling with the unaffected enthusiasm and vivacity so characteristic of a "good conversation." There would seem to be a kind of electronic garrulity informed by what Schon (Schon, 1983) referred to as "reflection-on-action." Schon revealed that time itself is a prerequisite for a newcomer to reflect and that such time is available and can be taken in the conversations recorded here. Internet conversations do not discriminate against those who like to or require themselves to take time to think about what they are about to say and be able to reflect on it by reviewing the text of their emails – a second "thinking over their thinking," or a revised draft of it.

I have often wondered if Jerome Bruner's thoughts have any bearing here. I think they do. He refers to the French cultural psychologist Ignace Meyerson's contention that "the main function of all cultural activity is to produce 'works/oeuvres' as he called them works that, as it were, achieve an existence of their own" (Bruner, 2005, p. 22). Bruner refers to "externalizing," the benefits of which he considers to have been overlooked. These collective oeuvres "produce and sustain group solidarity. They help 'make' a community, and communities of mutual learners are no exception (p. 22-23)." Such oeuvres yield a "metacognition" "and usually lead to lively discussion. Works and works-in-progress create 'shared' and 'negotiable ways of thinking in a group.'" He borrows the term "mentalite" from the Annales school of history/sociology to indicate such styles of thinking, or each community having "a mind of its own."

I recall many of Peggy's students commenting that such conversations were unique so far in the course of their undergraduate and postgraduate studies. In my re-reading of Peggy's book, whenever it is possible, I am going to try to observe how such a "mentalite" forms over time. I suspect I might be somewhat limited in doing so without the electronic records of conversations in their entirety or immersing myself in a similar electronically-documented conversation. But I will see what I can do in what here has necessarily been considerably abbreviated. Are the outsider witnessing practices, so integral to this training programme, implicated in the formation of any such "mentalite"?

Although I have left this to my last consideration, I consider it to be very important; how much bearing must be given to Peggy's obvious exuberant love of the practice she teaches and learns, and her unashamed exulting in it? I suspect that has a great deal to do with students and readers becoming boon travelling companions, traveling from place to place, teacher to teacher, seeking wisdoms.

NOTES

[1] Michael White invented the neologism "knowledged" to remind us there is a multiplicity of "knowledges" including "insider knowledges," and that so-called "expert" or "outsider knowledges" do not hold a monopoly.

REFERENCES

Luhrmann, T. (2000). *Of Two Minds – An Anthropologist Looks At American Psychiatry*. New York, N.Y: Alfred A. Knopf.

Pelliccia, H. (2001). Introduction (B. Jowett, Trans.). In Plato (Ed.), *Selected Dialogues of Plato* (pp. vii–xxii). New York: The Modern Library.

Plato. (2001). *Selected Dialogues of Plato: The Benjamin Jowett Translation* (B. Jowett, Trans.). New York: Modern Library (Random House).

Rilke, M. (1993). *Letters to a young poet*. New York: Norton.

Ross, A. (2007). The well-tempered web. *The New Yorker*, 80.

Schon, D. A. (1983). *The reflective practitioner: How professionals think in action*. New York: Basic Books.

White, M. (1995). Reflecting teamwork as definitional ceremony. In M. White (Ed.), *Re-Authoring lives: Interviews & essays* (pp. 172–198). Adelaide: S. Australia: Dulwich Centre Publications.

Section One: Re-authoring Teaching

INTRODUCTION

Posting from Kerry1

I loved that at any given time there were multiple threads to choose from. You could choose to join a conversation or simply start your own depending on what you were drawn to at the time. I think this really allowed each person to be engaged in what they were responding to and writing about rather than simply answering a standard set of questions. It also allowed us to dig in more with each other because there was a layer of safety in writing something down and not having to say it face-to-face. We had time to think about what people said and respond in a way that more accurately reflected our thoughts versus what first came to mind.

CREATING A LEARNING COLLABORATORY

The online medium has opened up vast new possibilities for sharing and learning that could be adapted by nearly any teacher, in almost any topic, but seems to be particularly suited for teaching narrative and other postmodern therapies. In fact, when I introduced the online aspect to my teaching, the interactive website became "the tail that wagged the dog." Rather than just being an interesting and somewhat useful adjunct, it has opened up entire new vistas of possibilities regarding inter-connections, learning communities, bringing in multiple voices in addition to the teacher and student, and bridging the gap between teacher and students.

"Collaboratory" blends the two words collaboration and laboratory to convey an environment without walls where participants use computing and communication technologies to connect with a sense of discovery over a shared project. Most commonly, a collaboratory is an experimental and empirical research environment where scientists work and communicate with each other to collaboratively design systems, conduct experiments, and share research findings (Rosenberg, 1991). In this book, I extend the collaboratory metaphor to illustrate how the addition of a website can turn a course into a vital collaborative learning community that combines an ethic of confidentiality with an ethic of circulation (Lobovits, Maisel, & Freeman, 1995). I provide guidelines for online reflections that make it possible for the teacher to take a decentered position, structuring discussion that encourages students to engage with each other in refreshing conversation with emotional intensity more akin to friendship than classmate. This approach to teaching allows space for everyone, including the teacher, to share stories and speak candidly about their learnings and questions.

The Internet is transforming possibilities for education. Colleagues have found enormous potential in teaching web-based courses where all communication takes place online. My personal experience is with constructing blended learning courses that combine face-to-face sessions and technology-based materials to deliver instruction (Bonk, Graham, & Cross, 2005; Heinze & Procter, 2004). While I use an interactive website to augment classroom teaching, I still believe the most powerful learning takes place through direct experience. Through storytelling, guest speakers and recorded interviews, students experience firsthand the spirit of inquiry and shared discovery that guide how I position myself in relation to people who consult with me. Students interact in person and online with people who have been in the client role, and who share stories about their preferences for more personal exchanges with service providers that do not hide behind a "professional" expert position. Together we participate in narrative interviews in which students practice speaking from a place of resonance and transport as outsider witnesses. I devote several chapters later in this book to describe the teaching stories, public practices, and intentional witnessing practices that are a cornerstone of my teaching.

My teaching has changed (and improved, I believe) in significant ways through using the online medium to augment classroom meetings and course readings. In lively classroom sessions, we discuss material, watch videos, practice interviewing, reflecting teamwork and narrative exercises, and meet with guest speakers. While these are all key pieces of the course, meeting online between classes at the course website offers an invigorating milieu for students and teacher to engage in frank and wholehearted conversation about course materials and experiences. This is reflected in their responses; most students overwhelmingly appreciate and express how much they have gained from this "new, improved" model of sharing and learning.

Most teaching guides are so far from students' actual experiences as to read like instructions in a manual. This book attempts to give readers a real sense of what happens in teaching situations where curiosity, wholeheartedness, and learning infuse the course. Archiving online reflections directly captures what students learn from guest speakers, recorded interviews, and storytelling, excerpts of which I share throughout the book. I provide examples from the classroom and the online class forums of how letters, reflecting teams, and archived websites provide public contexts for people to speak with knowledged[1] voices about life-shaping experiences in ways that significantly inform the lives of everyone involved.

Throughout this book, I strive to show how we "re-author" teaching from the concomitant roles of students and teacher. I give personal accounts of how students' responses energize and inspire me – as teacher, practitioner, author, and fellow traveler in life. I show a behind-the-scenes view of many effects of educational innovations on my thinking, teaching practices, and understandings of students' experiences. Together, students and I share experiences so memorable that we create what in some cases may well be lifelong bonds. Contacting students for permission to include their voices in this book, I was again reminded of the intensity of our connections, the genuineness of our exchanges, and of our care for one another. I learn from them; their presence enhances the quality of my life. I do not know if this is common practice. This book shows what is possible.

Rather than surveying multiple approaches, my illustrations are specific to teaching narrative therapy. I made this choice because narrative therapy has had the greatest impact on my own thinking and practices as a family therapist. By giving an overview of some of the most "sparkling" developments in my own evolution as a practitioner (White, 1992), I hope to contribute to students' commitment to pursue their own enthusiasms through further studies and into their professional careers.

Webs of Connection

I have always been intrigued by how people live and learn in complex webs of connection. I was fortunate to enter the field of family therapy just as a radical change was taking place – from a hierarchical to collaborative style of therapy (Andersen, 1987; Hoffman, 1993; McNamee & Gergen, 1992). My early home-based work with families of infants and toddlers with special developmental needs had ignited a passion for learning directly from and fiercely advocating for families (Bromwich, 1981; Brynelsen & Sax, 1980; Dunst, Trivette, & Deal, 1988). I learned to see community-building as an important aspect of our work – to strengthen social support networks that can include, yet not center on, professionals (Dunst, Trivette, & Cross, 1988; Kagan, Powell, Weissbourd, & Zigler, 1987; Schorr, 1997). Later, in my work as an organizational consultant, I was immediately drawn to the growing literature on creating and sustaining collaborative partnerships at work (Ellinor & Gerard, 1998) and building organizations based on a web of inclusion (Helgesen, 1995) I further describe the influence of these life experiences and others in Chapter Three, "Teaching Congruently."

It should come as no surprise that I seek in my teaching a similar congruence with collaborative ways of working. I take a relational stance in my teaching that strives for cultural curiosity, honors others' expertise and believes in possibilities and resourcefulness (Madsen, 2007b). I have been gratified to discover teaching colleagues with similar commitments[2]. Together, we have shared teaching ideas, practices, and dilemmas. Often a given exercise or course assignment goes through so many renditions, I lose track of to whom to give attribution. Wherever I have neglected to adequately give credit where credit is due, I hope I will be forgiven.

INTENDED AUDIENCE

This book conveys an interactive process in which students and teacher become partners in learning and teaching. My intended audience is teachers and students at the graduate and undergraduate levels, in formal classes spanning the range of social work, counseling and psychology, as well as workshop and seminar leaders teaching in community settings. I believe other programs that train practitioners may also find guidance here. Teachers can draw from my experience in devising their own highly interactive courses. The multiple strategies I use reverberate with students, create an engaged learning community, and facilitate new developments in students' thinking, approach to therapy, and even their worldview.

Originally, I envisioned writing this book solely for teachers of narrative therapy. However, I soon realized that my teaching approach applies to a wider readership. Postmodern therapies share an epistemological stance that questions expert knowledge and notions of "truth." The broad umbrella of postmodern critique (Anderson, 1997) includes three different yet overlapping traditions of family therapy: narrative therapy, collaborative language systems, and solution focused therapy. All attend to how knowledge and meaning are constructed in language and through relationship.

BOOK CHAPTERS

I divide the book's fourteen chapters into three sections: 1) Re-authoring Teaching; 2) Multiple Voices; and 3) Practice, Practice, Practice.

Section One: Re-authoring Teaching

In Chapter Two, "Opening the Online Lens," I describe in detail how I design a website for each course with an electronic syllabus providing an in-depth course description, links to online resources and materials on electronic reserve, and forums for discussion. I illustrate how the teacher provides the basic website structure and design, setting the stage for students to become active collaborators in co-authoring and co-editing evolving material. The online medium augments face-to-face classes to create a collaborative learning community facilitated, but not dominated by, the teacher.

Through a course website, students perform, witness, and reflect many times on each others' course assignments. I craft questions to draw forth their insider knowledge (White, 2004a). I strive to create an atmosphere in which no one is the expert and we are all learning together. This however does not, nor should it, deny a mentoring relationship between more and less seasoned practitioners. Often, this means getting out of the way so students can talk amongst themselves. Illustrations demonstrate how online pedagogy can be conducive to the ethics of collaboration and innovative circulation practices that are cornerstones of narrative therapy.

My goal as teacher is to model collaboration, transparency, and respect, and build on students' skills and knowledge. Chapter Three, "Teaching Congruently," gives a behind-the-scenes glimpse at how I work to make my choices as teacher as clear as possible. I describe influential developments in the fields of therapy, organizational development, teaching, and research that inform my striving for congruency in my teaching practices. I highlight concepts that influence my stance as a teacher and keep me honest in my exchanges with students: isomorphism; transparency; ethics of care; partnership accountability (Waldergrave, Tamasese, Tuhaka, & Campbell, 2003); and ethics without virtue (Welch, 1999). In the spirit of transparency, I give students more of a sense of me than the usual curriculum vitae by situating my ideas and practices in the context of my own life experiences. I demonstrate how I give students a sense of the events and abiding realizations that guide my commitment to my work.

I believe my approach to teacher-student relations is internally consistent with how I train practitioners to address their positions of power in relation to the people who consult with them. I strive to model practices that minimize hierarchy without obscuring power-relations in psychotherapy and other human services; that value all knowledges[3] including insider and professional. In Chapter Four, "Reckoning with Power" I explore how I reckon with power in the classroom and online. I expose students to reading materials, exercises, assignments, and conversation regarding understanding power and using it well. Together, we challenge traditional myths about insider knowledge, and examine "professionalism." I illustrate a more transparent approach to power with a section on learning from my mistakes and experimenting with evaluation.

Students often describe feeling excited, stimulated, and overwhelmed as they first meet the ideas and practices of narrative therapy through video viewing, exercises, classroom and online discussion, guest speakers, and class readings. I assign readings about specific narrative practices, give students hands-on experiences with the practices they are studying, and start an online forum for students to reflect on their experiences. In Chapter Five, "When Nice is Not Enough," I share some candid student reflections and questions they have posted online as they grapple to understand how best to position themselves in relation to the people they aspire to serve. As practitioners-in-training, they feel the pressure to "get it right," struggling with self-doubt and self-surveillance. They exchange stories that convey confusion and disorientation as they question previously held assumptions. Students and I become partners in learning as we interact online about key concepts: the culture of applause, cheerleading practices, and the strengths perspective – always striving to make room for complexities.

Section Two: Multiple Voices

A course website makes it possible to archive students' ponderings, questions, and realizations as they engage with course materials. I include many student voices; their stories as much as mine bring this project to life. Through anecdote and personal reflection, I share my own teaching stories, many of which have been archived through my course websites. I aspire to follow the advice of my mentor, Lynn Hoffman, when I told her about my intention to fill this book with students' voices: "Take your writing out of the homespun sack of materials that fills up magically behind you. I like the edge of wonder – of 'what ever will come next?' If that's not there, the work dries up."

In my teaching, I incorporate others as "living" resources to me and the students. Throughout the book, I show how the online medium makes it possible for students to interact not only with each other, but with visitors to their course. A "guest pass" makes it possible for guest speakers, authors and virtual visitors to engage in online conversation with students on the course website. Guest speakers come to class to speak from the perspective of the service seeker. Other guests visit the classroom and/or the course website to engage with students around their work as practitioners and authors. In Chapter Six, "Peopling the Course," I demonstrate how having guests join students in dialogue shifts and enriches experiences in the classroom and online. I give accounts of what becomes possible as well as what the teacher surrenders when choosing to instruct in this way.

I have discovered that students will go to far greater lengths to understand a concept or develop a practice when they have opportunities to apply it to the living of their own lives. In this book, I describe classroom exercises and online conversation through which students take up and live the actual ideas and practices they are studying. They develop a sense of a learning community as they share their reflections and assignments in class and online with one another. They apply their deconstructive listening skills to examine previously held assumptions about cheerleading and pointing out positives. In Chapter Seven, I offer the "Preferred Stories of Identity" assignment through which reflective practitioners directly experience the narrative practices they are studying. I share student's experiences as they learn the re-authoring conversations map that guides the interviewer to attend to expressions of initiatives in harmony with what a person holds precious (Thomas, 2002; White, 2004c, 2004e).

As a practitioner-teacher, I believe it is important not only to showcase the masters' work, but to share recordings of one's own. People who have come to consult with me graciously give me permission to share recordings of interviews, read aloud their poems, letters, and journal entries – anything that makes their stories come alive. I demonstrate in Chapter Eight, "Teaching Stories," ways in which people who have consulted with me bequeath to students compelling stories of their personal experiences in dealing with daunting challenges in their lives. I describe how I use class time to read aloud a riveting account of Kate's experience of "Hell & Back" - a descent into and recovery from a psychotic depression; I then show how I structure a letter-writing exchange between students and Kate. This chapter demonstrates the tremendous impact a story can have on students, who are moved both by the personal account and by the willingness of people to share their private struggles with such strangers.

Just as narrative therapy challenges assumptions about the absolute privacy of the client-therapist relationship, online learning challenges the academic tradition of prioritizing individualized confidentiality over community sharing. In this book, I demonstrate how innovative teaching practices can use therapeutic documents and "public practices" that incorporate audiences to consult with each other and with outside consultants around shared themes. In Chapter Nine, "Public Practices" (Lobovits et al., 1995), I share my strategies for practicing an ethic of circulation while still protecting privacy and allowing students to choose the extent to which they share their stories and personal reflections with others. I illustrate how I structure teaching environments that incorporate students as audiences to learn directly from guest speakers, recorded interviews and story-telling. In particular, I describe some of the far-reaching impact of one woman's story on students to illustrate the potency of public practices in teaching. Through journal entries, poems, and letters, I introduce the reader to Nicole and her struggle to overcome anorexia, self-harm and depression; I include letters by students and workshop participants that convey how Nicole's candid accounts ripple into their lives, like echos, inspiring them to connect some of their own stories with hers.

Section Three: Practice, Practice, Practice

In each class, I give students time to hone the narrative skills I have introduced. Chapter Ten, "The Power of Intentional Witnessing," is illustrated with students' online conversations about in-class experiences with live interviews. I demonstrate how students participate as outsider witnesses in a moving interview with their own classmate, Mohammad. I also include a transcribed excerpt of an in-class interview with guest visitor Nicole, where students artfully participate in an outsider witness team. Throughout, I show how online forums give students opportunities to reflect, inquire, and build community as they explore possibilities and limits for personal sharing in outsider witness practices. I conclude the chapter with reflections and commentaries from Mohammad and Nicole about their experiences with being the focus of interviews with a reflecting team format.

Therapeutic letters are an aspect of narrative practice with a wealth of possibilities limited only by the imagination. In Chapter Eleven, "Teaching Letter - Writing Skills," I offer specific tips for letter-writing that use note-taking of direct quotes to enable letter writers to ask questions from a stance of earnest curiosity. I give three exemplary examples of preferred letter-writing practices from teaching and therapy situations. Through archived online reflections, I show how students give voice to such complexities as breaking through an internalized therapeutic gaze and speaking from their own voices, reflecting their own hard-earned wisdom. I describe how students practice their letter-writing skills in response to hearing insider accounts through guest speakers, in-class interviews, video-viewing, and storytelling. Students appreciate writing letters to someone real, not imagined, as this forces them to practice this skill knowing their letter will mean something to its intended reader. I provide a glimpse into the vibrant online conversation that each of these classroom experiences has generated as people with experience knowledge teach students invaluable lessons about how much ethical, useful practice means to them.

Chapter Twelve, "Remember to Ask the Cook," illustrates the learning and understanding that results from students consulting with experienced service seekers about their preferences regarding service provision. I share insider accounts I use in my classes that include tips for practitioners from the following people: parents of children with special needs; Alan, an adopted teenager who experienced foster care; and Meghan, a survivor of sexual abuse, family violence, psycho-pathologizing, and psychiatric maltreatment. Students write letters and/or participate in reflecting teamwork in response to these teaching stories.

Students often struggle to integrate their studies of narrative practice with other cherished learnings, and to adapt practices resonant with their own personal styles.

I want them to understand that the narrative approach does not come "naturally," as it is so different from the psychodynamic therapies that many of them have been studying (White, 2001). In Chapter Thirteen, "Apprenticing to a Craft," I draw from archived correspondence and students' online discussion to give examples of how everyone, including the teacher, works on skill-building. Letter-writing assignments in the classroom and on the course website provide students additional opportunities to practice, critique, and revise their therapeutic documents. I illustrate with a "Take-Two" letter writing activity.

Finally, Chapter Fourteen, "Practice, Practice, Practice" explores how a teaching environment can encourage students to learn specific technical skills based on poststructuralist approaches in counseling while simultaneously developing their own unique ways of working. The possible applications extend well beyond the realm of psychotherapy to practitioners in a variety of community service contexts. I give an insider view of students' commitments to making differences in both the private and public sectors, and to moving beyond the isolated private world of therapy to join larger communities that share social justice concerns.

BOOK FORMAT

I intend for this book to be reader-friendly and written in a collegial tone. I quote numerous online exchanges where students, myself, and guest visitors explore aspects of the history and culture of psychotherapy, grapple with provocative questions, and learn about narrative therapy. By including interactive material gathered from the course websites, I aim for a dialogical experience rather than drawing on a traditional monological text (Bakhtin, Emerson, & Holquist, 1990; Lysack, 2006). Throughout this book, I weave in my ongoing consultation with students to keep in touch with how their learning is proceeding and do my utmost to assist their progress.

Student Voices

Students generously gave me permission to weave their voices throughout this book. I strive to capture the back and forth and zigzagging of online conversation by including reflections and postings in a consistent format. Single online postings are highlighted as follows:

Posting by Kerry1

> *Of course you may use anything I posted that you wish. I am flattered that I said something that may be helpful to someone else someday. This course has really been transformative for me and brought me to places I would not have gotten to on my own – at least not in this short period of time.*

I use pseudonyms for some students, while others prefer I use their real names. I distinguish between two students with the same name by using "Kerry1" and "Kerry2". Several students reviewed this manuscript and gave many useful recommendations. They became my "co-researchers" in sharing their preferred ways of learning, reflecting on specific classroom, reading and online activities, and actively shaping the learning environment. In narrative practice, "co-research" refers to the process by which people inquire together to create original research about insider knowledges (Epston, 1999).

I offer students' behind-the-scenes accounts as they make discoveries and reflect upon unique realizations in applying narrative concepts and practices to their own lives and work contexts. Their reflections and questions make us partners in learning, deeply impacting the choices I make as teacher, and now as author.

Insider Knowledges

As a practitioner, I carry a deeply held commitment to taking a position that does not privilege professional "expert" knowledge over client knowledge. The anthropologist Clifford Geertz is widely attributed for drawing the distinction between expert and local knowledge (Geertz, 1973, 1983). Professional expertise is knowledge that is written, published, and given cultural credibility; local knowledge is based on a person's knowledge that grows from her or his daily life. Local knowledge is synonymous with "insider knowledge" or "experience knowledge" (Walnum, 2007), the terms I most often use.

Throughout the book, I include powerful stories that people in the designated role of client have graciously shared with students through class visits, video recordings, and journal entries. People with "experience knowledge" have generously collaborated with me to review the chapters that include their stories. Together we have changed identifying information to protect their privacy. I believe their stories will enlighten you, the reader, as has been my experience and that of my students. With this book, their circle of influence widens and they become teachers for all of us[4].

In situations where these stories are from young people I worked with whose parents I got to know as well, I asked these young clients to invite their parents to join them in reviewing the manuscript and making choices about how to publicly tell stories that impact their family privacy. Through conversation, parents came to understand how important it felt to their children to speak out publicly so others could learn from their life experiences. Reviewing Chapter 8, Kate's mom described what "an emotional journey" it was to revisit from a parent's point of view her daughter's reflections on a descent into a psychotic depression at age 18. Still, she supported her daughter's choice to leave in some identifiable details: "Kate's ongoing concern to 'normalize' and almost publicize the mental health struggles that she and so many others have had to cope with is a frame of mind that I think our whole family honors."

Alan, who gives suggestions to social workers based on his experience being adopted from foster care as a young boy in Chapter 12, told me that using a pseudonym would symbolize that he was afraid to be who he really is. "I am proud to be who I am and nothing will ever change that." Through conversation, Alan's parents learned how much this meant to their son and gave their support to Alan's position:

> *My parents thought at first that because I live a small town, word would jump around fast about my life story and they wanted to make sure that what I was doing was the right choice. I talked to them about it because I think that it would be better if the news travelled faster than slower so it would get to more people in a short amount of time and would be heard of as a boy who has advice as a person who had a hard early childhood and wanted to help out as many people as he could.*

Again and again, students demonstrate how much they learn from hearing life stories directly from the people who have lived them. Through their letters and online reflections, students also share ways in which these stories resonate with their own experiences and transport them to new understandings.

My Voice

Writing this book has given me the opportunity to "show and tell" my approach to teaching. Throughout the writing process, I repeatedly faced my growing edge as a teacher and as a writer. I am more comfortable demonstrating than describing what I do and believe. In response to my reviewers' encouragement, I weave in my own voice, reflecting on how my teaching embodies the concepts and practices that I aspire to teach. In addition to bringing in multiple voices, I frequently return to my own voice, striving to ground each chapter in my experiences of teaching and witnessing this kind of learning. I reflect on my own edges of learning as I aspire to live the values and intentions that influence my chosen theoretical framework. I describe an interactive process in which I play the facilitator and guide – a process that strives to meet each student at her or his learning edge and has the flexibility to scaffold each person's learning from that point (Vygotsky, 1986). I try to show my thinking behind intentional choices, such as letting students know why I choose to incorporate many voices in the classroom. I explore the tensions of embracing a collaborative poststructuralist position within structuralist institutions and systems of care (Madsen, 2007c).

I openly position myself as a learner in the process. When I teach this way, I believe students are more likely to experience themselves as teachers, akin to how people who consult with therapists gain confidence in their own knowledge when they teach the therapist about what is most meaningful to them in particular life situations and relationships. Besides, I speak in earnest when I express how much I learn from my students.

Hence this book chronicles a personal journey of discovery in using blended learning methods to teach narrative therapy. My writing reflects a personal approach where I speak from my own experiences as teacher and practitioner. I do my utmost throughout the book to discern between this personal style and teaching rigorous practice skills. Every teacher must find her or his own unique teaching style; in this book, I show you mine.

TEACHING NARRATIVE PRACTICE

Posting by Bobbi

I have gained an intense awareness of the importance of asking questions that open the possibilities and knowing when to thicken the plot. There is an art to this. I try to take deep cleansing breaths and tell myself that I know this intuitively; then a nagging worry returns. Worry is interfering with my ability to feel comfortable with the practice. I am interested in slowing down and learning how to let others make connections for themselves and letting go of the pressure to be the expert "fix-it person." I was thinking here about listening as breathing...I am hopeful that the maps will provide me with some scaffolding about where and how to begin.

A learning "collaboratory" is highly congruent with the focus and values of narrative therapy, where there is a priority and an ethical commitment to develop practices in which therapy is a reciprocal two-way process (White & Denborough, 2005; White, 1997c). The online interaction has proven a rich source of give-and-take that immeasurably deepens students' understanding of concepts and practices.

My narrative practice has been – and continues to be – inspired by excellent articles and texts on narrative therapy (Epston, 1998; Freedman & Combs, 1996a; Freeman, Epston, & Lobovits, 1997; Monk, Winslade, Crocket, & Epston, 1997; Morgan, 2000b; Payne, 2000; Russell & Carey, 2004; Smith & Nylund, 1997; White, 1997c, 2000b, 2004b, 2007d; White & Epston, 1990a). Thus far, the published literature on teaching narrative therapy is primarily in article and book chapter form (Jorniak & Paré, 2007; Lewis & Cheshire, 2007; Marsten & Howard, 2006; Mckenzie & Monk, 1997; White & Denborough, 2005; White, 1992; Winslade, 2003; Winslade, Crocket, Monk, & Drewery, 2000). I hope this book will further contribute to this growing literature and hence further legitimize teaching narrative practice in academic institutions.

Narrative therapy provides the conceptual framework to think in terms of people's lives as "storied," and of considering possibilities for giving new meaning to such experiences (White & Epston, 1990a). Therapists in narrative explorations adopt a position of inquiry guided by the craft and art of narrative interviewing to assist those seeking their services to explore their own ideas developed over the history of living their lives (White, 2007c). Narrative inquiry brings forth a person's specific and unique ways to approach life's difficulties, and to articulate what they intimately know about their own lives and relationships.

"Narrative practice" is a term that is replacing "narrative therapy," with many applications beyond the therapy room. Many students who work in public sector settings such as early childhood care and education, social services, and community mental health have readily adapted this change in language (Hancock & Epston, 2007). The narrative therapy literature has begun to explore the application of narrative practices in community circumstances (Collective, 1999;

Hancock, Chilcott, & Epston, 2007; Madsen, 2007c; White, 2003a). Recent literature on social work education recognizes narrative therapy as a values-based practice approach, and explores its applicability as a model of narrative-deconstructive practice to bridge the gap between clinical and social practice (Epston, Gavin, & Napan, 2004; Ungar, 2004; Vodde & Gallant, 2003). In this book, students explore possible applications for narrative practice that extend well beyond the realm of psychotherapy into using family-centered practices in a range of public sector work settings.

Narrative pedagogy is guided by a particular set of intentions, ethics, and aesthetics. Teachers informed by poststructuralist inquiry seek to develop intentional understandings of what is most precious to us in teaching and what we stand for in our beliefs, values, hopes, dreams, principles, commitments, and ethics. My teaching intention is to offer opportunities for reflective practitioners-in-training to step into the experiences of those they aspire to help, to listen attentively, and learn to hold themselves accountable to the seekers of their services. I want students to move beyond traditional power relations to better understand help-giving practices that contribute to more equitable relationships between human service providers and the people they aspire to help.

Narrative Principles in Action

Narrative therapy course content brings together folk psychology traditions and formal academic training (White, 2004a). Personal accounts of experience are respected sources of knowledge. Within narrative interviewing practices, insider knowledges are privileged over expert vocabularies, and significant care is taken to ensure that language conveys people's actual experiences, rather than others' interpretations of these experiences. Teachers of narrative therapy face the challenge of deliberately accenting local knowledge and minimizing academic jargon, while learning concepts, values, and practices that fulfill standardized accreditation requirements.

Throughout the book, I illustrate ways in which the teacher's commitment to experience knowledge can inform learning experiences. Students read memoirs of pioneers in family therapy (Beels, 2001; Hoffman, 2002) and hear first-person accounts from people who describe their hard-earned preferences in therapy and other human services. Through exercises and assignments, students carry out and reflect upon the skills and knowledges they bring to their work as reflective practitioners (Sax, 2006).

In two-way accounts of therapy, the therapist takes responsibility to identify, acknowledge, and describe specific ways a therapeutic conversation contributes to his or her life (White, 1997c). This approach has emerged from a tradition of engagement that differs from traditional therapeutic practices in which the therapist examines his or her experiences of therapeutic conversations through the construct of counter-transference. I believe two-way and even multiple accounts of learning are important aspects of a learning collaboratory, as well as to collaborative approaches to therapeutic conversations. Multiple accounts make it possible for people to learn some of the real effects of their stories on others – including people in elevated positions of power such as professional service providers and teachers.

Online communication offers multiple opportunities to structure courses to move beyond a one-way account of learning. Students benefit from knowing not only the influence of their stories on each other, but on my work as their teacher. In writing and in person, I strive to render visible the powerful ways in which students' work and thoughtful exchanges touch my life. I illustrate this book with many examples of the "two-way accounts" principle in action. With students' permission, I often share their work with others. Students are generally not only willing to have me share their on-line postings and writings, but highly appreciative of being able to contribute to others' learning. As Olivia emailed back to me **"I feel like it wasn't an accident that my work traveled to other people. Every time I heard that my work was touching someone I also became touched powerfully. This is the beauty of narrative therapy isn't it? All parties end up being enriched by their work together."**

The interactive website offers opportunities for a network of multiple accounts – for students to see themselves through many eyes within a web of connection. By reflecting online together about real effects on each other, the students gain experiential understanding that sticks with them well beyond their readings about two-way accounts. Again, this conversation does not revolve around me. I see my role here as a facilitator, to create and monitor forums for such lively exchanges to occur. I am often moved by the clear acknowledgements students give to each other especially since the teacher's evaluative role can add complexity to the teacher-student exchanges.

The course website offers online opportunities for ongoing inquiry with students about the effects of a particular classroom, reading, or online activity on their learning experience. While I offer the students certain knowledge and skills about teaching and therapeutic approach, I am always learning from their experiences. Each semester, I build on what I have learned from prior teaching while experimenting with new possibilities. Students express intrigue in hearing about what I learn from them. I have collected interesting responses to the following forum I began during the last week of class. I posted this forum after students learned about "two-way accounts" in their course readings and classroom discussion:

If you could experience yourselves through my eyes, what do you imagine you might see? Does it surprise you to hear that the ways you have engaged with the course materials has affected me and my sense of identity both as a teacher and as a life-long learner? In reflecting on this learning experience, what stands out to you? What have you learned from each other? What would you like to know from me about my experience(s) of this class?

PEDAGOGOGICAL CONSIDERATIONS

Posting by Amy

For the longest time I viewed education from the dominant discourse of "filling a bucket" and writing down "facts" that I would later study and recite back on standardized exams. I learned how to work the system to meet the institution's expectations. Now, I have come to realize that education is so much more. It's lighting that spark of inquiry into alternative understandings that create space for multiple viewpoints with no ultimate "truth" or "fact."

I have been heartened to discover a burgeoning literature that has grown out of the seminal work of the Brazilian educator Paulo Freire on popular and informal education (Freire, 1973, 1994, 1996) and the relevance for adult education (Apple, 2000, 2002, 2003; Vella, 1995a, 1995b). Freire questioned a "banking" concept of education where teachers deposit knowledge into the students' depositories. Banking education maintains a teacher-student dichotomy where those considered knowledgeable issue one-way communiqués and deposit their knowledge into those who know nothing. Freire lists ten attitudes and practices as also mirrored in oppressive cultural forces (Freire, 1973) p. 54:

a) the teacher teaches and the students are taught;
b) the teacher knows everything and the students know nothing;
c) the teacher thinks and the students are thought about;
d) the teacher talks and the students listen meekly;
e) the teacher disciplines and the students are disciplined;
f) the teacher chooses and enforces his choice, and the students comply;
g) the teacher acts and the students have the illusion of acting through the action of the teacher;
h) the teacher chooses the program content and the students (who are not consulted) adapt to it;
i) the teacher confuses the authority of knowledge with his own professional authority, which he sets in opposition to the freedom of the students;
j) the teacher is the subject of the learning process, which the pupils are mere objects.

Freire proposed that education should instead seek to reconcile the student-teacher contradiction. I believe Freire's philosophy of education is highly relevant to adult education, including training practitioners in academic settings. His pedagogy highlights democracy, dialogue, and reciprocity as educational methods that situate education in the lived experience of all participants, including the teacher. As co-creators in "authentic thinking," the teacher partners with the student focusing on realities beyond ivory tower isolation. These educational principles orient everyone toward putting theoretical knowledge into practice or "praxis" – a synthesis of theory and practice in which each informs each other.

I too believe in working together with students to develop consciousness and committed action informed by and linked to values.

Postmodern Pedagogy

Postmodernism is a cultural phenomenon affecting philosophy, architecture, literature, music and other expressive arts. Jacques Derrida, Francois Lyotard, Michel Foucault, Richard Rorty and other postmodern philosophers offer an outlook on education that challenges conventions, fosters innovation and change, encourages tolerance of ambiguity, emphasizes diversity, and accentuates the social construction of reality. Many narrative practitioners prefer the more specific term poststructuralism to describe an approach to inquiry that questions the concept of "self" as a singular and coherent entity, and is in contrast to structuralism's truth claims (Thomas, 2002; White, 1997b). I am not an expert on current debates about postmodernism and poststructuralism. However, I do believe my approach to teaching shares pedagogical challenges with others who embrace a collaborative outlook on education. I sometimes chose the umbrella terms "postmodern" or "collaborative" therapies as an effort to unify a diversity of approaches – not to obscure distinctions.

In 2002, I attended a workshop[5] that piqued my curiosity about the pedagogical challenges for teachers and trainers of postmodern therapies in academic settings. It spurred me to consider the parallels in power relations between the therapist/ client and teacher/student relationships, and of the many institutionalized assumptions in academia that remain unexamined. How can teachers of postmodern therapies position themselves to teach and supervise in ways that are consistent with the values and guiding principles to which we aspire? Are there ways for teachers and students to respectfully discover and learn from two-way accounts of the learning experience?

As editors of a special issue of the Journal of Systemic Therapies on Teaching and Learning Postmodern Therapies, Paré and Tarragona contemplate pedagogical questions for teachers and trainers of postmodern therapies that "share a respectful, collaborative spirit that reflects a loosened grip on truth claims and purported expertise" (Paré & Tarragona, 2006, p. 2). They describe postmodern epistemologies as "reminding us that knowledge is not so much handed over as it is co-constructed through mutual talk." In this book, I respond to their question, "How might we teach conceptual frameworks and therapeutic interventions without simply duplicating modernist traditions that privilege instructors' knowledges"?

Lynn Hoffman drew from a specific exchange between students to reflect on her experience with the difference between "lions" and "lambs" in discussion groups. "Lions usually have their hands up and take strong stands, and they get called on and feel more and more intelligent. Lambs hold back, and don't often hold up their hands, and begin to feel more and more stupid. Gianfranco Cecchin called this result "systemic genius" and "systemic stupidity." In one group, a student objected that Lynn was against "open and honest discussion." When Lynn explained about the lions and lambs, the student reflected, "Oh, I see, it's like affirmative action for shy people."

Since that time, Lynn has become increasingly interested in conversations that do not require consensus, and allow many voices to be heard. She captured my students' attention with her online description of Jean-Francois Lyotard.

Posting by Lynn

The man who defined postmodernism, Jean-Francois Lyotard, called this way of talking "paralogical." He meant that rather than following the logic of reason, which says there is a right and a wrong answer, you bypass logic and open the doors to many voices often in contradiction to one another.

Interacting in the online conversation with students in my course reminded Lynn of poet John Keats' concept of "negative capability" – the ability to remain in the midst of doubts and uncertainties "without any irritable reaching after fact and reason." For Lynn, the virtue of this online conversation was that it never descended into escalations and arguments about who and what is right. "Even when people did take stands one way or another, they never put each other in the wrong. So, Peggy, I think you successfully set the stage for what I think of as a 'postmodern' type of discourse."

Ethical Considerations

"Stick to the 'heart of what matters to you' so that you teach not as a measurable performance but rather because you believe what you have to say has to be said" (Epston, 2006).

Ethics is an important content area in every course about therapeutic or counseling relationships. I have participated in many conversations with colleagues about creating space for discussing ethical considerations and dilemmas in our work as practitioners[6]. We note a common phenomenon – material about ethics usually focuses on professional codes regarding boundaries and confidentiality. Preventing breaches in confidentiality, exploitation, and dual relationships is indeed very important given the egregious violations that can occur and the very real litigious concerns for licensed professionals regulated by professional licensing boards.

In addition, teaching creates space for other ethical decisions that are often pushed to the margins. To whom are we accountable? What does it mean to be a professional and what does professional behavior look like? What about respectful greetings? What about services not available to people with low incomes or to the working poor? I illustrate this book with thoughtful and thought-provoking online exchanges between students, teacher, and outside visitors sparked by sharing favorite passages about the ethics of hospitality, accountability, collaboration, and professionalism (Bird, 2001; Buckley & Decter, 2006; Madsen, 2007a). Archived postings from the interactive websites from my classes afford the opportunity to often gather a vibrant glimpse into such dynamic conversation.

Ethical considerations in teaching collaborative therapies challenge us to:
- Teach in ways that are consistent with the philosophy and therapeutic stance to which we aspire;
- Offer our own knowledge and expertise without disqualifying students knowledges and skills;
- Be accountable to power relations between teacher-student; and
- Create contexts for collaborative learning.

The aesthetics of teaching postmodern therapies are based on personal style, preferences, and unique teaching abilities. We learn about our own special teaching skills when they are reflected back to us. Often this occurs through evaluation by supervisors, student feedback, and friendly critique from colleagues. In this book, I highlight learning about my own distinctive teaching abilities through exploration of special teaching moments. By sharing memorable experiences in the classroom and online, I strive to demonstrate how students actively guide my teaching preferences with a spirit of collaborative inquiry (Roth, 2007).

Respect for School Culture

Posting by Nan

I am both in line with others' affirmations of collaborative approaches to psychotherapy and, at the same time, questioning of these very same views of this newer form of therapy as being the one, right way of approaching the challenging task of helping people. Perhaps my unique respect for and skepticism of narrative therapy is rooted in my education in the area of psychology. Until now, I had yet to be exposed to this emerging field of thought, having instead been trained in the more traditional, individual psychology perspective. This unique experience of mine has shaped my accolades and criticisms alike of narrative therapy, and it is from this stance that I share my thoughts on the subject.

Students study narrative therapy within undergraduate and graduate programs with particular philosophical traditions. Teaching collaborative therapies in different academic settings – some with vastly different traditions and values – highlights the importance of respect for school culture. I have learned the hard way how my biases inform my teaching. I strive to learn directly from students' understandings about their particular school culture and what they most deeply value from their studies. In constructing course requirements, I vary my expectations according to different school cultures[7].

Students often share their dilemmas as they imagine putting narrative therapy into practice alongside other therapeutic approaches. For example, students learning transference-based therapies are particularly perplexed as they seek an eclectic approach that might encompass psychodynamic in addition to solution focused, cognitive-behavioral and narrative therapies. Social work students revisit their understanding of "the strengths perspective." Psychology students often struggle to understand the implications of post-structuralist notions of identity and development. In each of these situations, the online forum provides a safe haven for provocative conversation.

Not everyone is enamored with narrative therapy. I often feel a creative tension between making space for different voices and my responsibility to teach narrative therapy. How much room is there for complexity when questions come from contradictory points of view? How can I avoid the dangers of "group think" so students can speak candidly about their skeptical thoughts and feelings? Over the years, I have discovered some personal edges of learning as I strive to listen respectfully to others drawn to different therapeutic traditions. At the same time, I believe it does not work for students to continually attempt to interpret narrative practice through the language of a different approach. To the extent possible, I encourage students to temporarily check their competing beliefs at the door, so they can attend to learning this particular approach. For example, I was heartened when by the end of a semester a student from a Freudian psychoanalytic tradition told me that he had come to understand my encouragement to listen and experience narrative therapy without trying to see everything according to the id, ego, and superego.

Posting by Jordana

Engaging with this narrative material has been rather humorous for me because I have realized, to my surprise, how influenced by traditional psychology I am. Long-held assumptions that I took for granted regarding what is helpful to a client have been challenged. I am grateful to this class for having opened me up to ideas requiring a real shift in my thinking as to what is healing for people and communities. It is not that I should sit with my clients and "process" their emotions in a "narrative way" as I originally presumed. Rather, what is healing is the new story and its plot and the new way of being in the world that it allows.

Teaching narrative practice within a psychodynamic program poses particular challenges as students seek to integrate their psychodynamic studies with narrative practice. Narrative therapy introduces a paradigm shift in relation to the meaning and practice of therapy from intra-psychic, transference-based psychotherapies to a focus on historical and cultural context (McLeod, 1997, 2001). In this book, I include questions from students who are studying narrative therapy while also learning psychodynamic traditions. I believe there is much to learn from their thoughtful examination of theory and practice. Many of their questions remain unanswered and their confusion lingers throughout the course. I tell them that this "not-knowing" tension is something I greatly value. To add to the confusion, I introduce the concepts of "ethics with ambiguity" and "ethics without virtue." (Welch, 1999), encouraging students to develop skills to hold moral and political complexities without resorting to "Us against Them" thinking.

Teaching narrative practice in a postmodern social work program is a very different experience. By the time I meet these students, many have developed sophisticated knowledge of social constructionism, the strengths perspective, social justice, and human rights. Prior teachers introduced them to narrative therapy and now they are eager to learn all they can. In many ways, I feel with such students as though I have arrived in "teaching heaven." In this book, I describe my discovery of another set of challenges as students learn to put ideas into practice. I include reflections and questions by students steeped in the strengths perspective to convey how they work together to disengage from well-meaning practices of applause, to move beyond pointing out positives to "asking not telling" people their stories.

Throughout this book, I try to be transparent in describing my approach to the challenge as teacher of narrative therapy to convey respect and curiosity while not encouraging a forced marriage between narrative and psychodynamic practice. Many students of psychodynamic therapy have already committed to following another course of study and/or they hesitate before delving into learning an approach that is so different from their other courses. When students cannot immerse themselves in the course material, I strive to kindle a fire for pursuing the study of narrative practice in the coming years. Often students of psychodynamic therapy are taught a simplistic view of narrative therapy in comparison to the highly nuanced traditions of transference-based psychotherapy. In my teaching, I aim to demonstrate the depth and complexity of narrative therapy practice.

I invite you, the reader, to enjoy the exploration.

OPENING THE ONLINE LENS[8]

Posting from Christie

As many of you know from previous classes, I tend to be pretty quiet in class discussions. I think that I just need some time to sit back and chew on the material for awhile before I can offer my thoughts in any organized, intelligent way. This setting, while admittedly a bit unnerving at first, has become rather liberating. Besides, how else could I have gained such tremendous insight from all of your stories, opinions, and general brilliance?

Teaching practitioners-in-training effectively with technology requires significant course preparation, including an electronic syllabus, course site design, online forums for reflection and letter-writing, and course assignments. My experience using an interactive website to augment face-to-face classes powerfully demonstrates a collaborative learning community facilitated but not dominated by the teacher. Through a course website, students perform, witness, and reflect upon each other's course assignments. In this chapter, I share illustrations to demonstrate how I use online pedagogy conducive to the ethic of collaboration and innovative circulation practices that are cornerstones of narrative therapy (Sax, 2003, 2006, 2007a).

I am not someone for whom mechanical knowledge comes easily. Each step along the way has taken a lot of trial and error work with more moments of exasperation than I like to admit. Through practice, I eventually found a computer comfort zone, and the self-confidence that makes it possible for me to venture into new territory. Fortunately, I have been given invaluable technical assistance along the way[9].

Not every teacher finds moving into online teaching a natural or comfortable step. Colleagues have reminded me that there is no magic in online learning, any more than there is magic in conversation[10]. Good ideas, expressed initially in embryonic form, require others to express curiosity and inquiry. Rather than occurring by chance, good classroom conversations are facilitated by an instructor who structures the conversation to ensure that it goes somewhere and that participants do not get lost. This is equally true for online discussions.

Often when I share with other teachers my enthusiasm for using an interactive website to enhance classroom teaching, they respond with skepticism and concern about increasing their workload. Teachers inundated with daily email need a good reason to add even more technology to their lives.

Teaching online means major changes in teachers' distribution of labor. I put significant preparation time into launching an interactive website. Even when I am out of town, I stay engaged in the online discussion. But in my experience, using a website to complement classroom teaching has been well worth the time and effort it requires. Students' weekly postings keep them engaged with course materials throughout the course. For some classes, I have done away with assigning a final paper in favor of students' continuing online engagement through the numerous opportunities I provide on the course website. I no longer dread grading the pile-up of papers at the end of a course.

ONLINE PEDAGOGY

The online medium is redefining community, the networks of people with whom one forges connections, and ways of linking lives with each other. Email, instant messaging, live journals, blogs and wiki are transforming the landscape of connection and consciousness for people in the 21st century. Much has already been written about the use of online communication tools in higher education and applying design principles to course design. (Chickering & Ehrmann, 1996; Funaro & Montell, 1999; Ritchie & Hoffman, 1996; Salter, 2001; Simonson, Smaldino, Albright, & Zvacek, 2006; Tinker, 1997). With the rapid advances in technology, online possibilities seem limitless: as a storehouse for information, avenues for research, and interactive communication. However, "...as with other new educational technologies, it is not so much the tool that improves teaching and learning but how the instructor integrates the tool into the curriculum and into the educational setting" (Ragan, 1999). The key is to plan ahead how online communication will be used to meet course objectives and to choose judiciously among the many options.

In my review of literature on pedagogical roles for online discussion, I was excited to discover an enthusiasm for designing learning environments that are "...more authentic, situated, interactive, project-oriented, interdisciplinary, learner-centered, and which take into account the varieties of students' learning styles" (Berge, 1997)[11]. Communication and information technologies are viewed as tools for adopting principles of good practice for teaching and learning in higher education (Chickering & Ehrmann, 1996; Funaro & Montell, 1999; Harasim et al., 1997). These include active learning techniques conducive to reflective thinking and creative problem-solving, and isomorphic to the guiding principles of narrative therapy. Chichering and Ehrmann (1996) list seven principles: 1) Encourage contact between students and faculty, 2) Develop reciprocity and cooperation among students, 3) Use active learning techniques, 4) Give prompt feedback, 5) Emphasize time on task, 6) Communicate high expectations, and 7) Respect diverse talents and ways of learning.

COURSE PREPARATION

When I was first hired to teach a course using online technology to supplement classroom sessions, I was paid to take a training course titled, Teaching Effectively Online.[12] The course provided a conceptual framework and technical skills for teaching online, including readings, web resources, and peer discussion. It opened me to the potential for using online communication tools in higher education and helped me to apply design principles in planning my own course (Ritchie & Hoffman, 1996; Salter, 2001; Tinker, 1997).

In designing a course on narrative approaches to social work, I was guided by the following provocative questions:

- What tools of inquiry are available to make meaning out of cultural and professional assumptions about therapy, the role of the therapist and client, and the therapeutic relationship?
- What is important for social work graduate students to understand about the cultural history of psychotherapy, and in particular, developments in the field of family therapy toward collaborative approaches within the last quarter century?
- How might I foster students' curiosity about collaborative approaches to therapy, otherwise known as postmodern, social constructionist, discursive therapies, which have emerged as alternatives to psychoanalytic, psychodynamic therapies?
- Within an intensive course, how could graduate students develop understandings of the ideas and ways of working of "narrative therapy"?
- In the face of discouraging trends for therapists and other human service providers toward overworked, overstressed and underpaid "burn-out," how might I convey some of the possibilities for invigoration and creativity that these developments offer?

As I prepared my initial course, I thought about how online communication might augment classroom contact to accomplish course objectives. I sought to facilitate a collaborative learning community in which students would 1) be comfortable sharing curiosities and reflections, while minimizing the effects of what Michael White (1997) borrowing Foucault's expression, calls, "the evaluative gaze" (Foucault, 1973); and 2) practice their newly acquired narrative therapy skills, specifically reflection, outsider witness practices and letter-writing.

About a month before the course begins, I send a welcoming email to enrolled students with instructions on accessing the course website. I encourage students to explore the website as if on a treasure hunt, following the electronic links to the syllabus, content areas, assignments, reading materials, resources, and discussion board. This first email is intentionally written to arouse a sense of intrigue and discovery in students from the very beginning, to help set the stage for the active approach I hope will characterize their participation:

I am pleased to welcome you into "Collaborative Approaches to Therapeutic Conversations." The course is structured around this website. Please familiarize yourself with each section of the course site so you can readily follow the course design and get a feel for the spirit of it. I've had a lot of fun designing this course site, which hopefully sets the stage for a lively, interactive, intensive learning experience. In some ways, I envy you since you have such a wondrous world of exploration ahead. However, proceed with caution, as these materials pose provocative questions that can change the way you think about many things. Enjoy!

Electronic Syllabus

In preparing an interactive website to enhance classroom teaching, I closely reviewed my collection of narrative therapy materials, explored the Web for online resources, and then linked the two to design an electronic course syllabus. My first course, "Narrative Approaches to Social Work" was five weeks long, with five content units: 1) discovering our intellectual ancestors; 2) the guiding principles in narrative therapy; 3) narrative interviewing practices; 4) thickening the alternative story; 5) the ethics of collaboration; and 6) applications to practice. Over the years, I continue to tweak the syllabus, including adding further links to online resources as they have become available.

Course Design

The online component is organized around the course website. While nothing quite takes the place of coffee after class or meeting in the corridor, the interactive website provides a forum to keep conversation active between classroom meetings. I structure forums for students to reflect on assigned readings, classroom activities, and assignments. Initially, I pose questions to get the conversation started; soon, the website comes alive as students address these questions as well as start their own threads of inquiry. I select thought-provoking reading materials to stimulate reflection and conversation. From prior experience (both as teacher and student), I have learned to structure activities that foster ongoing discussion of assigned readings. I let students know that we will be discussing readings in class and online.

FOSTERING A LEARNING COLLABORATORY

Posting from Margot

> *The richest learning environments I have been in are those where we have created a safe space to learn, make mistakes, take risks, feel uncomfortable – knowing that those around me are doing the same thing and are respecting my bumbling humanness. Activities like role plays, fishbowl conversations and small group or one-on-one conversations around a specific, probing question seem to work best. I haven't had an online class before and I'm finding it hard to imagine this kind of learning can occur while looking into a screen rather than a human face, although I can see the value of reading and writing responses with time to think and process first.*

As teacher, I strive to create a hospitable atmosphere in which no one is the expert and we are all learning together. Often, this means getting out of the way so students can talk amongst themselves. As Danielle, an MSW student, reflected, "The use of the website really did deepen and move the relationship among our class along more quickly...The conversation was able to continue with such an unabashed depth beyond the classroom between class times, thus maintaining our connection with one another and shared thinking."

Preferred Ways of Learning

"Collaboration doesn't mean doing whatever the client or supervisee wants; it is a process negotiated among people where all the knowledges available are valued and considered." (Behan, 2003)

I create space for students to actively participate in steering a course oriented to their preferred ways of learning, with activities structured to enhance their learning and build community. By not being in the center of these interactions, I can sit back to keep my eye on many different aspects of learning and interaction, steering the course accordingly. In particular, I try to stay cognizant of the effects of unspoken power relations, and to seize opportunities to explore the influence of culture and context on our experiences with each other, and to share applications for these deconstructive listening skills in our unique work settings.

An interactive website makes it possible for students to participate more actively in decision-making that shapes learning activities. I do my best to build on their preferences – while at the same time, staying grounded in the planning that went into constructing the course syllabus. When students first join the online discussion board, they find several questions from me:

Have you experienced teaching environments where you have felt fully engaged in collaborative learning? What about any classes that have effectively used the online medium? How about any ideas that come from "learning the hard way" about what doesn't work? Sharing these "hands on" educational lessons will help us shape a collaborative learning community conducive to our most stimulating and satisfying learning experiences.

In reflecting on their preferred ways of learning from prior experience, students begin to share stories with each other. Often they speak about their desire for a teaching milieu in which atmosphere and relationships are conducive to taking risks and learning from mistakes.

Posting by Tawanna

I think it is possible to have a relationship that is mutually explorative. The times that I have felt fully engaged and challenged are during class discussions where people are willing to take risks by sharing their ideas and what drives or motivates them. I learn best in a collaborative setting, whether it be small group/class discussions or on an on-line forum. I expect that the course material along with the guest speakers will provide a supportive platform for all of us to learn and share ideas with one another.

I listen to the preferences that students bring to the course. Sometimes I join in by asking more questions. Similar to narrative interviewing, and letter-writing practices, I directly quote students' reflections rather than attempting to interpret their statements. Often, I compile the online suggestions as a way to acknowledge the particular meanings and life experiences valued by classmates; I then invite the students to join me in shaping the course, according to their preferences. I compiled the following list from what students have taught me to share with other instructors:

TEN TIPS FOR CREATING A COLLABORATIVE LEARNING COMMUNITY

- Offer multiple opportunities for students to shape the learning environment based on their own preferences.
- Assume students are knowledgeable and skillful – continually ask them to reflect on learnings from their own life experiences and how we might incorporate their learnings into the class.
- Get students personally involved in what they are learning. Structure exercises and assignments that invite students to apply practices to their own lives.
- Avoid the passive dry lecture format in favor of more active learning with-in-class exercises, letter writing, role-playing, interviews. Experiment with creative options.
- Provide opportunities to "decenter" the teacher's voice and encourage students to share their ideas and work with each other.
- Encourage reflection on readings, in-class experiences, etc. including implications, applications, ripple effects, inspiration and provocations.
- Give two-way accounts of learning: Let students know specific ways this learning experience is affecting you – how what they say and do impacts on your own thoughts, teaching, etc. Avoid the culture of applause. Use yourself as an example when you make mistakes – show how you reflect, acknowledge. and rise to the occasion.
- In academic settings, make the evaluative gaze transparent from the start. Share your dilemmas, intentions, and a behind-the-scenes view of choices you have made.
- Invite conversation with outside voices – guest speakers, virtual visitors, authors, etc. Include people who can speak with insider knowledge.
- Provide continual opportunities over the duration of the course for students to reflect on how the course is going and suggest how to make it better. Strive to make it as comfortable as possible for students to give constructive input and reflect on positive and negative ripple effects of provocative materials on various domains of their lives.

ONLINE CONVERSATION

Using an interactive website has exposed me to a variety of course management tools, all of which feature possibilities for interaction through a discussion board[13]. Online conversation revolves around specific forums that invite participants into dialogue. When students enter the course website, I give a description of the online forum and do my best to familiarize them with the course culture and expectations, as conveyed in the following instructions:

From time to time, I will join the online conversation. I look forward to reading your comments, and to adding my own. As well, please feel free to ask me any specific questions. However, the discussion should not focus on me and my thoughts. This is an opportunity for you to explore and express some of your own ideas based on your own studies and hard-earned knowledge about living and learning. My hope is that we can create a safe context in which we can explore ideas together. We will all be learning from each other, and co-constructing something unique.

Some of you may have had experience with classes that use online discussion as a teaching tool. I welcome any suggestions from your experiences that can make this work as well as possible. Feel free to try out this "discussion tool" by pressing the "discussion" link, and adding your comments here.

Similar to the role of the collaborative therapist, the teacher creates a context for conversation and extending invitations for meaningful engagement while giving space for individual exploration. As course developer, I provide the basic website structure and design. I construct the questions to introduce students both to the philosophical underpinnings of narrative therapy and to explore specific narrative practices. Each week I post several questions based on the in-class experiences, assigned readings, and course curriculum. I invite students to respond to any of these questions – or to start their own thread of inquiry. When I join the online conversation, I take care to keep the students' reflections at the center, to foster a collaborative learning environment in which we are all learning from each other and co-constructing a unique experience.

Students use the discussion forum to post and share reflections and questions about topics as they emerge. They begin engaging in the generous sharing, intimacy, and connectedness that becomes the bedrock of our online learning community. In response to questions, students become "co-researchers," (Epston, 1999) as they apply the ideas and practices to their own lives and work settings. Everyone is expected to participate in the online discussion with at least three postings each week that are based on course content and demonstrate familiarity with the readings. I welcome students to write more, "so long as we make room for everyone's voices to be heard."

Guidelines for Reflections: In addition to the introductory instructions, I post the following guidelines for online reflections:

I will open the discussion with a question. Someone will need to begin the online conversation with a response. The next person's comment should not just refer back to my original question, but rather reflect upon the preceding reflection(s). In other words, please do not put me at the center of your discussion. I want you to listen to each other, and engage in real conversation, which is different from simply waiting for space to say what you want to say. As well, I want to do what we can to minimize the power relations of the "teacher as authority" and learners as "empty vessels" – otherwise known as the "sucking up to the teacher" tradition.

At the same time, every posting need not link with the preceding post. There will be a lot to say, and before long we will have multiple threads going at once. Feel free to ask your own questions, and spontaneously respond to others. If you start a new thread, just give it a new heading, so we will be able to keep track.

After the first week, we will review how this is going, and re-evaluate accordingly. As the course progresses, we will be using the online discussion format to experiment with the guidelines for "reflecting teamwork" and "outsider witness practices." During the second half of the course, you will have the opportunity to share online one of your course assignments, and then to reflect upon each other's work. Instructions for this assignment will be thoroughly described in class. But for the first week, my main goal is to create a secure comfortable conversational context, to get the conversation going and for students to begin to engage with the materials.

Along the way, please feel free to add here any reflections and suggestions that draw from your experiences in using this online forum.

Topics for Online Reflection

Posting by Suzanne

For the first time, I feel like I have the time to really ponder the readings and to be involved in hearing other people's ideas about them so that I can truly immerse myself in the subject matter. I would much rather spend the outside of class time on this than on a research paper.

The questions I post serve as guideposts for the online discussion that is further explored throughout this book. The discussion board is used both for postings that are shared with the entire class, and for the small group work conversations that are later described. Figure 1 illustrates what one discussion board looked like by the end of a course with 20 students lasting five weeks.

SAMPLE QUESTIONS

After the first class, I post questions online to invite students to share their initial thoughts and questions with each other. I do my best to set a welcoming and nonjudgmental tone. I open forums for students to explore together provocative and potentially difficult issues that touch on their own lives and experiences. Here is an introductory question I pose under the forum "Questions and Ponderings:"

This is your chance to try out the discussion board. What are some of your initial thoughts as you begin this course? As you read the course materials, what stands out? What surprises you? What lingers with you from our class meetings? Do you have further reflections on any of the questions posed in class? What do you think about the idea of viewing theories like metaphors situated within a particular historic/cultural context? Which metaphors have you found to be most helpful in your work? What's it like to be asked to deconstruct what you might have otherwise experienced as sacred in your studies so far? Is the world ready for this way of thinking and working? What are your initial thoughts about what it might be like to explore this approach within your existing world? What in particular strikes you about the collaborative nature of this way of working? Do you see application in your work with children and families, and if so, how? Is there a different question that you wished I'd asked and if so, what is it?

Table 2-1. Discussions

Topic	Total
Description of online forum	12
Creating a collaborative learning community	16
Questions and ponderings	46
Identity	26
Narrative as living practice	36
Applications	43
Ethics and accountability	19
Practice	90
Video reflections	22
Preferred identity assignment	33
Tellings and retellings	11
Small group #1: Sarah, Ellen & Jill	17
Small group #2: Kevin, Brenda, Danielle & Julia	38
Small group #3: Amy, Lynn & Cally	23
Small group #4: Kayla T, Karen & Amy R	28
Small group #5: Stacey, Rachel & Danielle	21
Small group #6: Bobbi, Michelle, Carol & Sherry	31
Inspiration and provocation	19
How is this course going?	11
Ripple effects	37
Leftovers	9
Notes	0
Main	1
All	589

From the start, I invite students to grapple in community online with the edges of their learning experiences. I strive to create a space in which people do not need to show off what they know in a cut and dried manner, but rather allow for expressions of confusion, skepticism, and pondering. As students begin to study the specific practices of narrative therapy, I ask the following:

> As you learn about narrative practice, what do you find yourself most intrigued and/or puzzled by? What stands out to you as you learn narrative concepts and practices such as externalizing conversations, unique outcomes, decentering practices, remembering practices, and reauthoring conversations? What questions and/or areas of confusion do you find yourself puzzling over? If you could be in conversation with Michael White or David Epston, what would you want to say and/or ask them?

Deconstructive Listening

Narrative therapy teaches us to think about situations in their cultural and historic contexts, and to inquire into specific discourses such as class, race, gender, and sexuality (Freedman & Combs, 1996b; White, 1991). Students learn to question taken-for-granted beliefs, truths, knowledge, and power. A process of deconstruction is applied to the ideas and experiences that shape service providers' practices and the people who consult them and to their interactions. Professional ideas and practices can be "unpacked" as professional discourses within the cultural history of psychotherapy (Cushman, 1995) including "truth claims" underlying such assumed knowledges as identity, psychopathology, problem formation, and resolution (White, 1997c).

An online forum provides an opportunity for students to experience "deconstructive listening" with each other. They share stories, dilemmas, curiosities, and questions about applications both in personal lives and work contexts. I often begin a discussion topic that invites students to take a critical stance towards taken-for-granted knowledge about psychotherapy. Concurrently, I assign course readings that focus on the meaning of a discourse in social construction (Burr, 1995), the cultural history of psychotherapy (Cushman, 1995) and deconstructing conversations (White, 1991). Time permitting, I show video clips in class from a range of movies and television shows to provoke inquiry into cultural and historic discourses about psychotherapy depicted in popular media. The following online topic and accompanying questions I post have generated very lively discussion:

Cultural and Professional Discourses about Psychotherapy

- How can we take a critical stance toward taken-for-granted knowledge about psychotherapy?
- What part does psychotherapy play in the complicated cultural landscape of early 21st Century America?
- How can a critical inquiry of the helping disciplines influence the ways we think about psychotherapy?

– What are some of the cultural and professional discourses in the United States about mental health and mental illness, therapy, the designated role of the psychotherapist and client and the therapeutic relationship?
– What are some of the "absent but implicit" assumptions about power, gender and culture as depicted in portrayals of therapy in movies and television?
– What are the dominant discourses that circulate in the therapy room? How do these discourses influence the ways we construct meaning about people who consult us, their relationships and our approach to therapy?
– What does all of this have to do with Family Therapy?

I encourage students to step back and identify some of the social influences on their perceived understandings of psychotherapy. Sometimes I join in, sharing with students some of my own thinking and questions. At other times, I listen, reserving my questions for a later time. I share how I too have experienced shock waves in discovering that I could not simply rely on what I had been taught as truth claims — even when I wholeheartedly embraced the logic, wisdom, usefulness of a given concept or categorization. I recount my personal experience of paradoxically feeling discouraged and enlivened by "enlightening disorientation." In Chapter Five, "When Nice is Not Enough," I share student responses to the following questions posted on an online forum entitled "Is nothing sacred?"

If I cannot trust what I have been taught by people I respect, what can I trust? If all knowledge is subjective, does this mean I need to discount psychology's rich history and knowledge base? Will this pursuit isolate me and make me depressed and lonely? Will I alienate myself from respected teachers and colleagues when I apply the tools of critical inquiry to explore their ideas as well? Where is the ground to stand on? Is nothing Sacred?

Ethics and Accountability

Every course on collaborative therapy exposes students to a range of ethical considerations that supplement the practitioner's professional code of ethics. In particular, I design course materials for students to become accountable to their professional privilege as they explore the ethics of collaboration and the inevitable ethical dilemmas that arise in their work as human service practitioners. Throughout the course website, I provide opportunities for students to ponder their personal and professional ethics, as exemplified in my posting below. These key narrative therapy ideas and students' responses to them form a central theme in this book:

In this course, there is frequent reference to ethics and accountability. What are your thoughts about what guides the ethics of practice? To whom is a service provider accountable, and how is this put into practice? What are you noticing about yourself as you think about what informs your own ethical stance? What specific dilemmas come to mind, as you grapple with your concomitant commitments to professional, relational and personal ethics?

When given the opportunity, students have a lot to say about ethics and accountability. Committed to learning their professional code of ethics, they embrace the additional opportunity to talk openly about ethical complexities and consequent dilemmas. They often remark on the contrast with more traditional training in ethics for mental health practitioners, as expressed by Bobbi. "My earlier training was all about boundaries and not in any way revealing anything from my personal life." Online course forums provide opportunities for students' to share their own sophisticated commentaries on ethics.

Posting by Andrew

Ethics are often thrown out there like hard and fast rules, so that we often think of ethics and laws as one and the same. But they are not. I feel that if this is becoming more confusing to you, then you must be headed in the right place. To use the post-modern/social construction/narrative lens on this, why did we become so wrapped up in ethics? Is it to protect the disempowered clients from empowered social workers? Is it because of lots of previous litigation, in which professional organizations like the National Association of Social Workers (NASW) say, "We really need to crank up the ethics training?" Is it to protect our own vulnerabilities? Is it malpractice insurance companies determining what is ethical behavior? How do "template" ethics allow for individual cases where it's up to the person to determine what is/is not ethical? Is it the social work profession trying desperately to legitimize itself through language, professional literature, schools, and ethics? All rhetorical questions of course.

Philosophical Foundations

Classroom experiences, readings, and online discussion give students multiple opportunities to further their understanding of the philosophical foundations of narrative therapy. This book includes many student reflections and questions as they ponder the following questions:

The Narrative Metaphor: *What is meant by the narrative metaphor and how does this impact the way you think about your work? What are the implications for theory and clinical practice? What are your thoughts about the shift in metaphor from individual to systems to stories? What are some of your lingering thoughts after hearing the stories shared in class?*

Therapy as Social Construction: *Given all that you are reading, what are your thoughts about collaborative approaches to therapy and therapy as social construction? What are some of the implications and applications, particularly in your own work settings? What questions does this raise?*

Identity: *What are some of your thoughts about different approaches to identity – structuralist/internal state identity and non-structuralist/intentional understandings of identity? How might this impact on the ways you think about psychotherapy? What relevance might this have for your own life and your identity as a practitioner in training?*

Narrative as Living Practice

Teaching narrative therapy affects people's lives in ways that extend beyond usual academic studies:

Posting by Becca

> *Often course constructs remain in my mind just long enough for me to regurgitate them for the final exam, but soon after, they are quickly pushed aside to make room for new teachings. This time, this will not be the case. In encountering an entirely new way to approach the world through the lens of narrative therapy and its poststructuralist roots, my worldview (and more specifically my perspective on empirical psychology) has been eternally altered. The change in my thought processes that has driven me to question all discourses is in fact so fundamental that I don't believe I could do away with it even if I tried. I find myself continually attempting to share with my fellow psychology majors as well as my other friends the new ideas to which I have been exposed, and I would like to think that if every small event makes an impact on our society, by perpetuating the flow of knowledge, I am helping others to see a new manner of approaching our world from a critical, questioning, and analytical standpoint. Furthermore, I frequently spend time after class relating the stories of guest speakers to my friends and bragging about the fact that we are able to personally interact with the authors of the texts we study. Throughout my college career, I have never witnessed this type of direct involvement in the course material, and it has certainly had a lasting effect on me. If memories are ripples in the fabric of life, my experience this J-term is a tidal wave.*

Through reading assignments, classroom experiences and online forums, I constantly strive to render visible narrative as living practice. After assigning the article "To Do No Harm" (Bird, 2001), I start an online conversation:

> *Johnella Bird describes her way of working as "a living practice." In class, we spoke about holding ourselves accountable to the ideas and practices we embrace. What are some of your thoughts and questions as you reflect on power, language, meaning-making, transparency and the ethic of collaboration? As we begin this course of study together, what are you noticing about how this approach makes sense or does not make sense to you? What role would you like self-reflection to play in your work? What living practices would you like to further develop – and how might you distinguish this commitment from practices of self-surveillance? What else occurs to you as you ponder narrative as living practice?*

I demonstrate how teaching informs my work as a therapist and vice versa. As a practitioner-teacher, I share stories from my work as a therapist that breathe life into philosophical ideas. I then invite students to write letters and share online reflections with the people whose stories they hear. Michael White's attention to what we hold most precious to us guides our study of poststructuralist inquiry and intentional understandings of identity (Thomas, 2002). Class exercises and course assignments give students opportunities to "try out" narrative practices, applying them to their own lives and relationships. Students often share online their various challenges as they attempt to apply narrative practices to their particular work contexts.

PEOPLING THE EXCHANGE

With students' permission, I offer a "guest pass" to select authors, guest speakers and narrative therapy enthusiasts. Many students find this to be an invigorating, expanding approach that greatly contributes to their learning. I further explain and illustrate this teaching practice in Chapter Six, "Peopling the Course." Sometimes virtual visitors ask questions that otherwise might go unnoticed. For example, in the following exchange, Jo Viljoen, an online guest from South Africa, inquires into students' learning experiences:

> *Hi everyone, I would like to consult with you as students, if I may. I am teaching a short course in narrative therapy over here in South Africa and I would love to hear from you what it was that sparked your interest in the course. I would like to know this for my own preparation for my own students. What should a teacher of narrative do and not do for her students? How did Peggy manage to get you all so actively involved? What does it mean to you to be able to make such detailed contributions to the course through your papers and reflections? I would really appreciate some ideas from your side of the world. Thanks in advance.*

Posting by Becca

> *Hi Jo, There are a number of things that Peggy has done that have proved successful in sparking our interest in the material. For me, the most beneficial has been her intent on getting us personally involved with what we are learning. Be it in class discussion, Internet posts or paper assignments that relate the ideas to our own lives and studies, this approach allows students to get away from the passive, dry lecture format and into the realm of more active learning.*

> *The Internet reflections have been one of my favorite parts of this course. Through the posting process, we are given more time to prepare our thoughts. Secondly, posting not only provides us with the opportunity to continue discussions after class is over, but also allows for input from authors, guest speakers, and therapists or other knowledgeable individuals. In addition, posting gives the more reserved students an opportunity to express their ideas in absence of the pressure and trepidation of addressing a large group of people. Finally, posting allows us to make detailed contributions to the course, which has given me a great deal of confidence in*

my ability to share my own thoughts within a discussion setting. It is quite rewarding to see not only that others may have been thinking along the same lines, but also that classmates are able to expand the possibilities and bring to light new or different perspectives.

Sometimes, I am able to arrange for students to engage in conversation with authors of their assigned readings. At other times, I ask students to post the questions they might like to ask the authors. When guest speakers come to class, I start an online forum in which students can share further questions, reflections and acknowledgments. Often, the guest speakers will continue to engage with students by joining them on the online forum; alternatively, I serve as an online conduit, by emailing postings to them.

PRACTICE, PRACTICE, PRACTICE

A course website gives ample opportunities for students to reflect on shared exercises. Often, students start their own threads, posting reflections and asking each other questions. As students learn to distinguish the conceptual framework and guiding principles of narrative practice from other therapeutic approaches, they become familiar with specific narrative interviewing practices (Morgan, 2000b; Russell & Carey, 2004; White, 2007c). Throughout the course, I give students multiple opportunities to experience narrative practice "from the inside out." Students read about a specific narrative interviewing practice, try it out in class, and then after class share online the effects of these experiences. Following are examples of how I prompt the online discussion:

Statement of position map: Today we talked further about the "statement of position" map and externalizing conversations. From various perspectives, you had the opportunity to experience externalizing conversations within the in-class interviewing exercise. What are some of your lingering thoughts and questions? How do these reflections link to what you have been reading? What are you left wondering? What kind of practice would you like to experience more in order to feel confident with asking questions oriented by the statement of position map?

Reauthoring conversations: You have now been introduced to Michael White's "reauthoring conversations" map. What comes to mind as you begin to study this map and apply it to yourself? Does it seem relevant to your interviewing in specific work situation and if so, how? What seems confusing, unsettling and/or enticing about possible uses of this map in your work?

Outsider witness practices: Through your reading and in class, you have been learning about incorporating outsider witness practices and the four categories of response into narrative practice. What are some outsider witness skills that you would like to further develop? Can you envision creative ways to link people's lives with shared themes within your own work setting? What possibilities are you thinking about? Are there areas of excitement for you? Are there also dilemmas on your mind, and if so, how do you envision addressing them?

Interviewing practices: *Today in class we experienced a four-part narrative interview. Thank you, Sarah for volunteering and sharing some of your inner life with us. This forum is for any lingering thoughts about the interview. Sarah, you are welcome (but not in any way required) to share any reflections on the experience. For the rest of us, this is an opportunity to continue the fourth part of the interview – do you have any "debriefing" questions, thoughts, ponderings?....What was it like to participate in this interview? What was it like to be an outsider witness (in either the first or the second "tier")? What do you find yourself still thinking about? If you had it to do over again, is there anything you would change? What have I forgotten to ask that you would like to say about this interview experience?*

I then offer additional invitations for students to reflect online on their in-class experiences:

Today (in a very hot, humid room) you watched David Epston's interview with Sebastian[14]. You were also given a session transcript, with the instruction to take note of whenever in the interview you felt a glimmer of hope or solidarity, from the perspective of either Sebastian's mother or stepfather. What did you discover when you traced these moments of hope and/or solidarity to specific questions? What did you notice about this interview and David's practices of inquiry that really captured your attention? What do you think about his notion that "open ended questions invite dullness," and of David's proposal that the more specific you wish an inquiry to be the more specific the questions should be? What would you like to learn about David's approach to narrative inquiry and what questions does this raise for you? What have I forgotten to ask (blame it on the humidity) that you would like to address either online or in a subsequent class?

Letter-Writing

After experiencing a narrative interview in class – either live or on video – we often practice letter-writing. I then create an online topic to practice letter-writing skills, and as an opportunity to conflate training, supervision, and practice:

Narrative therapy offers boundless opportunities for letter-writing and other therapeutic documents. What kind of letter-writing skills would you like to further develop? What are your current thoughts about the potential for various kinds of therapeutic documents in your own workplace? What are you reading about and/or hearing in class that you find yourself pondering? Can you think of a particular story to tell that would illustrate how these practices have or might "thicken" the alternative story?

I invite students to bring their reflections and questions online:

What are you thinking about since watching the DVD of the interview with Meghan and me? What was it like to write the letters to Meghan? Do you notice any new developments in your reflections on boundaries and ethics? What if anything do you find yourself pondering about endings and new beginnings? How are these reflections informing your understandings of and questions about narrative practice?

Apprenticing to a Craft

Online forums for letter-writing provide multiple opportunities to practice revisions in honing letter-writing skills. I post the following question to encourage the students:

Today in class we spent some time crafting a "Take 2" of letters written to Meghan in response to having viewed the DVD of the conversation about our work together. Thank you to those of you who gave me these handwritten revisions. I really appreciate the specific ways you illustrate shifting from "telling" to "asking" in these letters. This is the forum for any of you to post any other newly crafted letters ("Take 2" or even "Take 3") and/or to share any reflections on letter-writing. What has been particularly interesting to you about our focus on letter-writing in this course? What do you find yourself pondering? How (if at all) do you think this practice might influence your work outside of this course?

When we repeat an in-class exercise, I create online space for further reflections:

During our final class, we did a "Take 2" of an interviewing exercise, as a way to practice the statement of position map. Thank you Sherry, Bobbi, Danielle, and Michelle for being our volunteers. This space is for reflections on this exercise. Bobbi, Danielle, and Michelle, as our scribes, would you be willing to share with us here what you wrote down about our questions? What was it like to be the scribe and is there anything about this experience that you'd like to write about? Sherry, what lingering thoughts about this experience would you be willing to share with us?

What was it like for the rest of you to participate in this group exercise, and what are your lingering thoughts and questions? Would you recommend doing this exercise again and if so, are there any specific adaptations with which you would like to experiment?

In Chapter Eleven, I further explore ways in which students apprentice themselves to the craft of letter-writing.

Inspiration and Provocation

I always create an online forum for students to share writings they consider their personal favorites: "Here is space for anyone to share inspirational (and/or provocative) poems, parables, songs, quotes, and any other modes of expression that engage the heart, mind and soul."

I am often struck by the common threads that link our lives and the generosity with which students share with each other when asked. Students freely share passages from their favorite novels, poems, songs or philosophers. Lynn offered a favorite quote by David Whyte that hangs in her home and work offices: "Whatever the hour of the day in our work, we must do the right thing in the right way, for the right end; work that makes sense of the hours that we are privileged to live."

As a participant in a Unlearning Racism Group, Sandra shared several poems that they had melded together into a beautiful spoken word piece.

"If you have come to help me, you are wasting your time.
But, if you have come because your liberation is bound up with mine
then let us work together."
  Lila Watson

"We are afraid to rock the boat in which we hope to drift safely through
life's currents, when, actually, the boat is stuck on a sandbar. We would be
better off to rock the boat, and try to shake it loose, or, better still,
jump in the water and swim to shore."
  Thomas Szasz

"What a delight it is to respect people!"
  Anton Chekhov

"When I despair,
I remember there have been tyrants and murderers,
and for a time they seem invincible,
but in the end, they always fall.
Think of it, always."
  Mahatma Gandhi

"I used to be a discipline problem,
which caused me embarrassment
until I realized that being a discipline problem in a racist society
is sometimes an honor."
  Ishmael Reed

Course Assignments

In addition to online forums, the course website offers opportunities for students to post and reflect on written assignments. I describe in detail my favorite assignment, "Developing Preferred Stories of Identity," in Chapter Seven. I designed the "Preferred Identity" assignment so that while students were studying outsider witness practices and definitional ceremonies (White, 1995b), they would experience the communal nature of narrative work with multiple online tellings of their own preferred stories as practitioners. Students apply Michael White's "landscape of identity, landscape of action micro-map of narrative practice" to their own personal stories of identity as practitioners.[15] Based on White's creative adaptation of Jerome Bruner's ideas about the dual landscapes of action and of consciousness (Bruner, 1986, 1990), landscape of action questions encourage people to situate influential events within the past, present, and future. Landscape of identity questions inquire into the meaning of developments that occur in actions, which can include perceptions, thoughts, beliefs, speculations, realizations, and conclusions (White, 1988).

Each student constructs a "personal micro-map" and a letter of commitment. The course website makes it possible to post the assignment instructions, illustrations from prior students' work and space for questions and/reflections. I assign students to online small groups where they post both parts of this assignment, as attachments. In addition, they are expected to read and post a brief reflection for the written materials posted by each member of their small group:

> *Each of you will be assigned to one of 5-6 online small groups where you will post the class assignment. In addition, you are expected to read and post a brief reflection for posted work by each member of your small group. The logistical details will be decided during our next class.*

I give students the choice of either posting their first assignments online or sending them to me privately. I hope they will take the risk of having their stories of identity as social workers publicly witnessed. However, I do not want anyone to feel pressured to do so. Nor do I want technological worries to be the deciding factor. Most students choose to post online, but I make sure that they know their options are open:

> *Many of you have now joined online small groups where you will post the class assignment. In addition, you are expected to read and post a brief reflection for posted work by each member of your small group. One group – Chappell, Kim, and Heidi – has chosen to share their reflections in person rather than online. Several students have opted not to join small groups, rather to keep this exercise more personal for themselves. Whether privately, in class, or online, I hope we can share some of these experiences with each other in class. Here is space for reflections about your experiences of various aspects of this assignment. I believe this is going to be an engaging assignment within a very busy week. Enjoy!*

Often, the words that make the difference come not from the instructor, but from a classmate. When Steve posted reflections on how much he enjoyed the exercise and learning about himself through it, he described how it "hardly felt like an assignment." He then encouraged others to share their maps, created and posted by computer as "a means to deepen our understanding of each others' unique stories and commitment to this art of social work." For anyone with questions, he offered to give pointers on how to design a map in Microsoft Word. In fact, the only times students did not post their work online seemed due to technological difficulties. I was awestruck by the quality of the students' maps and letters. One of the most perplexing aspects of writing this book has been choosing just a few illustrations from a myriad of possibilities.

STUDENTS AS CO-PILOTS

An interactive course website makes it possible to continually check in with students about their course experiences in order to co-create what emerges. After a given class, I start an online topic inviting students to engage in conversation on our recent shared experience. I listen carefully to what the students tell me; their reflections actively shape the emerging course structure, climate, and expectations. I bring forward what I learn from students each semester into how I structure future courses, building on the accumulating knowledge.

While involving students in shaping the course, I also do plenty of upfront planning. I take seriously my role in setting up the structure for an interactive space for shared learning. I want to involve students in making sure that the environment and methods are most conducive to their participation and sharing with one another in ways that will best help them learn and benefit from the course. However, I don't just throw out my syllabus in favor of giving a forum to whatever students want to discuss. I also let in students on my teaching challenge to do justice to the multiple theoretical and epistemological developments in the field of family therapy in preparation for teaching specific narrative practices.

I regularly post my intentions for a given class and ask students for any requests. The post goes something like this, "Here is what I am planning. How does that sound to you? What else would you prefer? While I cannot promise to incorporate all suggestions, I am most interested to hear what you think." Students respond with many excellent suggestions. They want experiential activities, role plays and practice with questions. They also appreciate illustrations in class and in their assigned reading. Often they give me concrete suggestions on bringing more practice and less lecture into our classroom meetings. Students not only give their own ideas, but respond to and build on one another's suggestions, all of which helps me structure the class in the way that they see as most beneficial to 1) create a collaborative learning community and 2) deepen their learning.

Class Rituals

As the course progresses, I give multiple opportunities for students to create class rituals. Students have excellent suggestions for both celebration and meaningful activities. Danielle captured the spirit of collaboration in this class in making the following suggestion while also asking classmates for their ideas. After reading about ceremonies, celebrations and acknowledgements (Morgan, 2000a), she asked her classmates: "As you look at this class, what would be a fitting celebration for you to acknowledge what you have experienced over the last 5 weeks?" I then compiled the suggestions into a proposed plan for the last day of class. I added:

Is there anything you'd like to see happen on the last day of class? Danielle and I have created one plan for the last class (under "applications" /"ceremonies and celebrations"). Let me know any other thoughts you might have. We really haven't had sufficient class time to discuss the readings for this course. I'd like to do something the last day with the eight articles assigned for the last day of class (these are listed on the syllabus). Could each of you commit to reading at least two of these articles? We can then share with each other some of what we've learned from these readings. Here too, let me know if you have any suggestions.

Leftovers

I encourage students to keep talking online even after the final class. Students are welcome to post anywhere. I start a leftovers forum: "Here is a space for whatever is leftover and still yearns to be said." Some course websites remains active for a week or two after the course ends. Students can continue to refer back to reread conversation and consult resources for as long as they have access to the website.

You've all now left – it's nearly 6 pm and I'm about to head home. The classroom feels rather empty without you all. I know that I have so many more questions and reflections to offer but right now I am not remembering what I wanted to say. Please don't hesitate to linger a bit longer in this rich conversation. What do you find yourself thinking about as you digest today's class? What were your thoughts about the (MastersWork) Lorraine Hedtke video, "Grief Takes a Holiday"? What stands out to you as we approach the finish line of this course?

CONTRIBUTION OF AN INTERACTIVE WEBSITE

I have found that the ease with which students weigh in on the quality of their learning experience is a unique and valuable aspect of the online approach, which clearly sets it apart from the classroom. The comments that students share online – their discomfort, enthusiasm, excitement, trepidation, and so on – greatly contribute to the sense that we are co-creating a learning community. Contrary to students' expressed concern about looking into a screen detracting from a positive learning environment, posting their thoughts on the course website seems to be a safer, more comfortable way for students to reflect on the teaching methods as opposed to focusing solely on content. This is one way in which I see the online resource as far more than just another communication tool – it has opened up a whole new dimension of participation and shared commitment to creating a collaborative learning environment.

While there is necessarily a certain amount of trial and error, my students have been quite forgiving. I consciously hold myself back from being in the center of online conversation, and find that students ably cultivate their own conversations without me. In fact, my voice as instructor seems to be only slightly elevated, which is different than what generally occurs in a classroom. Together we experience the democratization of the online medium, which is conducive to being equals in sharing a love of learning, a quest for knowledge, and opportunities for practice. There emerges a great sense of "we're all in this together."

Adjusting to the Changes

An interactive website provides a medium to explore and experiment with innovative teaching practices based on collaborative and relational ways of learning. With careful preparation and monitoring, the classroom that extends into cyberspace can become a playground and learning lab. As teacher, I am vitally engaged in dialogue that often transports me into new territories of learning. Simultaneously, I am responsible for structuring the flow and direction of conversation. I am accountable to course and workshop learning goals.

Reviewers of this chapter asked me to say more about my own experiences in shifting teaching paradigms: "Have you always taught in these ways? How did the old way raise its head or try to pull you back, with you, with your students and with the student-teacher relationship? What has helped you to make these changes? How do you fit in technology while preserving a sense of balance in your life?"

I have always been drawn to collaborative ways of working. As a human service provider, therapist, manager, organizational consultant and teacher, I am more comfortable in the role of facilitator than as expert. Whenever possible, I like to build dialogue and create bridges between people and to cross-pollinate ideas. Thus, the transition in teaching from "sage on the stage to the guide on the side" and toward networking is not a big a jump for me. I cannot speak to what this adjustment might be like for other teachers less comfortable with these changes. Technology breaks down the traditional hierarchy. The more traditional teaching strategies one is used to employing, the more challenging the introduction of educational technology will likely be.

I have been using an interactive website since 2001. Strangely, I now have trouble recalling what it was like teaching prior to this innovation. Email correspondence with friends and colleagues around the world has also become an integral aspect of my life and work. However, interacting in person with people in my daily life is also very important to me. I live rurally and deeply value an outdoor life where technology has no place. I try to closely monitor that balance.

Once I experienced firsthand the online possibilities, I became an enthusiastic convert. Maybe parenting is an apt metaphor. Non-parents might ask, "Why on earth would you choose to do something that takes so much work and poses such a time squeeze?" The extra work is secondary to the complex web of life-enriching contributions.

Most of my struggles along the way are related to frustrations in becoming familiar with technical details. I am far from a technological whiz and every step has developed through trial and error. Sometime in the 1990s, I realized that educational technology is here to stay – and I would miss out on a lot if I chose to ignore it. I made a conscious decision to stay open to possibilities. I am glad I have, and appreciate the opportunity to share my excitement and the strategies that have worked for me with readers of this book.

At the same time, I try to remember my privileges. By now, I have more than 15 years of experience with computer technology. I own a desktop and a laptop. I have high speed Internet service at home and at my office. I am a fast typist. I know resources to call on when in need of help.

While I embrace technology as a tool to reinforce my teaching principles (see Chapter Three, "Teaching Congruently"), I do not want my teaching to become dominated by technology. In fact, this is a possibility I intentionally guard against. For example, I pay attention to the interaction between technology and the teaching space. The configuration of technologically-enhanced classrooms can either reinforce or distract from collaborative teaching goals. In my experience, many technology support people do not appreciate the nuances of creating a safe comfortable environment that encourages conversations. I have moved out of many assigned classrooms in search of space that is an encouragement, not an impediment, to good conversation. When in doubt, I would always take a comfortable learning space before technology. Hopefully, I won't have to make that choice.

Teaching Challenges

An interactive website engages students to become active participants in their own learning. Yet the online medium does not motivate every student to take on rigorous study and practice of course materials. My highly motivated and hard-working students are not solely a reflection on my teaching skills and ability to engage them; the make-up of some classes works better than others. As with classroom teaching, some students are enthusiastic but unable to devote the necessary time. Others are distracted, or their interest in the course content is not fully sparked. Some who are initially reticent become more involved over time, once the online conversations get going. I have heard from several students who reviewed this manuscript that I kindled an intrigue with narrative therapy that lay dormant until a few years later when something shifted in their work lives.

I keep a close watch on the student make-up of a given course. Are most of them more interested in talking about guest speakers than discussing course materials? Do nearly all actually complete the readings? Have I given them too much free rein in their assignments? Is their thinking getting sufficiently challenged? Who is getting left behind? Whose voice is not being heard?

I find that the interactive course website gives additional opportunities for the teacher to get to know students' individual learning needs. By listening in to their discussion on online forums, I am repeatedly stunned by how quickly I become intimately acquainted with students, not only their names but their thinking, study habits, and particular interest areas. Because I consider it essential that I quickly connect online voices to classroom faces, for the first few classes, I ask students to use name tags.

Is creating an interactive website too much work? I have often heard teachers lament that they don't know how they could add something so labor-intensive into their teaching. It does take a significant investment of time to construct an interactive website, set up online forums, and regularly monitor conversation. Yet for me, creating and participating in the website is energizing; it so enriches the collaborative learning community I strive for that it is well worth the effort. Once the structure is in place, I experience joy and intrigue in performing teaching tasks that otherwise might feel laborious and protracted. I can't imagine going back to "before the course website."

TEACHING CONGRUENTLY

Posting by Emma

I am trying to embrace the philosophy of doing the best that I can, knowing that there is bound to be quite a bit of "failure" along the way. I want to embrace a path of conviction with my actions and words that are not without consequence. I see that happening with everyone [in the class], and I think that is the beginning (given our short period of time together) of a collaborative learning community. That's exciting.

Teaching particular content is only part of the teacher's responsibility. Recent literature on therapist training supports teachers and practitioners reflecting on their position for both ethical and pragmatic reasons (Paré, 2007). Teaching colleagues share a commitment to establish teaching practices that keep us alert to the complexities of social exchange – to what we attend to and what we leave out of conversations (Crocket, Kotzé, & Flintoff, 2007; Davies & Harré, 1990). New Zealanders Dorothea Lewis and Aileen Cheshire introduce the Maori term *Te Whakaakona* that includes in one word the concepts of teaching and learning; while the teacher and students learn side-by-side, the teacher is responsible for teaching practices that foster learning through discovery for both students and teacher, and, feedback on practice. Meanwhile, Nigel Parton and Patrick O'Bryne recognize process knowledge and product knowledge (Sheppard, Newstead, DiCaccavo, & Ryan, 2000) as informing any theoretical approach that aims to make a direct contribution to practice itself (Parton & O'Byrne, 2000).

Like these authors, I pay attention to the effects of my practices as teacher on students. The way I position myself as a teacher mirrors my favored approach to therapeutic work. As teacher, I want to think beyond good intentions (Bird, 2001) and to practice in ways that minimize discrepancies between theory and practice (Schon, 1983). In the previous two chapters, I discussed several aspects of the remarkable new pedagogical opportunities that an interactive website creates – how I structure online forums to provide space for students to share their experiences as reflective practitioners-in-training, and for exchanges that build on an ethos of respectful mutual discovery. Here I further reflect on principles that shape the ethics of my teaching practices.

This chapter begins with a brief description of six influential developments in the fields of therapy, organization development, teaching and research that provide "lenses" that inform my efforts towards this same consistency, or what I like to call "congruency" in my teaching practices. I further describe five concepts – isomorphism, transparency, ethics of care, partnership accountability and ethics without virtue – that guide my approach to internal consistency. I then show how I become a reflective teacher by applying these concepts and lenses to give students a more transparent and in-depth view of my story as a practitioner.

SIX GUIDING LENSES

The continuing infusion of new ideas from my studies as well as from students refreshes and energizes me as a teacher – I remain an active learner right alongside my students. I also draw from my cumulative understanding of developments in fields of study that have most influenced my approach to my work. I here highlight six lenses that influence my stance as a teacher and keep me honest in my exchanges with students:
- A reflexive stance (family therapy)
- Learning-centered teaching (adult learning)
- The reflective practitioner   (organization development)
- Family-centered practices (human services)
- Participative inquiry (research)
- Co-research (narrative therapy)

A Reflexive Stance for Family Therapy

Reflexive is defined in the Random House Dictionary as "the bending or folding back of a part upon itself." Lynn Hoffman suggests as a graphic synonym a figure eight, which is also the sign for infinity (Hoffman, 1992). She further describes that to her, "the word implies that there is equity in regard to participation even though the parties may have different positions or different traits" (p. 126). A reflexive stance for family therapy is one that is more participatory, less hierarchical, and mutually influenced.

I strive to bring into my work – as therapist, consultant, and teacher – the spirit and pragmatics of such reflexive processes as reflecting teamwork and collaborative inquiry (Roth, 2007). An interactive website offers additional opportunities to teach congruently with reflexive processes. Students practice skills of reflection and inquiry in the online discussion forums. As teacher, I continuously check in with students, "folding back" to steer the course towards promoting learning congruent with the actual collaborative practices I am teaching.

Learning-Centered Teaching

Excellent materials on adult learning offer first-rate tips collected by seasoned teachers who share their hard-earned wisdom toward facilitating active learning in higher education (Brookfield, 1986, 1990, 1995; Knowles, 1984, 1989; McKeachie & Svinicki, 2006; Vella, 1995a, 1995b; Weimer, 2002). Every time I consult these books, I learn something new from the higher education community about the passions, responsibilities, and challenges of teaching congruently while dealing with the political realities of teaching. I especially appreciate two trends: 1) learner-centered teaching that seeks to connect instructional practice to what is empirically known about learning (Weimer, 2002) and 2) critically reflective teaching through which teachers reframe their teaching to intentionally draw from their personal backgrounds and experience and become more aware of the effects of their own assumptions on teaching practices (Brookfield, 1995).

Stephen Brookfield suggests specific reflective practices for teachers to discover and examine their own assumptions (Brookfield, 1995). He organizes dozens of classroom illustrations into four distinct yet overlapping lenses for teachers: 1) autobiographical reflection; 2) students' eyes; 3) colleagues' perceptions and experiences; 4) theoretical frameworks reflected in the literature. I find this four-part system appealing because it proposes specific practices for teachers to become accountable to themselves, their students, colleagues, and their theoretical background. I too aspire to develop habits to reflect on my biases, to elicit and learn from students' experiences, to develop connections with teaching colleagues, and stay grounded in the various literatures.

The Reflective Practitioner

I consciously seek to align my teaching practices with my stated beliefs. I draw inspiration from the work of Argyris and Schon who have written extensively about "theories of action" – specific practices for "the reflective practitioner" – to think in action and put espoused theory into practice (Argyris, 1993; Argyris & Schon, 1974; Argyris & Schon, 1996).

When I discovered Schon's concept of "a reflective contract" (Schon, 1983, 1987) I was struck by similarities with Dunst's "participatory practices" (Dunst, Trivette, & Deal, 1994; Dunst, Trivette, Davis, & Cornwell, 1994), both of which orient practitioners to become more directly accountable to the client and consequently require new kinds of competencies. I aim for the classroom and interactive website to become places to reflect on our professional privilege and participation in systems and ways of thinking that elevate the expertise of those with more power over the resourcefulness of the people who seek our services. In my teaching, I actively seek to change habits, question assumptions, and explore new possibilities. Whenever possible, I share with students my discomfort that leads to self-questioning and actual changes in practices.

Family-Centered Practices

My teaching reflects my fierce commitment to a family-centered approach. I have been learning directly from the family members who consult with me since the mid 1970s. I am also a student and advocate of family-centered care and the family support movement. Family-centered approaches have evolved from a generalized reference to practices that emphasize the family rather than an individual, into a

49

coherent philosophy of care based on generally agreed-upon principles and practices which recognize, respect, support, and build upon the family's central role in caring for children (Adams & Nelson, 1995; Briar-Lawson, Lawson, Hennon, & Jones, 2001; Dunst, Trivette, & Thompson, 1991).

The human services field has developed a common language to describe service principles as "family-centered," "community-based," "culturally competent," and "consumer driven" (Kinney, Strand, Hagerup, & Bruner, 1994; Schorr, 1991; Stroul & Friedman, 1988). I strive to model a respect for families and commitment to these principles that extends beyond such buzzwords to experience firsthand participative practices that actively engage people in decision-making, community-building, cultural learning, and apprenticeship training.

In my teaching, I often draw from what I learned from a participatory action research project I co-conducted about more equitable participative relationships between the seekers of human services and the providers and planners of these services (Sax, 2000). The project explored how relationships between human service seekers, providers, and planners can move beyond the traditional medical and mental health models defined by clinical distance and hierarchical organization, with the professional in the position of expert. I applied narrative practices within a community context to guide parents and professionals to give detailed accounts from life experiences of preferred ways of being in relation to each other. This research offered providers and family-centered systems of care helpful strategies for inviting effective working relationships with parents of young children with mental health concerns, based on recommendations provided by parents (Sax, 2007b)[16].

Similar principles guide my teaching. I want to join students in a learning endeavor without taking over. I seek teaching strategies that support their active involvement with the course materials. Together we put great care into co-creating a learning environment conducive to learning from each other.

Participative Inquiry

My experience as an action-researcher has influenced me in ways I could never have predicted. I approach teaching as a form of "participative inquiry," which Peter Reason describes as collaborative processes *with* and *for* people rather than *on* people (Reason, 1988; Reason, 1994a, 1994b; Reason & Rowan, 1994). A participative inquiry worldview challenges the bright clearly defined line that investigators often try to draw between science and everyday life in human services, organizational development, and community studies. Researchers do not stand outside, but rather, are members of the researched community. Thus, participants become co-researchers to engage with experience and to integrate action with reflection. Rigor is developed through critical self-reflection and openness to outside feedback.

Four themes influence my teaching that Stringer described as fundamentals for community-based action research (Stringer, 1996):
- Rigorously empirical and reflective;

- Engages people who have traditionally been called "subjects" as active participants in the research process;
- Results in practical outcomes related to the lives or work of the participants; and
- Develops a sense of community in process as a condition for continuing action.

Co-Research

In narrative practice, "co-research" refers to the process by which people inquire together to create original research about local knowledge – to learn from people's direct experiences to discover what is most meaningful to them in learning from particular life situations and relationships (Denborough, 2004; Epston, 1999, 2004; Maisel, Epston, & Borden, 2004; White, 1997e). The narrative interviewer adopts a position of inquiry guided by specific "maps" to co-explore "insider knowledge" and skills of living learned by the interviewee through the experiences of living their lives (Epston & White, 1992). Participating as a co-researcher can bolster individuals' self-confidence and shape positive identity conclusions (Gaddis, 2004; White, 2001).

I have come to believe that co-research positioning – learning to move from a place of embodied curiosity – is the "powerhouse" of narrative practice, akin to learning to move from the abdominal powerhouse in Pilates, as the energetic center of the body. I further develop this theme in Chapter 13, "Apprenticing to a Craft." This book is filled with illustrations of how teaching narrative practice offers unique opportunities for students to engage in original co-research about course material. For example, classroom teaching coupled with a course website offers an engaging setting for ongoing consultation between students and teacher to guide coursework. I structure activities, conversation, and assignments for students to repeatedly practice inquiring into each other's experiences – and to experience the self-confidence that can emerge from participating in exchanges characterized by respect and earnest curiosity.

FIVE GUIDING CONCEPTS

Isomorphism

I first came across the term "isomorphism" in the literature on clinical supervision (Behan, 2003; Wynne, McDaniel, & Weber, 1986). Isomorphism is a mathematical term referring to the "same shape" between different objects in which the essence is the same. If two objects are isomorphic, what is true for one is true for the other. In mathematics, isomorphisms extend maps of theorems from solid ground where a problem is more understood into unfamiliar territory. Similarly, the practice of consultation parallels the practice of therapy, differing only in the context for the respective application (Anderson & Goolishian, 1986). Whether consulting with agencies or families, the consultant positions herself according to similar guiding principles and pursues matching actions.

My teaching is also replete with isomorphisms. Both in the classroom and online, I strive to reflect living practice of a particular stance toward all people including those who consult with me in therapeutic contexts. For example, my teaching strategies aim to inquire into students' experiences so that I can better understand their distinctive stories within the framework of the concepts I am teaching. I strive to learn from students with a spirit of "Ask, don't tell" inquiry just as I do with the people who consult with me in my practice as a family therapist. People have graciously given me permission to share accounts of their therapeutic journeys through recordings of interviews, poems, letters and journal entries. Through these teaching stories, I want the students to experience firsthand the hospitality, and respectful curiosity with which I approach people who consult with me.

Transparency

Transparency practices challenge the traditional therapist-client relationship characterized by professional distancing and one-way accounts of the help seeking relationship. In contrast, narrative therapists learn to share their organizing thoughts and assumptions with clients. Madsen (2007) describes "conducting therapy with subtitles that show our thinking" as the relational stance that is the foundation for clinical work. He includes examples, such as the question "Would you be interested in my thinking behind this question and why I'm asking it?"

Similar practices of transparency guide my pedagogy. In teaching narrative therapy, I strive to give a "behind-the-scenes" view of my thinking – to situate my ideas and practices in the context of my own life experiences. Later in this chapter, I excerpt an online account of some of the events and abiding realizations that have guided my work since the mid-1970s, when I first became a human services provider.

On the course website, I make every effort to make my choices as teacher as transparent as I can, asking questions in ways that model the concepts and practices that students are studying. In one course, I started an online conversation about "Teaching Congruently" with the following set of questions:

I have discovered that students will 1) work hard to understand a concept when they have opportunities to apply it to themselves; 2) make real connections between narrative ideas and their own lives and relationships; and 3) develop a sense of community as they share their reflections and assignments in class and online. As a member of this learning community, how do you experience this approach to teaching? What links are you making between the materials you are reading, classroom experiences, and your own learnings? Do you have ideas about how to further develop these links between your own lives and the materials that you are studying in ways that will be most helpful to you?

Ethics of Care

In researching this book, I discovered a burgeoning literature and hot debate about the feminist ethic of care. Nigel Parton identifies this debate as being at the center of the moral and political rethinking of constructive professional practice (Parton, 2003; Parton & O'Byrne, 2000). Authors identify the cultural devaluation of "care work" (Tronto, 1993) and propose that practitioners establish a relational stance with clients based on mutual interdependence, and value practices of attentiveness, responsiveness, competence, responsibility, negotiation and mutual recognition (Wiliams, 1999). Parton cites Davies as pointing to other characteristics that can emerge once an ethic of care is in place: "reflectively using expertise and experience; creating an active community in which a solution can be negotiated; recognizing interdependence with others; collectively being accountable for practice; an engaged and committed stance towards client or service user; and accept use of self as part of the therapeutic or professional encounter" (Davies, 2000) (p. 350). Other authors use the term "an ethic of care" to describe practices by people in a range of circumstances that evoke a sense of solidarity, extending and expressing care into wider communities (Crocket et al., 2007; Sevenhuijsen, 1998). This concept of solidarity also struggles to accommodate difference (Dean, 1996).

I believe these ethics of care are at the root of both therapeutic practice within contemporary mental health and social services, and teaching. Frances Hancock and David Epston refer to an ethic of hospitality – "older and somewhat 'wiser' traditions of the 'care' of and 'respect' for others, especially those in some sort of need or vulnerability" (Hancock & Epston, 2005). I encourage students to follow the aspiration described by Epston and Hancock[17] to become "a practitioner of hope and of respect." By "respect" I am referring to Sarah Lawrence-Lightfoot's definition of respect as "creat(ing) symmetry, empathy and connection in all kinds of relationships, even those, such as teacher and student, doctor and patient, commonly seen as unequal" (Lawrence-Lightfoot, 2000). She further describes respect "not only as an expression of circumstance, history, temperament, and culture, rooted in rituals and habits, but also arising from efforts to break with routine and imagine other ways of giving and receiving trust, and in so doing, creating relationships among equals." (p. 9-10).

Partnership Accountability

My teaching and therapeutic practices have been influenced by the work of the Family Centre in Lower Hutt, New Zealand and the concept of "partnership accountability" in which people are mutually accountable to each other, while those with more power take responsibility to amplify the voices less likely to be heard and hold themselves accountable to the people most affected by their actions (Tamasese, Waldegrave, Tuhaka, & Campbell, 1998; Tamasese & Waldergrave, 1993; Waldergrave et al., 2003). The Just Therapy team developed practices to ensure that people of different cultures in an agency or institution can be protected against gender and culture bias. They outlined possibilities for responsible partnerships so that subtle experiences of discrimination in the workplace can be named and addressed. Their radical approach reverses the usual modes of accountability in which management and decision-making are in the hands of those with more power in the organization. Instead, it is assumed that the groups that have been unjustly treated best judge injustice. In their New Zealand setting, this means that the Maori and Pacific Island sections are self-determining, while the Pakeha (White) section is accountable to the other two sections. A similar accountability structure exists for women and men.

In all of my work, I am acutely aware of my power and privilege. As a human services provider, I believe in questioning practices that make professionals primarily accountable to peers and supervisors instead of to those who seek their services. As teacher, I intentionally create learning opportunities that amplify students' voices. In designing activities in the classroom and online, I hold myself accountable to students, as they are most affected by my actions. I also expect students to practice accountability throughout the class – for example, to keep up with reading materials and assignments, even if they will miss any class time, to check in with me and other students to find out what they missed, and to actively work to ensure they get the learnings from others and thus don't fall behind.

Ethics Without Virtue

I am inspired by Sharon Welch's writings on "the feminist ethic of risk" and "ethics without virtue," otherwise known as "ethics with ambiguity." (Welch, 1989, 1999). I share with students Welch's valuable insight on this latter concept, which is that despite the best of intentions, we cannot predict if our actions will do more harm than good or if our actions will succeed; it is up to each of us to clean up after ourselves, accordingly. On the course website, I post a quote that I have practically memorized because I refer to it so often. Welch wrote the following in response to what she calls the "key issue": recognizing the difference between "accepting moral and political ambiguity in a way that is self-critical, and using ambiguity in a way that is self-justifying" (Welch, 1999) p. 123.

Faced with these ambiguities, we might give up on moral reflection altogether; acting boldly, but without the pretence of being moral, without any attempt to think through actions and their impact on others. Action then becomes sheer impulse, whim, the arbitrary exercise of creativity and power.

Imagine another alternative. We can take ambiguity seriously, making a best choice, and then being willing to accept the consequences of that choice. Basically, we become ready to clean up after ourselves, to re-evaluate actions, all with the style of humor and openness to failure. The key here is not being paralyzed by either moral failure or by political actions that are ineffective. We can accept that we can only do our best, with a style of not expecting perfection or saintliness from ourselves and others. It is then easier to act in ambiguous situations, not being defeated or paralyzed by the mere fact of ambiguity. (Welch, 1999) p. 121.

Students join me in applying "ethics without virtue" to our own lives. In an online post, Emma described her reaction to reading about working with ambiguity rather than being paralyzed by it. While she knows that intention alone will not remove the possibility of doing harm, she believes that critical thinking can help us all "meander through the ambiguities and hypocrisies which present themselves all of the time." She also believes in creating a learning space where everyone commits to group learning with a focus on both intentions and actions.

THE REFLECTIVE TEACHER

Reflection by Mohammad

Your story is what gives this writing a heart. It gives it warmth by sharing your light with the reader, the light of understanding, humanity, compassion, and awareness. Your emphasis on awareness of professionals not taking over when attempting to help families, and being mindful of not adopting the self-serving title of "expert" is very apt and needs to be heard by those who become seduced by the power that the status of a professional offers them. I recall sitting in a meeting and being introduced as a "know-it-all" and feeling very uncomfortable for the advantage that I was handed. It was a precarious position, a position that I was put in by those who somehow felt comforted maintaining the status quo. The status of expert pushed me into being an agent of control at the behest of the dominant socio-economic forces rather than being a catalyst for change. This chapter reminds me of Lynn Hoffman's "An Intimate History," in which she puts forth the events of her life and how they intertwined with the development of her perspective and her inclination to reach for what she did.

Many course websites offer a space for the instructor's introduction. An interactive course website gives opportunities for teacher transparency as a context for critical reflection and learning[18]. Rather than the more standard professor-distancing stance based on some version of an academic curriculum vitae, I post my story to provide students a more transparent and in-depth view of my story as a practitioner, consultant and teacher.

Each section of my biographical sketch gives space for students to respond with questions and/or reflections. I post the following:

There are many approaches to therapy, and many ways to tell the story. Each approach is informed by a particular epistemological stance, and then further influenced by the biases of the person telling the story. In this course, we will explore ·some of the ideas that inform developments toward collaborative approaches in the field of family therapy.

The choices I make in how to guide you through this exploration are inevitably informed by my own biases. These biases are shaped by my studies and experiences, which are influenced by the particular cultural-historic context of my life. While I cannot give a neutral objective account, I can offer a transparent "behind-the-scenes" glimpse of influences on my thinking. Thus, the following is an account of some of what informs my approach to teaching this course, and my enthusiasm for the particular course materials.

As you read my story, you will see that each section leaves space for "discussion." Please use this discussion tool to add reflections and/or questions, if something strikes you, or as the Quakers say, "as the spirit moves you." Feel free to try out this discussion tool as an opportunity to experiment with the interactive possibilities offered on this website. I would be happy to try to answer any questions and/or to hear any of your reflections. Later, you will have the opportunity to share and reflect online with your classmates and your own stories.

MY STORY

As a practitioner, I have experienced many professional roles that share a unifying commitment to supporting healthy children, families, organizations, and communities. Over more than 30 years, my professional development has evolved through several incarnations, including early intervention specialist, family support outreach worker, psychologist, administrative and clinical supervisor, project coordinator, family therapist, facilitator, teacher, researcher, organizational consultant, and now author. Stories from these firsthand experiences imbue my teaching with illustrations of narrative therapy in practice.

Learning from Families

Looking back, my early experiences as a practitioner in the 1970s set the stage for a "not knowing" stance and my deep respect for insider knowledge. I begin my online story with an account of how I discovered how much I learn from families:

Knowing virtually nothing about babies and disabilities, I answered an intriguing newspaper ad to initiate an "infant development programme" in Surrey, British Columbia. I think my naive enthusiasm helped me get the job. Suddenly, I was immersed in an entirely new world that involved home visiting families with infants and toddlers with developmental special needs. Home visiting was like being a field anthropologist. I was deeply moved by being welcomed into families' homes to witness their adaptation to having a young child with special needs within distinctive cultural contexts. I felt like a sponge soaking up experiences everywhere, consulting families, colleagues and the growing body of literature on infancy, infant-parent interactions, developmental disabilities and the parent movement. I fell in love with the families I visited, discovering a surprising ease in conversing about hard things with people who were in psychological pain, and an abiding love for babies.

I also became intrigued with the emerging parent advocacy movement, which was my introduction into an organized approach to counteracting the power dynamics and structural inequality inherent in traditional parent-professional relationships. I read every parent account I could find of life with a child who is different. I helped organize panels of parents of children with infants and toddlers with special developmental needs and a mothers' support group. This inevitably led to grappling with questions of how to truly listen to families' voices and to honor cultural diversity while acknowledging my own cultural biases. This self-questioning continues. I'll worry when it stops.

I share stories of my own experiences in graduate school, and as a mother:

In the late 1970s, I went to graduate school, to learn more of the theoretical underpinnings for the work I was doing. At that time, I was also ready to take a break from direct service work, having become a mother and discovering a whole new set of life priorities, commitments, and enthusiasms. I was able to tailor a graduate program at the University of British Columbia in Canada in early childhood special education based on the burgeoning literature on parent-infant interactions, systems theory and social ecology, using a transactional model of development in planning strategies for early intervention. I spent a lot of time observing interactions between mothers and infants, attending to the natural unfolding of mutuality and attunement, as well as disruptions in this process.

I reflect on what I learned by studying infants and families:

I thought a lot about when and when not to intervene and the effects of unnecessary interventions. I also began to look beyond the mother-infant dyad including relationships with fathers, siblings, extended family members and community. I studied such disabilities as visual and hearing impairments, cerebral palsy, mental handicaps and spina bifida, and their impact on families. I read and thought about cultural differences in approaches to raising children and in living with a child who is perceived as different. I also received a research grant to develop a handbook for strengthening parent-professional partnerships. I enjoyed being in an academic environment that was grounded in families' stories and everyday realities.

A Broadened Perspective

The mid 1970s was an exciting time to be studying early intervention, as there was much discussion about a multi-discipline paradigm shift. I still remember the thrill in discovering an article (Sameroff & Chandler, 1974) that outlined the conceptual shift from a linear uni-directional cause and effect model of development to what the authors called "a transactional model of development" which recognizes the effects of complex interactions over time. This affirmed what families already knew: not only do parents influence their children, but infants' behavior and temperament shape their caretaking environment; together, a "dance" occurs between parents and even very young children. In research, and in direct work with families, I was encouraged to develop a broadened perspective that highlights reciprocity and mutuality in parent-infant interactions. A transactional model of development affirmed my intuitions, and made me more confident to pursue them in my practice.

I had never trusted the North American tendency to simplistically blame mothers for children's problems. I studied the match between parents and infant, including what became identified as inevitable "missteps in the dance." My respect deepened for families' interactional strengths and unique resources and for the privilege of being a witness to families' interactions. I preferred to think of my work with families akin to that of a field anthropologist rather than as an early interventionist.

I describe in my online story how the conceptual understanding of parent-infant transactions (or interactions over time) became a living metaphor that I always take with me, laying down the foundation for later inquiry into family therapy, and in particular, collaborative approaches to therapeutic conversations.

It made intuitive sense to me to envision change as interactive, embedded in context, and evolving over time. By the time I became a family therapist, I knew down to my bones about possibilities that can emerge when least expected. In my special education training, I learned specific strategies and practices that build on family strengths. Over and over again, I felt privileged to learn directly from families how small changes could make room for big differences in their family lives. Families of young children with special needs taught me about the small miracles that can emerge from steadfast persistence, love, ingenuity and hard work.

My academic inquiry was actively shaped by the compelling stories of families I visited. I felt a kinship with others in the parent advocacy/developmental disabilities/early intervention movement(s). In the 1970s, parents were beginning to demand changes in models of service delivery to families, and were establishing parent-professional partnerships oriented to their family needs. I continue writing to my students:

I became particularly interested in further developing a family-focused approach that could draw from families' strengths, build community, individualize according to family needs, normalize special needs and efficiently gather information for families to use. I felt good being part of something larger than myself that was striving toward social change. I also felt empathy with people who struggle with being different and who feel like outsiders to the dominant culture.

I share with students the impact of my discovery of an ecological approach (Bronfenbrenner, 1979):

Bronfenbrenner used the analogy of a set of Russian nesting dolls to describe how an infant is embedded within layers of family and community. Until then, the field was primarily focused on the infant and primary caregiver, as though they exist separately from their familial and cultural contexts. Thinking ecologically broadened my perspective, raising questions about concentric circles within which a given interaction is embedded, including relationships with fathers, siblings, extended family members, and community.

While studying parent-infant interactions, I became enthralled with the unfolding phenomenon of turn-taking between primary caregivers and infants in the first year of life (Sax, 1981):

I surveyed the literature on normal infant-mother pre-language communication to draw implications for professionals working with parents and their infants with developmental delays. This research involved micro-analyzing videotapes of mother-infant dyads in their home settings, recording such measurements as the parents' sensitivity to cues, emotional and verbal responsiveness, and concomitant responses in the infant. "Turn-taking" has relevance for therapeutic conversations. A therapist needs to give serious consideration to the ways in which (s)he positions herself – when to take the lead, and when to listen.

Becoming a Family Therapist

I share with students my family's choice to move from British Columbia to Middlebury, Vermont in the early 1980s and the events that figured in my decision to become a family therapist. I was highly influenced by my discovery of like-minded people in my work at the Addison County Parent/Child Center:

I worked for a couple of years at a very innovative Parent/Child Center, visiting families with infants and toddlers in their homes. This included families with children with disabilities as well as adolescent parents. This was my introduction to rural poverty. I saw close-up what it was like to have fuel cut off in the middle of a harsh winter, to get evicted with no place to go, to worry about having food at the end of each month. Many families lived in trailers – if they were lucky. I witnessed first-hand the effects of teenage parenting, family violence, sexual abuse and substance abuse. This shattered my idyllic image of Vermont. I felt acutely aware of my own privilege. My interest in working with families expanded beyond developmental special needs, and the birth-to-three population I decided to go back to school to reorient myself, moving from the field of early intervention to becoming a family therapist.

While at Antioch New England Graduate School in the mid-1980s, I experienced once again how much I love being a student. I share this with students as one way to let them know what I value as both student and teacher in a learning environment:

I thrive in a learning environment that encourages rigorous inquiry, exploring ideas, and applying theory to real life situations. I soaked up all I could about different types of problems and therapeutic approaches. I was disturbed by trends to pathologize and hyper-analyse families. I was grateful to have my earlier experiences to help ground me.

I describe the seven years I spent working at The Counseling Service of Addison County, a fantastic community mental health center, where I was an outpatient clinician, coordinator of an intensive home based services program, and a clinical supervisor. Here I discovered another group of like-minded people who shared a life-long commitment to being of service in the most innovative ways to people in our county.

Most of the families I visited in their homes were rurally isolated, marginalized by poverty and multi-generational cycles of abuse and neglect, outcasts from the dominant culture. I had a string of incredibly powerful experiences, the kind of hands-on education that has profound effects. The greatest gift was to glimpse life through others' eyes; in doing so, I was forced to reckon with class issues, with my own classism and assumptions based on personal privilege. I developed bonds with people who lived in appalling poverty (such as in shacks with dirt floors, unreliable heat and transportation for Vermont's harsh winters, chronic unemployment, reliance on government programs to put food on the table), whose children were struggling with limited choices to find niches at school, often with reputations as troublemakers by the time they entered kindergarten. I learned a great deal about how socio-cultural injustice disrupts people's lives. I struggled to respect cultural differences in parenting and relationship practices while taking a stand against physical, sexual, and emotional abuse. I witnessed the seduction of substance abuse, as well as its pain and disrupting ripple effects on family members. All these experiences stretched me to ask myself hard questions, and to develop practices in alignment with my beliefs and values, while seeking to understand and respect cultural and class differences. This commitment to being accountable to the people I aspire to serve is an ongoing, life-long and most humbling process.

Becoming a family therapist "fit me like a glove." I briefly describe my journey to become a licensed psychologist and AAMFT Approved Supervisor. I was fortunate to work closely with Lynn Hoffman, MSW, some of whose work is reviewed in the coursework I assign my students (Hoffman, 1993, 2002) .

During this time, I further developed my personal approach to working with families as well as systems consultations. I spent a lot of time examining my underlying beliefs and values, working on developing an approach to supervision that mirrors my clinical work in highlighting strengths, inner and outer resources and natural helping systems. I further explored feminist critiques of family therapy and the burgeoning research on women's ways of knowing, which accent the centrality of gender in family theory. This deepened a commitment in my work to address gender differences and inequalities, challenge established power imbalances within the broader social context and try to make room for both male and female experiences.

I briefly describe my abiding interest in gender and women's studies. The writings of Jean Baker Miller, Carol Gilligan, Janet Surrey, and others from the Stone Center in Wellesley, Massachusetts initially helped me think relationally about women's development (Gilligan, 1982; Jordan, Kaplan, Miller, Striver, & Surrey, 1991; Miller, 1986). *Women's Ways of Knowing* (Belenky, Clinchy, Goldberger, & Tarule, 1986) further clarified for me how women have been culturally devalued, and the centrality of "finding one's voice" in women's development through circumstances that highlight connection and subjective knowledge.

My framework for family therapy has been greatly influenced by feminists in the field of family therapy – Virginia Goldner, Thelma Jean Goodrich, Rachel Hare-Mustin, Judith Myers Avis, Michele Bograd, Betty Carter, Monica McGoldrick, Peggy Papp, Marianne Walters, Froma Walsh, Olga Silverstein, Carol Anderson, Joan Laird, and Ann Hartman. These pioneering women raise the provocative issue of women and power, and ask hard questions about the interface between gender and culture. They focus on the confusing roles of women in families (vacillating between glorification and blame), the devaluing of women's voices, and the long- standing cultural tradition of mother blame.

Evolution of the Family Therapy Field

The 1980s were a vibrant time to study family therapy. I give students a sense of the ideas that had a powerful impact on many people's thinking and practices. Exciting new developments in the field of "systemic family therapies" were shaped by Gregory Bateson's conceptualization of 1st and 2nd order cybernetics (Bateson, 1972).

Studying Bateson's work provided me with the grounding to remember that work as a family therapist does not occur in a vacuum, but will automatically impact on the family system. The principles of autonomy, interdependence, and interconnectedness affect not only the family but the therapist's relationship with the family. This provides a further reminder that there is no such thing as neutrality as a family therapist, as well as the importance of respecting the family's need to maintain a sense of homeostasis as a family.

My understanding of systems thinking was greatly impacted by the book *The Aesthetics of Change* (Keeney, 1983). I introduce students to Keeney's interest as a cybernetic epistemologist and a family therapist in "the aesthetics of change" that extend beyond the pragmatics of story lines to uncover the essence of how we come to know what we do, how we become who we are, and how we can make changes for ourselves and others in this world.

Kenney presented cybernetics as a type of map to help keep people from feeling lost, and to maintain a sense of wonder about what one discovers along the way. Reading this book generated more questions than answers, yet celebrated the freedom to explore, giving me permission to cultivate a student state of mind well past my years of formal schooling. Keeney's metaphoric mind helps translate abstractions into concrete realities, and integrates concepts toward a more ecological understanding of the universe.

I share with students how studying cybernetics helped family therapists develop more awareness of the lens of a second-order view, which exposes a higher order perspective of life on earth to see that what we do matters and influences life in ways that may not be readily discerned.

Lynn Hoffman borrows the term "the lens of a second-order view" from the field of mathematics to describe "taking a position removed from the operation itself so that you can perceive the operation reflexively. These views are really views about views. They often make you more aware of how your own relation to the operation influences it, or allows you to see a particular interpretation..." (Hoffman, 1993, p. 91).

I give an overview of my current work as a practitioner. I also share developments that inform my approach:

As a family therapist, I work with a range of individuals, couples, and families. I honor a commitment to work with a socio-economic cross-section of people. I enjoy providing consultation and supervision to other therapists. I also work as a consultant with organizations that request facilitation in taking stock, getting into alignment with their guiding vision and mission, and taking specific steps toward making desired changes.

Working as a family therapist has presented learning opportunities to counsel literally hundreds of families, couples, adults, adolescents, and children over the years I have worked and lived in my small rural community. I appreciate the opportunities I have to witness developments over time, as we informally meet with each other while shopping at the local stores, recreating in the great Vermont outdoors, attending school events, etc. I marvel when I sit back and reflect on so many of the people whose challenges and wisdom I carry with me, along with the trust clients have given me in telling me their deeply personal stories. My heart and head are bursting with ways these stories have touched my thinking and my life.

Collaborative Therapies

I offer students a behind-the-scenes view of the theoretical changes that influenced my practice as a family therapist to step beyond the structural, strategic, and Milan-informed systemic foundation of family therapy into the realm of postmodern, collaborative therapies that embrace the idea of "therapy as social construction" (McNamee & Gergen, 1992):

Like many other family therapists, I had been secretly doing my own version of collaborative therapy all along, while gradually the theoretical literature became supportive and like-minded. This subtle shift occurred over several years, including our use of language. Working in a community mental health center in the 1980s, we talked about making "systemic interventions," sometimes even "paradoxical" interventions. Our energetic and creative family team experimented with uses of the one-way mirror, and pondered concepts such as hypothesizing, circularity, and neutrality. By the late 1980s, we had evolved from Milan-influenced systemic interventions toward embracing a new format, the "reflecting team." We began challenging assumptions of secrecy, hierarchy, and control, and highlighting in their place values of affirmation, transparency, and affiliation. I share some of the ways narrative therapy has informed my own work.

Reflecting Teamwork

Through telling my own story, I introduce the students to reflecting teamwork and outsider witness practices. I was fortunate to learn about the reflecting team directly from Tom Andersen, the Norwegian originator of this approach (Andersen, 1987) who visited our setting several times between 1986 and 1993, and from Dario Lussardi, of the Brattleboro Family Institute, who provided ongoing consultation (Lussardi & Miller, 1990).

Tom Andersen provoked a new image of self as constituted through language and conversation. More than a tool, the reflecting team is a philosophy that encourages dialogues, reflexivity, and inquiry. Reflecting teamwork moves away from theoretical certainty and objective truths to embrace openness to multiple points of view. Attention is given to how we socially construct meaning through conversation in therapeutic situations. I learned to listen carefully to the stories people tell about themselves, to how people who come to consult me give meaning to their requests for help.

I describe how therapists have adapted the reflecting team in action in numerous clinical situations, including family therapy, outreach services, and clinical supervision, as well as applications beyond mental health.

Reflecting processes have also profoundly influenced my work and life beyond therapeutic settings. This includes teaching and consultation with organizations and community groups. I believe my exposure to the reflecting team has also given me skills and understandings towards becoming a more reflective person.

Narrative Practice

Having situated myself in my own history, I introduce students to the influence of narrative therapy on my work as a practitioner.

My approach is highly influenced by Michael White and David Epston and their groundbreaking work in narrative therapy, otherwise known as a "reauthoring conversations" approach (White & Epston, 1990a). As a family therapist, I have been privileged to witness countless therapeutic experiences where the ideas and practices of narrative therapy have made significant differences in people's lives.

I introduce "outsider witness practices" as a unique approach to reflecting teamwork that generates both reflection and inquiry (Russell & Carey, 2003; White, 1995b).

In this course, we will study how White drew on the work of Barbara Myerhoff, an anthropologist who studied elderly Jews as they developed community through mutual storytelling in Venice, California (Myerhoff, 1986) Reflecting teamwork is envisioned as a type of "definitional ceremony" in which outsiders witness people's far-ranging, lived-in experiences. As "outsider witnesses," the reflecting team not only reflects on what they have heard, but further inquires into the alternative story.

I include a brief description of my commitment to the reflective practitioner (Schon, 1983) in teaching and my own work.

I am most interested in theory in practice. How can we continually increase our professional effectiveness? How can theoretical thinking contribute to becoming a better practitioner? What are the tools for a reflective practitioner? My thinking has been very influenced by the work of Donald Schon on The Reflective Practitioner (1983) and Chris Argyris and Donald Schon on Theory in Practice (Schon, 1983). I am also continually impacted by the challenge narrative therapy poses to step back to reflect on whatever is "absent but implicit"(White, 2000a) that informs a given conversation, and to remember to reflexively inquire into the ongoing effects of choices I make as a therapist, consultant, and teacher, and to make adjustments accordingly. In this course, I hope we can create a safe and reflective milieu where we can experience this kind of collaborative learning so we can construct knowledge together.

I then offer the following reflections in summary:

As a practitioner, I have moved between the professional worlds of early intervention, family therapy, children's mental health, and organization development. I am drawn to environments where professional services seek to become less professionally centered, more linked with the family support movement and more focused on strengthening and collaborating with community-based resources. I have an abiding interest in power relations between those who seek help and those who provide it: parents and professionals, clients and therapists. This has motivated me to explore how parent-professional relationships can move beyond the traditional medical and mental health models that were defined by clinical distance and hierarchical organization, with the professional in the position of expert. Throughout, I continually return to different versions of the same question: How can providers join families without taking over? How can professionals support the autonomy, active involvement and personal agency of people who seek their services? How can we create a setting conducive to learning from each other? What can narrative ideas and practices contribute to these conversations? In this course, these questions will guide our exploration of the field of family therapy.

Responses to My Story

Students express surprise to read such a detailed and reflective autobiographical account. Sometimes they ask specific questions or acknowledge some shared experience, such as having lived in British Columbia or a passion for home-based work. However, most students do not take up my offer to ask online questions about me. They tell me they feel a bit intimidated by my wealth of experience, and that it takes awhile to realize I am sincere in my request for their further inquiry. Reading my detailed account alerts them that this course will be different and adds to my credibility as teacher-practitioner, grounded in the theory that my practice both informs and draws upon.

While I welcome any response, I do not expect to engage most students right from the get-go. Students experience many competing demands at the beginning of the semester. I have also come to value their silence. Students have taught me that silence can mean lots of things. It can take them a while to articulate their responses. I want to keep finding ways to further inquire into their experiences.

The interactive website is only one way I share personal stories with students. I weave into every class illustrations as a practitioner. I try to give a behind-the-scenes view of my thinking. Students tell me this is one of my strengths as a teacher. They thank me in person and online for sharing so many of my own stories with them. Kerry wrote, "Those examples help me to feel the richness of your life and of narrative practice. It has made me feel that narrative is alive."

CHAPTER 4

RECKONING WITH POWER

Posting by Sarah

What I have often found is that with grading, I end up trying to please my professor, rather than engage in learning for the sake of the learning. Making the teacher "happy" becomes my priority as well by "sounding smart," "saying the right things," etc... It's often difficult to really engage with the material when you are so worried about "appearing" the right way. In this situation, I still felt like I wanted to please but I really had to ask myself why, since it didn't really matter...I could be more myself. I think for me at least, I see a grade as a representation of my worth. One of my professors reminded me this semester that grades reflect the work, not me...but it's difficult to break away from that. Anyway, I appreciated the chance to experiment with power in the classroom since it always seems a bit strange with all of this talk of social construction that we as students are graded. I don't think it affected the amount of work I did, and in fact I think it allowed me to be more enthusiastic about the material and more willing to take chances. Thanks!

As a teacher, I have at times struggled with power and at other times avoided thinking about it. However, I cannot naively think my good intentions are enough. In this chapter, I reckon with power in the classroom and online. How is it possible to aspire to create a collaborative learning community while acknowledging my position of privilege and the inevitable power relations with students? How can I reconcile a collaborative spirit with the teacher's responsibility for structuring course materials and moving a class forward to cover the given material? If I take up the mantle of power as a teacher, how do I use it well? How do students and I work together to negotiate a collaborative, co-learning situation given the inevitable power dynamics? What have I learned from others to assist me in understanding and using power? How have my teaching practices evolved over time and what have I learned along the way? I explore discoveries in the quest to model practices that minimize hierarchy without obscuring power-relations; that value all knowledges including from personal understandings, professional training, insider knowledge from the people we consult with and their unique life experiences/learnings, and the great range of experiences that we all bring from living or lives outside of these learning/teaching settings. In spite of our designated roles, we become partners in learning.

I believe my approach to power relations in the classroom is internally consistent with how I train practitioners to address their positions of power in relation to the people who consult with them. I structure opportunities for practitioners-in-training to experience firsthand an ethic of collaboration toward the people who consult with us. Both in class and online, I expose students to reading materials, exercises, assignments, classroom and online visitors, recorded interviews, and conversations that examine power relations in psychotherapy and other human services. In this chapter, I give a behind-the-scenes view into my approach to taking a position in relation to power. In the following chapter, "When Nice is Not Enough," I give a glimpse into the students' world as they too reckon with the politics of power, collaboration, privilege, and accountability.

POWER

I draw a lot of guidance from Sharon Welch's thinking on power and ethics without virtue (Welch, 1989, 1999). She describes power as neither essentially evil nor essentially good. "Rather power is intrinsically complex, and to understand power and to use it well is a matter of balancing its complexity, of holding in mind its possible manifestations and noting what the possibilities of that power are in a specific situation." She cautions us to use power well: "The solution is not an abdication of power but an exercise of power...that co-exists with a deep seated awareness of our limits and our own potential for error and harm" (Welch, 1999).

My approach to power is influenced by provocative writings by intellectual ancestors about their struggle with the question of power relations in therapy, supervision, and teaching. I have chosen to highlight two approaches that help me recognize and continually re-examine power relations that might otherwise become obscured by an egalitarian account of the relationship: 1) feminist pedagogy (hooks, 1989); and 2) the evaluative gaze (Foucault, 1973; Foucault, 1980).

Feminist Pedagogy

As a feminist, I have found inspiration in feminist literature that highlights politics of gender and power (Beasley, 1999; Freedman, 2002). I share with others the commitment to develop a consciousness and a network that recognizes women's special knowledge and unique contributions in families and in family therapy (McGoldrick, Anderson, & Walsh, 1991). I take note of the dual tendency to ignore women's voices and experiences, and to hold women primarily responsible for what goes wrong in families (Caplan, 2000). At the same time, I have come to deeply value "women's ways of knowing" through growth in connection (Jordan et al., 1991) and diversity (Jordan, 1997). All of these writings insist on taking seriously women's knowledge and how women come to know what they know. Many men wish to join women in the feminist tradition of striving toward a more equitable balance of power in families, and toward going beyond traditional ways of knowing.

What are applications of these traditions in teaching? I found no single definition of feminist pedagogy but rather some shared beliefs (Cohee, 2004; Del Piero, 1983). While feminist teaching identifies gender and gender identity as important influences, other considerations such as race/ethnicity, culture, social class, age, and geography are each attended to as impacting classroom dynamics. Feminist pedagogy encourages reflection about the relationships among students as well as between teacher and students – how the teacher organizes her classroom; who is included and excluded from discussions.

Bell hooks' approach to feminist pedagogy focuses on the issue of power (hooks, 1989). She emphasizes that being a teacher is a position of power over others, regardless of the difficulty many women have in asserting this power. In response to her question "How can feminist teachers use power in ways that are not coercive and dominating?" Bell hooks offers ideas for how acknowledging power can enrich teaching. For example, the teacher can elect not to assume the posture of the all-knowing professor with her students, being "open and honest about what we do not know as a gesture of respect for them."

The Evaluative Gaze

My teaching has been influenced by the writings of Foucault, who examines the central role of power and practices of power in influencing all relationships, including teaching relationships. Systems of modern power reproduce what Foucault called "the evaluative gaze" that highlights relationship practices of evaluation, documentation, remediation, and correction. In this teaching situation, I am the person with more power within an inherently lopsided context that elevates my voice, and places me in the role of evaluator. It is as though the instructor is fully formed and knowledgeable in contrast to the students, who are vulnerable and in need. This attitude not only discounts the knowledge and skills of the students, but shapes instructors' relationship with their work, how they story their lives as "professor," and their professional identities.

I have thought a lot about grades and the hypocrisy of teaching Foucault's "evaluative gaze" and Michael White's "modern power/addressing personal failure" (White, 2002) while simultaneously being required to grade students. In the midst of rigorous discussion of White's critique of the professions' reliance on formal and expert knowledges to control and shape behavior, and Foucault's discussion of how the established hierarchy of knowledge fosters teacher-student relationships that perpetrate modern power and "the evaluative gaze," it is a dicey proposition for an instructor to explain to her students what they need to do to get an "A." I find that it works best to make this contradiction as explicit as possible. I let the students know that I want most of all for them to engage with the material. I have little patience for people just showing up. They needn't share my enthusiasm, but I strongly believe in the privilege of education and that they will need to work hard to understand complex concepts and to develop narrative interviewing skills. I like approaching evaluation with an air of innovation. Later in this chapter, I share a couple of ways I have experimented with evaluation.

CHAPTER 4

TAKING A POSITION

I want practitioners-in-training to approach their therapeutic position with intentionality. We spend a significant amount of time in class and online exploring how we choose to position ourselves in relation to the people we aspire to serve. I find it very helpful to have guiding principles, such as those I describe in the subsequent chapter, to orient me toward living my values. Often, I refer back to the overarching rule, to strive to "do no harm;" and to Johnella Bird's caution that a well-intentioned eclecticism is not good enough.

> *The eclectic therapeutic practice is unaccountable and potentially dangerous unless the practitioner can articulate the ethics that underpin this eclectic practice. The ethics are then available for review, reflection, challenge and change. We cannot stand in a multiplicity of places at the same time. I stand in one place while making that place available for reflection and review from time to time.* (Bird, 2001) *p. 4*

Online, I share my thoughts in response to students' questions about eclecticism. Given my belief in "both/and," students ask why I do not embrace eclecticism. I reply:

> *I embrace an array of therapeutic practices and ideas, and I try to stay open to new possibilities. I also know many therapists who do really decent, caring work who do not follow any particular theoretic school of thought. And even more importantly, I can think of many people who have been helped by therapists who probably think of themselves as 'eclectic.' However, I cannot speak for others experiences — as therapist or client — only for my own. Since I have chosen to study a particular approach, my work feels infused with a overflowing vitality that is in stark contrast to the 'burn out' or 'compassion fatigue' that has become an occupational hazard for so many therapists. It's as though I have a ground to stand on, from which I can make my own modifications. The best I can become is "Peggy Sax," not "Michael White" or "David Epston" although I continue to learn a great deal from each of my mentors — and others. Without this kind of overarching theoretical framework, I think it is much easier for therapeutic work to become sloppy — sort of 'anything goes' without tools for noticing discrepancies that become evident when accountable to a particular theory and practices.*

Students ask for specific examples of how I draw from my breadth of professional knowledge while staying true to an overarching therapeutic position. I sometimes offer particular understandings or resources that I believe might be useful. I do my best to situate this particular offering in a given circumstance, sharing with a tentative tone that leaves space for others to take whatever fits and leave the rest. For example, I might say "I learned something in my studies of developmental psychology about temperamental differences that might be of use to you here (you could also insert postpartum depression, trauma and recovery, leadership in organizations, etc.). Would you be interested in hearing this?" My belief in collaborative approaches orients me to keep in touch with the actual experience of someone consulting me. I demonstrate how I guide the spirit with which I offer that information, categorization or construct with my overarching belief in collaborative, post-structuralist, social constructionist approaches. "Otherwise, I worry that practitioners can elevate professional knowledge—however learned and/or empirically based-- at the expense of building upon people's hard earned experience-near accounts of what they have learned themselves through life experience."

As a course gets underway, I invite students to engage in online discussion about what is meant by "therapeutic stance" (Hoffman, 1992):

> *Lynn Hoffman writes about taking a particular stance when constructing lenses (such as a reflexive stance, an ethical stance, and a non-expert stance). Michael White describes the intention of the therapist to take up a "decentered and influential posture" in conversations with the people who consult them. What is meant by stance and why is this so important in therapy? What stands out to you about the stance in narrative practice and how might this influence how you approach your work?*

Students reflect online as they engage with provocative materials I introduce that question their assumptions about their therapeutic stance. Johnella Bird's (Bird, 2001) condemnation of the "You (the client) know and we (the therapist) don't," shocked Luke. It was a "light bulb" moment for him when he realized how a "therapist-not-knowing" stance could obscure the power balance; not talking about power relations or dismissing the expert position doesn't make power relations vanish. As he conveyed in the posting that begins the following chapter, When Nice is Not Enough, Luke saw a progression in the field – replacing the expert position of "We know, you don't" with the "nice" position: "You know we don't." He saw further explanation in Freedman and Combs' writing on the issue (Freedman & Combs, 1996a), how a not-knowing position is not an "I don't know anything" position. The therapist's knowledge is about the process of therapy, not the content and meaning of people's lives. Luke asked his classmates for ideas: "Is there a "third way?"

Taking a Decentered and Influential Position

Through letter-writing, classroom exercises, and shared interviews, I give students multiple opportunities to practice developing "a decentered and influential" therapeutic posture (White, 1997a). I quote Michael White directly to describe his notions of "decentred" and "influential."

> *"Decentered" refers to the therapist prioritizing the personal stories and the knowledges and skills of the people who consult with the therapist. The therapist is "influential" not in the sense of imposing an agenda or in the sense of delivering interventions, but in the sense of building a scaffold, through questions and reflections, that makes it possible for people to a) more richly describe the alternative stories of their lives; b) step into and to*

explore some of the neglected territories of their lives, and c) become more significantly acquainted with the knowledges and skills of their lives that are relevant to addressing the concerns, predicaments and problems that are at hand (White, 2003b).

I share with students Michael White's four-quadrant chart on Therapeutic Posture:

Table 5-1. Therapeutic Posture (White, 2003b)

**(From Michael White's Workshop Notes:
http://www.dulwichcentre.com.au/)**

	Decentred	**Centred**
Influential	Decentred and influential (potentially invigorating of therapist)	Centred and influential (potentially burdening of therapist)
Non-influential	Decentred and non-influential (potentially invalidating of therapist)	Centred and non-influential (potentially exhausting of therapist)

Insider Knowledges

I was first alerted to the distinction between expert and insider knowledges more than thirty years ago, at kitchen tables and living room floors of families of children with special needs. I simultaneously learned a deep respect for mothers' knowledge of their children and family lives while being appalled to hear stories of their feeling discounted and disempowered by some of their contact with professionals. My later experience with consumer movements for parents of children with disabilities and psychiatric survivors further instilled a desire to dispel the myths that dismissed the value of insider knowledge.

I was delighted to discover that narrative therapy centers people as the experts in their own lives, and assumes they have many skills, competencies, beliefs, values, and commitments to reduce the influence of problems in their lives. (Epston, 1999; White, 1997d). For example, David Epston aptly describes how the women he has worked with over the years have been nothing like the "anorexics" he read about in professional texts.

Even those who had abandoned all hope became feisty and wise beyond their years. I began to realize that these young women were in possession of knowledge but had no means to represent it. It was as though they had been gagged. However, I was soon to learn that even those who had been mute were capable of becoming fluent (in anti a/b), which for many has become their second language. (Maisel, Epston & Borden, 2004) *(p. 6).*

Other approaches also embrace a respect for client knowledge. Nigel Parton and Patrick O'Byrne propose a constructive approach to practice that emphasizes the "plurality of both knowledge and voice, possibility and the relational quality of knowledge (Parton & O-Byrne, 2000)" p. 184.

I encourage students to question cultural assumptions that grant a monopoly to professional knowledges over "local" knowledge. I strive to dispel the following myths about insider knowledge.

TABLE 5-1. Dispelling Myths about Insider Knowledge

Myth #1: Effective and ethical psychotherapy depends primarily upon a unique relationship between client and therapist that takes place in a solely private and protected context. *Ethical practice can include non-transference based therapies, which go by a different set of rules. It is possible to simultaneously protect privacy while strengthening a person's sense of community and giving back. A person's sense of social interconnectedness contributes to her or his identity and sense of self.*

Myth #2: Only professional therapists have the ability to help people in psychic pain through their difficulties. *Therapists are not the sole or central source of support and knowledge for clients. In fact, people live within a web of connections. Therapists are often the last resort. Therapists come and go, but informal supports can be sustaining throughout a lifetime. Prudence, whose expertise is based on her years of being a service seeker, now providing services to others, has taught me a lot about how therapists can be of use. "They can strengthen communities of concern and help link people to their circle of support."*

Myth #3: Expert knowledge is of higher value than insider knowledge. *Common sense tells us that different knowledges are all important. Experience makes people authorities over their own lives, hence potential collaborators in lives of others. In the "Finding Common Ground" research project (Sax, 2007c), parents consistently speak about the healing power of ally-to-ally connections. Sharing knowledge/giving testimony profoundly contributes to our understandings of suffering and living. Practitioners are accountable to the people we aspire to serve.*

Myth #4: The helping relationship between the healer and the healed goes one way, with only the lives of the consulting person(s) changed by the therapist's application of expert therapeutic knowledge. *We are all co-learners: service seeker and service provider are designated roles within a particular situation. Practitioners learn in countless ways from the people who consult with us. Experiencing oneself as impacting another person's life in specific ways can be a powerful source of healing. Public practices (see Chapter Nine) demonstrate how ripple effects can go beyond two-way accounts to contribute cascading influence on many lives.*

CHAPTER 4

Professionalism

I invite students to reflect on professional discourses, not as polarized dichotomies but rather in terms of assumptions and practices that inevitably effect our preferred ways of relating to clients and their families (Madsen, 2007a). I like to read to students a favorite passage from Bill Madsen's, *Collaborative Therapy with Multi-Stressed Families.* He invites the reader to consider alternate definitions of "unprofessional" behavior within a new paradigm.

> *Our work can be enriched when we examine the discourses that organize it, and consider how those discourses fit with our preferred ways of relating to clients and families. While professional identity has traditionally been rooted in client deficits, professional expertise, and professional responsibility for clients, it is interesting to ponder what a definition of professionalism might look like grounded in possibilities, collaboration, and professional responsibility to clients. The accusation of acting "unprofessionally" has often been used to police professional actions. Imagine if a definition of professionalism included standards like the following:*

- It is unprofessional to inquire about difficulties without having first built a foundation of competence, connection and hope.
- It is unprofessional to not actively elicit client or family wisdom that could contribute to resolving difficulties in their lives.
- It is unprofessional to use objectifying language in any clinical discussion without considering how clients might experience it or how it might shape our thinking about clients.
- It is unprofessional to not actively think about the ways in which our own assumptions about race, gender, class, and sexual orientation affect our interactions with all clients.
- It is unprofessional to not routinely solicit client feedback about their preferences for the direction of therapy and the effects of our actions on them (Madsen, 2007, p. 331).

The above passage has fueled some lively discussion in which students express their mixed feelings about "professionalism." Ella wrote about her discomfort with what that word has come to represent. While she understands that a code of ethics can be important as a protection and safeguard for clients, she wonders what experiences and possibilities it excludes. She thought about the discussion about the ideas of boundaries and sharing of oneself. "Do these ideas have detrimental effects of their own? What happens when we insist on strict boundaries and distance our own stories from the conversation at the expense of all else?" Conversely, having her classmates share personal stories "demonstrates that really powerful effects can come out of deviations from this standard code of behavior."

RECKONING WITH POWER

Reckoning with power means reckoning with privilege. As a teacher, I have seniority, experience, and status. Practitioners-in-training are in a similarly privileged position in their relationships with their clients. If we let our good intentions obscure these power relations, we risk losing opportunities to monitor the real effects of the power relation on our work within teacher-student and therapist-client relationships.

I teach with a spirit of collaboration that brings me immense enjoyment of my students and our interactions. I learn a tremendous amount from them, and experience us as partners in a mutual process of discovery. As a result, I tend to emphasize an egalitarian account of our relationships, making me less likely to monitor the real effects of unspoken power relation on my students. While I do believe these power relations are diminished compared to typical student/teacher relationships, I cannot deny that as teacher, I am in an elevated and privileged position. For example, in reviewing archived postings, I notice that students join me in using particular language preferred in narrative and poststructuralist worldview. They also overwhelmingly mirror my expressed preferences for a collaborative approach to learning. A colleague has repeatedly reminded me not to be too naïve: "Students want to get good marks...and you are their marker in spite of the fact that you are kind, thoughtful and interested in what they have to say."

I find inspiration in Johnella Bird's writings about the unspoken power relations in both supervisory and consultation relationships (Bird, 2001, 2004, 2006), which are equally relevant to the teacher-student relationship. While everyone needs to be alert to these power relations, the person with more power "holds substantial responsibility for maintaining this vigilance" (Bird, 2006) p. 76. She cautions us to reinvent rather than obscure the boundaries of the power relationship.

Students also teach me about ways my enthusiasm can inadvertently obscure power relations. One student told me she thought it was hard for students to challenge me because my animated expressions did not leave enough space for skepticism. Sometimes it takes the entire semester for students to feel comfortable contributing opinions that differ from mine. For example, a student stayed after class on the last day to candidly share with me what he likes about power. This left me wondering how next time I might open more space in class or online for frank discussion of such complexities.

The more seasoned I become as a teacher, the more importance I place on developing open space for different voices to speak. I notice a growing confidence in my teaching style and content knowledge, which perhaps paradoxically makes it more possible for me to listen to a range of students' expressions, including their frustrations, dissatisfactions, or confusion.

Using Power Ethically

My connections with students are informal, yet clearly differ from those of their classmates. I genuinely enjoy my students' company and learn a great deal from them. I also use my facilitative and relational skills to deepen their connections with their classmates, rather than their individual relationships with me. I believe the distance gives me perspective to stay cognizant of my responsibilities as teacher. I know that my decisions are highly influential in co-constructing a learning environment conducive to learning.

MAKING MISTAKES

Posting by Kerry2

> *What touched me most about your teaching was your willingness to share your own stories and especially the times when maybe something didn't work out or maybe you didn't have the exact right question. Knowing that we can each make a positive contribution without always knowing the perfect thing to say is really powerful. I also appreciated you saying that we each can use our own voice and personality to make it work for us.*

I make plenty of mistakes in my teaching. Having an interactive website provides a public forum for me to demonstrate accountability practices. I welcome students' feedback, including that which might be hard to hear. I have discovered that lessons learned the hard way are often the ones we remember the best and that others can learn from as well. While some of my mistakes go unnoticed, others impact students to the extent that they bring these to my attention. Here I introduce an online exchange to illustrate this self-reflective teaching practice and students' responses. After class, I corresponded with a student who respectfully sent me some candid concerns. I then posted the following on the website:

> *Since yesterday's class, I have been thinking about a mistake that I made – I invited a guest to participate in our class without letting everyone know ahead of time. I also shared some of your posts with someone (albeit on the other side of the world) outside the class without asking your permission. I want to apologize for this inconsiderateness. This is sloppy teaching, which runs counter to everything I believe about creating a collaborative learning community. I want to reassure you that I will not do this again – either in class or online. It is really important for us all to feel safe and comfortable knowing that this learning space is protected. Please feel free to respond to this apology if you feel that there is more to be said.*

> *What else do you think might be important to keep this learning community as vital and protected as possible? How might a mistake be best handled within such a learning community? Are there other reassurances that might be important for me to make?*

I am often surprised by students' reactions. Celia responded to my apology by conveying how hard it is for her to trust when a teacher says she is open to admitting mistakes, examining her own practices, and earnestly attempting to live in congruence with what she believe and value. Celia described prior negative experiences with professors who did not practice what they preached:

> *Thank you for modeling for me that it might be possible one day for students to expect respectful treatment and accountability from all their professors.*

I'm also really glad that we all make mistakes in life, as sometimes the best gifts come from them – e.g., this email exchange about apologies and respectfulness has been really healing for me.

Behind-The-Scenes

Often, I try to give students a behind-the-scenes view of my teaching, akin to watching the extra footage on a movie DVD that shows how the movie was made. I let students know that my apologies are in earnest:

I take very seriously when anyone tells me that she or he experienced discomfort in any teaching circumstances where I am responsible. I wish I didn't make mistakes, but I do. I try to be thoughtful in my actions. In the teacher role, I must live with a certain amount of creative tension – doing what I can to create a collaborative learning community that feels safe enough to stretch oneself, and the push toward developing practitioner skills. I need your voices to help me navigate, to know when something fits and when I miss the mark. In this instance, your earnest responses have alerted me to cutting too many corners. In attempting to teaching narrative practice in such a condensed time, I have been moving too quickly. From the posts, I realize that we haven't really had time to get to know each other. I skipped ahead from the readings in order to make a schedule work.

I let students know some of the challenges I face as teacher. I offer this view in the spirit of transparency, not as a justification or rationalization.

For me, it is a great privilege and challenge to teach narrative therapy to you all. I am grateful to the social work teaching faculty for the ways they have introduced these studies to you, sort of like preparing the soil, maybe even planting the seeds that we now water, weed and fertilize. No MSW program can cover everything. I take seriously a sense of responsibility to teach areas that I believe may otherwise be less developed in this MSW program. That is why I am accenting experiences that draw forth an "embodied response." I am a practitioner-teacher, and I want to work on putting concepts into action. I want to create a learning environment where we can make mistakes together, learning through trial and error.

As teacher, I purposely make myself available to students and show my humanness:

As with many of us, my greatest strength can also be one of my greatest vulnerabilities. Have you noticed that I jump right in and express myself with enthusiasm? I want to get right down to the material and work together on learning these practices – this summer, that enthusiasm seems to be getting in my/our way. I am hoping I can now slow down and try to better meet you where you are, to give you time to practice in ways that will feel safer to you.

Together, I believe we can steer the course to make the absolute most of this precious time together. I wholeheartedly appreciate your contributions.

I continue on the forum entitled "Whoops":

One of life's greatest, most challenging, and elusive balances is finding/ creating/nurturing circles of support in which to feel secure enough to find our voices, and at the same time, learning/stretching outside our comfort zone to embrace edges of new learning and discovery. I have learned that I cannot ask others to do this if I don't apply the same principles to myself. Yes, even after many years of practice and studying narrative therapy, I continue to make lots of mistakes. I cut corners. I miss opportunities. I say things that could have been said better – or better left unsaid. I forget to ask. I bark up the wrong tree. Still I strive to "do no harm," and to hold myself to high standards, while simultaneously remembering my own humanness. I am often amazed and inspired by how, when given the chance to glimpse "behind the scenes," people can be very forgiving.

I strive to render visible my process of noticing and cleaning up after mistakes while maintaining perspective:

Often now, I experience a kind of silver lining in "eating humble pie." As a friend once said to me (when I was worrying about how my actions might have inadvertently hurt someone else), "You're important, Peggy – but not THAT important." In other words, life does not center around me (or you for that matter). We all do the best we can and we all fall short. Fortunately, we humans are breathtakingly resilient creatures.

Several students wrote thoughtful and kind responses. Kerry2 wrote to acknowledge my role in helping to set the stage for "what has become and will continue to inspire each of us." This online exchange contributed to collectively creating an open, collaborative space. I further responded by acknowledging their contribution to my own learning and awareness.

Now that I am older and wiser (!), I am so much better able to speak my voice/live how I want to be in the world in ways that feel supportive to seeing and honoring myself in my "Peggyness." In this way, the presence in this class of each of you, your engagement with the course materials, and with each other have really helped me to achieve this "Peggyness" commitment. I hope that this course experience will inspire each of you further into your "Kerryness," "Heidiness," "Cathyness," etc.

Emma responded:

Reading all that Peggy has expressed in her behind-the-scenes thinking on all of this, I feel inspired to share a little bit of how that touched me, especially because I have not made my voice present in our conversations on-line about mistakes and the "how-tos" of not doing harm when differences of power create much of the context of rapport building. I am thoroughly moved by everyone's willingness to take the risk of expressing thoughts that are not easy to express. It really helps me to be a witness to everyone's voices in this class, and the challenging and powerful dynamics...witnessing and expressing that is helping me to team up with the strength I have often sleeping by my side and challenge the reticence, both to express those feelings of discomfort, and also to recognize and bounce back on the world of my relations when I have been one to contribute to the pool of offenses.

EVALUATION

I begin an online forum on evaluation as follows:

Foucault wrote about the inevitability of "the evaluative gaze" in modern culture, which is more evident in some settings than in others. In this teaching context, I have been in the designated role of teacher, and you have been my students. As much as I wish I did not have to grade your work, we all know that this is a required responsibility of my role. Evaluation and grades are an unspoken and implicit undercurrent of many interactions between students and teachers at this school. We have acknowledged how good you must have become at "the game" in order to have made it this far in your academic studies. At the same time, our classroom discussion and your written work have hopefully encouraged personal reflection beyond seeking my approval or telling me what you think I want to hear in order to go for the "A." But I would be naive to think this dynamic was banished from our class just because I wished it did not exist.

At the end of the course I sometimes start an online forum to learn from students about the effects of evaluation on their engagement with the course. I ask: "What do you imagine would have been different if the course had been pass/fail? Were there times when you forgot about grades, and if so, what helped make this happen? What do you wish I was asking, but have thus far neglected to ask?"

Catherine responded that she thought about grades quite a bit less during this class than she does in other classes and experienced relatively few negative effects of grading in this class. "I believe it was because there was such an emphasis on contributing to class and participating for our own benefit, rather than to achieve a particular grade. I tried as hard on my papers in this class as I do in other classes, but I did not work myself into a nervous fit over ensuring they were perfect."

On my computer, I keep a file of each student's postings. I do this for several reasons. Since I rely less on formal papers than is typical, the online postings become an important source for understanding and accessing students' learning. I notice when a student does not fulfill the required number of postings and/or only posts minimally. These patterns often emerge quite early, making it possible for me to privately urge those who have been most silent to increase their postings. When a class gets off to a slow start, I remind everyone – in class or through a posting – of my expectation for them to chime in fairly often. Their online participation usually goes up dramatically when I ask them if they would prefer the more traditional approach of writing a formal paper. At the end of the semester, I create a document that I give each student with her or his compiled postings, reflections on their posted work from students in their small group (see Chapter 7), and some of my own reflections. Students often express surprise to see such evidence of their contributions to the classroom "collaboratory."

An Experiment in Innovative Grading

I prefer to teach within a pass/fail format, which can free the teacher from feeling like a hypocrite and help students keep from continually looking over their proverbial shoulders. Early one semester when all students in a graded program were actively involved in course materials and with each other, I invited them to join me in an experiment. I would commit to giving them all "A's" based on the assumption they would all give 100% to the class. I asked for individuals to contact me privately if for any reasons they could not fully participate; together we would decide upon an appropriate grade. I found students honest and forthright and when appropriate, they did indeed contact me to negotiate a different grade. At the end of the course, I posed this question:

> *In this class, we experimented with a different approach to evaluation. As co-researchers, what are some of your reflections on this experience? What did you notice about any effects of our different approach to evaluation on your participation in the class? Do you think this approach had an impact on your relationships with fellow students, with the course materials, and/or with the course website – and if so, how? What do you imagine might have been different if we had approached grades in a more traditional way? Do you have any recommendations for my future work with students in academic environments?*

Students responded with their reflections on my questions.

Posting by Danielle

> *Peggy, I have thought a lot about this question this week and am trying to think how things "might have been different" for me had you chosen a traditional evaluation method. I tend to participate fully in any class I am in, so I don't think my participation would have been different. I think the difference for me would have been how I felt about the course work – especially the on-line work. I would have been more conscious of getting postings "right" as opposed to just pondering things online. So I would say that this evaluation method allowed me to really relax into the work and respond in a thinking way rather than a strategic way... I am not sure if this makes sense... I don't know how to put it into words... I guess the long and short of it is that I would have done the same amount of work – but it would have felt more like "work" rather than my just feeling free to enjoy thinking with my classmates.*

Classroom Tellings and Retellings

When a student misses a class, rather than taking an evaluative stance, I like to use this as an opportunity for further practice. For example, when Carol missed the interview of her classmate, I suggested that she post the class requesting a retelling of what she missed. This gave her the opportunity to formulate specific questions. "What transpired in the interview? Is there a way to briefly summarize it? What did you take away from the interview in regards to your understanding of narrative practice? How did this interview help in the re-membering and understanding of your development as a social worker?" Carol then posted what she had gathered from phone, face-to-face, and online conversations. Each telling and retelling added to the richness of our shared experience of the original interview.

I start a separate online forum where I ask students, "What do you think would most help someone who had to miss the class to catch up on? What has stood out most about what you have been learning about such narrative practices as letter writing, the class interview, the David Espton/Sebastian tape?[14]" In addition to catching up on accumulated online postings, I ask the student who was absent to practice asking questions of clarification. Such an expression of earnest curiosity adds a rich thread to our online tapestry of narrative discovery.

Due to illness, Nancy missed a class filled with experiential exercise. I then started the following forum: "I have a couple of specific questions to help Nancy ease back into the course. Which small group would be able to graciously invite Nancy to join you? Who is available tomorrow to share in person with Nancy anything that might help her catch up with what she has missed?"

Nancy responds:

I am excited to be rejoining the class, and thank everyone for allowing me to do this. I will hopefully be adding to the discussion later this evening. I looked quickly at the posts and realized that I first need to catch up on reading before I am able to respond substantively. So, I am off to do that, and will see you in cyberspace tonight!

Nancy later posted several questions to the class and thanked her classmates for welcoming her back to class and offering to help her catch up.

WHAT REMAINS UNSPOKEN

In her widely read postmodern analysis of therapy, Rachel Hare-Mustin alerted therapists to developing a heightened awareness to "discourses in the mirrored room" that influence the ways therapists and family members make meaning out of their conversations (Hare-Mustin, 1994). She defines a discourse as "a system of statements, practices, and institutional structures that share common values...The ways most people in a society hold, talk about, and act on a common, shared viewpoint are part of and sustain the prevailing discourses" (p. 18-19). Not all discourses are equal – some have a more dominant influence on language, thought, and action. Once a particular language community accepts a dominant discourse, certain constraints are inescapable.

> *When a group of people talk and relate among themselves in familiar ways, much of their talk reflects and reinstates dominant discourses. Moreover, because dominant discourses are so familiar, they are taken for granted and even recede from view. It is hard to question them. They are part of the identity of most members of any society, and they influence attitudes and behaviours. (p. 19).*

Many therapists have striven to develop sensitivity to muted yet prevailing ideologies of culture, language, and community such as gender, power, ethnicity, and race. For Kathy Crochet and her colleagues, the ethic of care in teaching practices involves continually attending to everyday practice and how teachers and curriculum shape each other (Crocket et al., 2007). Sometimes it takes outsiders to notice common assumptions that otherwise might remain unspoken. For example, my manuscript reviewers alerted me to a similar language borrowed from narrative therapy in online posts by my students throughout this book. They use "knowledges" and "re-membering" and "discourses" and "learnings" and "thickening the story." How much are students influenced by me and other like-minded teachers to try out this new way of thinking and expressing themselves? Do we leave enough room for a dissenting viewpoint?

I believe in rigorous training where a practitioner becomes accountable to a set of over-arching ideas and practices. At the same time, I am uncomfortable joining any kind of movement or approach in ways that impinge on individuals' personal style and creativity. As teacher, I hold this tension – embracing an apprenticeship model that exposes students to maps of practice without communicating the kind of rigidity that stifles self-confidence and ingenuity.

GROUP THINK

Throughout this book, I illustrate how online forums can create space for candid dialogue about provocative topics. I believe it is the teacher's responsibility to ensure both classroom and online conversation makes space for complex and even contradictory perspectives. Students and I strive to co-create conversation unusually inviting of expressions of uncertainty, contradiction and fresh eyes. However, I am also aware of the risk of inadvertently encouraging consensus thinking otherwise known as "groupthink" (Janis, 1972). Groupthink is a kind of rationalized conformity that happens when group members minimize conflict and reach consensus while avoiding viewpoints outside the comfort zone of consensus thinking. A group is particularly vulnerable to groupthink when three characteristics are present: members share similar backgrounds, they are insulated from outside opinions, and there are no clear rules for decision-making (Janis, 1982). Janis documents the symptoms of groupthink; primary among these are an illusion of unanimity, self-censorship, and direct pressure on dissenters not to express arguments against any of the group's views.

The writing on groupthink alerts me to certain risks in teaching practices that strive to create a collaborative learning community. I strive to attend to creative dangers of group think, when group members avoid promoting viewpoints outside the established norm of narrative practice. Crocket (Crocket et al., 2007) p. 40 brought to my attention Maturana and Varela's question (Maturana & Varela, 1987) p. 19 "What might we not see that we do not see?" In particular, I try to stay alert to unintended silencing effects in my teaching style: Do I inadvertently encourage language that supports homogeneity of thought with a pressure to conform? What are the implicit rules that students must follow to succeed in my courses? Do I misinterpret silence as an illusion of unanimous agreement? When do enthusiastic expressions of my personal and theoretical biases interfere with students sharing conflicting points-of-view? How do we know when we might get a bit too comfortable with each other – creating a collaborative comfort zone that is hard to disrupt? I want to keep asking myself these questions and will worry when I stop.

CHAPTER 5

WHEN NICE IS NOT ENOUGH

Posting by Luke

An entirely not-knowing position still leaves us in the power position because power relations are not being openly spoken of (we are just deciding to lower ourselves). We have already dismissed the expert position (we know, you don't) and now the "nice" position (you know, we don't). Still...any ideas of what would come after "We know, you don't" and "you know, we don't"? Maybe "we know something, you know more/other stuff" or something like what Freedman & Combs write: "We know about this therapy (or social work) thing, you know about your life (story.)" I am growing increasingly concerned with just being the nice therapist and ending up another benevolent patriarch. I also love that this program and class has me questioning being only nice (especially as a male).

As a teacher of narrative therapy, I expose students to a variety of experiences that lead them to examine their therapeutic stances. They have plenty to say after guest speakers Betsy Buckley and Phil Decter share their thoughts about distinctions between content, relational, and personal ethics (Buckley & Decter, 2006). I structure experiential exercises, assigned readings, and online forums for students, teacher, and invited guests to interact with each other. I provide students with online questions that encourage them to challenge traditional myths about insider knowledge, and explore what it means to take on a decentered and influential therapeutic posture (White, 2003b). Finally, students ask provocative questions as they try to see the 'family resemblances' between the strengths perspective and the narrative approach. All of these experiences conspire to expose students to a variety of experiences that lead them to examine ethical considerations and power relations relating to therapeutic stance, professionalism, and expertise.

Rather than being professional therapists resorting to an expert position, I invite students to practice thinking of themselves as partners in learning, linking their lives across shared themes with the people whose stories they witness. I want them to develop skills to inquire further into others' experiences. The online forums become like a learning lab for students to experiment with taking a position in relation to their therapeutic stance. Students appreciate and respond to this partnership approach. They share with each their contemplations as they reflect on disturbing experiences with psychiatric and mental health services.

In this chapter, I illustrate how a course website offers an engaging place for students and teacher to meet at the edges of learning about course materials. I learn along with the students, as we discover new ground in our explorations of concepts and practices. I share some student reflections and questions as they grapple to understand how best to position themselves in relation to the people they aspire to serve. Through archived online postings, I give a behind-the-scenes glimpse into candid discussion of prevalent student challenges: confusion and disorientation in questioning their previously held assumptions; self-doubt and self-surveillance as practitioners-in-training feel pressure to "get it right"; and moving beyond cheerleading and pointing out positives. I then show how they apply their deconstructive listening skills to take a position on "The Carefulness" that informs their lives and work. The chapter concludes with a frank discussion of everyday challenges a practitioner faces when intentionally making room for complexities – sharing a commitment to ongoing, rigorous, reflective studies while at the same time refining a personal style.

STUDENTS' BEHIND-THE-SCENES VIEW

When used well, an interactive website gives students opportunities to candidly engage with each other, opening up and sharing their growing edges. Students tell me conversations such as these that synthesize the personal and professional are preciously rare. It is equally uncommon for the teacher to be privy to such intimate dialogue. I become more familiar with the realities of their experiences and develop sensitivities to their preferences, insecurities, commitments, hopes, and dreams. For me, this behind-the-scenes glimpse greatly enhances my ability to meet students where they are, assist them to navigate through course materials accordingly, and address particular and pertinent learning issues that rise to the surface.

The beauty of an interactive website is that not everyone needs to actively participate in order to benefit. Some students express discomfort with such public openness and prefer face-to-face exchanges. Others listen from the sidelines in one forum while actively engaging in another online conversation. I remind students that the website is restricted to students enrolled in the course and those to whom – with their permission – I give guest passes. Still, sharing intimate thoughts on a website takes some getting used to – for some students more than others.

Is Nothing Sacred?

Students of narrative therapy often describe the sense of groundlessness that can come from re-examining assumptions they heretofore assumed were sacrosanct or inhere in nature. The discussion forums add opportunities for students to reflect on their experiences as they question taken-for-granted beliefs, truths, knowledge, and power. Amy, a social work graduate student, articulates her experience of reading material that is "totally stimulating but a little off-balancing for me, as feminist theory and family systems theory and psychoanalytic theory keep getting deconstructed away."

Posting by Amy1

I am left feeling empty, but not in the Buddhist sense, rather in a lost and scared sense. What are we left with, without all the radical innovations and techniques of these and other theories, many of which I think are being reformulated in post-structuralist thinking? I keep asking myself, if we make meaning through discourse and we change meaning by reprioritizing discourses, how do we make a jump from helping people re-story their narrative identities (with language) to really experience those new stories? I think of a friend who will not allow others (friends and therapists alike) to take away her narrative of abuse and pain: when I try to help her externalize it, she responds with appropriate rage.

I posted a response on the course website:

Amy, I know my own version of the groundlessness that can come from unpacking discourses heretofore assumed as sacrosanct. Is nothing sacred? I too am challenged in an ongoing way by the question of how to join people in their own process of "restorying narrative identities" without imposing too much of my own biases. And I too have been unnerved to realize how much I influence meaning-making, prioritizing and re-prioritizing in any therapeutic context – no matter how good, gentle, and/or inadvertent my intentions. While I have not yet discovered any easy answers, I do believe that asking questions like this is deeply rewarding, keeps the work vital, stimulating, humbling, and accountable to our aspired desire to truly be of use. The best way I have found to keep on track is to check in with the people I seek to serve – to create circumstances where it is (hopefully) safe and comfortable to be guided by their experiences. Amy, you have me on the edge of my chair...looking forward to your next installment. And I hope we can find ways to bring this discussion into the classroom.

Deconstructive Listening

Sometimes students have studied deconstruction in other courses. I invite them to bring this knowledge into their current studies.

Posting by Sarah1

I've been thinking about the idea of deconstruction that lies at the heart of narrative therapy. Recently (in another class) I watched an interview with bell hooks, who spoke with great eloquence about our education system's failure to offer critical thinking skills and tools of cultural criticism to people of color. She said when she taught students in largely white, prestigious colleges, they were given these more abstract tools and exposed to various ideological frameworks, but in the college in Harlem where she later taught, there was a sense that education was simply a vehicle for a better life, for a job. hooks saw this practice as deeply patronizing, and worked to undo it in her pedagogy. It seems the deconstruction inherent in narrative therapy – the way clients are encouraged to examine larger social forces and their impact on individuals – speaks very much to the need that hooks identified. I find this one of the most appealing parts of this practice.

Partners in Learning

The following exchange took place online after students viewed a narrative interview and responded with letters. Sarah2's posting described a deepening appreciation of the narrative therapeutic approach and the strengths and resilience that people possess. She felt moved by the thoughtful letters that people wrote and a growing sense of excitement about facilitating positive changes. At the same time, these powerful experiences sadly reminded her of some recent experiences on an inpatient psychiatric unit. During the weekly psychiatry "case conferences," a "case" was presented to an "expert" in a room full of students and residents. Following this presentation, the patient was brought in and interviewed in front of the large group. Afterwards, the patient left without receiving any feedback from the group or the "expert," and the patient was discussed again behind closed doors. Sarah reflected:

Posting by Sarah2

Though these sessions were often interesting, I always felt uncomfortable with this process and how it was affecting the "patient" and everyone involved. Now, seeing the power of reflecting teams, and a way of approaching this work that seems more respectful and helpful, I am saddened and angered that this practice continues. I feel like these sessions and similar practices end up further stripping a person of what may help them to heal and recover. The medical system seems so wedded to using these methods to teach...what can we do?

Sarah1 also worked in an inpatient setting in which cases were discussed by "experts" behind glass.

Posting by Sara1

Clients often later reported that they felt shunned or humiliated by the process (though these reports were sometimes understood by staff as a manifestation of illness). This interview/consultation process seemed clearly to exacerbate the client's sense of unease, anxiety, frustration, inefficacy – often the very concerns that brought the person to seek intensive treatment. It seems that finding a way to use a reflecting team ethos (regardless of whether general narrative methods are used) would offer some kind of corrective, and would diminish the tendency for clients' concerns to be intensified by the treatment process itself.

Their classmate, Alison, could identity with both of these experiences. While learning about narrative therapy, she tried to imagine the application in a work setting such as in her first year placement – a hospital's day-treatment unit for adolescents. "The language that was used, the tone of discussion, was so 'problem saturated.' It left me feeling quite distressed with the hospital model." The following year, Alison worked in an agency that "appeared much more invested in creating a working relationship with families but even then there was a sense of superiority about the way some clinicians worked with their clients." She described her experience presenting a case and hesitating to make too many assumptions because it was early in treatment.

Posting by Alison

The psychiatrist exclaimed, "C'mon, be more confident...you're the expert." At the time, I felt incredibly uncomfortable with that statement but only now do I realize why that felt so "icky" to me at the time. In some ways, the tentativeness that many of us still experience as novice clinicians can be destabilizing but in other ways, it provides some necessary humility in avoiding becoming the "expert."

Jordanna had also experienced case conferences and expert consultations that seemed "insulting to the people we're trying to 'help.'" As a first year intern, she was not completely aware of how obnoxious these practices were, but looking back, she felt offended. Luckily there were some clinicians at her placement who practiced "client-centered" ways of being as best they could within the medical model. She found that narrative practice was very much affecting how she thought about her work. This was most noticeable to her in her practice class, reading case studies: "We apply theories and hypotheses about what are going on for the client and what has happened in his life that needs to be 'corrected.' I find myself unable to join the conversation and keep thinking that the presumptions we are making are irrelevant; we are not experts in this client's life and therefore do not have the privilege to make such statements."

Sometimes students boldly bring these concerns closer to home. Abbie reflected online about her discomfort with how in other classes "we discuss our 'cases' and put them into 'THE four psychologies.'" She had just come from a practice class where they spoke about a client from a vignette and treatment based on one of these psychologies.

Posting by Abbie

My eyes sort of glazed over at points when people started talking about "transference" and "ego-syntonic defences" and "the need to be a good object for the client to internalise." These are people we are talking about! I feel like we get so far removed in these classes from seeing them as people, just like us. "Conceptualizing a case," as my supervisor this past year termed it, set up a huge us/them hierarchy that felt contrary to how I approached them in the room. I believe in collaboration and empowerment and get tripped up in what is, in a sense, a kind of privileged language as to how we talk about them. Couldn't what comes out of our mouths influence how we feel about them and interact with them, even if they are not the room? How would they feel to hear us talking about their "pathological character traits?!" I'm struggling with how to talk about clients when they are not in the room in a way that feels comfortable to me. Also, I find that the more I distance myself with language and get into theory, the harder it is for me to make useful interventions. I feel like I'm often left wondering, "what does that look like in the room"?

Abbie ended her posting with the invitation: "Reflections and/or counter-arguments are welcomed and appreciated." Again I was reminded of what an online forum makes possible. Where else could such candid conversation take place?

REFINING THE STRENGTHS PERSPECTIVE

Posting by Luke

Just before the letter-writing exercise, Peggy said something that struck me. It was that we were to move beyond the mere strengths perspective to a more personal stance (i.e. what resonated and how will we be different for hearing this story). I was initially shocked to be so simply told that the strengths perspective was not enough (and possibly oppressive), but it seems to make sense to me. It makes me wonder what is beyond (more progressive) than narrative. How do we question even narrative approaches in this class in a way that helps us move forward and not back to traditional oppressive practices?

Online discussion forums offer space for students to apply their deconstructive listening skills to question assumed philosophy and practices. Many students gain inspiration from what has become known as "the strengths perspective" in social work (Saleebey, 2002) and in particular concerning children's mental health (Poertner & Ronnau, 1992; Stroul, 1996) and emotional difficulties (Kisthardt, 1992). They embrace the fundamental principle of emphasizing strengths in helping relationships, bringing into the forefront the knowledge, skills, and experiences that people can contribute to solving a given problem. My approach has also been deeply influenced by the strengths perspective. I am grateful to practice in an era when practitioner training highlights the value of the contributions of people themselves. I appreciate the accent on resiliency and possibility. However, I also want practitioners to be cognizant of the dangers these approaches carry with them. I want students to differentiate between supporting/helping people and remembering to let the clients themselves lead the way. I want the help-giver to be cautious about pre-determining that his/her role should be that of the positive, cheerful optimist, rooting for the client. I encourage them to resist the urge to point out positives, or to optimistically re-interpret clients' words or feelings. For this discussion, I introduce the practices of "applause," "cheerleading," and "pointing out positives" – all of which Michael White cites as potentially problematic (White, 1997c).

Amy put into words what she cherishes about the strengths perspective and what invites caution, further inquiry, and considering of context.

Posting by Amy2

The strengths perspective is a philosophy that I really embraced, mainly because service providers (based on my own experience and experiences within my family) often are problem oriented, and tend to start talking about the deficits in relationship to the problem, rather than focusing on the strengths that people possess and ways in which they can and do use those strengths in their daily lives. For example, when I was "depressed" in high school, I felt as though all the people around me were focusing on my "symptoms" and the things that depression was getting in the way of me doing. In a sense, I felt as though the focus on what I couldn't do only made me more dependent on my family and friends to help me get through the days. Not many people helped me point out the things I was still able to do, for example, I was still getting through school and learning. Those who did point out positives, would simply say "You're strong, you'll get through this." As we've talked about in class, these free-floating compliments just floated over my head, because I didn't feel strong. If someone had said that a particular thing I was doing was a strength of mine, I might have received it better.

When the strengths perspective is situated in the person's context or story, rather than just general strengths such as "you're nice" or "you're smart," it can be a source of support for the individual that could potentially help the person realize way they can take those "unique outcomes" and link them in time to create an alternative story. With people focusing on the things I couldn't do at the time I was depressed, I internalized the depression more and felt like it was a part of me.

Who identifies the strength in the collaborative relationship? I always thought of the strengths perspective as a philosophy in which the therapist or service providers helps the person with whom they are working to identify their strengths, and helps provide the person with some hope. However, I have been thinking recently that it seems to be more effective if the service provider asks questions that encourage individuals to recognize and name their own personal strengths, ...putting them in the driver's seat.

When Stacy first read the question about the strengths perspective and narrative work, she also reflected on why it's not necessarily a good plan for the service provider rather than the service seeker to highlight individuals' strengths. "What if the client doesn't see that particular attribute as a strength, or one they want to be associated with? If we are giving individuals the opportunity to name their obstacles it seems only fitting that we should be giving them the opportunity to name their strengths as well."

A Culture of Applause

Posting by Paula

> *When I sat down to write my first letter, the first thing I wanted to do was offer some applause...It took a few minutes for me to rework my thoughts. It is ingrained in our culture and is an easy way to ease into or out of a conversation. I liked how Lynn Hoffman called narrative applause "unthinking addiction to the positive" (Hoffman, 2002). I agree with you, Amy, we are quick to "gloss over a problem" with praise and try to make someone feel good, when really we may be just dismissing their experience. But if you have a compliment for someone in narrative therapy should you really hold it in?*

A lively discussion often emerges when students contemplate "the culture of applause" that creates a sweet but rather thin story description. This contrasts with narrative therapy's constant refrain, "How can we best speak to one another to co-author rich story development?" Katherine reflected on personal situations where she turned to others to talk over a concern she had, only to be applauded. She was left feeling as though her feelings were not real. Not being given the space to express her negative feelings made her feel worse.

Posting by Katherine

> *I was informed of all these great positives or told, "no you're not that way...you're this..." These conversations did not help me. Yes, at times I may not be thinking rationally and maybe I do not truly believe some of the things I say in a moment of self-doubt, but those feelings are real to me. Talking with someone who just wants to fix it or tell me the positive things is not listening to me. [I want to be] able to express my thoughts without others telling me my feelings are wrong and pointing out only positive areas of my life. I end up feeling worse because I have these negative thoughts but should be happy because of all the good things I have going for me. My question is, how do we balance out the compliments with room for the other person to tell their story without feeling it was as Katy described, "glossed over"?*

Michelle shared her belief that she saw some applause as a necessary piece of her work as a social worker. "I wonder if it's more in what we applaud, when, and the nature of the relationship with those people. I feel that this realization will be an important foundation in my future work." A good friend of Michelle's wrote a letter to confront her older brother who had sexually abused her. For years, the family avoided and denied the events. Michelle knew that the letter was the culmination of six years of her friend's hard work, impacting her identity, life goals and relationships with men.

Posting by Michelle

> *This week she called to share her letter with me and get my feedback. Prior to taking this course I would not have hesitated to praise her hard work and*

offer feedback and suggestions. As she was reading the letter, I reminded myself that "these are her words and how she intended them to be." The narrative concepts resonated with me as I listened to her emotional story through letter-writing and as she asked me my opinion. All I could think to say was how the letter reflected all of those things she's talked with me about through the years. I offered several positive statements; however, I made it a point to describe why I felt that way based on certain lines in the letter or previous conversations. I really felt that my ability to pull myself back from praising and offering my personal opinion made her feel empowered and strong in that the letter was exactly as she intended it to be.

Michelle's posting is a clear example of students understanding how the culture of applause plays out in their own lives and exemplifies my goal of helping students to realize there are ways to be supportive in positive ways without "taking over" and putting your own ideas/words in place of the person they are helping .

Discussion about the culture of applause often leads into further contemplation about "cheerleading" and some cautions about using it as a helping strategy. In one class, I posted the following:

In some situations, I think of cheerleading as a really positive image. In sports, I imagine teammates are inspired to do their best when they hear the cheers. And in social work/helping professions, it is a great step forward for humankind to switch from a pathologizing to a strength-based approach. However, as Michael White points out, it is less helpful when we sometimes find ourselves having finished the race when the person consulting you isn't even out of the starting gate. In practicing narrative therapy, the person in the role of the service provider strives to walk side-by-side, rather than ahead of the person who is coming to us for help. If we get too far ahead, the story becomes ours and we create our own meanings (albeit with good intentions) while leaving behind the person whose live is our focus. What are your current thoughts about "cheerleading" – when you imagine cheerleading to be useful or not useful?

I strive to help students discern the sometimes subtle difference between cheerleading and acknowledging positive developments. Danielle posted about her work with a preschooler where she was able to see positive developments while the teachers seemed unable to see other than negative behaviors. At the end of the day, she would be the "cheerleader" for the child, pointing out the positive choices and hard work she had done that day. For instance, whereas the teacher might only see the child's tantrum, Danielle would say, "Yes, she did get quite frustrated with that...and then in the hallway, after she had time to be mad and to get all the mad out, she was able to talk about how it frustrated her and this helped her learn names for the emotions she was having, which, at four years old, she doesn't have yet. It was great seeing her trying to figure it all out, including how to talk about it."

Lynn shared a story from her work:

Posting by Lynn

Sometimes when I am sitting with people sharing the space with their pain, such as when they are having a rape exam, or physical exam because of the injuries from an assault, or much later, when they are still processing what has happened a year later as we sit in court and they are testifying, it has also seemed to me instinctively that to pull something out positive just for the sake of pulling something out positive, would not be helpful. I think writing and reflection for themselves alone, have much value in that they can read [what they wrote] later or destroy even in a ceremony for themselves.

This posting and others from students grappling with how to make sense of this new way of thinking propelled me to ponder what I have learned about practices of applause, as giver and receiver. I join in with my own posting, letting them know how their questions, reflections, and expressions of confusion resonate with my own experiences. I first acknowledge the complexities, underscoring that the intention is not that we stop giving compliments or positive statements, or throw out the strengths perspective as important steps forward from the pathologizing foundations of many approaches to psychotherapy. I share a story from my experience of watching many interviews and videos with Michael White:

When I focus on Michael White's therapeutic interactions, I am amazed by the number of acknowledgements he gives. These are very concrete acknowledgements of what he is witnessing and what he has heard others say they have accomplished. He also often checks in with people – variations on the theme of "How is this going for you?" and "Do I have this right?" I think this is something to aspire to – to do the best we can to create an environment in which people feel witnessed in their sorrows, their fears, as well as in their developments toward becoming more of whom they want to be.

Because of the prevalence of practices of applause in western culture and human services, I invite students to apply the considerable skills they have learned while studying narrative inquiry to unpack and question our assumptions. I also encourage them to ponder their own experiences. "What do we personally experience as being helpful and not helpful and in which situations? And why? The intention is not to blithely dismiss the practice of applause as a "bad thing" but rather to take into account more complex accounts of experiences and apply these learnings to our ongoing development in the various contexts of our lives as social workers, friends, partners, etc." I further reflect on what I learn from students putting themselves in the shoes of the person receiving "applause."

I appreciated reading Katy's contemplation of how you might feel as the recipient of applause – the danger of feeling patronized or as though your concerns are being glossed over, as well as acknowledging that there are situations when a compliment, word of encouragement, or support might feel appropriate. Reading your post reminded me of the importance of defining what we mean by "applause." Where are the lines and what about the grey areas? I try too to remind myself that it is the receiver, not the giver, who defines success.

I encourage students to remember the importance of context:

Here we are primarily talking about becoming more cognizant of how the culture of applause might inform our interactions in therapeutic contexts (including therapeutic interviews and letter-writing). There were times when watching my son play hockey or a friend's musical performance that I have enthusiastically indulged in applause. While there are some similarities with parenting or friendship, therapy is a unique context. As therapists, our role is to assist people to more richly describe their lives in ways that help them shape new stories that extend well beyond sugar coating/feeling glossed over – into new territories that offer new possibilities.

I share some of the particular effects of their postings on my own thinking:

Michelle, you gave such a wonderful illustration of ways to think about the real effects of "applauding" and to contemplate alternatives to giving praise and offering feedback. "These are her words and how she intended them to be" will be a mantra I will try to remember in my interactions with others both in and out of therapeutic contexts. I feel somehow linked with you in your efforts to pull back from praising and offering personal opinion. Thank you for reminding us to attend to what we applaud, when, and the nature of the relationship with these people.

GETTING IT RIGHT

Posting by Kerry2

I am struck by how many of us seem to feel self-doubt that penetrates us to a point that we become (nearly) verbally paralyzed. So often, I feel like I must be the only one who feels this way. I wonder if it has something to do with patriarchy? The "Carefulness" we've spoken about? Or a result of often times only communicating what's "important" in abbreviated forms like text messaging and email instead of having full blown conversations with each other? It makes me sad to see that so many kind-hearted souls feel nervous about communicating thoughts.

Students share volumes of compelling reflections about how the pressure to "get it right" influences their identity and self-confidence. I believe this tension has particular relevance to students of narrative therapy, who strive to learn maps of practice while simultaneously developing their own styles of working. I try to set the stage for them to understand that getting things right is not the focus. I continually invite students to embrace the metaphor of apprenticing to a craft. I hope they will use the class as an opportunity to stretch themselves, try new approaches, test new skills, and in the process likely make some mistakes, which are all part of the learning process. I highlight trial-and-error learning as the mainstay of such an apprenticeship. In the following post, I try to enlist my students' help in easing their anxiety about making mistakes to learn and grow:

Do you have any ideas about what we can do as a group and/or me in the role of teacher to make this course as comfortable as possible to practice on each other and to learn through trial and error? What might help us lighten up with each other to resist letting Self-surveillance and Perfectionism interfere? How can we best notice and take advantage of the ideal learning environment we now find ourselves in?

Often students realize a sense of solidarity through sharing their experiences with living with and overcoming self-doubt. Emma wrote about her love for reading, yet recalled feeling stifled and nervous when she was asked to identify and write about major themes in a book. "We were always graded by what our teacher and state/federal policies had decided the meaning of the story was, leaving little space for students to make their own meaning." Now, Emma thinks about "how my attention to people's stories gets wrapped up in what people with influence and authority would want us to believe in order to preserve the status quo."

Kerry2 wonders why it is that she holds herself to standards that she would never expect of others. "What's worse is that I'm pretty good at beating myself up if I don't succeed at meeting these outrageous self-standards." Since becoming a mother, she has started to be a bit less self-critical and hard on herself: "I look at my daughter and see this beautiful child who doesn't know about embarrassment or rules we and our culture place on us. I want to live by example for her. I don't think I could bear having my self-imposed rules become rules that she inherently imposes upon herself."

Kerry1 admired her classmates "for being what I consider to be very brave" in their sharing. She boldly wrote about her struggles with sharing. She reminded others that everyone contributes and "just because others share does not mean that we must share as well unless it feels right."

Posting by Kerry1

I am continually moved by what people share...I truly appreciate and hold everyone's stories close to my heart and I thank you for so bravely presenting us all with this gift. I resonated with what both Luke and Foresta described as the unworthiness of our stories. I have often felt that in my own life...I am somewhat protective of my stories and experiences and often hesitant to share them. I think this has to do with people then "using" my story in ways either against me or in circumstances when I myself would not have shared. It's tough to describe but I have felt it even this past semester. I have yet to share anything very personal, as I am not there yet, but I can feel the possibility of doing so; it is very powerful for me to feel that connection with this class. Thank you everyone for being so real and allowing this space to be so safe and caring. Thank you Peggy for bringing this out in all of us.

Her classmates immediately responded with appreciative support. For Luke, it was important to hear another voice added to the "unworthiness" camp. "This forum makes it very hard for those voices to tell me I'm alone in this." He added:

Posting by Luke

When you write, "I have yet to share anything very personal" I think, "to me, that very post was very personal." I think of what Ken said when he wrote that voices of inadequacy (my word, I don't have his post in front of me) come up for him when others share very "personal" stories. I can relate to what I hear both of you saying. Sometimes it seems that more detailed or "heart wrenching" stories get placed higher on the hierarchy of "personal stories." . I like to think (or am convincing myself to think) that since we can only speak from our own realities, we cannot help but be personal in whatever comes out. Having experiences with you inside and outside of class over the last year Kerry, I see you in every post. I feel you on this site. Thanks again.

In her post, Foresta shared her respect for Kerry1 "knowing the limits of what you are willing to share, to whom, and at a pace that makes sense for you." She referred to a parallel in her conversations with service users, where "we often talk about each person being the expert of his or her situation and the importance of remaining in control of that knowledge." Like Luke, she expressed concern about the hierarchy that can rank "worthiness" of personal stories. "I think that the danger of this kind of hierarchy is that people may feel compelled to share something that they are not ready to. I really appreciate that you have chosen to resist this idea and that you are being personal without putting yourself in a place of vulnerability."

Emma brought in another strand of complexity to this thread of the online conversation. She questioned whether the aloneness of certain experiences, "especially given our culture of individualism and competition" can ever be completely re-authored. "I find there are some days of seeing the big picture, and feeling like the world is my home, shared with everyone else, and on other days like I'm a stranger, where no place feels like home, and no one can quite get what I'm feeling, nor do I try to facilitate understanding." She reflected on how the therapist/client roles seem to denote one giving and the other taking, and not sharing in the responsibility for that which is created. In contrast, "I feel like something really beautiful that I cannot articulate is being created every day through this website, and I feel everyone's voices so strongly." She further acknowledged to her classmates "how strongly I connect with all that you have shared and inviting me and everyone else to be there as you navigate your way to a place that fits your preferred self. It is helping me connect with my reserve of strength and realizing that we can all be in this together. The aloneness is already dissipating a little."

Students gather courage from each other. Melissa began her post by thanking a fellow student for volunteering to be interviewed in class. "Your willingness to share gave me the courage to volunteer later in the day." She spoke about the self-doubt that so many students seem to carry. "When we divided into small groups and slowly began to share what thoughts we had for the day, it was like this great release. We all discovered that we were nervous and not sure what to expect."

The online conversation often goes places I could never envision. When one student speaks candidly about her self-doubt, others respond accordingly. Kerry2 described coming to class feeling inadequate and unsure of how she was going to get through the day without others noticing she wasn't "getting it." "Having read everyone's brilliant and thoughtful posts from the weekend, I felt like you all were Jacques Cousteau (or Steve Zissou – any other "Life Aquatic" fans out there?!) and I was a little rubber ducky bobbing and floating on the surface." Online, she chronicled others' contributions that made her feel a bit better, reminding her "that there are no 'right' questions, just different ones."

The Carefulness

Posting by Foresta

> *In my personal and professional life I have spent a lot of time thinking about what I am saying, how I am saying it, what the other person will think of me for saying it, or whether or not I will offend the other person. This used to be like an internal voice that I would hear in my head when I was working with service users when I first started at my internship last fall. This "voice" diminished over time but it is still there sometimes, especially when I talk with my family, because on the one hand I want to be myself and say what I am feeling, but I also don't want to offend them or be taken the wrong way.*

As students learn externalizing and deconstruction practices, they apply these skills to their own lives as students. An online forum makes it possible for students to engage with each other around themes that are relevant to them. For example, in one class students referred to "The Carefulness" as an unspoken presence in the room that influenced how they interacted with each other. Several students had talked about this "Carefulness" in another class with a different teacher. I post a number of questions to spur online discussion:

> *I continue to contemplate what we have come to refer to as "The Carefulness." What feels important to you in "thickening" our understanding of The Carefulness, putting it in a social context, influenced by culture and history? What have you been noticing about the effects of this Carefulness on the ways that you think about yourself and your approach to your work? Which of these effects are your preferred ways of being, and what would you like to change? Why? As we approach the home stretch of this particular course, are there some learnings about The Carefulness that you would like to take with you into other contexts of your life? What comes to mind? And how might you do this?*

Amy2 responded:

I think that one of the important things to do in "thickening our understanding of The Carefulness" is to think on an individual and group level how this "carefulness" came into play...I think that the first time I made a pretty large mistake when I was young, and then felt the teasing that came from peers thereafter, I started to incorporate The Carefulness into my daily life. I did a lot of self-surveillance, and thought long and hard about doing something before acting, for fear of making a mistake and being judged for it. The Carefulness became a protection for me from the harsh world of perfectionism.

We can begin to think of the Carefulness in terms of how it has affected our personal relationships, relationships with clients, relationships with co-workers, and relationships in group settings. Other ways in which we can thicken our understanding of The Carefulness is to look for unique outcomes in which we let some of The Carefulness go and have had positive experiences or outcomes as a result. Basically, by applying narrative practices to our thinking about The Carefulness and our individual relationships to it, we can begin to see what aspects are beneficial and which are not, and more deeply explore how The Carefulness impacts us as individuals and as a group...

In regards to the effects of The Carefulness in my work, I often second guess my decisions, or go through an internal dialogue in my head of whether or not to say something, ask a particular question, or take a particular route with a client. I worry that what I say will be misinterpreted, and then think about the ripple effects. I try to articulate my points in a clear way in attempt to avoid this. But, often, The Carefulness prevents me from asking a particular question or taking something a client says and trying to develop it further. I feel that The Carefulness holds me back, and convinces me not to explore certain avenues with clients. Another aspect of The Carefulness is that I sometimes get caught up in my own internal dialogue and get lost in it, and I'm no longer fully present with the person I am with. This is something I'd like to change.

One aspect of the Carefulness that I do like, is that I think about what I'm going to say, and in doing so, I try to avoid making assumptions. The Carefulness also leads me to be transparent with clients, which is one of my preferred ways of being.

Students' reflections and questions piqued my intrigue with the unspoken effects of "The Carefulness" on our lives. The following year, I experienced something similar in students' initial sensitivity to criticism and reluctance to speak with earnest curiosity. I then structured the course to highlight responses that move people beyond theoretical understandings of the material. Molly shared the effects of The Carefulness on her life:

In general, I find that The Carefulness consumes me. I am always worried about what others will think, if I'll upset someone, and if my curiosity is inappropriate... I struggle with The Carefulness in both my personal and professional life. I often find that I'm so worried what others will think and if I will offend someone that I ultimately choose not to share my thoughts and opinions...The Carefulness consumes me and I shut down. I stay away from conflict even if it means compromising my ideas.

Our culture values the idea, "think before you speak." I was told this many times as a child. I have seen the few clients I have worked with experience this as well, along with the struggles associated with it. What a huge burden it is to be carrying around so much worry about being careful. There are times when I actually speak and what has gotten through The Carefulness filter is nothing like what I originally wanted to say. Does this happen to me and other women because of the role of gender?

I have only recently been able to acknowledge The Carefulness and what a large role it plays in my life. I'm in the process of discovering how I can balance The Carefulness while being able to express myself. I know that the more comfortable I am challenging The Carefulness, the more open and available I am to clients.

However, transparency is really difficult to grasp. How can you be both professional and real?

Through online conversation, students became aware of the influence of gender on The Carefulness. Emma wrote about the relevance of carefulness to her life as a woman:

Molly, I really appreciated your sharing your thoughts on how The Carefulness has influenced your life and has at times led to you not being fully able to express what you're feeling for fear of offending, being misunderstood, feeling judged, the fear of conflict. All of these ideas resonate deeply within me and how I've seen myself for most of my life.

I've recently begun seeing my life story as one constructed by others more than by me and what my identity meant to me. I let others' labels of me, whether peers, adults, men, women, family, close friends, boyfriends, become my self-perception. I did not have an active voice in my life in high school and some of college. I was so unsure of everything...Fear, anxiety, and self-doubt were some of my common internal stories, which I expressed through external kindness, people-pleasing behaviors, and a passive voice in my relationships.

You brought to light the influence of gender and how this might be an influence on The Carefulness. From my own experience, my filters or my perception of men originated from early abuse and from relationships I had with men who devalued me as a person...I never learned how to name any of that as oppression, or to feel some sense that I was not alone or that it wasn't only my problem, or that it wasn't "my" problem at all.

I would like to explore The Carefulness in the classroom setting by taking more personal risks. I have often defined risk as anything that is self-revealing. I am starting to construct that differently, realizing that by revealing stories, we are bringing forth a way to connect, and my hope is to find in this class (which I feel already, by the way) a sense of community, openness to difference, and a curiosity and sensitivity to the challenge that sharing poses for some.

Bronwen added a cultural perspective to the discussion about carefulness:

Working in social work for many years has brought me into contact with people from many cultures. Even people who don't appear to be from a different culture often are. I come from the Irish culture where people talk constantly, emote frequently, and tell everyone their opinion about everything...Irish family gatherings are noisy affairs; my grandfather was the king of all narrators with stories that could last for hours. I have had to learn to be quiet, listen, and learn from what people share with me. Some cultures are loud. I can be loud with them. Some are quiet. I have to notice that and be part of the quietness. It takes much carefulness to be with people in a way that they can accept and be comfortable with.

The people that I work with have impaired mental abilities due to addiction problems and altered reality problems (what do we call it if we don't use a diagnostic name like "schizophrenia"?) I find that I have to be so very careful. Even an expression or a laugh can be taken the wrong way and cause much emotional agony to the other person. So there is the dilemma – how to be genuine and caring and generous with ourselves but know how to act so that people feel safe and comfortable with us as the social worker. Someone mentioned in one of these responses about not adding to anyone's burden. Many times, supervisors have advised me, "share your own story if you are clear that it will be of some use to the other person. And share your feelings if they are gentle and kind and will not overwhelm the other person." That is my guiding motto. Perhaps the narrative ideas we are learning in this class will help us to further develop the stories that we do share and help us find a way to deepen connection as we do it. But carefulness will always have to be a part of it for me.

EDGES OF LEARNING

The online conversation makes it possible to situate my reflections without resorting to a stance of "teacher as expert." I do not want to add to students' internalized pressure to "get it right." I strive to render visible my process of noticing and cleaning-up after mistakes while keeping perspective.

Whenever possible, I remind students that we cannot be brilliant all the time. I share heartfelt reflections on an online forum that in person I would worry might sound too preachy:

> *The bad news is that we can't always be the one to "make the difference that needs to happen" for a given person or family. The good news is that none of us is alone – we are part of a much larger circle of humanity. We take turns in making differences small and large. When we do human services work, we (hopefully) become part of a kind of safety net for families and individuals. Together we can catch people who might otherwise fall through the cracks if there was only one of us trying to offer support. Often it's not even the service providers who make the main difference – it's family, community, friends, and other informal supporters.*

A couple of weeks after this posting, Kerry1 wrote to say how much she appreciated this milieu in which she felt safe and protected, while also comfortable enough to continue to challenge herself.

> *I can see this class transforming the way I hope to interact in other classes. I definitely want to continue this apprenticeship. Thanks for being so open and allowing yourself to be vulnerable along with us. I appreciate the open dialogue we have achieved here rather than what I have felt at times is a one-sided talk with people agreeing. This class allows us to talk without the fear of offending and hopefully in a way that is not too personal. I really hope to continue some of what we have accomplished in this class in the coming year.*

Making Room for Complexities

Posting by Amy2

> *I want to...[bring narrative practice] into my way of living and future work. I still have an appreciation for the strengths perspective, but I want to ask more questions in my practice rather than give advice. I think there is great value in helping people come to their own realizations rather than simply giving advice and tips on how to work through problems.*

Students often express gratitude that their narrative studies have taught them not to jump to conclusions. For example, Danielle1 posted her reflections on a conversation with her classmate, Julia. When they mentioned to others that we were going running, their listeners responded, "Oh, are you trying to lose weight?" Having both taken the narrative course, they had similar responses, "Why is it people assume, when you tell them you are running or working out that you are trying to lose weight? Do they assume you are unhappy or dissatisfied with your weight?" They decided that the "normative" way of considering running and working out by those who do not have the same habit is that the purpose is weight control.. Julia practices meditation; as someone who doesn't practice mediation, Danielle1 immediately assumed that Julia meditated to relax. With these two examples in mind, they pondered whether having a particular experience gives insight into another person's motivation.

Posting by Danielle1

If, for example, I am working with a client who was abused as a child, since I had some experience of abuse myself, I would have some ideas based on personal experience that would quell the assumptions I might otherwise make about that person's experience. Yet, what if I have a client who has a substance abuse problem? How do I work with that person effectively and not make normative assumptions about their experience?

Danielle1 sees narrative practice as awakening her understanding of the influence of normative assumptions on their roles as human service practitioners. She aspires to keep in mind that she cannot possibly have had similar experiences to every client she serves – "even if we have had some similar experiences, that does not inform us wholly on the other person's experience." Her narrative studies helps her ask, "How do we get beyond the normative assumptions to truly understand the person from their perspective of their experiences? We would have to ask specific questions to really get at that person's experience of the issue and the meaning THEY make of that experience!!! This would be living narrative practice."

As teacher, I strive to makes space for complex and even contradictory perspectives and to hold that space open. Students learn to question long-held cultural, historical and professional assumptions. I strive to apply similar deconstructive listening skills to question my own teaching practices. Hence, I responded:

I will be learning about these complexities for the rest of my life. Maybe you have noticed that I am a person who carries a lot of enthusiasm; I continue to train myself to hold back from well intentioned yet not particularly helpful "Bursts of the Positive." Yes, this is so much better than "Bursts of the Negative," and I think the good intentions do make a difference. Yet, in therapeutic situations, I have found that it really does help to discipline myself to speak more specifically and from a stance of inquiry.

As a postscript, I shared a draft of this chapter with a couple of people who have consulted with me in the therapy room. Reading about my intention to restrain bursts of enthusiasm brought forth a similar response of laughter. Apparently I am not as good at concealing my reactions as I envisioned. However, people tell me that they actually appreciate the genuineness of an energetic response, as long as I make room for them to share a different experience or perspective. Again, I am reminded of how the therapist and teacher must hold multiple and at times contradictory guiding principles. We each have a personal style that expresses our humanity. As an eternal optimist, I see possibilities in predicaments and have confidence in people's abilities to rise to occasions. Yet no matter how genuine, a positive spin can feel discounting to someone in distress. In Chapter Seven, "Stories of Identity," I further describe how narrative practice trains the practitioner to "double listen" to and against problems (Epston, 2003a), to foster conversations that highlight "unique outcomes" (White, 2007a) and to engage with a person's history to draw forth "the absent but implicit" (White, 2000a). Again and again, I want to develop skills to ask questions rather than assume I know what it is like for others in a range of roles including as therapist and as teacher.

Section Two: Multiple Voices

PEOPLING THE COURSE

Posting by Morgan in online conversation with guest author, Chris Beels

If Dr. Beels gets a chance to join our conversation again, I'd like to convey my thanks for responding to my question. It's so exciting to be able to have dialogue with the people that we read about. I think this online thing is really useful and should be used in a lot more classes.

THE VALUE OF MULTIPLE VOICES

Through classroom visits and online exchanges, I incorporate many voices in my teaching. My pedagogy is a reflection of the material I teach. Bringing in multiple points of view reflects the postmodern ideas that 1) there is no one truth and 2) identity is multi-voiced. Moreover, I want students to experience firsthand how personal identity is tied to significant people in their lives.

Some teachers might worry about introducing multiple voices into a course. What exactly is their role? Will they lose control? Does it take too much effort? Is it too messy? I recall entertaining such concerns. Facilitating multiple voices shifts the teacher's role. Other teachers who embrace these ways of teaching say they are no longer "the sage on the stage," but rather become "the guide on the side." The teacher spends less time lecturing in front of the classroom and more time as a hospitable host who facilitates conversation. Certainly, by bringing in other voices, I reduce the amount of time to teach from my own point of view. Similar to facilitating a group, I use a light touch that might otherwise go unnoticed, so the interaction between the participants is highlighted.

In this chapter, I describe some of the specific ways I create space and gently guide these conversations. As conversations become more complex, I make room for multiple voices while moving forward with course material. While this role might sound time consuming, I believe the benefits are well worth the effort. Inviting online guests frees the teacher from being the sole content expert and allows her or him to become a participant learner. I become entranced by the lively exchanges where everyone – myself included – is both a teacher and a learner. I no longer teach in isolation. Instead, I am accompanied by an entourage of team-teachers, available for support, collaboration and problem-solving.

GUESS PASS

Reflection by Mohammad

I think the guest pass is what puts this course in a category of its own. It is one thing to have guest speakers but it is another for them to be able to read postings and participate in the online conversation. I remember Beth and Steve had already entered our online world and spoken with us before even coming to the class in person. This is an important aspect of this course. The community that is created by first establishing a sense of trust among students expands as guest speakers enter the arena of discourse. Since the guest speakers are persons who have thought about, written about, and practiced narrative approaches, the class transforms into a community of learners. Practitioners, teachers, and students all engage in a conversation dissolving the barriers and prescribed hierarchies setting them apart.

I use the online medium to offer opportunities for students to consult with knowledged people outside of the actual course. With permission, I give a "guest pass" to select colleagues to join our online discussion – people who share an interest in collaborative approaches to therapeutic conversations, and an enthusiasm for narrative therapy. I welcome the guests to join the online discussion as follows:

The students have given me permission to give a "guest pass" to select people to visit our course site. You are most welcome to join in the discussion. Please introduce yourself so that students will know who is reading their reflections. Feel free to ask any questions of your own. Thanks – and welcome!

I create online forums where students can converse with the authors whose writings they are studying as well as continue conversation with guest speakers. For example, students have conversed with the authors after reading Lynn Hoffman's first-person account of becoming a family therapist (Hoffman, 2002), Christian Beels' memoir about the rise of narrative in psychotherapy (Beels, 2001), David Paré's article on the shift in metaphors in family therapy from systems to story (Paré, 1996), and Chris Behan's article on using reflecting teamwork in group therapy (Behan, 1999).

I also give guest speakers "guest passes" so that they may join the online conversation after class as their schedules allow. Every time Lynn Hoffman visits one of my classes, she leaves an indelible mark on students; soon after class, their reflections fill the screen.

Other class visitors have included Pam and Prudence, seasoned veterans as seekers of human services; Peter and Marc, practitioners from the local community mental health center and Chris, Betsy, and Phil, experienced narrative practitioners and teachers. Early in the course, I sometimes invite former students to share some of their experiences in learning narrative therapy within a psychodynamic culture. Students post their reflections and questions and guest speakers respond with further reflections. This also gives me, as instructor, the opportunity to add a few of my own reflections without dominating the conversation.

Often – and with students' permission – I invite narrative enthusiasts from elsewhere to join us online. Olivia, one such online guest, remarked, "I feel like it wasn't an accident that my work traveled to other people. Every time that I heard that my work was touching someone I also became touched powerfully. This is the beauty of narrative therapy isn't it? All parties end up feeling enhanced by their work together."

A caution is warranted. I make sure to continue asking the students' permission before opening up the class to new visitors and sharing their work with others. "Is it okay for me to give out the guest pass to others who teach narrative? Is it okay if I link you to someone else who would be interested in reading your work? How would you feel about having your assignments and/or posts included in this article? Would you prefer to be anonymous? Have I given you enough freedom to say no, for whatever reason?" It is important not to presume or take liberties based on earlier conversations when no objections were given. I also let the students know I will share with them any reflections from invited guests about their work. Then I follow through with this promise.

Knowledged Prior Students

Learning about narrative therapy poses particular challenges for students amidst an intensity of demands and exposure to divergent approaches. Students otherwise studying transference-based traditions are understandably confused and even overwhelmed in their attempts to integrate new learnings into existing psychodynamic and psychoanalytic frameworks. They ask:

> How does narrative therapy fit into the evolution of the field of family therapy? What are distinctions between narrative therapy and other therapeutic approaches? Is narrative therapy really that radically different and if so, how can I cope with this affront to heretofore cherished constructs? What can I keep and what will I need to change in order to embrace these new concepts and practices?

I have found it useful to invite former narrative therapy students to share some of their experiences, learnings, and survival tips to help students find their way through the confusion. Sometimes I bring in classmates who have already taken the course. Guest speakers have also included narrative practitioners who are graduates of the program. By inviting people with local knowledge, I can interview them about learning narrative practice within their own school's culture. Afterwards, I begin an online forum to continue the dialogue:

> **Welcome to Guests:** *A heartfelt thank you to both Beth Prullage and Stephen Bradley, our first guest visitors to this course. I feel grateful to each of them for opening space for conversation about some of the particular challenges for students studying narrative therapy at Smith's School of Social Work,*

where psychodynamic therapy is the dominant culture. What are some of your lingering reflections and questions as you embark on this course of study of narrative therapy at Smith? How might we break away from the either/or dichotomous thinking to honor the spectrum of therapeutic experience, while also drawing necessary "apples and oranges" distinctions between different ("inside-out" and "outside-in") understandings of "the self?" What is it like for you to enter this dialogue? Does anything come to mind that you would like to contribute to this conversation?

After class, students posted their reflections online. Mohammad noticed how "Beth talked of being at a work setting that many of her friends have come and gone from and Steve spoke of the narrative therapist feeling the need to speak and take action to bring about structural change." He further noted, "They seemed like ordinary people, listening with interest to stories about life, loss and in between, helping the storytellers make meaning out of their experiences so as to go on and write new stories of their lives, perhaps reaching for the extraordinary."

Sarah reflected on distinctions between psychodynamic and postmodern therapies: "Since I've gotten deeper into the readings, my initial need to hold these models next to each other, to compare, has diminished." Sarah appreciated Beth's summation of the "interpretive turn" and "her clear way of illuminating why these two models (narrative and dynamic) may not effectively or logically overlap." Her question aptly articulated an important edge of learning.

Posting by Sarah

If one roots oneself in a social constructivist framework, and sees reality/interactions/self as invented by the interplay of external forces, it is hard to imagine reconciling this with a theory that depends upon notions of internal, innate forces. However, it seems to me that external forces (whatever they are) must in some way get "internalized" (albeit in deeply personal, relational ways, which may not be "known" by the "expert.") Though the place of inception of the forces (inside or outside) remains contentious among theorists, I feel like dynamic theories which look at the inside may still have some resonance within this postmodern model. What am I missing?

Practitioners-in-training often describe how much they savor opportunities to learn directly from people who work in a variety of settings. As Bruce reflected, "I don't know when I am going to get over being afraid of things I don't know much about, but it was comforting to hear Beth and Steve talk about the journey from our program's psychodynamic approach to the more narrative approach." In particular, he was glad to hear Beth describe how she was creatively using a narrative approach in an otherwise typically medical model hospital setting.

Laurie also appreciated hearing from Stephen and Beth that narrative therapy informs how they live their lives and understand the world. "By spending time doing some political action, or as Beth said, being able to use less problem-saturated language with an insurance company, I think we can influence systemic change, in addition to the changes that take place on the personal level in therapy". Laurie then asked a practical question about how narrative therapy works within current mental health/insurance systems: "I wonder what measurable, concrete treatment goals that will get services authorized for a client would look like within narrative therapy?"

Students notice a different approach to self-care as expressed in the guest speakers' "freshness and evident passion." Sarah noted a stark difference between this experience of narrative therapists and "more cynical, jaded therapists I've known (especially in inpatient units), whose basic therapeutic stance seems rooted in reactivity." Melissa further reflects:

In my last two placements I was reminded over and over again to "leave work at work" as a means of self-care. I was struck at listening to Stephen's and Beth's stories about how they incorporate a narrative approach into their everyday lives. I found myself wondering, was this something they intentionally began doing, or did it slowly and unconsciously become part of who they are both in and outside of their clinical roles?

Other students immediately notice a stance that embraces transparency:

Posting by Sandra

I continue to be struck by the transparency that both Stephen and Beth gifted us with during their visit last week, and how accessible as people and colleagues they were. I appreciate Stephen's awareness of the privilege he carries as a white, straight male and his need to use that privilege to alter the punitive systems he works within. Beth, as well, brought in issues of gender and the construct of femininity which I welcome greatly.

In this term more than ever before, I am better able to recognize the intersections of various forms of oppression. I challenge myself daily to be mindful of those intersections, and to allow space and energy to give voice to the struggles of all who suffer. As Jan Willis reminded us in her lecture, we are all connected, and we must all take responsibility for the safety and well-being of one another. What will you do today to take up that challenge?

ONLINE CONVERSATIONS WITH GUEST AUTHORS

When given the opportunity, students and authors often engage together in lively conversation. After assigning a reading, I ask the students specific questions to guide their studies:

What stands out for you as you read Lynn Hoffman's illustrative and thought-provoking memoir (Hoffman, 2002), David Paré's article about the shifting paradigm of family therapy (Paré, 1996) and the selected chapters from Sharon Welch's book about living with ambiguity and "ethics without virtue (Welch, 1999)?" Which particular stories, images and ideas stay with you? What are the effects on how you think about yourself and the possibilities that lie ahead in your own life? If you could be in conversation with any of these authors, what would you say or ask? (Amazingly, we'll have the opportunity to talk person-to-person with Lynn Hoffman next week. I have given David Paré the "guest pass" to enter this online conversation. Alas, I haven't yet figured out how to contact Sharon Welch....)

After reading Christian Beels' memoir, Morgan, an undergraduate psychology student, gained a new appreciation for the practice of narrative therapy. In particular, the chapter "Marriage and its Therapy" stood out to him as an especially poignant example of how, "instead of focusing on the past as the origin of our problems in relationships, we can make the most progress by changing our conception of how we would like our lives to be in the future."

Posting by Morgan

When discussing John and Mary's predicament, Dr Beels says, "One way of thinking about these impasses is to look for a new image of the marriage, different from the symmetrical image of trade, bargain, negotiation or deal. There is another kind of economy, little discussed in our culture, that has been called the gift economy," (Beels, 2001) (p 148). Thus, rather than focusing on what is wrong with John's and Mary's previous economic relations (which clearly don't work), it is more useful simply to alter the overall dynamic of the relationship. As the author remarks, relationships are always unfinished works in progress, and we must continuously be writing the next chapter.

In response to the online question, Morgan asks the following:

I would like to ask Dr. Beels how he knows when to concentrate on a relationship's past and when to concentrate on its future. Not every problem in a relationship requires a complete change in interpersonal dynamics; some may require simply minor adjustments within a past framework. How do we know when to make minor adjustments within a framework and when to alter the overall framework?"

Morgan later had the opportunity to converse with the author. After sharing his reflection with Chris Beels, I posted Beels' response online, which I include in part:

I was thrilled to read that my book is required reading in your course. Thanks for your question, Morgan. It got me thinking about what clues I follow in organizing the imagery of change with different couples. Part of it has to do with the language they are already speaking. A lot of couples have already been taught that their problems should be discussed in terms of their traumatic childhood stories, and it works best to join them in that discussion at least in the beginning. The next step can be a discussion about how they want to continue these stories in the present, but with different projected impersonations of figures from their past. And even with a couple who don't have a childhood model of the past...it still makes sense to take the recent past as...the starting point for change. Most people need an alien model for the starting point of change – otherwise they get startled by the way the past repeats itself. Is this what you meant by "a minor adjustment within a framework"?

The couples that come to mind when you said "alter the overall framework" are those trying to make an intimate relationship out of enormous differences of philosophy, temperament, goals and so on. I'm continually amazed at the determination with which some people stick together in defiance of all the common predictors of separation. For these brave people I mainly help them to find and protect areas where the intimacy has a chance of working, and quarantine the others. Let me know if I've understood your question correctly. Thanks.

Morgan was equally thrilled to engage in this conversation. He continued:

I was very interested by what Dr. Beels said about having an alien model for change. We have been learning that social context plays an absolutely enormous role in the way people relate to the world. Is an alien model necessary because it forces the [client] to see his/her world in a new way/from a new context, which allows them to see the changes they wish to make? Also, to what extent do you think that childhood experience plays a role in people's relationships? I know that...narrative therapy de-emphasizes the role of childhood experiences in shaping the "self," but do you think these early experiences can be completely ignored? I'm very interested in what you all have to say.

As teacher, I facilitate exchanges such as these between author and students. Sometimes authors prefer that I send them student postings rather than their using the guest pass. Either way works well as long as the teacher is prepared to be the go-between in connecting people. This approach embodies a reflexive stance that is more participatory, less hierarchical and mutually influenced.. Everyone – even the author – becomes partners in learning. My commitment to this approach was reaffirmed by Chris Beels' reflection upon reviewing this chapter: "Reading my letter in answer to one of your students who inquired about the use of the past in narrative vs, psychodynamic work, I was reminded of one of the important benefits of your process for me – the way student questions provoke new thoughts for "experts" like me. Writing that letter concisely was certainly one of my best experiences."

I am delighted by the generosity with which guest authors make themselves available to students. The authors are touched by having the unusual experience of being in direct contact with enthusiastic and inquisitive readers. In turn, the students become more alert to the ideas conveyed when they have direct contact with the author.

Even when Lynn Hoffman cannot visit my classroom, I have sent her students' reflections on reading her personal history of family therapy. I then post her generous comments on the course website, part of which appears below. Given her life experience, she speaks from a perspective that I could never offer on my own:

Your students are a grandly responsive lot. And it's fascinating to run into myself, first from long ago, and then from more recently. I'll do some summarizing and also some comments. l. The subject of "stance." Julia sums up one of my earlier identities when she says "the therapist 'bounces his stance' off his patient in such a way that it does not cause the patient to recoil but causes him to unleash and undig his own stances in a reflexive, give-and-take manner." This was my Constructivist Period, when I was thinking that we were all imprisoned in our nervous systems, like people in bathyspheres, bumping into each other and trying to send signals. Then Martha says that it is important for therapists to be transparent because "it is impossible to separate yourself and your opinions from your own life experiences and be completely objective." Again, this was one of our huge insights from the mid-80s – we always put the "eye" in the corner of the blackboard, as the constructivist Humberto Maturana did, to remind us that we are always part of what we observe. Amanda brings up a very good point when she points out that this focus on taking a stance clarifies for her the conflict between remaining "consistent with these beliefs," and "letting the circumstances of the situation determine my choices." That sums up the current quarrel between the modernists, who say there are ethical absolutes, and the postmodernists, who hold that "truth" depends on context and circumstances.

GUEST VISITORS

When guests come to our classroom, I start an online forum for students to share their reflections, questions, and acknowledgements. After students have read her memoir and articles, I am sometimes able to bring Lynn Hoffman into the classroom. Following one such visit, I started the following online forum:

I am happy for the opportunity to share Lynn Hoffman with you – by now you have been able to read some of her writings as well as to experience her in person. Now I am quite certain you understand why I feel so privileged to have Lynn as a mentor. This forum is for you to share reflections and questions with Lynn. She is eager to hear your thoughts and to the extent possible, engage in continued dialogue with you.

Students often post very moving accounts of their experiences with Lynn.

Reflection by Mohammad

This course provided me the opportunity to meet Lynn Hofmann not only in class, where she went around and shook everyone's hand, but also online. Knowing that she had shaken the hands of many of those who have given life to the practice of family therapy and narrative therapy in particular then made it as if we met without even having read them extensively I somehow made contact with them as well. A nugget of her knowledge, the essence of years of experience, was passed on to me when I witnessed her interview my classmate. I was, as Sandra put it, given the gift of her presence, and her knowledge was passed on to me in the oral tradition, much the same way that Persian culture was preserved, from the source to trusted others.

Kim chose to write a letter to Lynn that she posted online.

Posting by Kim

DearLynn,

Your very first action, shaking hands and going around the room, was quiet and radical at the same time...For me it established the tone of a relational interaction that honors the uniqueness in each of us...I think what was exciting about your visit (and hopefully, some future correspondence with you and your colleagues through our discussion board) was the ability to blend our worlds – that of your rich professional experience with our sense of just beginning.

Through your consulting with our pods, I was able to experience what it feels like to work with the questioning style that is unique to the narrative approach, and how the questions carried so many messages: these are questions to help get the ball rolling, so that the dialogue can continue, even after today; there are no right or wrong answers to (nor judgments in) these questions; and there is most likely something in our experience that will help us answer these questions (which makes us the author of the answers, in fact).

In attending to the sense of ambiguity about the narrative approach, your demonstration of the experience, (the sense of touch/feel) really resonated with me. It seems as if the notion of being present with the client's feelings is embedded in the approach. In fact, I get a sense that all of the other "things" that we "do" in therapy that are rooted more in the therapist-as-expert approach, get in the way of really knowing how a client feels.

Thank you for coming to speak to us.

ACCOLADES, PONDERINGS, AND QUESTIONS

Students report their excitement and awakening to new possibilities in response to my bringing people from various roles in the evolution of narrative therapy together in the classroom. They express particular appreciation for the opportunity to together practice an interview with reflecting teamwork.

Posting by Sandra

I am so grateful to Lynn, Peggy, and Caretia for the opportunity to see a narrative approach with a reflecting team not only LIVE but also co-occurring within the same room! In my last placement, I had the opportunity to be on reflecting teams, and to do therapy while a team observed my session and fed suggestions to me through an earpiece. However, the reflecting team and the family were always kept separate...The experience always felt a bit surreal to me. How could we be privileged to listen to a family therapy session, and then reflect in a group on what we heard in the session, but not allow the family any direct interaction with anyone on the team other than their therapist?

Having the reflections occur in the same room, even when the team was not interacting directly with Caretia, was so much more powerful and palpable than any of the other live sessions I had at my placement. Certainly the reflection I gave that day was far more personal and compelling than any I have made in the past. I walked away feeling that I had both contributed and gained from the process. What a gift!

THE DESIGNATED ROLE OF THE SERVICE SEEKER

In my courses, I make sure to expose students to the voices of people in the designated role of service seeker. I devote Chapter Twelve, "Remember to Ask" to further describing how I structure courses to train students to hold themselves accountable to the people they aspire to serve. Two guest speakers, Prudence and Pam, who have profoundly influenced my own development as a practitioner, make a powerful impact whenever they visit my classes. Having experienced many services, service providers, and social workers in the service-seeking role, they speak passionately about how professional helpers have been both helpful and unhelpful to them along the way. After one visit, I posted the following question:

Having had the opportunity to hear more about first hand experiences as a service seeker, what are your lingering thoughts and questions? How might this inform your own approach to being of service to others? What would you like to say to and/or ask Pru and Pam?

Students share their reflections online:

Posting by Diana

You reminded us that there is no one broken, no one can fix it, and that the gift that is needed is the "connection" of "community. We as social workers should be used as a helping hand to stabilize someone into a community...You talked about your friendship and how you both drew strength from your lives and experiences. This reminded me of the tremendous strength and power of women!

Undergraduate students have been particularly moved by Prudence's and Pam's class visits.

Posting by Molly

The discussion with Pru and Pam, to put it in Pam's words, knocked me on my ass. I literally walked out of class and back to my room, and sat down at my computer to write this. The power of these women's stories is truly amazing. It seems like a once in a lifetime experience to sit in a classroom and have two people open up their lives to you, to show you what they have overcome, who they really are, and give us a small glimpse at what it is to be on the other side of the story....Peggy, thank you for having them come speak to us. Most of all, Pru and Pam, thank you for your stories and your advice. It truly made a lasting impression.

Posting by Becca

Never before in my Middlebury College career have I encountered such an inspirational, emotional, and moving classroom experience as I did last week during Pru's and Pam's visit. All I wanted to discuss with my friends for the rest of the day was how affected I was by their stories and their ability to achieve success in the face of so many unbelievably challenging tribulations.

Being profoundly inspired by their visit, Becca took away "so many essential life lessons, that it was difficult for me to articulate in the duration of one post the impact that their talk had on my life perspective."

One of the most important messages was this: "You can't fix us, we're not broken." "You can't rescue us," Pam explained, "You can be a guide or a tool we use to help us get to the next step." Until this moment, I had naively believed that with enough education and enough technical training, one could do anything, solve anything, fix anything. Pru's and Pam's words still reverberate within me and explain to me that no matter how many courses I take, or how many degrees I earn, I will never truly understand what the families that social workers are attempting to "fix" are actually experiencing.

When Pru commented on the importance of looking at a problem from all angles, I suddenly realized the grave and naive mistakes that so many service providers must make due to their inability to truly comprehend the situation of the families for whom they are working. For example, as Pru said, removing an abusive husband from a family in order to "solve" the family's problems...might lead to a lower income, perhaps the lack of a car, and thus the inability to go to the hospital or the grocery store. Every action has so many ramifications....

The Community Practitioner

I like to structure opportunities for students to dialogue with community practitioners committed to and engaged in their work (Epston, Rennie, & Napan, 2004). Nan, an undergraduate psychology student, was floored by the honesty and unique perspective offered by Peter and Marc, practitioners devoted to innovative work in community mental health.

Posting by Nan

I felt their ups and downs, regrets and excitements, and the stress and joy that has made their work so unique. In an important way, their continued optimism and sincere commitment to a job that is so taxing on the mind and soul was an encouraging experience for me as an aspiring therapist. I think that sometimes I get wrapped up in the study of psychology and the idea of helping people, and overlook/minimize the actual hardships this job entails that make it so unique a profession. Peter and Marc's visit and comments reminded me of the liabilities of being a therapist, and yet, to see them 20 years into practicing still saying that they "fall in love with their clients" and truly get excited about their work, have aspirations to start new programs, and have expanded their work in myriad directions that have proved helpful and fullfilling, instills a true sense of what is possible when you love what you do, are committed to a cause and a community, and put your heart on the line in a way that is at once scary and fulfilling in ways that other professions cannot offer.

After class, I invite students to continue the conversation online with their visitors:

After Peter and Marc came to our class, they told me how much they enjoyed coming to the class and meeting you. They especially appreciated how many of you participated in the conversation, which was different from their experience in other classes when only a few students tend to speak up. Marc said how enlivening it felt to experience your earnest curiosity in his work, which, as he said in class can be a source of sustenance. They both wished there had been more time to hear your thoughts and reflections. I wonder if we could use this space for such continued conversation. What was it like to hear Marc and Peter speak about their commitment to their work, and what thoughts and/or questions continue to reverberate?

Students were glad to have this opportunity, and the entire class was able to benefit from reading the online dialogue that continued after class. In their discussion, the group opened up and explored the difficult and somewhat abstruse idea of discourse. In the following online exchange, they expand upon their understandings of assigned readings and classroom discussion:

Posting by Philippe

As Peggy said, it is a lifelong challenge to find ways to keep questioning the unspoken assumptions that inform our identity, interactions, relationships – even our questions themselves. After our discussion with Mark and Peter, I began thinking about the effects of discourses on therapy where both therapist and patient are participants in the same social environment. Towards the end of our conversation, we brought up considerations of practicing within a small community as compared to let's say, having a private practice in New York City. Although I appreciate the benefits of being in a smaller community, I wonder how a therapist's involvement in the same community as his clients would affect their discourses...I'm wondering if this might make it harder for therapists to identify these assumptions, since there is nothing with which to contrast their perceptions. I know it is wrong to assume that simply by having a small community, everyone's experience would be the same, but even still, there must be some similarity. Therefore, I wonder whether or not it would be more beneficial to a client if the therapist already participates in similar discourses as his or her client? I think it is beneficial to a client since the therapist is already equipped with much of the language that a client might use in describing his/her own reality. In this way, a therapist can become a much more effective listener. On the other hand, having been exposed to similar social and cultural experiences, it might become harder for a therapist to identify and question certain assumptions as he/she may hold them as well. Although it is important to understand the language and meaning that a person has given to their experiences, I can't help but think that a therapist's role as providing a new space for conversation might be hindered by the similarity of their experiences.

I thanked Philippe for illustrating the ongoing practice of questioning assumptions on which we construct our realities, which he applied to exploring the unique contributions and challenges for the rural practitioner. Although I generally take a decentered stance in my postings, in this instance, I took the opportunity to offer my expertise more directly:

Philippe, I think you are onto something here. In small town practice, how can the therapist question the assumptions upon which he/she constructs realities if and when the therapist and client function within a similar social environment and thus similar discourses? How might this be different from practice in a place like New York City? Is it better or worse to be entranced by similar cultural discourses?

My answer is that it isn't really better or worse, just different. This difference calls upon us to develop a range of skills. For example, sometimes people will come to consult me with whom I discover I share some unique cultural, familial or ethic feature – maybe they are Jewish, they moved to Vermont from Canada, or we discover a shared area of interest. This experience of connectedness is hard to put into words but feels very engaging and attuning. I welcome this kind of connectedness, which goes well beyond "joining" with mutual two-way effects. Growing up in "women's culture," I have a lot of experience with this kind of connectedness, relational practices that encourage this kind of mutuality and I thrive in this. At the same time I have learned to be careful of the illusion that our experiences are similar. I have learned over the years that our experiences are often much more different that initially meets the eye, and to encourage expressions of/embrace/enjoy/ such differences. Often this is what can get longstanding couples in trouble –

we think they know each other so well we "mind read" and jump to conclusions and have to relearn the skills of seeing each other with fresh eyes.

As a result, I have to monitor myself to try to really listen and inquire into the other's experience. I might preface what I say by something like, "I have this thought or image that I would like to share. Honestly, I can't tell if I am talking about you or me here. We have a lot in common, yet I don't want to jump to conclusions that my experience is the same as yours. Please help guide me here."

What about discourses on psychotherapy and in particular power relations between therapist and client? While we can come from very different sub-cultures, we do live with media portrayal and Freudian historic traditions within U.S. culture. Here too we can strive to notice, identify, and inquire into the effects of such discourses. What about discourses about socio-economic class, sexual orientation, race – and the effects of the 'isms' of sexism, classism, homophobia, racism, etc.? Even if you were working in an urban center, in many ways you would be living in a similar cultural environment under many shared discourses. Living rurally and/or in a small town offers many opportunities to practice these skills of deconstruction – unpacking the discourses, and finding ways to speak about them and their effects on our lives and relationships.

People in rural practice can learn a great deal from those in city practice. What about the reverse? I get more of a sense of tolerance for the exception that can be made for rural practitioners because of their unique situations. Sometimes there can be a patronizing tone as though those country bumpkins are cute but not especially sophisticated – with the "real therapy" occurring in environments where it's possible for lives to not be so interconnected...Yet rural practitioners do real work, and develop skills and knowledge that could be useful to others. I wish this could become more reflected in the professional literature.

Marc joined in, by describing how much he enjoyed reading Philippe's post and the thoughts it provoked:

In an earlier post someone alluded to Marshall McLuan's thought – (paraphrased here) "Never ask a fish about water." I'm taking the water to be the assumptions on which we construct our realities. That seems to support your thought that an urban therapist would have an easier time identifying assumptions than a small town therapist. On the other hand I think one of the major tasks of all therapists is to remember that we are all fish and that as fish we can easily fall into not noticing or into an illusion of knowing. I have never practiced in a city but my guess is that a therapist could just as easily fall asleep in the city as in the country. As I write this I'm thinking that this conversation is reminding me of my fishness. A major part of the support I surround myself with, (individual and group supervision, etc.) serves to remind me of my fishness. I assume that at this point you all have the image of group supervision at the Counseling Service beginning with us all standing together and with our hands over our hearts saying in unison, "I am a fish, I am a fish, I am a fish." In fact this does not actually happen.

CYBER-VISITORS

Sometimes students engage with virtual visitors. Visitors can use the guest pass to introduce themselves to class members. Betsy joined in the online conversation: "Betsy Buckley here, from Boston, coming to class with you all next week. I really love this preliminary description of the use of self in post-modern therapy. I am often at a loss to describe how I understand 'self-disclosure' as valuable in my work – I like the idea of fluidity, discovering new stories, and a mutually creative journey."

At other times, the visitor and students never meet. The following exchanges took place between South African narrative therapist Jo Vilgoen and students in both undergraduate and graduate programs:

Posting by Jo

Hi Peggy and Students:

I am a white Afrikaans speaking woman from South Africa. I practice as a psychiatric nurse and narrative therapist. Narrative therapy not only brought me new ways of working and thinking about my work and life, but also made a friendship between Peggy and myself possible albeit via email. Amazing what becomes possible with new technology!

I recently completed a PhD. in Religious Studies, using a narrative research design and methodology. What a ride that was! I explored the effects of dominant religious power discourses on the lives of Afrikaans women and found that religion can be a very powerful and healing but also very harmful discourse.

Your course seems amazing. I am honoured to be a guest on your list. I would love to pop in from time to time if I may and share in your learning. Hope that's ok with all of you?

Having studied abroad in Namibia, Alexis described falling in love with the South African people and culture. She posted many questions for Jo – asking where Jo was located, what type of people she worked with, whether she interacted with any tribes in particular and how she dealt with the more evident gender and race discourses that Alexis saw while there. She further inquired:

Is there a great difference between what has been emphasized in the U.S. versus South Africa in terms of psychology being initially guided by structuralism? If there is a great difference, do you believe that it is easier to practice narrative therapy without the preconceived notions that a therapist will "cure" or "fix" the client's internal problem that some therapists struggle with here in the States?

Jo responded by giving a more detailed account of her life and work living outside Pretoria, in a predominantly white residential area. When counseling at the spinal ward in Kalafong Hospital, she had met people from all over the country. She explained that "The racial and gender discourses permeate our society in ways Americans probably don't know. I deconstruct them as far as I can, bearing in mind all the time that the client has to go home or to work and face those issues again. It is a slow process, this transformation of ours, and I guess it will take many years before the pain has left the political wounds we all suffer from."

In response to Alexis' questions about the acceptance of narrative therapy and the role of structuralism, Jo wrote a thoughtful and detailed response, included in part below:

First, narrative therapy is by no means an accepted way of working in South Africa. It only migrated here in the late nineties, and the people who were drawn to study these approaches were theological students (perhaps because the course was initially offered by the Department of Practical Theology!). Psychologists and psychiatrists generally pooh-pooh the narrative approach, claiming that it is nothing new as they believe all therapies are narratives! My background training was in nursing, so I had my fair share of learning how to "fix" it. I found it a great relief to be able to step out of the expert position, although I must say my wide and rich nursing experience gave me a good head start as a therapist. I believe no knowledge is lost, ever.

The majority of psychology is still situated in a structuralist worldview. I was delighted to hear a few weeks ago though, that the final year psych students at Pretoria University have been introduced to poststructuralist ways of working and that the narrative approach also received some attention. Certainly when I read psychology it was all about the inner self and the ego and the improvement of the self...In my practice I find it very hard to work along structuralist lines, as the context of our lives in South Africa is so complex. The political story of South Africa's past and present cannot be ignored if we want a good future. I think to do that would just be plain unethical.

Generally people still go to therapists to be fixed up here; that is if they can overcome the stigma associated with mental illness and actually take the step to make an appointment to see somebody about their problem. Did I answer your questions? If not, let me know and I'll try again! From a wet and rainy Pretoria.

Students seize the opportunity to converse online with someone from another culture. Often they post further questions about cultural discourses. Amanda reflected on the month she spent four years prior in a Catholic school east of Johannesburg:

Since my new interaction with narrative therapy I have reflected back on my experiences with African children and the drastically different perspectives that they taught me. More specifically they articulated to me a conflict between their cultural desire to be more western and the ways that their parents still believe in more traditional beliefs. I wonder if you ever see this discrepancy in your practice.

REMEMBERING MENTORS

As students study narrative therapy, I encourage them to link their learnings with prior meaningful learning experiences. This includes connecting with significant people in their own lives. Often they recollect people who have taught them valuable lessons. When Chappell began to read about narrative therapy, she wrote about an English teacher who first exposed her to deconstructionism and Foucault[20]:

In my junior year of high school I had an English teacher who taught us about Foucault and Derrida and encouraged us to approach "texts" in a different way. This was very bold to do in a large public high school where most teachers stuck to the same books year after year and taught the five-paragraph essay. I remember my teacher taking the book The Scarlet Letter and shaking it by its spine and shouting, "The author is dead! Is he here? No! You can not find him in the book!" In this class we also read One Flew Over the Cuckoo's Nest and discussed Foucault's ideas about the social construction of madness.

This teacher was a mentor to me. Her courage and passion inspired me... to study literature in college and go on to become an English teacher. It felt so liberating to be empowered to respond to or interpret texts the way I wanted to rather than trying to decode a message left there by the author. As a teacher, my exposure to these ideas helped me encourage my students to put themselves on equal footing with the authors and engage in conversations about the literature instead of feeling like they could not possibly question or criticize or even really engage with what "great" writers like Shakespeare or Faulkner wrote.

This class is bringing back all these memories of my 16-year-old self and of a time of profound intellectual growth and curiosity for me. Narrative therapy seems to provide me a link or a bridge between my past (English teacher) and my future (clinical social worker) careers and it certainly excites my intellect.

In another class, Lynn "re-membered" a teacher's living testimony to risk-taking[21]:

When I was in my first year of core classes as an undergraduate, a comment included on a class syllabus struck a chord with me... The instructor holds a very special place for me as he helped me see the many places in our lives where quiet compassion and steadfastness working for change can hold a place with those who work in other ways more bold and obvious. He wrote, "The courage to risk one's self is critical to all social change." His class shook me up to realize I had a responsibility to work for social change when I thought I was going to "just" work with people one on one. I did not visualize that working one on one could make one a social change agent. I had never allowed myself to be a risk-taker because I had so much family responsibility all my life. I felt risks were only for those who were very self-confident.

I copied this saying into every class folder for the next two and a half years. I still keep it close to my heart to remind myself when I falter or hesitate, that changes might not be obvious in my lifetime, but I have to continue to risk myself to try. It also serves to remind me of the power of words, even if they are few.

Teaching Congruently

As described in Chapter Three, I believe teaching should embody the actual practices being taught. By choosing to "people" my course in the classroom and online, I actively take a de-centered and influential posture (White, 2003b). As teacher, I do not position myself as a singular and influential expert - rather, I bring in multiple voices to facilitate an interactive process that strives to meet each student at his or her learning edge. Students' understanding of the concepts of narrative therapy is not being interpreted only through another source (me, the teacher), but rather they come in contact with real people who are doing, writing about, and experiencing narrative practice. This approach to education rejects a banking system metaphor where the teacher deposits knowledge into the students; mind (Freire, 1973). Instead I prefer a network metaphor, where the student can learn from people in a web of connections.

Like many students, I am an experiential learner. I believe that firsthand experience of theory-in-action is the best way to learn a concept. I try to live up to a preference Ellen, an MSW student well-versed in postmodern theory, expressed for teaching practices that "make all of those "floaty" ideas come closer to earth." I want students to understand from the inside-out how multiple voices enhance conversation.

Through experience, I have learned to resist the temptation to lecture before we can all gather around a shared experience. Instead, I structure classroom and online opportunities for reflection following a shared experience. I invite everyone to draw links between classroom experiences and the materials they are reading. I have discovered that it is all too easy to overlook and consequently miss these exquisite teaching moments.

It is important to me to let students in on my intention for incorporating many voices in the classroom. I make it clear that I do not want the knowledge to center on the teacher. Rather, I seek to value all the knowledges in students and guests as living resources. By doing so, I also reap the benefits of feeling accompanied by colleagues and friends in webs of connection throughout my teaching adventures.

PREFERRED STORIES OF IDENTITY
AS REFLECTIVE PRACTITIONERS[22]

Posting by Ali

*I really appreciate the preferred identity assignment for the way that it allows
me to relate narrative ideas to my own life and to begin to see my life as
many stories that can be read, written, spoken, shared many times with new
meanings emerging each time.*

As an educator of therapists and human service providers, I have discovered that
students often better understand and integrate a concept when they apply it to the
living of their own lives. Students become "reflective practitioners" (Schon, 1983)
by learning specific practices through which to think in action and put espoused
theory into practice (Argyris & Schon, 1974). This chapter describes a four-part
assignment through which students apply narrative ideas and practices to their own
lives and identities[23]. Through mapping and expressing their personal values and
perspectives, students directly experience the practices they are studying. Rather
than studying in isolation, students develop a sense of community as they share
their commitments and offer each other reflections. The stories generated by this
exercise are so compelling as to demand to be shared (Sax, 2006, 2007a).

By publishing this piece, I receive credit for a collaborative creation[24]. This
assignment reflects what is possible when teaching colleagues share their material
with each other. We are committed to a generosity of spirit in which we freely
share our teaching practices with each other, and build on each others ideas.
Geographically dispersed, we exchange ideas and practices through email and
occasional meetings.

My hope is that I can contribute to a growing body of literature on teaching
practices that afford students that all too rare space to make real connections
between classroom teachings and their own lives and relationships (Epston, Rennie
et al., 2004). Through the "Preferred Stories of Identity" assignment, social work,
counseling, psychology, and family therapy students directly experience the
narrative practices they are studying. I offer the "Preferred Identity" assignment as
a vehicle through which to teach five aspects of narrative practice: (1) Re-
authoring conversations; (2) intentional understandings of identity; (3) double
listening; (4) re-membering practices; (5) outsider witness practices and
definitional ceremonies. Throughout the chapter, excerpts of students' work

illustrate the capacity of this assignment in aiding reflective practitioners to become clearer about their own personal values and perspectives, and about the applicability of narrative practices within the teaching process.

While this assignment is designed for masters of social work students, I have adapted a version, "How Do I Want to be in the World?" for undergraduate psychology students[25]. I introduce it approximately halfway through the course, by which time students have already been given a grounding in the theory and practice of narrative practice, and have generally developed into a supportive, collaborative group. This exercise further connects them to their own personal values, beliefs, passions, commitments and ethics, and encourages them to imagine the effects of these preferred ways of working on (near) future directions as a social worker, psychologist and/or family therapist[26].

The assignment has four parts. Briefly, they are as follows:
- Participation in an in-class four-part interview;
- Developing a personal micro-map of preferred identity as a reflective practitioner;
- A letter of commitment; and
- Online posting of assignments in small cyber-groups of three to four students who also reflect on each others' work.

PREFERRED IDENTITY ASSIGNMENT

Part One: In-class Interview

Prior to applying the assignment to themselves, students participate in an in-class four-part narrative interview with outsider witness practices. The exercise, adapted from the work of Michael White (1992), helps students to experience the themes of their lives linked together (White, 1995b). The steps are as follows:

With the rest of the class as audience, I interview a student volunteer about turning points in her career as a reflective practitioner, the realizations that have emerged over time, and the subsequent effects of these understandings on the evolution of her career. Guided by White's map for outsider witness responses (White, 2003), the students then reflect aloud on and actively interview each other about ideas and questions sparked by the first interview. I then interview the initial volunteer about her experiences of hearing the reflections, while her fellow students again take up the audience position. Finally, everyone debriefs their experiences of all parts of this interview.

After the interview, I draw two horizontal lines on the blackboard. With the interviewee's permission, I invite students to help me plot present, past, and future events on the bottom line, and meaning-making on the top line. This is how I introduce students to the "re-authoring conversations" map (White, 2007e) (see Figure 1).

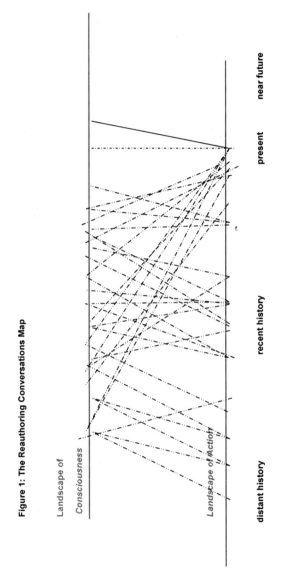

Figure 1: The Re-authoring Conversations Map

Re-authoring conversations is a key concept in narrative practice, which I address in detail further on. "Landscape of action" questions encourage people to situate influential events within the past, present, and future. "Landscape of consciousness" questions inquire into the *meaning* of developments that occur in actions, which can include perceptions, thoughts, beliefs, speculations, realizations, and conclusions. In the re-authoring conversations map, both types of questions inform the individual's exploration.

It took me some time to grasp the re-authoring conversations map based on Michael White's creative adaptation of Jerome Bruner's ideas about the dual landscapes of action and consciousness (Bruner, 1990). I have been amazed at how readily these theoretical constructs come alive when students use this map to contemplate turning points in their own development on a timeline stretching from the past to the present as well as their preferred near future.

The assignment requires each student to conduct a self-interview based on the classroom experience. I encourage them to create a comfortable milieu for personal reflection by taking a long walk, soaking in a hot bath, or conversing with a good friend. Some students arrange to interview each other outside of classroom time. Other students ask for help from a family member or a friend.

Part Two: Personal Micro-map of Preferred Identity

I give students an electronic template of a micro-map that applies the "re-authoring conversations" map to their own personal stories of identity as reflective practitioners (see Figure 2). At their computers, students use this template to construct their unique development as reflective practitioners in training. Over the years, I have collected over 100 individualized micro-maps. Some computer-savvy students create their own versions of the original template, adding personal touches such as color coding and sophisticated formatting. With their permission, I provide several illustrations created by past students, some of whom created their own versions of the original template. Students less comfortable with technology can choose to use paper and colored pencils.

Olivia's micro-map illustrates her preferred identity as a social worker. (see Figure 3).

C.J. created her own version that some later students have used as their template. (see Figure 4).

Each student maps a recent time in which her[27] actions resonated with how she aspires to perform her work, traces a brief history of her commitment to helping others, and thereby explores her preferred identity as a reflective practitioner. For example, by situating influential events in their identity as social workers and unique realizations that emerged from these experiences on a timeline, social work students learn how the storyline of their own lives can be "re-authored" according to their preferred ways of being as a social worker. I tell students that there is no right way and it is up to them to decide what they wish to share. I share some of what prior students have told me about the personal memories that this assignment brings forth, and their expressions of enthusiasm despite the challenges their disclosures posed. I try to assuage students' fears and arrange to communicate privately with students who express concerns.

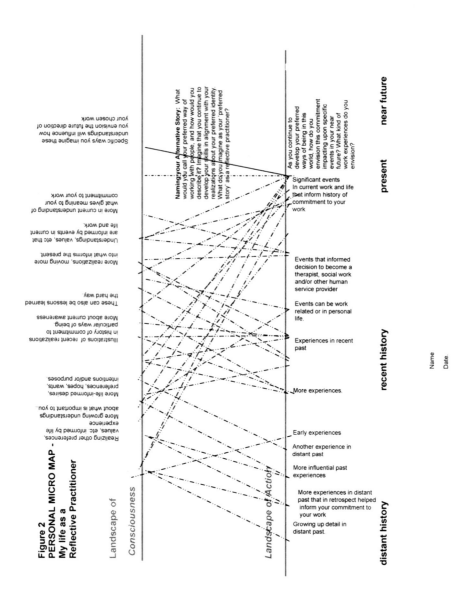

Figure 2: Micro-map Template (see attachment)

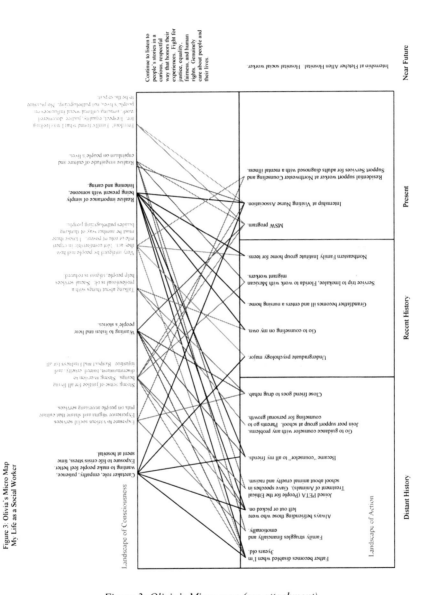

Figure 3: Olivia's Micro-map (see attachment)

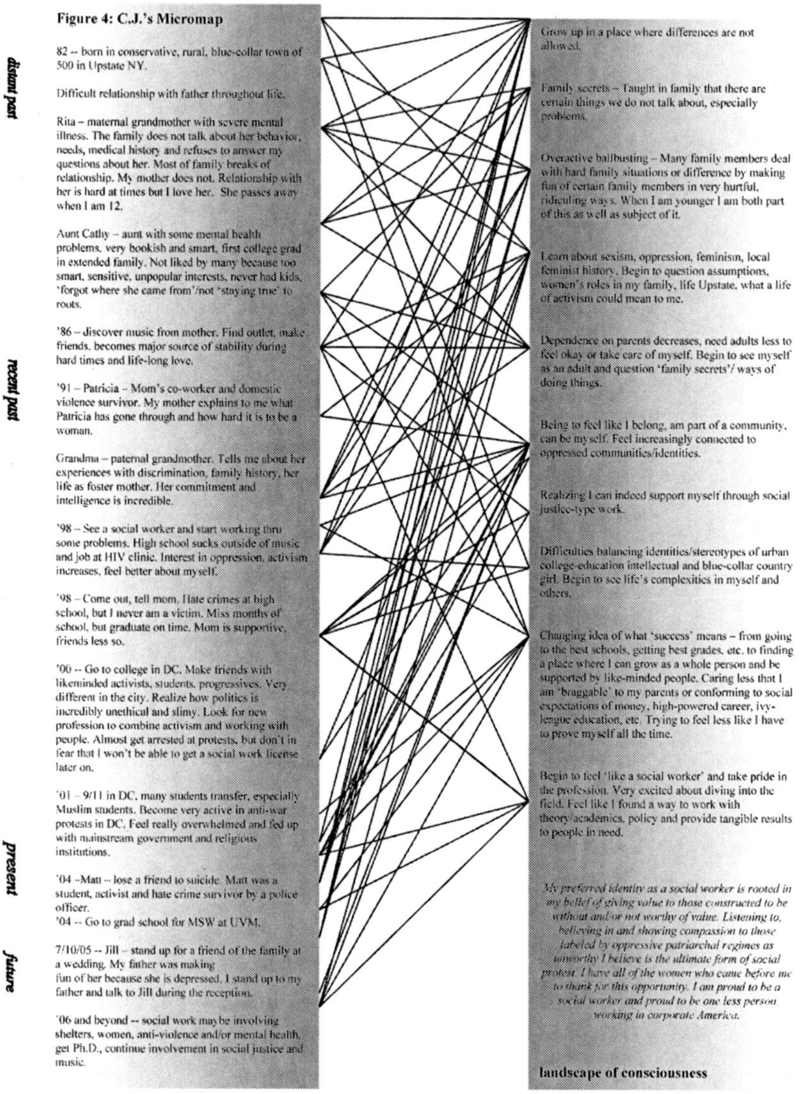

Figure 4: C.J.'s Micromap

distant past

distant past

82 -- born in conservative, rural, blue-collar town of 500 in Upstate NY.

Difficult relationship with father throughout life.

Rita -- maternal grandmother with severe mental illness. The family does not talk about her behavior, needs, medical history and refuses to answer my questions about her. Most of family breaks of relationship. My mother does not. Relationship with her is hard at times but I love her. She passes away when I am 12.

Aunt Cathy -- aunt with some mental health problems, very bookish and smart, first college grad in extended family. Not liked by many because too smart, sensitive, unpopular interests, never had kids, 'forgot where she came from'/not 'staying true' to roots.

'86 -- Discover music from mother. Find outlet, make friends, becomes major source of stability during hard times and life-long love.

recent past

'91 -- Patricia -- Mom's co-worker and domestic violence survivor. My mother explains to me what Patricia has gone through and how hard it is to be a woman.

Grandma -- paternal grandmother. Tells me about her experiences with discrimination, family history, her life as foster mother. Her commitment and intelligence is incredible.

'98 -- See a social worker and start working thru some problems. High school sucks outside of music and job at HIV clinic. Interest in oppression, activism increases, feel better about myself.

'98 -- Come out, tell mom. Hate crimes at high school, but I never am a victim. Miss months of school, but graduate on time. Mom is supportive, friends less so.

'00 -- Go to college in DC. Make friends with likeminded activists, students, progressives. Very different in the city. Realize how politics is incredibly unethical and slimy. Look for new profession to combine activism and working with people. Almost get arrested at protests, but don't in fear that I won't be able to get a social work license later on.

'01 -- 9/11 in DC, many students transfer, especially Muslim students. Become very active in anti-war protests in DC. Feel really overwhelmed and fed up with mainstream government and religious institutions.

present

'04 --Matt -- lose a friend to suicide. Matt was a student, activist and hate crime survivor by a police officer.
'04 -- Go to grad school for MSW at UVM.

'7/10/05 -- Jill -- stand up for a friend of the family at a wedding. My father was making fun of her because she is depressed. I stand up to my father and talk to Jill during the reception.

future

'06 and beyond -- social work may be involving shelters, women, anti-violence and/or mental health, get Ph.D., continue involvement in social justice and music.

Grow up in a place where differences are not allowed.

Family secrets -- Taught in family that there are certain things we do not talk about, especially problems.

Overactive ballbusting -- Many family members deal with hard family situations or difference by making fun of certain family members in very hurtful, ridiculing ways. When I am younger I am both part of this as well as subject of it.

Learn about sexism, oppression, feminism, local feminist history. Begin to question assumptions, women's roles in my family, life Upstate, what a life of activism could mean to me.

Dependence on parents decreases, need adults less to feel okay or take care of myself. Begin to see myself as an adult and question 'family secrets'/ ways of doing things.

Being to feel like I belong, am part of a community, can be myself. Feel increasingly connected to oppressed communities/identities.

Realizing I can indeed support myself through social justice-type work.

Difficulties balancing identities/stereotypes of urban college-education intellectual and blue-collar country girl. Begin to see life's complexities in myself and others.

Changing idea of what 'success' means -- from going to the best schools, getting best grades, etc. to finding a place where I can grow as a whole person and be supported by like-minded people. Caring less that I am 'braggable' to my parents or conforming to social expectations of money, high-powered career, ivy-league education, etc. Trying to feel less like I have to prove myself all the time.

Begin to feel 'like a social worker' and take pride in the profession. Very excited about diving into the field. Feel like I found a way to work with theory/academics, policy and provide tangible results to people in need.

My preferred identity as a social worker is rooted in my belief of giving value to those constructed to be without and/or not worthy of value. Listening to, believing in and showing compassion to those labeled by oppressive patriarchal regimes as unworthy I believe is the ultimate form of social protest. I have all of the women who came before me to thank for this opportunity. I am proud to be a social worker and proud to be one less person working in corporate America.

landscape of consciousness

Figure 4: C.J.'s Micro-map (see attachment)

Part Three: Letters of Commitment

After completing their personal micro maps, students post a letter of commitment online, addressed to whomever they select to witness their written statement. In preparation for writing this letter, I give them a series of questions, originally constructed by Betsy Buckley and Phil Decter:

- What did you learn about yourself and your commitment to the work through this assignment?
- How did these learnings relate to aspects of your own experiences?
- What does this reflect about yourself as a practitioner and about future directions in your work?
- Who and what stood by you in working this way?
- What kind of effects do you envision this way of working will have on the people who consult you in the future?
- Who and what will help you feel supported in the future, and continue to 'thicken' your alternative story?

I ask students to close with a personal statement of their ethics and commitments, describing how these ethics are connected with past experiences, and how they imagine they will be carried into the future.

The letter of commitment provides students' firsthand experience with performing an alternative story based on their cherished values for an audience of their choice. Students write letters of commitment to a wide array of people who are uncovered through their micro-mapping process: parents, family members, classmates, colleagues, mentors, teachers, friends, clients, and spiritual guides. Some students write to themselves and to their future selves. Wendy provides a good illustration of the power of this experience in a letter to her parents:

> *I had no idea that this path as a social worker started early in life. Did you? I realize that I started caring for other people and being concerned about their wellbeing in grade school. I was always looking for the person who was down and out. Once I found them I would try to comfort them. As an adult, I had always believed that my work in this field was just that, my work. I now realize that this "social work" is something that I bring into almost everything that I do.*

Part Four: Reflecting in Small Cyber-Groups

Students are assigned to small groups in which they become "outsider witnesses" to each others' assignments. Students post their work and share their reflections on each group's online forum. Some small groups choose to meet in person in addition to or instead of meeting electronically. Reading each others' work sparks new ideas and questions. Through responding online to each others' work, they learn from each other, and their reflections convey accounts of "two-way effects" (White, 1997). Students often comment on the personal meaning of discovering similar themes when they read fellow students' micro maps and letters of commitment. Students acknowledge relief in hearing words put to shared experiences, as illustrated in this online reflection from Jen to Lisa:

The first thing that stood out to me on your map was the clarity with which you described the person you want to be in this world. Your landscape of consciousness allowed me deep into the world of Lisa and I felt I had a "birdseye view" of who you are in practice as well as who you want to be. I found myself thinking, "Hey why didn't I think of that?" often and then incorporating some of that into my ever-changing story of myself as a social worker. Perhaps that is one of the greatest gifts of this project and by extension, this class, to me...the ability to be part of the transformative nature of dialogue. It still amazes me how my story about myself can change (although it seems that my foundational beliefs do not really) as a result of witnessing others' stories.

TEACHING KEY ASPECTS OF NARRATIVE PRACTICE

All four parts of the Preferred Identity assignment focus on key aspects of narrative practice (White, 2007c). These five "maps" for guiding therapeutic conversations into new territories are as follows;
− Re-authoring conversations
− Intentional understandings of identity
− Double listening
− Re-membering practices
− Outsider witness practices and definitional ceremonies.

Re-authoring Conversations

The entire assignment takes place as students are studying "re-authoring conversations," which invites people to link some of the more neglected events of their lives in sequences through time to recreate an alternative story line based on their preferred ways of being (Carey & Russell, 2003; White, 1995a). The re-authoring conversations map helps people develop alternative storylines to address and fill in gaps in their own history and provides options for people to re-engage with what they value most in life.

Throughout all parts of the assignment, I ask students to focus on their preferred ways of performing their human service work. Thus, someone whose memory of himself at school was as the "troublemaker" who could not seem to do anything right might "re-author" the conversation by recalling instances when he resisted archaic traditions and rules that he experienced as unfair and oppressive, which contributed to a lifelong commitment to social justice and human rights, and paved the way to his current choice of a career in social work.

In her letter of commitment that she chose to write to her parents, Rebecca described how she used the re-authoring conversations map to trace her history that led her to present path, becoming a social worker:

In this assignment, I had to start with a "unique outcome" in the present in my practice with people and trace my history back through recent and distant time to find where my beliefs and commitments came from. From you, Mom, I certainly learned about compassion and a commitment to volunteering...

Remember when I went off at a young age to volunteer in an institution for children with severe disabilities? And then I had a fascination with mental institutions and volunteered in a few? These were not your interests, but the spirit of sharing oneself with other people I clearly learned from you. From you, Dad, I developed an early sense of social justice, fairness, and honesty. None of us will ever forget you holding forth at the dinner table each night about the latest injustice in the business world, and these values have been an integral part of my growing into an adult. My determination to be an effective advocate for the elders I work with comes out of the fire I saw in your commitment to social justice.

Intentional Understandings of Identity

Students of postmodern and relational therapies are generally familiar with structuralist understandings of identity and their influence on psychotherapy. As a rule, students expect to learn theory and tools with which to interpret behavior, so as to get to "the truth" of the inner self – the ultimate, fixed essence of a person's identity. Alternatively, narrative therapy encourages students to question whether people actually have fixed identities at all, and asks "What are we today" (Foucault, 1988) (p. 145)? Narrative therapy views identity as a public and social achievement, supported by communities of people, shaped by historical and cultural forces as well as by ethics, beliefs and values (Thomas, 2002). Through therapeutic conversations, individuals are encouraged to co-author intentional states of identity, based on their own hopes and dreams, intentions, commitments, purposes, beliefs, values, and principles (White, 1997b).

The personal identity assignment enables students to directly experience how conversation and the stories we tell about ourselves actually shape the ways we think about ourselves. Students become personally familiar with how their own lives have been shaped by particular life events, which in turn guide their hopes and dreams, underpin their beliefs and values, and influence their ethics and life commitments.

In her letter to herself, Sara offers herself encouragement to develop and stand by her own values, to learn from her experiences and to have confidence in herself as a social worker and a person: "From early on, my parents, brothers, and grandparents (four of whom were teachers and social workers) encouraged me to develop my own identity, speak my mind and do what makes me happy." She genealogically links how her family's values and their belief in her informed the decision she made to become a social worker as well as her current view of herself: "They modeled caring and generosity in their daily lives and supported my interest in learning about and developing relationships with people. They consistently shared their belief that I could do anything I set my mind to, and urged me to be persistent and courageous in pursuing what is important to me."

Double Listening

Students of therapy and social work are typically taught to examine how people's families of origin have negatively impacted their lives and relationships, and to develop analytic skills to overcome the obstacles of growing up in "dysfunctional families." This psychopathologizing practice in training contexts is often culturally expressed through unspoken assumptions of mother-blame (Caplan, 1998; Coll, Surrey, & Weingarten, 1998) that are further reinforced through unexamined adherence to the foundations of psychoanalytic theory.

Trained to "double listen" to and against problems (Epston, 2003b), practitioners of narrative therapy pay particular attention to "the absent but implicit" experiences (Derrida, 1978) in which people are guided by an unspoken adherence to what they hold as being most precious in life, their intentions for their lives, the particular skills and knowledge evident in a person's unique response to life challenges and to the social, relational and cultural genesis of these responses (White, 2000a). Hence, a therapeutic conversation that addresses trauma in a person's history attends to psychological pain and emotional distress in response to the trauma as well as to experiences of violation that can give testimony to cherished beliefs, values, personal ethics, hopes, and dreams (White, 2005).

In this assignment, students often reflect on their parents' positive influences on their hopes and dreams, beliefs and values, ethics and life commitments. I could fill an entire book with poignant illustrations from students' letters to family members. Letters of commitment to parents continually defy the common practice of mother blame and psychopathologizing of dysfunctional families of origin. Students often attribute their most preciously held values and turning point experiences to one or both parents' positive influence. They express profound gratitude for their parents' guidance, human kindness, sacrifices, social conscience, determination, modeling of steadfast commitments, generosity, hard work, strength of character, selfless contributions, loyalty, dedication, gifts and small gestures, and expressions of love. As a tribute to her mother, Laura wrote,

> *The presence of my mother in my life is very deep, as an independent, caring, strong survivor; she has made me a more aware, respectful person. Having to take on a caretaking role early and being "adultified" by the reality of my father's mental illness and thus being raised by a single mother has a direct correlation to my working with people. My advocacy work for women's rights and being drawn to crisis-oriented work has to stem from experiencing my mother's own strength to leave my father. I knew my passion for work with women came from my own life experience, but seeing it on my map re-affirmed how strongly I feel that people have the right to live free from violence and abuse and to be treated with respect and dignity.*

Morrie, an undergraduate psychology student, acknowledged his mother's and sister's contribution to his desire to help others. "When I was two years old, my parents went through a violent divorce, after which I had to become used to living in two separate (and radically different) households, each ultimately furnished with an abusive stepparent. From the support that I received from my mother and sister, and as time went on I was able to give to them as well, I came to see what a difference people can make in the happiness of others. When my parents would argue, my sister would take me upstairs and play a game with me to keep me distracted. I learned to appreciate the support people can give to each other to get through hard times."

Re-membering Family Members, Friends and Mentors

Through this assignment, students learn firsthand about "re-membering conversations" (Russell & Carey, 2002; White, 1997c) by applying these practices to their own lives. Michael White draws the "re-membering" metaphor from the work of the cultural anthropologist, Barbara Myerhoff (Myerhoff, 1982). Re-membering conversations invite people to purposefully engage with significant figures that have contributed to their lives, to contemplate how this connection has shaped or could potentially shape their sense of who they are and what their life is about, and to imagine what they may have reciprocally contributed to the life of this significant figure. Figures and identities can include significant or potentially significant people in one's present life or the past, as well as heroic figures such as favorite authors, actors or athletes, and even animal companions or stuffed childhood toys.

In constructing their personal micro maps and letters of commitment, students explore the influential people who have contributed to their discovery of preferred ways of being as an aspiring social worker and human being, as illustrated in this excerpt from Rebecca's letter to her parents:

> *After tracing back the roots of my social work values to both of you, I recognize that you "stand with me" in my way of working with people. Along with you stand my supervisors Carol, Heidi, and Fiona, all of whom have affirmed their belief in me as a person who brings a lifetime of experience of meeting people with disabilities where they are, and offering them my help along the path to their potential. That has helped so much when I have doubted my "lack of experience" as a social worker.*

Carol, who works in a public high school, wrote her letter "to those who may seek help from me... so that you can understand a bit about me, what is important to me, my commitment to you and to the social work field." Instead of a resume, imagine reading a letter like this in a waiting room:

> *When I was young, my mom kept me busy with stories and make-believe. She had a kind of pre-school in our home for me, my sister and some of our friends. We learned about Japan – kites, festival of dolls, rice and green tea (it was actually green 7UP!); Holland – windmills, wooden shoes and tulips. This was in our home, where everyone gathered, and we learned and played. My mom was teaching – although she never had a teaching license. She loved us in a way I did not understand until years after I became a mother myself, years after she died.*

> *The most important lesson I carry from my mom is the idea that there is no such thing as a bad kid. As a children's librarian and story hour lady, she was in daily contact with kids. Sometimes, especially on rainy days, they*

*drove her crazy. But still, she was able to separate the behavior from the
child. She told me once that before each story hour, she would say a little
prayer and ask that she would not say anything hurtful to a child.*

*I didn't realize how deeply connected I am with my mom's ideals until doing
this exercise. She continues to guide me in my work, even though she has
been gone for many years. And in my re-membering of her, I have come to
appreciate her values even more. My mom is, I believe, the single greatest
influence on my development as a social worker.*

Often, the letter of commitment links students to important figures from early in
their lives. Linda credits a number of those who influenced her decisions about
educational pursuits and career choices:

*I haven't thought about or seen some of those people in such a long time. I should
try to track down a few of them and let them know how they influenced me. I can
see how that could be quite powerful and affirming for them and for me.*

Anne wrote to her former guidance counselor, who has since become a mentor and
a friend:

*You, my friend, are by far the best listener I have yet to meet. You allow me
the room to make mistakes over and over without feeling ashamed. You have
helped me to see my own strengths and to realize that I have been fighting for
the underdog ever since I can remember, and that this field is a natural next
step. You taught me that all emotions are okay, which allows me to accept the
whole range of emotions in others, and that just being present, listening, and
witnessing is perhaps the best thing to do at times.*

Sometimes students give voice to their spiritual connections through this
assignment. Maggie wrote to God, "I want to do this right, I want to do this well,
and with your help I can. Please be patient with my mistakes and keep those gentle
reminders of how to do it right coming my way. You know I believe every
individual voice is as important as every other and has a right to be heard....The
better I get with myself, the more present I can be with others."

Definitional Ceremony and Outsider Witness Practices

Narrative therapy draws from the "definitional ceremony" metaphor to structure
rituals that acknowledge people's lives (Myerhoff, 1986). The definitional
ceremony draws from intentional understandings of identity to create contexts in
which to publicly acknowledge a person's preferred claims about her or his identity
and history. In this assignment, I extend Michael White's therapeutic applications
of the "definitional ceremony" metaphor (White, 1995b) to teaching.

The Preferred Identity assignment enables students to experience the communal
nature of narrative work with multiple online tellings of their own preferred stories as
social workers. Students' online reflections of each others' work in their small groups
are guided by White's map for outsider witness responses (White, 2003b). They readily

identify aspects that catch their attention, capture their imagination, and resonate with their own experiences. They describe images that strike a chord, and embody their responses with images from their own lives. They acknowledge what White refers to as "transport," describing how they have become other than who they were at the onset through witnessing these expressions from their classmates. Often, their reflections are as sophisticated as those of a highly trained outsider witnessing team.

Amber posted online her letter to Paul, a young foster child whose enduring memory contributed to her decision to become a social worker:

Thank you Paul, for all you have taught me over the years. You have had a huge impact on whom I have become both as social worker and as a human being. I met you when you were only two years old and I was ten or eleven; 18 years later you remain fresh in my memory. When we met, you had been taken out of your home because of constant physical abuse; I was helping out at your foster home. I remember the connection we developed where you felt you had finally found a safe place in my arms. I wanted to care for you, undo your pain, and protect you from harm. As a young girl these seemed realistic goals. However, I did not understand the multiple systems at play. I had to witness you be returned to your original home and I was filled with fear and hope. I soon saw you again, as you were returned for once again suffering abuse. I was filled with frustration and anger at the injustice of it all.

You taught me lessons of love, being present and available, how to let go when needed and about my responsibility to do my part for other people. I also learned to accept some doses of reality of the injustice and pain that people face all around me. These have been hard, but have made me a fuller person. I don't see people as one-dimensional. I know they have stories of pain and strengths, joys and sorrows that are not always apparent. Over the years I have committed myself to be available to people and to welcome their differences and strengths. This has made me a richer person.

I encourage students as outsider witnesses to experiment with asking questions with earnest curiosity. Joanne and Leslie were in Amber's online small group. In response to Amber's further description of her struggle with "not being able to protect those that need protection," and her experiences of wanting to "undo the pain that (Paul) had suffered," Joanna queried:

I was reminded of the many times that I just wanted to reach out and hug a youth that I was working with, take away their pain, stop their sadness. I try to remember some of the "sparkling moments" with them and wonder if you recall some of your sparkling moments from your time with Paul. What are they? How do they sustain you and give you hope? How will you nurture and support yourself? What are some things that you are doing now or have done to support yourself? How would you like others to support you?

Leslie expressed her appreciation for the opportunity to get to know Amber on another level, to see her in a role "we don't get to see just by being classmates." She further inquired:

It was incredible to see how the majority of your landscape of action focuses on helping people from an early age. I wonder where you got this urge to be such a strong force and touch so many lives. In our hectic lives it is so easy to let people slip away and so impressive that you were able to stay active and present with so many people. Your map also shows your strong belief in the worth of all people. I wonder where you think this came from and what drove you to be so available to others.

REFLECTIONS

Faced with multiple invitations to re-examine cultural and professional discourses and their relevance for family therapy, one student aptly described the experience of learning about narrative therapy as "confusing and in some ways goes against many of the concepts I have previously been taught." Yet students often remark on how much their understanding is enhanced by their firsthand experience of many of the narrative concepts and interviewing practices they are studying. What is it about this assignment that works so well?

After students completed their "Preferred Identities" maps and letters of commitment, I posted the following questions:

I once heard Michael White draw a distinction between 1) pointing out positives/identifying strengths and 2) practices that strive to bring forth a sense of legacy that opens space for people to become more cognizant of who might have contributed to emergent self-understandings. In what ways has the course assignment provided entries into responses/skills of living the histories of your own lives and brought you into the realm of imagination and new possibilities? How does this experience feel similar or different from thinking of yourself from "a strengths perspective?" Is there anything you are learning here that you think you will bring into your work with people who consult with you?

The assignment helped Amy take a fresh look at some of the events in her past that she had always thought of as "bad," and wished had never happened. As she interviewed herself, and created her map, she understood that many of the events in her life that were most challenging, and which she felt at the time she'd never get through, also contributed to the person she is today.

Posting from Amy

I started realizing that in all these events, despite what was going wrong, there were things that I was doing that felt good to me, and that I consider to be some personal strengths I used to get me through those hard times. I guess I made the rather simplistic realization that no matter how difficult the time or problem may seem, ...those strengths that are situated in my own personal story will help me get through that hard time, and possibly hard times that might lie ahead.

In class discussion, several students mentioned a shift in attitude from "getting the assignment done" to finding an entryway into self-discovery. The exercise seemed to create an atmosphere of intrigue for almost everyone. Hence I started the following discussion forum:

> *What do you think is helping you make the assignment into something meaningful to you? Have you made any discoveries about how you have resisted having your preferred story silenced by Self-Surveillance, Performance Anxiety, Comparison, or other intruders? Several of you mentioned how much more intense this assignment has been than you anticipated. Would you have preferred a less personal project, or do you think it is worth it? Why do you think this is? Do you have any suggestions for how to fortify a sense of self-protection and calmness as you share such personal details with each other? What makes it worthwhile?*

In her response, Danielle reflected on what helped her to relax into the assignment, be honest with herself, and "be genuinely curious about all the good, bad, and ugly that have contributed to my preferred identity so I could cultivate that throughout my future." She is often protective of her personal story, not wanting comments that can feel empty despite how well-meaning people may be. "You know, the ones that go 'Oh, I am so sorry you had to go through that... and what-not.'"

Posting by Danielle

> *But what made this exercise so worth the risk was: 1) it wasn't about those group members reading it. They were positioned only to help me think more deeply for myself; at least that's how I viewed the group. I saw myself not as being there to critique what someone wrote, but rather to ask questions to help my group-mates think more deeply – to get out of their own ways, if you will...; 2) I trust and respect my group-mates and realized that if anyone from another group reads my map, chances are they would not tell me for fear that we "aren't supposed to do that," so self-censorship will keep negative/well-meaning sympathy at bay; 3) I see this exercise as so strengths-based that I realized after a while that I will only benefit by being honest with myself, and if others read it, they are doing the same exercise and so we will have mutual respect for the depth and risk of each other; and 4) I don't have any government secrets or criminal behavior to protect, so what the heck! It's a very liberating thing to not take oneself so seriously. :o)*

It is impossible to exaggerate the significance of this assignment, the generosity with which students share their lives with each other, and the potent effects of acknowledgements through small group reflections. Students use terms such as "profoundly life altering," and "one of the three most important experiences of my life." When I share these experiences with others who teach narrative therapy, they are surprised at the apparent sophistication of students' understanding as demonstrated by the quality of their work.

Rebecca expresses the impact of writing to her parents:

For me, writing the letter of commitment came after quite a bit of thought about the roots of my gratitude to both of my parents. That is not something that came easily over the years in my very Protestant family – meaning we had great difficulty expressing our emotions. We have always been better at writing these things to each other than verbalizing them, so the letter was a perfect vehicle for me! I have been feeling some urgency lately about not letting more time go by because of my mother's gradually growing dementia; she will still grasp my gratitude at this point, although she may not remember it for long. With my father already gone before I had a clear vision of his influence on my ethical development, I have some regrets. But it was deeply satisfying to publicly express my gratitude to him, to my classmates and through your reading the letter, as a way of honoring him after his death.

The Preferred Identity assignment affects people's lives in ways that extend well beyond usual academic studies. Catherine appreciates the bonds formed among classmates. "What stands out most is the relationships I developed with the other class members." Many students maintain contact with me well beyond the end of the course, which I take as testimony to the impact of this teaching approach. Morrie described his experience as transformative:

After we finished our class, I felt more confident and sure of myself and more able to roll with the stresses that I encountered in my relationships and everyday life (I think because I began seeing these stresses as external and not fundamental to my identity). Sometimes, I feel myself slipping back into the old way of being, at which point I re-read my letter of commitment. It's been an amazing help and I think will continue to be so in the years to come.

Next Steps

This firsthand experience with narrative concepts and practices gives students a base of understanding from which to expand their explorations. Some are inspired to continue their studies of narrative practice. Whether or not they decide to pursue further formal learning about narrative practice, I remain convinced that experiencing the Preferred Identity exercise provides students with the means to apply these concepts to themselves and will make them better reflective practitioners, clearer about their own personal values and perspectives, and more able to relate to people who come to consult with them in whatever their future roles might be.

I have experienced a similar influence on my practices as both teacher and reflective practitioner. Reading students' micro-maps and letters of commitment is a privilege that enlivens my commitment to my work. The generous witnessing with which students reflect on each other's maps and letters inspires me to similar practices of acknowledgement to people throughout my daily life.

CHAPTER 8

TEACHING STORIES

Reflection by Lynn Hoffman (following viewing a home-made recorded interview):

Does your class know that they were the first audience to see that particular performance and do they know how precious these artifacts are, that usually just disappear?

Posting by Lauren (whose class watched the videotape and then responded by writing letters to the interviewee):

I appreciated your reminder, Lynn, that the video is such an important artifact! It is true that I have never seen anything like it before – unrehearsed reality. Also, I have never had the opportunity to correspond with a person whose therapy I witnessed but did not participate in within the moment. It was truly magical and inspiring.

In my practice as a family therapist, I have equipped my office to record interviews with reflecting teamwork, using closed-circuit television from an adjacent office[28]. People who have come to consult with me graciously give me permission to share recordings of interviews, read aloud their poems, letters, and journal entries – anything that makes their stories come alive. Guest speakers come to class to speak from the perspective of the service seeker. Other guests visit the classroom and/or the course website to engage with students around their work as practitioners and authors. In the next three chapters, I further describe several of these practices, which significantly contribute toward a collaborative spirit of co-research.

This approach is in dramatic and stark contrast to the tradition of professional distancing that customarily animates case presentations. Family members' stories transport students into intimate experiences of people's lives and relationships. Letter-writing and outsider witness practices enable students to link their lives around shared themes with the people who generously share their stories. I want students to resist the so-called "professionalism" that draws sharp distinctions between practitioners' lives and the lives of people who seek help. Instead, I want us - teacher, student and therapist - to position ourselves as earnestly learning about life experiences from the people who seek our services. I aspire to inspire practitioners-in-training "to constantly confront the fact that if faced with circumstances such that provide the context of the troubles of others, they just might not be doing nearly as well themselves" (White, 1993) p. 132.

PREPARATION

Before they witness someone tell his or her story in person, in writing, or through a video recording, I instruct students on practicing their reflections through letter-writing or reflecting teamwork. From experience, I have learned that complicated instructions can flummox students' initial experience of resonance. Instead, I initially give only a few basic pointers. I ask them to listen carefully, staying as close as they can to the words and sentiments of the story being told, taking *verbatim* notes of anything they hear that particularly catches their attention.

Our shared experience becomes an opportunity to teach specific narrative practices, I provide handouts on outsider witness categories of response (see Chapter Ten) (White, 2003b) and letter-writing tips (see Chapter Eleven). Following a letter-writing or reflecting teamwork exercise, where students have had the opportunity to hear some of their classmates' letters and verbal reflections, we review these guidelines and highlight the considerable skills students demonstrated as well as areas for further tweaking. Always, students are invited to respectfully continue their conversation and inquiry online.

Students take seriously being invited into people's real life experiences. Ella posted the following online after writing letters to a woman, Chava, who I introduced to the class as someone emerging from a dark depression.

Posting by Ella

For me, the fact that this was going to be read by a real person who is dealing with real hardship in her life made the activity a lot harder. I found myself thinking very carefully about the effects of my words. I was concerned that what I had to say wouldn't be useful or important to her. It was a big deal for me that I was invited to be part of this assignment. Whatever insecurities I had about the value of my own experiences and of my voice, it suggested that perhaps I had a role to play in our friend's emergence because we existed in the world together and could shape and share stories and realities. The activity leads me to believe that resistance and emergence are relational and communal projects, which is something I kind of talked about in my letter. I also really want to thank Emma, Kerry, and Foresta for reading their letters out loud and allowing all of us to experience them together. Thinking back on the activity, I regret that I didn't share mine. It was hard for me to get over the convention that it's wrong or embarrassing to share personal stories and feelings in class, even though I definitely don't agree with this concept. The assignment helped me to form connections in a very meaningful way with our friend and with the other students that were able to read their responses out loud.

In this chapter, I share a story taken from my own practice. Kate generously gave me permission to read entries from her journal, after which I invited the students to use class time to write her letters, some of which were shared aloud. I also include a letter that Kate wrote back to the class as well as a postscript reflection.

KATE'S STORY

At age 18, Kate experienced what she named "Hell & Back" – a descent into and recovery from a psychotic depression. Six months later, she experienced what has been diagnosed as a manic episode. Through her talent for writing and the sensitivity of her detailed recollections, Kate teaches us about her experiences of psychosis. After hearing her description of her first experience with psychosis, students wrote letters in which they shared their reflections and asked Kate questions. I then shared with the class Kate's letter in response to theirs. Kate's generous sharing of her insider knowledge has contributed immeasurably toward expanding students and my own understanding. Now with this book, Kate's circle of influence widens.

My impression of Kate matches her own self-description: "I'm a peaceful happy young woman who goes to college and likes to play the guitar and write poetry and learn new things. I want to climb on rocks, make friends with trees, love other people." Nothing prepared her or her family for "the crisis" that changed her life.

In this excerpt, Kate grapples with her experience of psychosis:

I'm lying on my bed in my dorm room looking up at the ceiling between the words that I'm writing. I'm thinking about several things. One is how my bedside lamp casts a pattern of light up on the ceiling that's like the weaving of a basket. I can appreciate that it looks interesting but there was a time not long ago… maybe a week or so… when it looked so incredibly divine. It seemed like the work of a great artist rather than Walmart. I'm thinking also about this morning when I did a search on Wikipedia about psychosis. I learned that "psycho" is a term used both for people who experience psychosis and people who are psychopaths.

Psychopaths are people who seem to have no sense of empathy for others and for some strange reason become things like serial killers. Psychosis is when experience becomes too profound for words. I've never been a psychopath but I've experienced psychosis. It is a process of being lost in nothingness until little sparks of real life begin to show up again. It is an experience of not knowing where you are, whether you really exist, or whether you are lost. Psychosis. Psychopath. The word "psycho" labels us both. I hate the definition of the word "psycho."

Students are riveted when I read Kate's journal entries aloud in class. The following excerpt offers a glimpse into Kate's experience of the crisis that landed her a two-week stay in a hospital psychiatric ward.

Hell & Back

It's not entirely a bad memory, thinking of the time I spent in the hospital. It was kind of like, "Whoops, I left this life for a little while and had to go through a kind of 'training process' to get semi-near to where I left off." It was like a purification process – a whole system shutdown and then a gradual rebooting. I came in with overwhelming pain, hopelessness, confusion and crazy thoughts and ideas. My inner pain seemed to cause muscle spasms. In my hopelessness and confusion I would lose balance and fall to the floor. Everything around me seemed at times to take place in slow motion. It became difficult to determine whether the people around me were real, whether I was real. I could not make sense of my own thoughts and emotions. I tried many times over and over, spinning in circles, coming to conclusions and then rejecting them. As my lens looking out into the world became increasingly scary to look through, I began to stop peering out. That's one way to put it. It was more like I stopped responding to what I saw. I did not recognize my world. I didn't feel connected to it. I honestly didn't know if it was the world I had known or if it was heaven or hell or an alternate universe. All I knew was that I was somehow not in the right place and I had to either find my way back to my old life or move on to something better, even if that meant through death.

In this terrible time, it was like my physical body was there, but my spirit felt it did not belong. It couldn't find its place and for a day or so it seemed to disappear... or to reduce itself to the smallest flicker of a flame.

This was the Monday after I had been admitted to the hospital, the worst day of my life and in the lives of my parents. The doctors listed me as "mute catatonic." I stared blankly at nothing. I said nothing, ate nothing, did nothing. I showed no sign of recognition towards anyone or anything. I was frozen and lost. I remember hearing the words "We're going to get you back Kate. You're going to come back to us." These words were the only thing that felt real.

In the following journal entry, Kate further describes what led up to her psychiatric crisis.

In the days before going to the hospital, when my depression began to get very serious and debilitating, I was not overwhelmed with pain or sadness. I was more overwhelmed with confusion – constantly unsure and aware of myself. I knew that what I was dealing with was depression. Any time I was struggling with a symptom – difficulty concentrating for example – I would remind myself "it's just the depression. I'm not going crazy." But it became too confusing to constantly identify myself with depression. Was what I was feeling and thinking real or was it just an illness temporarily taking control over the "real me?"

I've known depressed people in my life and I remember sometimes wanting to just shake them out of it or somehow clear their vision. Now that I was depressed could I trust my own thoughts and emotions? In everything I did I would check myself: is this normal? Does this make sense? I couldn't stop monitoring myself.

What I hate more than anything about my experience with depression is that I could not stop talking inside my head – and all the talk was about myself. It was like my mind just kept trying to analyze and understand itself. I would come to my own conclusions about what was happening with me, thinking if I could just explain it, I could solve it. "I'm depressed because I'm too anxious and self-conscious right now to connect with anyone so I feel alone. I'm anxious because I know people are noticing me acting differently and are worried so I can't stop wondering what they're thinking. They're worried because I am depressed...."

When I realized I had gone in a circle with my thoughts I would say "Stop it! You're not making any sense." And at that point sometimes I would panic because there seemed to be no solution – nothing I could console myself with. Sometimes I could tell myself "have patience" but this didn't stop my mind from running.

They say that when you are depressed you should try to do the things you would normally enjoy doing even if you don't feel like it – unless it is too difficult or unpleasant. People will tell you it is very challenging dealing with depression – you really have to fight it. And some will tell you, "Be gentle with yourself."

When I was depressed, I couldn't figure out what to do with myself. This was partly because I lacked creative energy and motivation, partly because I had trouble focusing on one thing and partly because there were so many options and no guidance. I had graduated from high school. There was no daily community of people expecting my presence – nothing to provide me with structure and social interaction. I was in open space. There was no obvious goal or direction. I had planned to take a year off to work, travel and volunteer but hadn't made specific plans. For some reason the wealth of opportunities, the infinite choices, overwhelmed me. Plus, I began to fear an inability to function if I put myself in a situation of responsibility, which was certainly not normal for me. This led to the avoidance of actually finding something to give myself daily structure and social interaction. I didn't know where to start and I was afraid that if I did start my symptoms of depression would humiliate me and lead to deeper depression.

I spent my hours mostly alone, trying to solve the problem. I wanted to feel better before I jumped into a new environment with responsibilities but I didn't know how to make myself feel better while being alone all day. I began to feel like there was something I was supposed to do, something that had to happen before I could feel better. I thought maybe I needed to "fix" my relationship with a best friend from whom I had begun to feel very distant. "I need to write to Sandra. I need to talk to Sandra. I need to connect with Sandra before I can feel better." But I couldn't do it. My symptoms of anxiety and depression made it too difficult. And perhaps there was no "fixing" that could be done. Things were changing. People were leaving. It was time to move on to the next thing. But what was my next thing? I imagined my friends and I standing in a circle. Normally we'd all be facing one another but now it was like everyone was facing out into the world. I was the only one still facing inward. And all I saw was a bunch of backs.

That summer I went directly to a camp in Maine where I had been a camper and now had a job. About two weeks in I came home, after experiencing for the first time symptoms of depression that made it too difficult for me to live and work on the island camp. Not realizing I was experiencing depression, I described my troubling symptoms to the director as "having a mental breakdown" based on the fact that I couldn't concentrate enough to get any work done or pay attention to other people, needed to cry two or three times a day, and couldn't explain what was going on with me. I left camp feeling totally bewildered and embarrassed.

What I didn't realize was that my fear of deeper depression, which caused me to avoid new challenges, actually itself led to deeper depression... or so it seems. Upon returning, I was afraid of people noticing my symptoms of depression. I didn't want people to see that I was anxious about talking with them, especially when talking about camp. What should I say when they ask me why I had left? "I didn't feel up to it. It wasn't the right job for me. I couldn't do it. I didn't want to be there." How could I say this. When I returned home after being a camper, I thought to myself, "I belong here. I have to come back." So what do I say to people when I chose to be home over camp? If they know me they will know something is wrong with me. If they don't know me they will misunderstand something very important about me. My parents reminded me, "People understand. These things happen to everybody. You've been dealing with a lot lately and you're just in between jobs right now. That's all you have to say." OK. I could deal with that. But that didn't make things any easier. I had escaped responsibility by leaving camp but I hadn't really escaped.

I had decided that I would take several days after returning home to just re-coup and not worry about anything. I wouldn't even tell anyone I was home. After about the fifth day back I got a message on the answering machine from Sandra: "I heard a rumor that you were back in town...." And I knew I couldn't stay in hiding forever. Already my friends were thinking about me, possibly worrying about me. And I couldn't avoid the anxiety of wondering what they were thinking.

Usually the best way to deal with anxiety is to go through with the things that make you anxious even if you do end up failing or embarrassing yourself. I've always known this. Fear doesn't go away by avoiding it. Why then did I spend hours, even entire days, holding a phone in my hand and not dialing? Why then did I stand in front of the calendar staring at the days, trying to prepare myself for the weeks ahead, hoping that if I could just imagine them, I could survive them?

I never needed my friends so badly than during that time and yet I had never isolated myself more. I desperately wanted to connect with someone on a deep level and therefore couldn't sleep at night thinking about them and how I hadn't talked with them in what felt like so long. "What the hell am I doing?" I would sit up in bed and say out loud to myself. Sometimes I would panic, stiff as a board in bed, heart beating rapidly, as I thought to myself, "I'm ruining my life. I'm losing all my friends because they think I don't care about them because I haven't called them or talked to them in so long." When I'd get up to go to the bathroom I'd sit on the toilet and feel as though I were flushing not my waste but my vitality down the drain. Weak in body and spirit, sleep-deprived, my muscles ached and trembled. When I did see my friends it was as though all of my need for them, all the pain and suffering that had built up suddenly came to the very top. I felt as though my whole body were throbbing with it. I couldn't concentrate on anything except the desire to connect with them, to share with them what I was going through and for them to know how much I needed and cared about them and would miss them when they left. But to converse with them I had to be fake. If I touched on anything real I would feel dizzy, and for some reason I couldn't cry in front of them without panicking, because I couldn't explain why I was crying... there were no words to explain my suffering. Why was I even suffering? I couldn't think of a good enough reason. Nothing tragic or traumatic had happened. So what was wrong with me anyway?

Here, Kate describes her experiences of anxiety and confusion, and the effects on her relationship with her parents:

Kate's Journal Entry #3

Normal, everyday anxiety most people can talk themselves out of, right? If I'm anxious about something I just say things like "It's ok. Don't be ridiculous... you've done things much more difficult in the past. You'll be fine." I breathe deeply, put myself in others shoes, that sort of thing and I usually feel better. During this particularly difficult summer, I realized at some point that I was talking to myself non-stop, day and night, trying to talk myself out of my anxiety and ultimately out of my depression. After a while, instead of comforting me, it was just noise inside my head that prevented me from sleeping, reading, conversing, and experiencing life. I would jump out of bed in the middle of a sleepless night when in the midst of my thoughts I realized my problem was really that I was thinking too much.. There was no solution. I couldn't heal myself with my will. I couldn't find my own escape. I needed someone or something else to find it for me.

Days and nights like these I started to "hover." I would get up in the night and stand outside my parents' bedroom trying to decide whether I should go in or not. "I need help," I would say to myself, but when I tried to think of what I would say to them I went blank...The wall of miscommunication between us was such that this ordinary act of asking for help was a miniature of what I actually needed.

Before long, I was hovering during the day as well. My dad would be cooking dinner and I would be pacing back and forth outside the kitchen doorway. My parents knew that I was suffering: grieving the loss of high school, difficult relationships and thinking of camp. I don't think they realized as soon as I did that time alone was not going to heal me.

Sometimes I wouldn't even notice that I was hovering and whoever it was would say, "Kate, are you ok? You're kind of pacing back and forth..." This made me feel like crying and I would say, "Yeah, I'm just thinking," and then retreat to my room, deciding that I had to and would figure it out on my own after all. One time when I was hovering outside the kitchen, my dad said, "Kate, I'm listening if there's something you feel like saying."

"I don't know," I said, and I didn't.

I remember my dad taking me to the new Dunkin' Donuts that had just opened in town to spend some father-daughter time drinking Coolatas. "I wish I could just snatch you up and free you from all those little demons or whatever it is that seem to have such a hold on you." He said at some point. This was no metaphor to me. "I need you to," I replied.

This was one of the many times when I began to feel there was a pane of glass between the world and me. I was on one side and the people I loved were on the other. I could see to the other side but I wasn't there. I was somewhere else... and the glass was getting thicker.

A few days after the last words she wrote in that journal, Kate was in the hospital. She asks, "*Is it too extreme to say that I was losing my mind? I don't know.*"

In Journal Entry #4, Kate describes the difficulty she experienced in attempting to adequately describe what she remembers of her period of crisis and hospitalization:

Kate's Journal Entry #4

This is the most difficult place to return to in writing. Not because it's painful but because words seem hopeless in their ability to explain or express the experience. But I'll try because if there are any experiences of mine that feel important to relate to others, this is one of them. There are many things, which though confusing and difficult at the time, can be understood and described in hindsight. I've been able to do this with a lot of memories from when I was depressed. To a very small degree I think I can do it with that deepest and darkest time. But for the most part it is a mystery to me – as it would be for anyone. Our bodies and brains, like most things in nature, may have scientific explanations for their miraculous and unbelievable ways, but they don't necessarily satisfy the soul. I'm sure I will seek meaning and understanding from the memory of that time for the rest of my life.

There are so many lenses to choose from when deciding how to look back at that memory. Interpretations of it can be almost contradictory and yet I find myself at different times believing all of them to a degree. If I were asked now to explain what happened I would say, as I have said, "Something was happening inside my brain having to do with chemicals and neurotransmitters that affected my conscious state. In cruder terms I went crazy, and though the experience of it was real I can look back now and recognize how utterly confused I was then.

However, there is much more to be said if I am to get at how I really feel and deal with that memory. I guess I could start with this: Say that you come to a point when everything in your immediate experience signifies to you that you are dying. Regardless of reality, your interpretation of your emotional and physical experience is that you are dying, perhaps have somehow already died, or worse yet, are living in some literal form of hell. If this is the case, as it was at one point for me, explanations of chemicals and neurotransmitters will probably satisfy very little of your curiosity of what's happening.

Kate reflected on her philosophical and religious ideas about what happened to her:

What really happened to me? I do believe that to an extent I did die and am now alive again. There must be ways in which a person can die besides that of the physical and ultimate death of the body. And if this is true, as it seems to be, then hell exists and it is not an eternal punishment for the sinner but perhaps just the turmoil of feeling disconnected from Creation (whether deserved or not).

I'm not sure if I believe that when we die (truly die) that we somehow maintain an individual experience. I do believe however with certainty that we stay eternally connected and alive with the creation we are a part of. I think of the earth as a recycling machine; just as rain can be lifted from the ground and made back into clouds so can our souls evaporate into life as beautiful if not more so than the life we experience now.

When I think back at how I felt then...it was as though not my body but the spirit of life within me (which lives on even after the death of the body) was dying. This thought terrifies me. As you can see I have religious and philosophical ideas about what happened but of course I don't have a clue. It is so completely strange to me. All I really have is the experience.

Kate then described the events that led up to her hospitalization:

Several nights before the real crisis, I was babysitting my little friends Andrew and Aaron. I remember feeling disconnected from what I was doing. Nothing came naturally but instead required a decision... If I reasoned that I ought to feel a particular emotion, I would decide to feel it. I was aware of the sensation that my brain was functioning differently than normal.

I don't know if it was one night or several, but I remember lying in bed and feeling that it was a physical impossibility for me to sleep. Instead I would stay conscious but have dream-like visualizations that I could control. I remember visualizing something like a bar graph of people in my life and if the bar went high enough for one peson it meant that I should think about that person. Similarly I would imagine a web of stick figures that I was in. I would look at the web in my mind to see with whom I was most strongly connected. It was as though everything that would normally come naturally now took a conscious effort to grasp. Who were the people in my life that mattered? Was there anything in those relationships that I was supposed to be doing that I wasn't doing? I felt very uncertain of myself and for a good reason because clearly I was not functioning the way I normally would.

Yesterday I got out the calendar from when this all happened and tried to piece together that time, especially the week before the hospital. On September 1, 2004, a week and a half before I was hospitalized, I talked with Peggy (the therapist I'd been seeing since I came home from camp) about how I was doing much better. She suggested that I write a letter to myself for a future Kate in case I ever went through that depression again, which I did when I got home. Here is a short excerpt from that letter:

"For a future Kate who may find herself struggling: What feels so impossible to heal is really quite fixable. When it seems like no one can possibly understand, when it feels like you are disconnected from the world, or hovering like a ghost, or empty, or hurting... it is only a matter of time and faith. Hopefully it will never come to this again."

That same day I had an appointment with my regular doctor to check up on my medications. We decided that I could cut back on the Lexapro I was taking. Clearly this was a mistake, though it seemed to make sense at the time. The following week I was doing relatively well. I went twice to community soccer, I babysat twice and I went to a poetry workshop session at the library. The following Sunday, a week prior to the crisis, I babysat Andrew and Aaron as I mentioned above.

It wasn't as though the confusion came out of nowhere. Even though I had reported feeling better I didn't feel "recovered" or anywhere near better enough to say that I felt fully like myself again. I think the first sign that things were becoming worse again was when a mother of a friend called that Sunday to ask if I could walk her dog. Already feeling stressed and a bit overwhelmed I said no but by the end of the conversation had shifted over and agreed to walk the dog. During that conversation it was like my own needs felt so weak against the needs of others. At the same time, I felt ashamed at my own sense of feeling overwhelmed. It was like I was embarrassed to say, "You know I really can't handle another responsibility right now." Normally I would be able to say this. Perhaps that feeling I was getting, the heavy warning that I might be dealing with too much, was so real I was afraid to acknowledge it. It would be like showing weakness in the face of danger, thus proving the danger to be real.

Kate's writing gives students an insider account of a growing gap between a person's inner life and what is projected to the world. She wrote the following journal entry the day before she went in the hospital).

I seemed to have created a gap between what was going on inside me and what I projected to the world. What I projected was what I wanted to be true or what I thought ought to be true, while what really was going on could not have lived up to that alternative I had created for the outside. There is a breaking point I think, when the gap between your inner reality and projected reality becomes so wide, that a person can look you in the eyes and it is as though they are not looking at you at all. When this happens, it may seem that you have lost sight of yourself, that your inner reality no longer exists, because you can no longer see yourself in the eyes of those who look at you.

"Are you hungry?" My mother asks. Oh God, it is like she is talking to someone else but I am the one who needs to answer. "Yes." I say. I take the pizza. Like a robot I lift it to my mouth completely disconnected from the idea of hunger, a triviality at the moment. The sensation of its taste is one more signal sent to my brain out of so many that are just too much to handle. It is an overload of experience. Wrong decision. I swallow it anyway.

Looking back on herself on that night, Kate saw someone "running on the fuel of a fake reality."

I see someone sprinting in darkness when they should be feeling each step to test if it's safe to continue in that direction... Not that the fake reality I was running with was an impossibility... more likely, the true reality was so unexpected, so unusual, and so successfully hidden from others, that it was just too easy to overlook and pretend did not exist. The true reality was that I was suffering. There was pain inside me, so deep it was eating away at me without my even being aware of it. That pain needed to be seen. It needed to be touched and felt and held before it could be let go of. It needed a finger pointed at it with the words, "YES! That is sharp and hot and a reason to stop what you are doing, drop everything, kneel over it, pay attention to it, and hold it till it subsides."

I don't think my failure to project my inner reality to the world, and to myself for that matter, is really a failure or a fault that I could have prevented. You see, it was so deep and hidden that even if someone had pointed at it and said, "Look, you are in pain. That is why you can't function the way you normally would." I wouldn't have been able to see it. Of course I knew I was in pain to some extent.... I just couldn't fathom that feelings of hurt and sadness, something I had always been able to keep at bay, could build up enough force to break up on the shore and disable me where I had always otherwise been safe.

In my fake reality, the one to which I clung so desperately until the final breaking point, I saw no reason for feeling overwhelmed, no reason that I should have to stop and pay attention to myself. Or if I did, I saw no alternative but to go forward as I always had, to be seen as I had always been seen. I imagine this is why my emotional experience changed from doing and feeling what came naturally to constantly having to decide what to feel and do as though there were a right way and a wrong way. "What do I need to do and feel in order to maintain the level of emotional strength, normality and acceptability... that others and myself expect me to be at? How I am supposed to feel and act? This is how I will decide to be." When I tried to force my inner reality to the confines of what the outer world saw or to what I thought they saw or wanted them to see, disregarding my true reality, this was when I began to sprint in darkness. This is when I convinced the world I could see clearly when in fact I was sprinting at a brick wall and had no idea.

STUDENTS' LETTERS TO KATE

After hearing these accounts of Kate's story, I invite students to write letters to her "from the heart" that convey ways in which they are moved by hearing these accounts of Kate's experience. I encourage them to ask questions that express their earnest curiosity. I let them know that I will screen the letters so they need not get caught in worrying about "correctness."

It is hard for me to choose between the many letters that students have written to Kate.

Finding Resonance

I encourage students to write about what particularly caught their attention. I let them know that in narrative practice, we are seeking "an embodied response," which links lives through shared themes. Several students' letters focused on a particular aspect of Kate's story that resonated with their own experiences. Anonymity makes it possible for students to reveal personal stories they might not otherwise share with classmates.

Letter from Nina

Dear Kate,

I really don't have words to express how beautiful your writing is and how meaningful your story was to me. Your description of your experience as death and rebirth of the spirit was so powerful. I have struggled with depression at various times in my life, but depression and other mental health problems have never been acceptable in my family, so I have never really explored the experience. Hearing your descriptions of your experience was so moving to me because it is some of what I have felt. I really hope you continue to write your story, and publish it, because I think it can help so many people. It also helps me as a social worker in training – hearing your descriptions of your thoughts and feelings, while in the hospital and how the staff responded to you and how you hoped neighbors would respond gave me greater insight into the experiences of clients and hospital patients. I think this will help me be more responsive and helpful to people I work with in the future.

> *Thank-you,*
> *Nina*

Letter from Andrea

Dear Kate,

I'm not sure I can write much because your story is very close to my own. It was difficult and painful to stay present (to really listen) and pay attention as Peggy read your words to us. But I did stay present and I did my best to listen.

I know well what it is to be in a psych hospital, to have people trying to help and yet experienced the "pane (pain) of glass" between me and them that you described for me. Returning to the world was like coming slowly and uncertainly out of a fog. Indistinct shapes, muffled sounds, gauzy under-standing.

I too have longed to write my story – in part for myself, in part for those who want to understand. But I am not good with words, I'm good at listening. So that is what I hope to do. I will trust you to write for all of us who have been in – and come out.

> *Thank you for your words.*
> *Andrea*

Rich Description

I am often amazed at how readily students' letters written from the heart put into practice principles of narrative therapy to freshly describe what strikes a chord. Their letters reflect back in Kate's words what has caught their attention, the images evoked, and how Kate's behind-the-scenes account transports them to new understandings. For example, after hearing Kate's journal writing about her experiences with depression, Chappell described her amazement at Kate's ability to capture the confusion and paralysing effects of depression and anxiety:

I am struck by the details that you remember from this time and your willingness to sort through them piece by piece. I have an image of someone, with love and patience, piecing back together a broken piece of china that

155

means a lot to them. It is sometimes so much easier (at least for me) to sweep the pieces up and toss them away. It seems like sometimes the piecing back together can serve as a powerful reminder of the breaking of the thing rather than its state of wholeness. Your story and your writing push me to look at the wholeness of a thing.

Sarah was struck by Kate's images of "a glass getting thicker between you and those you love," and "all of your friends facing out of the circle as you faced their backs." These images gave meaning to and resonance with Sarah's experience of depression 10 years prior. "Your images are powerful messengers to remind me of that time." Sarah further described the relevance for her experience as a social work intern working in a psychiatric unit the previous year:

Your description of the highs and lows experienced in your brief contacts with the woman in the hall told me so much. What I heard as intense driving for connection even in the simple (yet not simple) questions you were asking reminded me of the importance of someone's mere attempt to listen. It reminded me of the necessity of trying to listen even harder when someone seems confused and unsure. Thank you for your powerful story and writing.

Several students connected with the spirituality theme in Kate's account, such as conveyed in the following letter:

Hello Kate,

Your writings conjured up for me those thoughts and images at the fringe of human experience and understanding – those moments of what some have called existential dread. That sense of being utterly cut off and separate from the rest of creation and our sense of solidity with in it. That sense that has been crazy-making for me too.

I am particularly struck by the level of cognition you retained throughout your trial. No doubt it was different than what we rely upon during most of our waking moments, but there it was nonetheless. In listening to your words, images of mental gymnastics came to mind. It was as if your mind were bending and twisting, spinning and jumping, all in an attempt to make meaning of its new landscape.

How does the spiritual lens through which you understand those early moments of coming back to this reality impact your understanding of our world now? Are the "angels" who were on the unit with you still felt as experienced in this reality or were they inhabitants of that in-between place you describe so well?

Thank you for sharing part of your story with me. I hope to read of your continued adventures someday. Peace and blessings.

Often practitioners-in-training are taught to use their professional knowledge to analyze others' experiences. Narrative therapy instead encourages its practitioners to connect with their earnest curiosity. When given a fresh opportunity, students ask many questions about Kate's experience. They situate their questions in the specific context of what they heard Kate say and its relevance to their own professional and personal lives. Rather than through a professionalized expert-in-training lens, their expressions of curiosity convey human-to-human connection.

In her letter, for example, Allison described how Kate made her experience understandable:

Letter from Allison

I pictured you standing outside your parents' room wanting to tell them "I need help," and remembered feeling that way myself many times throughout my life. When you described going to Dunkin doughnuts with your dad, his attempts to help you and your wanting his help but not knowing how to tell him to help you (and not knowing what that would look like) made me cry. Your revisiting of this difficult period is courageous and I will take this courage with me to revisit difficult periods in my own life. I know you will continue to do so and that inspires me. Thank you for sharing so much of yourself.

In their letters, students chose something in particular from the many images that stood out to them. Ann commented on the following:

I was moved by your description of how your inner feelings became expressed through your physical self, how your inability to manage emotional distress was translated into physical immobility. I have sometimes experienced a similar feeling (although not as severe as you). I want to ask you, what did it feel like to begin making progress toward physical movement and emotional expression? How were you able to begin that process of healing and change?

Beyond Pointing Out Positives

Students frequently express a deep appreciation to Kate for sharing her writing with them. However, their acknowledgements do not simply point out positives; they give concrete examples of the impact of Kate's story on their lives and relationships. In Ann's letter, she offers the following acknowledgement:

I was struck by your bravery in being willing to make yourself vulnerable to a group of people you have never met. In hearing your story, we gain greater knowledge of how many different paths to healing there can be. I also hope that for you, the act of communicating and sharing your story is part of your own healing.

Melissa's situates her question by first describing what she heard Kate say about her experience of meaning-making and how this account resonated with her own experiences:

Letter from Melissa

Dear Kate,

Thank you for sharing some of your story with my class. I was particularly struck by your description of how you were making meaning of your experiences up to and including hospitalization. If I got this right – I understood that for you, biological explanations (more making logical sense) are not enough. You spoke of living and dying, not just as biological events, but as acts of Creation. These concepts speak to me of a certain richness of experience I imagine you bringing to everything you do. It resonates with my own belief in living my life to the fullest (whatever that means) and my feeling of satisfaction in the attempt even when frustration threatens to overwhelm me.

As a soon-to-be social worker, your story has helped me to understand that I want to try to listen to people who may lose their voice. And I'm left to ponder how I can do that. Did you have the experience that there were people trying to understand what you were going through? And if so, did it matter in any way?

Thank-you,
Melissa

KATE'S RESPONSE

Kate was delighted to receive these letters. She expressed puzzled appreciation to think that her experiences could help train aspiring therapists:

Wow... Thank you so much for your letters in response to my writing. I thought of that writing mainly as a release for myself – to get off my chest some powerful memories that stick with me, but to see that it has an effect on other people, that it may mean something to others besides myself and people close to me means a lot to me. It is such a gift to risk sharing something personal and frightening and then to receive a response of such understanding and curiosity. Thank you so much.

A lot of the letters asked such really good questions that I want to make an attempt at answering them.

Kate then listed the many questions that students posed in their letters to her:

Students' Questions

- Could anything have been done (by you, your therapist, by your community) earlier on in your depression to keep it from becoming so disabling or do you think that you needed to follow your feelings to their completion and begin again?

- Did you have the experience that there were people trying to understand what you were going through? And if so, did it matter in any way?

- Did the outside world penetrate your world? Were you processing what people said and did? Were you aware of your own body and your own physicality?

- How did "touch" feel to you and when/how and by whom it was helpful and when it was not.

- I know for myself there is certain music with which I feel a very deep, in a sense spiritual connection, and I imagine that if I were in a similar situation this music would help me stay connected to what I love about this life. In your writings you mentioned playing the guitar, so I wonder what role music might have for you in this way?

- How does the spiritual lens through which you understand those early moments of coming back to this reality impact your understanding of our world now? Are the "angels" who were on the unit with you still felt and experienced in this reality or were they inhabitants of that in-between place?

- I am so curious to know what, if any, contributions your religious beliefs made to your understanding of what you were going through. Did this experience lead you to a new place in your understanding or your spiritual identity? Or did it confirm understandings that you previously believed?

- What did it feel like to begin making progress toward physical movement and emotional expression? How were you able to begin that process of healing and change?

- I would love to know when you felt you were ok again and how you knew that.

- I wonder what your old life was within your family and your surroundings. I wonder also what your new life is like and how your loved ones reacted and responded to you.

- You mentioned that you felt as though you were dying. Do you feel as though some part of you has died? Have you laid something to rest?

- I wondered how you will continue to bring yourself closer to that experience, and what you hope to gain from the experience of revisiting and retelling your story. Where do you want this journey to bring you?

- How did you come to choose this (parent/child center) experience in your life? What does the volunteer work bring to your life? Particularly working with children"?

Kate then begins with a detailed response to the first question:

One of the questions was whether something could have been done (either by me, my therapist, my community, etc.) earlier on in my depression to prevent it from becoming so disabling, or whether I had to follow my feelings to their completion and begin again. This is a very important question for the sake of a person at risk of going through what I went through but also for myself in the future. It's also an extremely difficult one to answer. I think in my own case, it's easier to consider the possibility of prevention for future scenarios than it is to look back and imagine how things could have gone differently. It was such unknown territory for me and for those close to me. Even though my dad is a psychologist, I don't think he could have imagined a week or even a day prior to the crisis that I would end up in the psych ward of the Rutland hospital for two weeks. It seems almost as though it had to happen as it did in order for me to learn from it and heal.

One of the things I think about when I look back is how the crisis wasn't really the worst thing that happened during my depression. In fact it was more like the climax that provided me with the force to heal. During my depression, which lasted several months, it was like I was being chased by this constant fear of what it could do to me. Behind every anxious feeling there was also that feeling that I might just go crazy, become mute... or maybe my brain would just decide to shut off at some point. I think of my "crisis" as the point when I couldn't run anymore and those fears caught up to me. The thing is, and this is what is so liberating, the fears caught me, even had a hold on me, and yet here I am. I now have an answer to that haunting question: What happens if the things we fear do catch us, look us in the eye, and say, "you can't escape me now?" I can't say it wasn't a challenge – a frightening one which I thought I might never come out of. But by having those fears catch me, I could look them right back in the eye, see what they were all about, and learn that ultimately I had the power to conquer them. Someone in the hospital told me, "sometimes things have to get worse before they can get better," and that was absolutely true for me. I had to hit rock bottom before I could push off and come back to the surface.

So could it have been prevented? I wonder what would have happened if I hadn't reduced the amount of medicine I was on two weeks prior to the crisis. Would I gradually have healed without such a dramatic downfall first? I don't know. I was on medication, I was seeing an excellent therapist, and I was meeting with my doctor...I didn't know at the time how I could possibly have prevented it because I had to learn from experience. But I think if it were to happen again I would know how to do things differently, as would the people around me. I know now that the medication I've taken is much more likely to help me then harm me (as was one of my fears). I have resources now that I didn't have before, such as information packets from the hospital, a written safety plan, a daily schedule I can follow if I need to, a crisis phone number and of course support people I may not have otherwise been aware of. Also, the more I share about the experience, the less I'll feel ashamed or embarrassed about seeking help if I need to in the future. I hope that answers your question.

Kate's Recommendations for Practitioners

Given her unique personal experience, I asked Kate if she had any additional recommendations for practitioners. Here is what she said:

The best things that therapists did for me was help me to rediscover self-expression. For me this is what I feel was lost during the time I was in the hospital for major depression. Depression for me in general has the effect of losing my sense of self and my ability to be expressive. It seems like for many mental illnesses an essential piece of the healing that needs to occur is the process of expressing oneself. The classic idea that when someone is having problems they need to "talk about it" is part of this idea that self-expression is healing. However, I think it may be really important to know that there are some other effective ways of helping a person find positive self-expression. In my case I needed help recovering from a depression that put me into a mute, catatonic state. Both time and medicine helped me recover but these would have been useless without certain exercises that helped me regain confidence in my ability to "be me again."

One of these exercises was sitting in a circle with a group and tossing a ball around. I remember at that point believing myself to be a ghost that no one could see. I literally believed that I had no physical connection to the world that I was looking at. When one of the therapists threw a bean bag in my direction (calling my name out as she threw it), I did what I thought at the time was impossible - I caught it. What's so amazing about depression is that we don't realize the things we are still capable of. I truly in my heart did not think that I was a part of that group - that I was in any way connected to them - until I was put in this position of having the opportunity to catch the ball and throw it back. It was part of re-learning that I could in fact interact with people. It also may be good to point out that little experiences are keys to larger concepts. For example, in this ball exercise I remember that I kept passing the ball right back to the person who passed it to me. Soon this therapist pointed to someone else just as I was about to pass it to her, indicating that I could choose to pass it to someone new. To me, this moment contributed to my re-learning that I had the ability of "creating something new" in a sense. It's hard to explain but it was like a reminder that I could be creative. I could do more than merely react to my environment. I could add my own spontaneity.

One of the worst things that practitioners can do to someone suffering from mental illness is to forget that they are still a real person who deserves as much respect as anyone. I clearly remember the way in which practitioners often talked to one another about me as though I weren't in the room or didn't inform me of what was going on. I think they assumed I didn't understand (which perhaps I didn't but the way they acted made me feel as though I didn't exist which was already part of the problem I was dealing with and that feeling did not need to be encouraged). I remember being taken to see the head doctor in his office and there were two nurses in there as well. As I replied or didn't reply to the doctor, one of the nurses would make a concerned face at me and then type something on the computer. The other nurse was also writing something down as I talked. They didn't even introduce themselves when I came into the room. I felt like they were analyzing me and testing me, and it made me very uneasy and certainly influenced my nervous behavior. Remembering my experience, I think it's important for practitioners to do all they can to try to see the person behind the illness – we are really under there somewhere and we need more than anything to be recognized. One of the simplest ways to connect with that person is to have a picture of something they love and ask about it. Or to have a picture of something the practitioner loves. My favorite practitioner in the hospital showed me a picture of her with her dog and she asked me whether I liked dogs and if I had one. She shared with me something about herself and gave me that opportunity as well. I liked her because she treated me as a real person who was worth talking to, not some object for tests and pills.

Postscript

I emailed an earlier draft of this chapter to Kate, which she shared with her parents. We then met in the local coffee shop to catch up and review her responses. More than a year had passed since we last saw each other. I was immediately struck by Kate's radiant health and poise. A reflective young woman, Kate knows herself well and is fully engaged in living her life as a college student. In a couple of months, she will spend a semester abroad in Asia. I would like to give Kate the last say in this chapter, thus ending with her words, which she entitled, "Looking Back Again."

It's been three years since I graduated from high school and thus three years since the beginning of the depression that led to my first episode. After I read a draft of the chapter Peggy put together of my writing and the responses her students wrote, she asked me if I had any more thoughts or reflections now. When I look at this writing again, I remember that period of necessary reflection and how important telling my story was. I felt like I needed to share it as much as I needed food to eat. It was so important and Peggy helped me to do it. Though I don't always write about it, I often still reflect back on the experiences I've had with psychosis and depression. Chappell wrote in her letter to me about how when something is broken it is often easier to sweep up the pieces and throw them away, rather than try to piece them back together. Piecing back together often reminds us of the experience of the thing breaking. As she hinted at, and what I experienced, is that piecing together a thing to make it whole again is a gift even if it reminds us of something difficult that we wish had never happened. When I reflect and tell others my story, I make it impossible to sweep the pieces away. This is okay because I need that story to help me understand who I am. It helps me see a bit more wholeness in myself than I would otherwise see. I am not depression. I am not psychosis. I am Kate and there are so many things I want to do with my life besides deal with that diagnosis I was given three years ago. Surprisingly, talking about it helps me do those other things.

CHAPTER 9

PUBLIC PRACTICES

Posting by Emma

I am really interested in the idea of linking experience with people I do not necessarily know. Meaning is relational and gets renegotiated with all of our interactions...I believe it is important to break through isolated borders of individual experience to feel connected and supported – to realize it is not taboo to be heard through our struggles, and to recognize that the struggles are just one part of the rich stories of our lives. Connecting to Nicole's story is something that seems, given my prior understanding of therapy, a new and uncharted feeling of freedom in the domain of helping professions.

Teaching narrative therapy offers opportunities to build on the ethic of circulation and innovative public practices that narrative therapists use to incorporate audiences into the therapy process (Lobovitz, Maisel, & Freeman, 1995). In this chapter, I offer stories to illustrate how I design teaching contexts to circulate insider knowledge in which unexpected opportunities, potential solutions, and creative ideas unfold. Archiving online reflections is a highly effective approach to capture what students learn directly from guest speakers, recorded interviews, and story-telling. I provide classroom and online examples of how letters, reflecting teams, and archived websites provide public contexts for people to speak with knowledged voices about life-shaping experiences in ways that significantly inform the lives of everyone involved.

Students glean a great deal from hearing service seekers speak with conviction about their relationships with professional helpers. After learning "at the feet of parents" about their experiences of parenting a child who is different, students interact online about their most memorable impressions. I also share students' reflections of their in-class opportunities to witness such insider accounts as living through and "unsuffering[29]" themselves from psychiatric crisis, severe depression, and sexual abuse.

By augmenting classroom teaching with an interactive course website, I structure numerous contexts to give students access to a wide range of input and social support. A course website offers particular possibilities for circulation practices based on social interdependency and a diminished hierarchy. Students gain immeasurably from the experience of expressing, sharing and witnessing - rather than evaluating - each others' work. They also gain a great deal from being able to link and consult with each other and with outside consultants around shared themes. We become partners in learning, as students intently listen to insider accounts of journeys of self-discovery in overcoming complex problems, aided and abetted by communities of support that include human service practitioners.

Safeguarding Confidences

Just as narrative therapy challenges assumptions about the absolute privacy of the client-therapist relationship, teaching with technology poses challenges to the academic tradition of prioritizing individual learning experience over community sharing. Access to a course website is password protected, restricted to either registered users or people to whom I give a "guest pass" – only after the students' clearance for the request. In designing the course site, the privacy of the students' postings is still operative unless the students decide otherwise; any forum can readily be set up to be either public or private. However, there is a key difference here from live discussion: all participants must understand that there is no real guarantee that online conversations will remain private, since any electronic posting or private email can of course be copied and sent to others. In my opinion, the benefits of the online medium far outweigh the risk of one's online communications becoming public. I seek to build a culture of trust and confidentiality to limit the likelihood that online communications will be disclosed to others than those granted permission to participate in them.

I create several online contexts in which to ask students what is acceptable to them. I ask them a number of related questions: "Is it okay for me to give out the guest pass to other teachers of narrative therapy?" "Is it okay if I include your assignments and/or posts in this article?" "Would you prefer to be anonymous?" "Have I given you enough freedom to say no for whatever the reason?"

It is important not to presume or to take liberties based on earlier requests when no objections were given. Students rarely object, but regardless, I think they want to be included in these decisions.

I also guarantee that I will share with them any reflections I hear back relevant to their work. It is important that I follow through on this promise.

AN ETHIC OF CIRCULATION

Upon reflection, we find that the use of audiences has sharpened our focus on social interdependency. Unexpected solutions to problems may be found as we access a wider range of input and social support for change. We are no longer burdened by feeling as if we are the sole source of support and knowledge for clients. We have become more conscious of how privileged we are to interact with clients and witness their journeys of change. We gain from a greatly enriched fund of creative ideas as well as stories of pain and hope, to inform us and to share with other clients (Lobovits et al., 1995), (pp. 254-255).

More than ten years ago, Dean Lobovits and his colleagues introduced the term "an ethic of circulation" to describe practices that provide audiences for preferred accounts of self and identity. Storytelling involves both a storyteller and an audience, with everyone engaged as an active collaborator in a personal process of meaning-making (Bruner, 1990). Rather than instruct or provide expert knowledge for clients, the therapist's role is "to enter the social space where meaning is shaped and support the development of alternative meanings to oppressive stories" (Lobovits, Maisel, & Freeman, 1995, p. 224).

Lobovitz, Maisel and Freeman (1995) discern two kinds of audiences, both with relevance to teaching narrative therapy. "Known audiences" include family, friends, teachers, human service providers, and/or significant persons living or dead, who interact with and influence a person's unfolding story. An "introduced audience" is drawn from the community of people who have insider knowledge about a particular problem and its social context, yet who are not necessarily personally acquainted with the person. A good example is the anti-anorexia/anti-bulimia "Archive of Resistance," an online forum that "introduces the reader to a wider community of those who have struggled to resist anorexia and bulimia, who understand its social context and who are dealing with the problem successfully" (Lobovits & Epston, 2007) (p. 225).

I share the delight expressed by Lobovits and his colleagues of no longer considering myself to be the sole source of support and knowledge, but rather reveling in the privilege to witness, interact with, and learn from students' journeys as adult learners. "According to an African proverb, it takes a village to raise a child. Similarly, it may take an audience to solve a problem. A community of those who have experience with a problem will contain just what is needed. So let us sow the seeds of belonging with stories of pain and hope and harvest liberation" (p. 255).

Protecting Confidentiality

The "ethic of circulation" that characterizes narrative practice challenges our traditional assumptions about the need for absolute privacy in psychotherapy. In the words of Lobovits, Maisel, and Freeman (1995), "Ethical and effective psychotherapy is commonly thought to depend on a unique relationship that unfolds in a private and protected sphere." They propose an interesting thesis: "the need for privacy increases when people's experience of problems is viewed in terms of illness/pathology or other problem-saturated descriptions" (p. 224).

The ethic of circulation does not in any way exclude an ethic of confidentiality.[30] When working this way with families, the service provider thinks carefully about ways to link lives while protecting privacy. Circulation practices are always offered with the option to say no.

I feel deeply grateful to the people who give me permission to share their stories with students. Their generosity conveys a trust in me and my ethical stance. My code of ethics as a psychologist keeps me very sensitive to not being exploitative in any way. In addition, I carry a strong sense of responsibility to safeguard confidences and protect privacy. I continuously check in to align with what works best for the person with insider knowledge.

NICOLE

I chose a story about "Nicole" to illustrate the potency of public practices in teaching. Nicole is a young woman who in the course of our work together experienced six hospitalizations in her struggle to overcome anorexia, self-harm, and depression. Nicole has generously allowed me to share aspects of her story in my teaching, including journal entries, poems and letters. Throughout this chapter, I illustrate pubic practices in teaching with accounts of tellings and retellings of Nicole's story that rippled into students' lives, connecting their own stories with hers.

Each time I present aspects of Nicole's story, supplemented by her writing, I ask her for permission. In preparation for a workshop in New Zealand, Nicole responded, "I am absolutely fine with you sharing my story. There isn't anything in particular I would, or wouldn't, want you to share...just the truth as you see it, I suppose." A few months later, when I asked again for permission to share, Nicole had begun speaking publicly about her story to help others understand some of the challenges she has encountered. She volunteered to come into my class as a guest visitor, presenting her writing – an unforgettable experience for us all, which I further describe in Chapter Ten. I subsequently asked Nicole, who is a talented writer, if she would like to work with me to include some of her story in this book. She responded, "I would be honored to work on the writing with you. Continuing to write will give me something to hold on to."[31]

This retelling relies on her generosity in giving permission to intimately share her story with others. I include here several transcribed excerpts from the in-class interview as well as pieces I have read aloud in class. Here is how Nicole introduced herself to students:

> *In the spring of my senior year of college, I started to feel bad. It wasn't really the first time; it was always kind of there. I just pushed it away with academics and that kind of thing. But it started to get to the point where it was affecting my work. I was having a lot of eating issues – restricting...also a sort of binging and purging. Right after I graduated I went to Romania to volunteer for the summer. I was okay at first, and then...I don't know how to describe it. I felt a sense of futility. I was working with children, orphans with AIDS who had nothing to eat and were cold. It was so incredibly overwhelming. I remember one night when I really thought that I would just kill myself and it would all be over. From then on, things just seemed to get worse. I started cutting that year...it wasn't really too bad, it was no big deal and it was actually a great sense of release. Then I started...it became this thing that grew on its own sort of inertia. It got to the point where I needed stitches.*

By the following summer, self-harm had begun to threaten Nicole's life. Over the next year, she had several in-patient hospital experiences for bodily harm, anorexia, and depression. In this journal entry, she looks back on the history of her struggle with self-harm:

> *It's raining. I've turned the music off so I can listen to the thunder. Looking down at the scars on my arm as I type, I wonder whether or not I should*

cover them with long sleeves. How does the shame of hiding compare to the shame of exposure? Why, not at all. If you could have seen the look on the check-out woman's face today as she handed me my change, not really sure if she was seeing what she thought she was seeing, you would know what I mean. Perhaps one of her friends has done it, perhaps she has toyed with the idea a time or two, or maybe she's just wondering how to make it home without stopping at the liquor store. Maybe she's just repulsed. Regardless, my cheeks redden from a smoldering voice telling me I should have known better than to wear short sleeves in public. I should have used the other hand to accept my change. You piece of shit, begging for attention again; my own voice betrays me.

If I hide, I have the shame of a secret. This shame occasionally pokes me in the side if I turn the wrong way; a dull ache I can soothe with my own reassurances. So why suffer? The answer is, I don't know. I only know that I'll die a little today if I pull a shade over my pain. Without air it will feed on itself and grow into something uglier, something devastating. Bringing pain visibly out into the world diminishes its power over us because it's suddenly in a context; it is no longer its only reality. I don't think anything will ever take the shame away. If I must feel this shame, I want it to be a testimony to my story; the story of how I cut to save my life for a day, how I starved to save my life for a little longer, and how I realized I must stop cutting and starving in order to save my life forever.

It's difficult to say where I am now. Three months ago I lay in a hospital bed wishing I were dead, furious at those around me who insisted on keeping me alive. I cursed myself for not taking enough of the meds I had taken a few days before to actually kill me. I went to bed at night praying to God, the Goddess, the Higher Power, whatever, that I would die in my sleep. Two months before that, I stood naked and freezing in a paper gown at five a.m. every morning for five weeks while a nurse weighed me and watched me pee. There were two times before that in Vermont hospitals and before that, a hospital in Chicago. And now, I'm in my apartment, sitting in front of the window watching the lightning, willing myself to live. Willing myself to live a little longer, just to see. Just to see if there's something else that makes my coexistence with depression worth enduring.

So many stand on the opposite shore beckoning, each battered by his own struggle. I have to believe they see a horizon that I cannot, and perhaps by reaching the shore I can offer my hands to those still in the water.

A few months prior, Nicole wrote the following after hearing that a dear friend had overdosed:

Something has shifted inside me, and more than ever, I feel the sensation of "no going back." I do not feel a forward impulse, however, I just know there's no going back to where I came from.

Shelly overdosed. She got too tired. Abandoned AGAIN. I pray to all the spirits of this world that this will be the last time for her. She won't survive it again. And I won't blame her when she decides it's time to rest. There is a certain kind of fury I feel now toward those who have persecuted her... My dearest friend in the hospital because of someone's horrible manipulation of her, and the story of that manipulation seems too unbelievable. That just couldn't have happened. But it DID happen. This world is capable of making it happen; so why shouldn't I believe my stories? Even if there is a component of these stories that is constructed, that's my experience. Peggy asked me what it would be like to forgive myself for being human. What would it be like to be allowed to have my experience, my terror, my stories? Can I have my stories and all the ones I can't remember?

It did happen, and Shelly almost died. Just as much as I believe people are capable of good, I believe them equally capable of evil, so why shouldn't I believe my stories?

I even feel guilty just for writing these words, but I'm trying to secure whatever has shifted inside me so I can live in peace and the embrace of my chosen family. I have to believe something, or I'm going to die; and death is an indulgence I believe myself capable of falling for. And even the curiosity of whether or not I'm capable of such a thing pushes me toward exploring it.

To live in postured confidence, within a whole, peaceful when I shut my eyes, bedded down in the security of my chosen family, LIVING MINDFULLY AND GENTLY; that's what I wish for. I wish to live mindfully and gently, please don't forget, mindfully and gently, mindfully and gently, mindfully and gently, mindfully and gently.

To Be of Service

Throughout her young adult life, Nicole has aspired to be of service to others through her work and friendships[32]. Witnessing children's desperation in Romania re-stimulated her own childhood experiences of trauma. I share with students the following journal entry that Nicole wrote in response to my question, "What are you learning about how to balance this desire to be there for others with taking-care-of-yourself skills? I think what you have to say here could really be of value, not only to yourself, but to others." Here, Nicole shares what feels good to her about using her experience to help others.

Nicole responded:

My desire to care for others came partly from a deep self-hatred. Though lacking any sense of self-preservation, I still retained the desire to love and be loved. Since it was, and often still is, my perception that I could never be lovable, what I had left was the option to give love. And no one could deprive me of that; except depression, and those were some of my darkest moments.

Living as the "hated" within my own body, betraying my own self as vile and revolting, the only way I could survive was to honor the humanity in others. It was a way of giving thanks for what I knew must be extraordinary and beautiful about creation, about nature, about the capacity for life; life with a big "L." Not just eating, breathing, and sleeping, but the potential for **experience.**

Selfish? Yes, though I doubt anyone can truly say that he does not thrive a little on the intrinsic satisfaction of sustaining his brother or sister. And why shouldn't he? Why shouldn't he be allowed to love himself? Won't his connection with others be richer, more meaningful if he understands the value of the self?

And I love people. With that comes the desire to alleviate their suffering, but more importantly to bear witness to their experiences. For now, I keep myself alive because to think of leaving people who I've met and have yet to meet alone in their suffering is almost too painful. At the very least I can say, "I see you, I honor your struggle, and in recognizing and loving your humanity, I honor myself; as part of you, as part of the greater community, as worthy."

I asked Nicole for any suggestions for practitioners working in different settings with people who are suicidal and dealing with life-threatening situations, such as self-harm and anorexia. She responded:

What's helpful for me is when I have a doctor or counselor who...doesn't immediately jump to ask, "Where are the razors? We have to get rid of them right now;" or "You have to eat right now." Or "We have to get you somewhere before you hurt yourself or kill yourself." I want to work with people who don't try to remedy the situation immediately with whatever they think will work. I always appreciate someone who sits with me and recognizes my pain and my experience in that moment and who acknowledges that it's my experience. I always am frustrated when someone I'm around starts pathologizing everything that comes out of my mouth. So if I say something that has a lot of meaning for me and someone says, "Oh that's just because you're depressed right now; you won't feel this later," I can't stand that because this is me – my experience – and this is how I feel. When someone says something like that, it devalues what you're going through at the moment. It just makes me more frustrated. My friends sort of still see me in my sick place. I have told them, if I say I don't want to do something, I really appreciate being recognized for my preferences rather than as acting through depression.

Circulating Nicole's Story

With Nicole's permission, I have shared a shortened version of some of what I have learned in our work together in classrooms and workshops in places as varied as Vermont, New Zealand[33], Cuba[34], and Boston[35]. I tell students and workshop participants stories of Nicole's struggles to overcome urges to anorexia/bulimia, self-harm and suicide, how she has responded to her challenges, what is working for her now, and what continues to trouble her. I read aloud some of her compelling journal entries and poems. Becoming witnesses to Nicole's life deeply moves people to link their lives to hers across wide distances of geography, language, work, and life experiences. People have written letters and posted online reflections in response to listening intently to these accounts. Each time, I bring back to Nicole evidence of a growing community of support. One participant sang her a song that I recorded on my digital camera. Hearing letters, online postings and video recordings, Nicole cannot deny the impact of her story on others.

Letters to Nicole

After telling the class this account of the current challenges that Nicole faces, I invited the students to write her letters. With only about 20 minutes of writing time, students wrote articulate and well-crafted letters, responsive to Nicole, sharing their own resonance with her story. I only wish I could include all eighteen of the original letters here.

I sealed each letter in its own envelope and wrote Nicole's name on the front. I showed her a class photo and gave her the stack of letters in the hope that she could add these letters to her growing stash of things to draw from when she finds herself alone fighting self-hating urges.

Sandra's Letter

Dear Nicole,

First, I want to say thank you for allowing Peggy to share a bit of your story with our class. I felt I could relate to many of the beliefs Peggy told us you hold. For example:

– knowing what you're talking about is real
– it is okay to feel bad (especially in relation to your parents)
– you have decided on "no more secrets"
– you have a right to your own experience and healing
– things can be different for you in your home despite the memories contained there
– you want to bring people into your life
– you love your job
– you want to instill a sense of self-worth that will be long-lasting
– you want to not hate your body so much
– you recognize the value of one more day, one more hour
– your life and your healing stem from your choice to hold out continued hope for improvement/contentment.

Had I more time, I would try to help you understand how powerful your story was for me. As it is, I want you to at least know these things.

I found comfort in hearing that you have questioned reality as I, too, have often felt unclear about my memories of past abuse. Your story reminded me to honor the truth I know in my soul.

I have, and continue to, struggle with wanting something different, more affirming, in my relationships with my parents. Despite the pain and anxiety I felt in unlocking family secrets, and despite the guilt my family has attempted to instill in me for breaking the silence, I have now come out the other side and feel so much better about myself because I'm honoring my truth.

I feel/felt I have spent far too much of my life passively living for others. My decision to come to graduate school was my first major departure from that pattern. This was my choice, and as difficult as the journey has been at times, I feel that following my own path was the <u>scariest, but best, gift</u> I could offer myself. You are now part of that gift!

So, thank you, thank you, thank you. Keep striving to move through the next day and the next hour. I will be thinking of you as my journey also continues. Cheers, Sandra

Katy's Letter

Dear Nicole,

Thank you for allowing Peggy to share some of your story with us. Although we have never met, I feel as though I can sense who you are based on Peggy's words: a strong, brave, quiet presence. One image that resonated with me was the idea of you returning to a home that held some hard memories for you, but knowing you could transform it into a room of your own. I too had that feeling when I returned to live in a city that was filled with painful memories for me. I felt scared and worried I would not be able to find joy and create a life that I desired. Nicole, I was able to find happiness there. It took some time, and there were days I cried and thought to leave but I stayed on, creating a new, different experience for myself. I imagine you too can do this.

Soon I will graduate from this program at Smith and again decide on a new place to be. I will be asked again to create a room of my own, and like you, I will. Together we can each fill our space with community, friends, plants, books, walks, laughter, love. Perhaps we can think of one another on our journeys and help each other transform the scary unknown into a welcoming home. I will think of your brave spirit, learning to feel feelings good and bad and share them in your group and with your family. I will draw on your strengths, an inspiration to help me venture out again and create a new home. Thank you. Warmly, Katy

I asked Nicole to share with me what these letters meant to her and requested her permission to share her reply in subsequent classes and workshops. Nicole's response was a powerful testament to the impact of letter-writing on the recipient.

*Eighteen letters, soft with wear. Eighteen letters, always in my pocketbook. Eighteen letters, from people validating **an** experience they have only heard about through storytelling. My eighteen letters, my eighteen flickers of hope.*

I have eighteen letters I keep by my side at all times from people who don't know me. Wrapped tightly in a rubber band, they are tucked into my bag, my jacket, and their rectangular pressure against my side helps me take one more step forward, even if that literally means putting one foot in front of the other. I've even slept with them under my pillow. At times, it's the only way to fall asleep; by holding onto something of this world, something real, something of kindness and love. They create my silk thread that leads me back time and again to my chosen family, to a life that must be lived because there are others; others who have broken off small pieces of themselves and with those pieces, fortified a small glimmer of hope inside me.

Eighteen people wrote to me, some sharing their pain, some reflecting on the human condition, some offering their light, all of them giving me something so genuine I protect them as one would a velvet bag of diamonds. Rare, but there, and a great privilege to hold in my hands, they gently push me in the direction of life or at the very least, they whisper they'll go with me no matter the direction I choose. They are too genuine to destroy, and so they will follow me, always at my side.

I have eighteen letters that help keep me alive.

While Nicole thanked me for sharing her story, she could not see the power of her personal contribution to students.

I don't know if this is helpful...I couldn't quite remember what you needed, so I just wrote the first few paragraphs that came to me. Let me know if there is something else I can do to help, or if you need me to write something different.

I have shared Nicole's "18 Letters" reflection at subsequent teaching commitments. A New Zealand workshop participant wrote:

Tess's Letter

Dear Nicole,

Thank you for allowing Peggy to tell some of your story. It has touched my heart immensely. I hear your struggle loud and clear. I also hear your determination and will to live. I am in awe of your strength in remaining alive as I have struggled with depression and other demons in the past. I know that people can live in very dark places in this world sometimes.

I was touched hearing about the eighteen letters that are precious to you, and I noticed many people in the room were too...I wanted to connect with you in this special way too; it felt so therapeutic for me to hear about this sharing of hope and compassion amongst strangers.

When I think about it this way, "strangers" seems the wrong word. Perhaps when people link like this, they become allies and unknown friends instead? It gives room for thought.

That you have generously given me the experience of having heard your story means a lot to me. It speaks of your compassionate nature in caring for others, and it will influence the way I experience people in the work I do. I feel grateful that you care enough about people to extend this to me. And all the way over in New Zealand!!! Such a random connection, but so meaningful.

I am happy you have dreams of being a therapist. I had dreams of being a therapist too, even in my darkest depths of despair and sadness. I thought that if I could make a difference for one person the way my counsellor had done for me it would all be worth it. I now think, "Why stop at one!"

Nicole, I think as a therapist you would have a unique understanding of other women who might be facing the struggles you have faced, and are facing. And the reason I believe it is because I know I have things to offer those who have faced struggles similar to my own. There is nothing like being properly, really understood; people like you and me... have that gift to offer.

In the dark times, I used to tell myself that when it rained, no matter how hard, eventually the sun would come out again...I hope that the glimmer of hope you have from your eighteen letters, eighteen reasons to live, brightens into warm rays of sunshine that nourish your soul. I hope that today you will have nineteen reasons to live. I hope that others will get to benefit from your struggle and your wisdom and that it makes the world a lighter place for them. We really need people like you in this world.

I dearly wish this for you and send you lots of appreciation, hope, and sunshine today, and every day. Best wishes, Tess

Online Reflections

The course website provides space for students to reflect on the experience and the ripple effects in their own lives. I am often awed by how students use what might seem a very impersonal medium-electronic text-in such deeply personal and open expressions of their thoughts and lives.

Posting by Heidi

Oftentimes I go about my daily life suppressing my emotions just so that I can get through the day and then move on to the next. I was really inspired by Nicole's honesty. I felt as though she was speaking to my soul, just like when I have these dreams about my dad, who is now deceased, and he is reminding me to live every moment like it's my last. This interaction stirs up all my emotions to the point where my entire body aches with pain and I awaken with tears in my eyes. The pain is good to feel on occasion, as it reminds me that I'm real, and that this life is real. Yet, I still go back to a place of numbness, as the pain is simply too much for me to bear on a regular basis. Nicole's honesty about her experience gives me hope that I too can be honest with others about my experiences, that it is okay for others to witness my pain. Thanks to Nicole's sharing, I have realized that the more I conceal my thoughts and feelings the more harm I may be doing to others by perhaps suggesting that my life experiences have been easy to deal with. I do not want others to feel shameful of the thoughts and emotions that their experiences evoke, so I will challenge myself to be more open with others. Thank you Nicole.

Posting by Laura

I used to write a lot; that was my way of dealing with things. But at some point I started writing less and less and I started denying certain feelings even to myself. Recently I started writing again. Hearing Nicole's writings was particularly helpful to me because she showed me that it is okay to "be real" and that there is no reason to deny myself or call into question the legitimacy of what I am feeling. Even if no one else believes it, it is real for me.

Many students start their postings by expressing appreciation for their classmates, "to everyone so far who has shared so honestly and personally about how the experience of hearing Nicole's and Peggy's interview and the process of witnessing and reflecting this experience have effected them and transformed them." Over and over again, they share how moved they are, feeling challenged to put words to their experience. Laura expressed appreciation for being part of the live interview with Nicole and being part of the reflecting team. "While I was very nervous about participating, I am really glad that I had the opportunity to have this connection with Nicole and witness her story, which is helping me to come to terms with my own. I would like to thank everyone for being open and receptive in creating spaces like this, where I feel comfortable being open with all of you."

Finally, Kerry2 wondered if Nicole recognizes her own courage, stamina, and the impact she is having on the world. "I know she mentioned a few times that she feels she 'tricks' people, including a 'room full of students.' If I've been tricked, then I'm all the better for it. And I'll bet the people in her life, specifically her chosen family, feel the same way."

REFLECTIONS

These public teaching practices – interviewing someone in front of the class or sharing a video of a session and then writing letters and sharing reflections – go beyond an artificially constructed demonstration of narrative skills. In my view, genuine participation in an ethic of circulation provides a lived experience that extends much further than one-way accounts of therapy and in teaching. When I share students' letters with people who have shared their stories with them and students share their writing online with each other, the walls of isolation and privacy break down. This clears the way for lives to connect and influence each other, often well beyond the classroom. Furthermore, participating in the four-part narrative interview with Nicole gave us all a unique and powerful learning opportunity – as I further illustrate in the next chapter.

Postscript

Nicole has taken significant steps in taking her life back from depression, self-harm, and anorexia. Every step along the way has taken steadfast effort and leaps of faith. Sometimes it feels like two steps forward and then one step back. We take nothing for granted. For Nicole, the definition of family is ambiguous. Her therapeutic support team – that includes me as her primary therapist- is part of her "chosen family," which she defined here:

> *My family carefully watches me consider two fruits, one healthy and one poisonous, though I know not which is the better fruit. They teach me what they know about these choices and reassure me that my own thoughts on the matter are valuable. I grow frustrated with indecision. They say they cannot choose for me. They urge me forward, "go on" they say, "we're here."*

> *My family doesn't know how to speak the word 'failure' because such a thing doesn't exist; should I choose the poisonous fruit, I will each time thereafter know how to distinguish the benevolent juices from the belly ache of their brother's, and that, in and of itself, is a success.*

> *My family doesn't make me pay for my choice, but celebrates the right by giving it to me, almost as a gift, and finding beauty in the furrow of my brow as I decide what to do with it. My family doesn't punish my choice and promises only to use their fists to pick me up off the ground should I fall ill from the bad fruit. My family doesn't judge my choice, doesn't kick dirt in my eyes to shame their mistake. Rather, they praise the discretion of my heart for having instincts, for its lack of indifference, for doing the best it could with what it had.*

> *My family says, "let's drink to the beauty in all of us, give what there is to give, work for the rest, love recklessly, bless the body, and praise the gift of choice and all the diverse and wonderful manifestations of greatness it provides." This is my definition of family.*

Recently, Nicole reminded me of a question I asked her about the effects of depression's loosening its grip on her connections with the cherished people in her life. "What's it like for you now to give and receive love?" In the following excerpt, she responds to that question, having come to the conclusion that love is really what compelled her to put her trust in her recovery, chosen family, and therapeutic support team.

> *Giving and receiving love; I can hardly believe how much the acid of depression can dissolve one's ability to volley emotions. Now that I, with much help, have pried the fingers of depression from around my throat, I can*

allow the freshness of the air to revitalize me, to remind me what it is to feel, what it is to be alive in a world full of "alive" things. It's almost disorienting to be suddenly bombarded by the emotional inflections of the world.

Imagine the absence of feeling one must experience in order for her to drag a razorblade across her skin; she feels nothing, and because she feels nothing, she pushes harder and depression helps itself to her life force as it runs from her body, licking her wounds, demanding just a little more. And she gives it. She gives it because she feels nothing and can't remember what it's like to receive a kiss upon her cheek from warm lips, can't remember what it's like to have a friend caress the trouble from her brow, can't remember why it's worth it to fight for her own life. She feels nothing and therefore, believes there's no incentive for her to stay. There's no emotional currency bargaining for her life. And so it's easy, when depression complains of thirst, for her to tilt its head back and empty herself into its jaws. It is this numbness that is depression's greatest weapon. In my darkest hour I felt no one's love for me, and I had no love to give.

But now...now I feel depression loosening its grip, and the more fresh air I breathe in, the weaker it becomes. The more I feel, the more love I'm able to receive, the more I value my own life, and if I believe myself worth saving, depression will never win. When I feel someone's love now, I'm no longer scared, as I once was. I don't fear the consequences of that love (attachment, obligation, pleasure, and pain) because I don't have to dig a razor into my arm or starve myself to feel them anymore. They are finally guests at my table and they have come just as they are, in all their original splendor, mine to experience. And so it is, I'm able to receive love, the love that has saved my life.

I will close the chapter with one more reflection by Nicole, which she sent to me after reviewing this manuscript:

Peggy, thank you so much for sending me the chapters. What an interesting experience it is to read them now after some time has passed. Has all of this really happened? It's weird, as I was reading the chapters, I suddenly had this image of myself from a few years ago. I was sitting alone on the beach in a foreign country, freezing and starving. God, I was so hungry. All I could think about was my weight, and I remember wishing I could just enjoy the sea. But the tyranny was unbearable, it literally ruined every part of my day. So much has happened since then and I never ever want to go back to that. Our writing helped remind me that we have really been working toward something, haven't we?

THE POWER OF INTENTIONAL WITNESSING

Posting by Chappell

I had no idea how much it would affect me to be a witness to an interview. I was touched by many things I heard and saw in class, but even more surprising was the effect that the class continued to have on me for the rest of the day. After class I found myself really thinking about courage; I did (or said or was) three or four things tonight that I might not have done if I hadn't been a part of that experience and witnessed Mark's courage and the effect it had on him. I don't just mean the courage it took to be vulnerable during the interview (which was no small thing) but also the courage involved in each of the acts of self definition that Peggy asked about and that he spoke about during the interview. I was literally and directly inspired!

Typically in North American society, testimony occurs in courtroom, religious, or political contexts in which a community bears witness to hear accounts of spoken truth. I consider interviews with witnessing practices are within the tradition of giving testimony (Weine, 2006). Experiencing witnessing practices within a classroom context can be similarly powerful for participants. In this chapter, I situate outsider witness practices as a particular approach to reflecting teamwork based on the definitional ceremony metaphor in narrative practice (Myerhoff, 1986; White, 1995b).

Narrative reflecting teamwork is like a conversation within a conversation or an interview within an interview. Reflections are in response to specific accounts that resonate with audience members, often transporting them "to become other than who they were on account of witnessing these expressions and responding to these stories in the ways that they do" (White, 2003b).

As outsider witnesses, students learn to situate their comments in their own contexts, linking their reflections to their own experiences of living. Simultaneously I give exercises for students to practice "decentering" their comments, always bringing the focus back to person(s) at the center of the original interview. Michael White offers specific instructions to create a structured forum for outsider witness practices according to four categories of inquiry (White, 2007b):

– What *expression* did you hear that most impressed you?
– What *image* did this expression evoke in you?
– What kind of *resonance* was set off between this image and your own experience?

- In what way were you *transported* or moved to a different place by what you heard?

In this chapter, I share students' reflections in two situations where they experience firsthand the power of a four-part narrative interview. These include 1) their classmate Mohammad exploring events and realizations contributing to his commitments as social worker; and 2) Nicole, whom I introduced in Chapter Nine, in her recovery from anorexia, self-harm and depression. I converse online with students about some of the challenges to incorporating outsider witness practices in their work settings. Together, we contemplate Celia's question: "How do we respond authentically from our own experience with enough detail to be helpful and real toward the person without going too autobiographical?" Throughout, I show how online forums give students opportunities to candidly reflect, inquire, and build community. The chapter concludes with reflections by Mohammad and Nicole on their experience being at the center of a four-part narrative interview within a classroom setting.

REFLECTING TEAMWORK

Before learning Michael White's guidelines for these retellings, I want students to know something about the history of reflecting teamwork. Outsider witness practices are a unique development in the history of reflecting teamwork as reflexive practices within family therapy (Andersen, 1991; Friedman, 1995; Lax, 1995; Lussardi & Miller, 1990). These narrative witnessing practices are structured by a specific four-part tradition of acknowledgement that provides the foundation for retellings (White, 2004d).

I think of reflecting teamwork as akin to bringing a Greek chorus into a modern-day context. In the ancient Greek tradition, the chorus gave background commentary to help the audience follow the performance. Through song and speech, the playwright choreographed the Greek chorus to accent particular ideas, perspectives, and themes in a tragic play. While they share similar roles, rather than focusing on tragedy, the "reflecting team chorus" reflects on and inquires into human experiences according to specific intentional witnessing practices. Each interview aims to create possibilities for new discoveries – acknowledging developments, making room for complexities, and resolving impasses.

The idea that a team could provide consultation to the therapist in a therapy session began with the Milan School of Family Therapy, when a group of therapists sat behind a one-way mirror watching an interview, and phoned in their suggestions to the therapist. A number of students have shared stories with me about their internships in agencies that still use a Milan-based reflecting team.

Other agencies use Tom Andersen's format – having the team switch places with the family, with the family then observing the team discussing the interview. Andersen's approach makes it possible for clients to hear conversation that traditionally occurs "behind closed doors." It also separates the listening and talking positions, giving a kind of freedom of choice. The witnessing group listens carefully to the stories told, and then the positions are switched so the persons whose lives are at the center of the interview form an audience to the reflecting team sharing what they heard according to particular reflecting guidelines. After the reflections, the roles are again switched so that the persons in the original interview have the opportunity to reflect on what they heard.

Having first learned reflecting teamwork from Tom Andersen, I still refer back to his respectful guidelines that emphasize:

- Positive or logical connotations, rather than negative attributions or blaming;
- Ideas presented tentatively with qualifiers such as "I was wondering," "perhaps," "possibly," or "it's just an idea;"
- Ideas often presented as stories or metaphors;
- No correct interpretation, so that many ideas can be presented, and the client can choose whatever fits or doesn't fit.

STUDENT INTERVIEW

With sufficient preparation, I believe the classroom can offer an ideal setting for students to practice the power of intentional witnessing. In class, I structure an opportunity for students to play various roles in a four-part narrative interview. As I describe in Chapter Seven, "Stories of Identity," the interview explores turning points in one student's career as a practitioner, the unique realizations that have emerged over time, and the subsequent effects of these understandings on the direction of his or her work. Students practice narrative interviewing from the role of interviewee and/or outsider witness.

Through this interview, students begin to learn how to use the Landscape of Action and Landscape of Identity within the reauthoring conversations map. Afterwards, they are ready to try out the reauthoring conversations map on themselves through the course assignment described in the previous chapter, "Stories of Identity," in which students trace a brief history of their commitment to helping others.

I have chosen Mohammad's interview to illustrate the potency of this experience. Before interviewing Mohammad, I instructed the class about White's four-part format for narrative interviews with outsider witness practices, as follows:

- I interview a volunteer about his or her stories of identity as a practitioner – present, past and future – that draws from turning point events as well as beliefs, personal values, and commitments.
- Acting as outsider witnesses, several volunteer classmates share their responses to what they heard in the interview. These responses are guided by White's four categories of response, as previously described.
- The original interviewee is interviewed about which of the outsider witness reflections stood out for him or her and why.
- The remaining classmates become witnesses to the entire interview. The entire group then shares its experience of this process, discussing which understandings became more richly developed and what kinds of steps or actions these understandings might inspire.

In addition, I start an online forum where students share further reflections on the outsider witness experience. Sharing reflections online is particularly helpful, as there is never enough time to fully debrief the experience in class. For one class, I introduced the forum as follows:

> Rather than going back into the actual content of the interview, the fourth part of the narrative interview is a time to inquire into each other's experiences. Feel *free to ask the interviewer (me) questions like, "Why did you choose those* particular questions?"* "Were there others you might have also asked?"

> To the outsider witnesses: "What was it like to be on the reflecting team and what did you learn from this experience?"

> To the class witnesses: "What was it like to witness this interview and what are any of your lingering questions/reflections?"

> And of course, the interviewee should get the last word: "What was it like to engage in this interview and what do you hope will stay with you?"

> "What have I forgotten to ask that you would like to say?"

"The Coming Out from Underground!"

In his interview, Mohammad publicly shared details of his life for the first time. A few days later, he reflected online on his experience:

> *I had not spoken openly about having been an illegal alien for those 20 years of my life, at least not to such a large audience. Much torment, intense fear, anxiety, and vulnerability were associated with the experience. Though it did put me in touch with my strength, the ability to master a craft, the opportunity to find out that I could use my hands to create well – made functional structures, it also put me in touch with my pain, both physical and emotional. In becoming familiar with my pain, however, I began to recognize and appreciate the pain in others.*

> *I have not spoken much about that experience because of the shame about it. It took much energy to tend to the need to hide it, the need to become invisible by not standing out, deflecting the suspicion somehow, and the question of "why an educated laborer?" Being an imposter, a feeling I had known from childhood, having to maintain a facade of worthiness, deserving of the pedestal I had been put on despite my feelings of unworthiness, caused a rift in my whole being. I felt responsible for creating a convoluted, no exit, bureaucratic legal trap for myself that affected every aspect of my life and the lives of many who were close to me. It inhibited me from doing much of what I had passion for and stopped me from speaking openly about what mattered to me... That the detour is behind me is a most welcome and liberating experience.*

> *It was not long ago, however, while at my internship, that a question about this experience became real for me. I had told my supervisor about my*

experience early on. She later assigned me the care of a foreign born patient who did not have proper documents. We discussed how close to my heart my patient's predicament was, and I described to her the feeling of shame I had. A lesbian, she had known that feeling too. "Society has its way of keeping us down through shame," she said. Her words for the first time helped me see it was not just me who felt that way. I was not the only source, the only cause for the feeling inside me; there were external sources and purposes for the shame I felt. In speaking to you now, I am putting the shame further outside and behind me. I am coming out from underground, letting the light of the day shine on my back, as I turn to face the Sun. I am, as you are, a piece of the Sun, walking on this Earth, it too a piece of the Sun, alive and conscious as we are.

Several students reflected on the impact of being outsider witnesses to Mohammad's story. They shared acknowledgements and posed questions. Over and over again, they described feeling touched by his story and honored to witness his "coming out." Melissa left class thinking about how close she felt to Mohammad.

Posting by Melissa

I felt like I got to know a part of him that not many people know. I questioned if Mohammad could feel the connection he made to those around him even when words were not exchanged. So I was struck when Mohammad stated his appreciation to those listening to his story for "holding" him. Because I felt myself listening and holding on to his words and his story and all of the meaning that he made out of it. Thank you.

Posting by Mohammad

I too will remember this event perhaps as long as I live. My heartfelt gratitude to the reflecting team for their meaningful reflections, the connections they helped me make, to the rest of the class for pulling around me to listen, for holding me, and to you Peggy for your genuine caring presence and curiosity. I felt like you really wanted to know. The experience of sitting amidst all of you, some of you whom I don't even know by name, and having a conversation about my life, so intimate, was exhilarating. It felt as if I was talking with a friend I have known forever; who I had shared moments, stories, and breath with. I wanted to say more, not so much about the events of my life, but how I have made meaning out of them so I could hear also how it is that you make meaning out of all that goes on in you. The human event is what I want to know, hear and talk about. The possibilities are endless, and perhaps only a few can be explored in the domain of language and time. Perhaps much will always remain unsaid... I feel as though I made such a leap out of a conversation witnessed by all of you. It could not have happened without you witnessing silently. Thank you for pulling my name out of your hat and indulging me.

WITNESSING NICOLE

I was moved when Nicole requested to come to my class as a guest visitor, to share her story with students in person. In preparation for the class, I instructed her about a four-part narrative interview with outsider witness practices. She agreed to videotape this interview, which turned out to be one of my most memorable teaching experiences.

Here I offer a transcribed excerpt of Part 2 of Nicole's in-class interview, where the outsider witnesses reflect on the interview they have just heard. Four students were on this narrative reflecting team: Jane, Ginger, Laura, and Andrew. I chose this excerpt because it demonstrates the skillfulness with which students learn to reflect on and inquire into each others' experiences. Jane set a personal tone, candidly linking her life with Nicole's. Ginger's question helps Jane give a more robust description of the impact on her own life of hearing Nicole's story. Their ensuing conversation illustrates personal sharing from a decentered position – striking a balance between speaking candidly while always bringing the conversation back to Nicole, the person at the center of the interview.

Jane: *I came in this classroom today as a social work student and to be on the listening team. I didn't know what the interview was going to be about but once Nicole started talking, I...felt like I was coming as a student but also...I guess I could say ally to Nicole...What Nicole did for me is beyond me being just a social worker. I have this bracelet on, it's from the Anti-Anorexia/Bulimia League and it says "No Surrender." The women who made these bracelets said they weren't going to surrender to the voice of anorexia that wanted them dead... If they were to die, everyone would know they were against anorexia and that would go with them. My therapist gave this to me when I had problems with anorexia for years, and I almost died.*

I've been so confused in social work school wondering where the meaning in this is. Nicole brought it back for me today when she said, "I just want a counselor who doesn't pathologize me as though everything that comes out of my mouth is from my illness." I remember people doing this to me all the time. I share that so much with her but in this intellectual banter craziness of school and all this competition, she brought it back for me today...I thank her so much because I felt really, really lost and it's beautiful.

Ginger: *Do you want to talk a little bit more about how through hearing Nicole's story you've regained your sense of where you stand right now?*

Jane: *When Nicole talked about her depression, suicide, and cutting, she said she sometimes feels like "I am making it up and I don't believe my own experience." And after she saw her friend Shelly after Shelly had overdosed and nearly died, she said she started believing her own experiences. I think...anorexia still does that to me. Nicole also said, "I can't trust my own voice – maybe I'm just trying to manipulate people." When she said that it makes me think about how that voice talks to me like that and I realize that's not me. When she saw Shelly it helped her believe her own stories and when I hear Nicole talk about it, I feel like I can believe in myself and my stories and that what comes up for me is true.*

Ginger: *I don't know where to begin. I feel like Nicole really was able to verbalize things I've been feeling for so many years. One thing was being recognized for my preferences – that I'm not acting through my depression by deciding to stay in for a night, not staying up late – having it be okay to just be with myself right now. I've never been able to really grasp that idea for myself and that held a lot of meaning for me.*

Jane: *How do you know when you're home and you want to stay in the house for Ginger? How do you know it's yourself that wants to stay in?*

Ginger: *Sometimes I look back on all the times when I've made decisions for myself against everybody else's judgments or interpretations...wanting to believe what they were saying..., but also knowing that something, even if I couldn't verbalize it, was strong within me. To just hear it being said with such clarity and confidence, that really gives me a lot of strength. Nicole said so many things so beautifully, I feel stronger because of it.*

Laura: *Nicole talked about how she really felt good when she could use her experience to help others. She talked about how even in the very darkest place of hating herself she still had the capacity to love others; that was her way of surviving. I really connected with that. I feel like my love for others is what really brings me into this work. It was clear that this is what carried her through her experience even though all these really tough things are happening and she's being confronted with the self-hate.*

Andrew: *I'll continue with that theme. My initial reaction before Nicole even started to talk was to wonder, "What would it be like to be driving up here knowing you were going to sit in a classroom full of social work students? I can't imagine. Sometimes it's nerve-wracking enough when you're starting a new course with people you already know. As I listened to Nicole talk and to some of the things Peggy read that she wrote so eloquently, I thought "That's why she has the ability to write." I wrote down quotes about what Nicole loves. "I love people," "staying connected with my chosen family," "when I can use my experience to help others, to extend a hand to those still in the water."*

Jane: *I remember times when I would go with Melissa, my therapist, to talk in front of people and it became so important to me to speak out about anorexia. I had to battle it so much to come anywhere; it became so important to me - I became so committed to killing this problem - it didn't matter whether the anorexia wanted me not to come...I wondered what was so important for Nicole that she came here today and talked about things that were really important for her, like living mindfully and gently. I wonder if being here today is in service of those kind of commitments...I just wonder about that. What did it take for her to be here and sit there not knowing any of us?*

Ginger: *Nicole decided to retry going abroad to Nepal to be in the service of others again after such a harrowing experience in Romania. That reminds me of what she said about no going back; there's no sense really of what the future is going to be or that you're definitely moving forward; there just is no going back, not knowing exactly what that is. I wrote down her words, "I'm trying to embrace what has shifted inside of me." I'm just trying to be present with that, it's profoundly courageous.*

Jane: *Is there something that strikes you about "No going back to things in your life you feel like there's no going back to?" What struck you about that?*

Ginger: *It's a philosophy that I embrace too. I've experienced depression. At some times, it's closer to me than others – but it is always there. The nature of it changes every time it comes to me. I recognize that physical response like the flu Nicole was talking about, not knowing what to do beyond the comfort of knowing there is some relief. Also just being able to sort of talk about it with myself too. It's not going to be how it was last year or last month. It's not going back; I'm not sure what it's going to be next time.*

After hearing these reflections, I interviewed Nicole about what she heard that resonated with her – images evoked, new realizations, and deepened understandings. Hearing others reflect how her experience affected them reaffirmed for her that she was not alone. "You know, you're laying on the bathroom floor because you've just made yourself sick from eating or from hurting yourself, you're not really all alone. It just dissolves that idea that no one's ever going to understand." She further described how she experiences the link with others.

Peggy: *So you feel like by sharing their experiences that they understand? That your lives are linked in some way? What's your sense of what that link is?*

Nicole: *For me it's a refusal to sort of live a life in a way that's fake or falsely okay and in doing that I'm stronger for it and there's company in that.*

Peggy: *You refuse to live a fake life and feel connected to others around you who also have struggles.*

Nicole: *The big part of depression is refusing to say "I won't get up and go to work and pretend that it's all okay. I just won't do it."*

Peggy: *Something that pops in my mind, Nicole, was something someone from New Zealand said after hearing our interview on tape. Do you remember what the man John said about you hanging by a thread and your needing to thicken the thread? Do you think – and in what ways do you think – this sense of feeling connected to others, might be something that helps to thicken that thread?*

Nicole: *Definitely. In my hearing how it helps bring perspective and how it helps people through the same struggles, I feel like I owe it to these other people who are going through the same thing to fight a little bit harder because they are.*

Peggy: *Like wearing the bracelet?*

Nicole: *Yeah.*

I asked Nicole what it was like for her to hear the students' responses to her writing.

Nicole: *Well I think for me, writing is just the only thing I can do to...it's like I can create a witness when I don't feel like I have one. I can say, "Okay, this thing that I've written down has seen what it's like....it's funny in hearing this stuff I don't remember writing it. It's like my way of saying I won't let depression put me through that and then make me forget.*

Peggy: *Are you standing up to depression with your voice and by having your life linked with other people?*

Nicole: *Right, it's like...I'm reading this play right now for class and one of the images in it, they're talking about the hole in the ozone layer. They talk about these souls coming together and linking arms to create this net that rises up and covers the hole. It's a really beautiful image for me and the way it's played on the stage.*

Nicole chose to stay for the fourth part of the interview. Together with the students, we formed a circle for reflection. We stepped back from the content of the interview to debrief the experience. It was not a time to ask Nicole questions. Rather, I invited students to ask me, the interviewer, any questions about why I chose the questions I did, and to ask questions of the reflecting team such as what was that like to speak so personally. While students shared some observations and questions, there was a noticeable stillness in the room. It was evident that we had shared a powerful experience, which would take some time to digest. Fortunately, the online forums offered the invaluable opportunity for students to share further reflections after we'd left the classroom.

REFLECTIONS ON OUTSIDER WITNESS PRACTICES

Through their reading and in class, students learn about various ways to incorporate outsider witness practices and the four categories of response into narrative practice. After an in-class interview, I post the following questions:

What are some outsider witness skills that you would like to further develop? How can you envision creative ways to link people's lives with shared themes in your specific work context? What kinds of possibilities are you thinking about? Are there areas of excitement for you? Are there also dilemmas on your mind, and if so, how do you envision addressing these?

Sometimes a student readily steps into the position of asking questions to other members of the outsider witness team. Luke appreciated how his classmate Kerry's questions helped him find his words. "I had something to say and I knew what I was leading to, but for some reason I couldn't get there on my own. Thank you for taking the step to ask, Kerry. I believe you then gave me the confidence to ask you why as well."

While there is no "right way," students notice reflections that seem to deepen or thicken the richness of the account. Melissa described finding it difficult to bring in both resonance and transport: "I'm not sure if this is due to a discomfort of sharing, thinking too much of the steps we had just learned, lack of words to adequately describe, or worrying about what my classmate needed from the reflecting team. I know there is no right way and kept that in mind during reflecting but still couldn't quite shake it."

Students ask me about my experience with outsider witness teams in a North American context. I respond:

I have thought a lot about possibilities of bringing in known and unknown audiences. In counseling, it is easier to invite known audiences – family and friends – since this is something that is of course only done in collaboration with the person whose story will be witnessed. I am also very careful in a teaching context when some people I work with are willing to have a class full of strangers as outsider witnesses to the live interview I conduct in class. Here in the USA we have to be particularly careful about ensuring confidentiality and safeguarding against exploitation and dual relationships. As a result, I tend to bring in "insider knowledges" and "experience consultants," a newly coined term in the narrative literature (Walnum, 2007), via letters, video and audio clips[36].

In Katie's post, she asked when reflecting teams are called in and whether they are standard practice. I weave in my own voice from an influential yet decentered position, posting from my own experience as a practitioner:

You asked about ways in which narrative practice is currently being used, whether there are narrative groups in agencies, how often reflecting teams are called in and whether that is standard practice. I'll start with your last question first. Reflecting teams are only one way to incorporate outsider witness practices into therapeutic contexts. When I left community mental health 15 years ago, I left behind a wonderful family team (which did not continue). In independent practice, I have discovered my own creativity in seeking contexts to support a reflective stance in therapy – for example, some years back, I realized that without a team, I could even reflect out loud to the Aboriginal picture on the wall or the stuffed toys on my couch. I have gotten excited about practices that embrace an ethic of circulation such as using therapeutic documents and other ways to link the lives of people with shared themes. It's only recently that I've been able to create a community consultation team with additional opportunities in my office for four part narrative interviews with outsider witness practices. Indeed, there are many other options. You have to get creative.

Sometimes I bring along a video camera so students can get additional experience. Often, it takes some time for students to get comfortable with being recorded. The online forum offers space for students to ask questions of each other. For example, Amanda posted her question after participating in a full-class interview with her classmate, Kelly.

Posting by Amanda

This question is somewhat aimed at Kelly, but not necessary for Kelly to answer if she opts not to respond. I wonder if and how you felt that your answers and your part of the exchange with Peggy this afternoon had to do with having an audience of over-attentive and interested peers, the video camera in the room, and/or perhaps your relationship with Peggy having some degree of power to it...I could see my own behavior shift slightly, even in my observer role. How do other people feel about this? Do you feel like your behavior and participation might vary in an outsider witness practice scenario?

Kelly responded candidly:

Posting by Kelly

Amanda, at first I felt slightly uncomfortable, but after 15 minutes I completely forgot about the other people in the room. I actually experienced a weird zen-like moment while Peggy was interviewing me. I did, however, have a minor bout of the insecurities when it was time to listen in on the outsider witnesses. I thought to myself, "Oh God, why did I let that all out about myself"? I'm not sure my story would have come out any differently had it been just me and Peggy in the room. I think the moment I forgot everyone else was there was the moment I really got interested in my own story; or maybe it was the way Peggy got really interested in my story. It was probably a little bit of both. I do know that when I left that room I felt really good about myself. There is something to finding the absent but implicit in our own lives. It was refreshing.

Going Autobiographical

When students hear Michael White's caution about "going autobiographical" in an outsider witness context, they post interesting online reflections. Celia describes experiencing worry as she reflected on her response to what touched and transported her as a witness to a recorded interview.

Posting by Celia

I felt quite transported during that conversation. It made me think about some new steps I might take in my own life and a lot about the abuses of power I suffered in graduate school and what more I might choose to do with that story in this stage of my process around it. But I had recently read Michael's thing about "going autobiographical" and felt worried about that. I was worried that if I shared too many details of my own story or what I might be thinking of doing next that would be "autobiographical" and yet I have heard Peggy and the class in general saying how they feel being willing to share personal details makes the outsider witness practice more powerful and meaningful for the individual at the focus of the session. Does anyone have feedback on this?

Celia remembered from her reading (White, 2007c) that White recommended "sticking to quotes from the individual a lot and sharing about what particularly that they shared brought up an image, a new idea or a transformation internally." However, she still contemplated how to respond authentically from her own experience without going too autobiographical. This query arose partially from Celia's prior experience in 12-step programs in her younger years "where people were often very good at listening closely and respectfully to people and then sharing how what they heard touched their own lives and process." The 12-step format discourages "cross-talking" that occurs when people focus on others without dealing with their own issues; instead people are instructed to only briefly mention another person's comments before moving quickly to how it connects to one's own life. Celia expressed confusion about what is different in narrative practice. "I know I'm not supposed to move so quickly onto myself in this practice, but to hold the gaze more on the other. So I've been trying to do that. But then I wonder if I am getting personal or revealing enough. Does that make sense to anyone?"

Ginger responded by saying she too was contemplating these ideas.

Posting by Ginger

I was just thinking about why it can be that "going autobiographical" can take away from the experience or diminish the meaning making that a person is trying to express in his or her own story. I almost think that when we talk about what to do and what not to do, it creates a tension. Each person has a unique set of experiences and preferences and preferred ways of re-membering stories. It seems a bit stifling to ward against "going autobiographical" since to share, one must talk about oneself, and that is in itself autobiographical, I think. But, in reading some of the dialogues in

White's book when he talks about going autobiographical, I can to some extent decipher what he means...In some ways, outsider witnesses may be transported to a place of unfamiliarity, perhaps remembering an experience that was never before acknowledged, and the re-telling, or the conceptualization of the thoughts evoked therein might be quite raw, and because it is personal, difficult to keep from exploring in an autobiographical way. But it seems like that can go in a direction that takes the focus away from the person being interviewed. When thinking about reflecting, even though the outsider witnesses are sharing their own experiences, reflecting seems to keep the interviewee very present so that their meaning making in reflecting on reflections can somehow add another dimension. Going autobiographical seems to steer away from the meaning of the story of the interviewee to the plot line of the outsider witness, which may or may not be applicable when linking stories and making those connections. But it is a fine line, and I don't have it figured out.

The "Fifth Part" of the Narrative Interview

Whenever possible, I ask the person(s) at the center of the interview about their experience. Sometimes these reflections take time to percolate beyond the scope of immediate debriefing during the fourth part of the narrative interview.

Mohammad's Review

In reviewing this manuscript, Mohammad reflected again on his interview. The interview began by my asking him about a recent experience when he experienced himself as acting in preferred ways of being of service with someone – a client, friend or family member. Mohammad told a story about how as an intern at a treatment center he took a sunset walk with a teenage boy, as an ending to their work together:

Every time I think of that day I think of the sun. I remember the setting sun in my client's room, blazing orange behind him, making it difficult to see him as we said goodbye for the last time. I had wanted to hug him but, his being a teenage boy, he had too many fears and doubts about who he was and the hug would have suited my ending not his. I walked away feeling as I have often, that something was left unsaid.

I was pleased when someone in the reflecting team resonated with the imagery of the setting sun and spoke of it. From where I was sitting it almost felt like the room was filled with light that day. I could almost see the shades of light when the reflecting team was sitting in the back ground and then when they were being interviewed by you the spotlight was on them and they were lit up.

What was different about that moment as I sat in front of you was that you smiled and seemed to be genuinely interested in me and what I had to say at that moment in time and nothing else was of any consequence. I remember how a number of students sat on the floor around me so to hear me better. Their curiosity, their genuine attention was what was holding me, inviting me to explore with them, for them, for me, a new vision of my story. A new version that was not laced with shame, one that did not apologize for having placed myself in harm's way, rendering me unable for all those years to pursue my dreams. I trusted them to the point of not necessarily caring that they were there, almost letting them fade in the background and just focusing on my conversation with you as if I was sharing a breath, words, with my kin.

That morning I felt that I could have shared any dark, unspeakable secret with you, and you would have just beamed back your intense loving gaze with a contagious smile without judgment and reflected back to me the view of it that was shining. The shame was not there because it was not going to be reflected back by you. With all that present somehow we, the entire class, became ready to take a leap, a leap toward the sun.

Transcript of Conversation with Nicole

A few days after the in-class interview, I met with Nicole. I asked her about her experience with the reflecting team format – an experience she had never had before. I brought a transcript of this conversation to class the following week to further demonstrate questions in a narrative interview. Two volunteers read aloud the parts of "Peggy" and "Nicole," an excerpt of which follows.

Peggy: *What was it like for you, Nicole, for us to share such intimate stories of your life with the students?*

Nicole: *For awhile, it felt as though I was not in the room but simply telling an impersonal story about someone else. In brief moments, I began to feel like the stuff really happened. At first, this was overwhelming and scary.*

Peggy: *What kind of scariness were you experiencing?*

Nicole: *It was frightening in a good way.*

Peggy: *What do you mean by "frightening in a good way"?*

Nicole: *For a second, I was seen by people who weren't obligated to see me. It was weird. I thought I might change my mind about sharing things, but I didn't feel reticent at all. Instead, I felt completely open, like I could have said anything and felt okay about it. I felt like I was a person rather than the experience of a troubled mess of things.*

Peggy: *What did it feel like to be seen as a person rather than a case, sharing your hard earned wisdom with the class?*
(Pause)

Nicole (speaking through the tears): *It felt like what laying your head in someone else's lap is like.*

Peggy: *Tell me about your tears. What are you feeling now? Or as I once heard Michael White say, "If you could unpack your tears like little suitcases, what would we find there?"*

Nicole: *I feel tremendous sadness. So many times, I have wanted to fall into someone else's lap. You don't know what it is like, what you are missing, until you experience it* (more tears).

Peggy: *Experiencing this sadness of what you have missed all these years, have you managed to resist the urge to do bodily harm to yourself?*

Nicole: *Yes. Sharing with your class was so intense. When I left, cutting tempted me as a way to release the tension. Instead, I sat with the intensity. I drove to see Don and Tony. I tried to tell them about the experience but I couldn't find the words. Don seemed really excited to know what I had done.*

Peggy: *Nicole, what was it like for you to share of yourself in the way that you did with my class?*

Nicole: *I really liked it a lot. I can't find adequate words to describe it. It was cool to see self-realizations in others. I love watching people discover things.*

Peggy: *Do you think that your presence – what you had to say – had something to do with their self-realizations.*

Nicole (pause, then tearfully): *Yes.*

Peggy: *What about the format that we used? You had never before been witnessed by a reflecting group like that. What was that like for you?*

Nicole: *I thought the reflecting team format was good. I like how someone else could relate a story without it being on my shoulders to present an answer. I could respond if I wanted to. I liked hearing from another perspective rather than having to respond with my own voice. I didn't have to concern myself with how to accept what was said. Instead I could just experience it.*

Peggy: *What else did you notice about the format?*

Nicole: *I was glad there was a man on the reflecting team.*

Peggy: *Why do you think that is?*

Nicole: *I usually feel like guys are not safe. It felt nice to have a male who gets it. Having read his online reflection, I thought it was cool that he is comfortable with silence. People usually can't stand the absence of noise.*

Peggy: *What if we had used a question and answer format? What do you think that might have been like?*

Nicole: *That would have been fine but more restrictive. The reflecting team format allowed them to just say their responses without having to pose a question or an academic comment. We could all speak more freely. I wasn't concerned with constructing responses but rather I could take it in and have my own experience.*

Peggy: *What would it have been like if you were asked to respond more directly?*

Nicole: *If I were obligated to respond, I would be pushing away my own experience to be able to answer the question. It was more helpful to not have to be productive but to become the conduit for something freer.*

Peggy: *And what was the experience like for you to receive these reflections in such a free way?*

Nicole (tears): *It was empowering. I like the sense of shared self-discovery, being able to relate experiences to each other. For example, I liked being able to talk about what writing does for me, and what I use it for.*

Peggy: *I have heard you speak about writing as a way that you experience yourself as someone who has some things to say, as a conduit for something that flows through you. Are there some similarities with your reflecting team experience?*

Nicole: *Yes. It felt like we were conduits for some things that needed to be said. Writing is also a way I can relate to others through which I can say, ""Screw you, depression! You want to put me through this and to make me forget but you can't take away the moments of discovery that I can share through writing and talking."*

Peggy: *What else did you appreciate about the experience with the class?*

Nicole: *With my friends and at work, I always try to break down the fear or uneasiness with differences. I think we did something similar here. I like how freely people spoke and shared about themselves.*

Peggy: *Do you have a sense of what you might have contributed to making this happen?*

Nicole: *I work hard to make people feel comfortable, to not be afraid of engaging with me. I want them to not have a sense of fragility – to be comfortable enough to show how they feel. For example, if I am speaking with a student of color, I ask, "What is it like? Can you tell me about your experiences?" I am not afraid to ask questions for fear of offending someone. I want people to not be afraid to ask questions. I believe it's okay for different struggles to be expressed.*

Peggy: *What was it like for you to have the camera there, and for the experience to be recorded?*

Nicole: *I think the camera was important. If the tape turns out to be productive, we have a teaching tool.*

Peggy: *I remember that you said that when you first saw the camera, you thought of voyeurism. Did that change and if so, how?*

Nicole: *Yes, I had to get used to the camera. At first it was a bit nerve-wracking. But then I came to understand the idea of witnessing oneself through someone else's eyes. Everyone can be so harsh on themselves. But soon the experience became something more.*

Peggy: *What do you mean by something more?*

Nicole: *It became about honesty and truth. When speaking truth, we are not trying to construct, analyze, or manipulate. It just comes out. We react to each other as human beings, which allows everyone to join in. No one is excluded.*

Peggy: *Looking back at all that we/you shared with the class, is there anything that you wished we had kept private?*

Nicole: *It felt good to share everything with the class. Before then, I didn't realize how much we influence each other, how we are all influencing each other in a never ending cycle.*

Section Three: Practice, Practice, Practice

TEACHING LETTER-WRITING

Posting by Emma

I hadn't imagined that in our first class we would be given an opportunity to actually do something that would connect us to a person outside of the classroom. Using letter-writing to connect collective experience and to show a person support and understanding is a practice I want to continue.

Therapeutic letters as an aspect of narrative practice present a wealth of opportunities limited only by the imagination. David Epston sees letter-writing as so central to narrative practice, that he recently wrote, "Reflecting on the contribution of letter-writing to narrative practice is like asking an adult to describe the influence of learning how to walk on everyday life". [37] David Epston and Michael White offer a variety of therapeutic letter-writing possibilities, specific guidance in constructing letters, and even a therapeutic documents checklist (Epston & White, 1992; White, 1995c; White & Epston, 1990a). Other authors offer innovative practices using therapeutic documents and an ethic of circulation to incorporate audiences into a variety of work settings with children, families, teens, and adults (Fox, 2003; Freeman, Epston, & Lobovits, 1997a; Lobovits et al., 1995; Madigan, 1999; Madigan, 2007; Morgan, 2000b; Rombach, 2003). In this chapter, I explore how I invite students in-class and online to join me as apprentices to the craft of letter-writing.

I share with students how letters can assist people in a variety of contexts. Students learn specific tips for letter-writing that use note-taking of direct quotes – from someone being interviewed, speaking to the class as an invited guest or whose writings they have read – to enable them to write a letter to that person with curiosity and question-asking based on the person's own words. They practice their letter-writing skills in response to hearing insider accounts through guest speakers, in-class interviews, video-viewing, and storytelling. Letter-writing assignments in the classroom and on the course website provide students additional opportunities to practice, critique, and revise their therapeutic documents. Often students describe finding themselves reconnecting with a lost art.

Posting by Laurie

I used to write so many letters when I was younger, and though I write countless emails in a day, it seems different somehow to connect paper and pen to communicate with someone. I think a lot about how email and technology affects the way folks communicate with each other – it is faster, more convenient for sure. But I think something is lost.

I give students a handout of letter-writing tips distilled from preferred practices and references (Freeman et al., 1997a; Roth, 2002; Roth, Epston, & Weingarten, 1998; White, 1995c; White & Epston, 1990a, 1990b).

LETTER-WRITING TIPS

- Speak in your own voice. Above all, keep the letter simple and from the heart. Remember that there is no "right" letter and that your letter will be uniquely your own.
- Strive to enter into the other person's world with her/his own language and metaphors. During an interview, take notes in the words of the person(s) you are interviewing and quote verbatim from these notes in your letter.
- Insert earnest questions throughout the letter that open up possibilities for fresh reflection and speculation. "Are you saying that?" "Do I understand what you want me to know about you?" "Is there a story or two (or three) that could further my understanding?"
- Try to be specific in describing the images conveyed, what resonated with you, how this experience/these thoughts make a difference to you. Whenever possible, include specific accounts from your own life/work as to why these particular expressions struck a chord for you. Think about and acknowledge "transport" – how this particular experience (witnessing these expressions) has taken you to somewhere new/different in your own thinking. It can be helpful to refer to Michael White's *4 Categories of Response for Outsider Witness Practices* http://www.dulwichcentre.com.au/
- Try to resist the urge to give applause: affirmations, pointing out positives, congratulatory responses, etc. To quote Michael White (workshop notes), "It is not the place of outsider witnesses to give opinions or to make declarations about other people's lives, to hold up their own lives and actions as examples to others, or to introduce moral stories or homilies under the guise of a retelling."
- Remember that narratives develop over time and space. Try to make references to past, present, and future in various domains of living – feelings, actions, relationships, sense of identity, imagined possibilities as well as envisioning events in various geographies.
- *Past*: where people have been, i.e., their problematic situation as they described it when they came in, and the effects of the problem on their feelings, actions, relationships sense of identity, or imagined possibilities.

Future: how they wish to be now and in the future (hopes, intentions, aspirations, values, purposes, etc).

Present: where people are during the witnessed conversation, looking at the present as part of the journey that the past has led up to.

Questions that involve future speculation should give the reader a chance to ponder possibilities – to take a position – including the possibility to agree or disagree. While future speculations can be wishful, try not to get caught in the "practices of applause."

EXEMPLARY LETTERS

While everyone's style is (and should be) different, I encourage students to search online for well-written letters that give ideas for how to integrate letter-writing into narrative practice. Some exemplary letters are written by therapists; others by family members or intimate strangers. By reading others' letters, students can see how a narrative letter includes a lot of verbatim quotes and asks questions that respectfully puts the last best word in the recipient's hands.

I encourage students to visit the website "Narrativeapproaches.com" (Lobovits, 2007) to read letters under "Narrative papers:" I also recommend reading several letters on the same website under "Archives of Resistance: Anti anorexia/anti-bulimia (Lobovits & Epston, 2007); 1) Letter of Apology to Jenny (David Epston). 2) Eight letters in an anti-anorexic journey. (Anna, Sara and Ann Epston); 3) Anti-anorexic/anti-bulimic co-research in action: Upping the anti-and planned retreats. (Lorraine Grieves, David Epston, Eva, Rhonda and Rebecca); 4) Relationships – pro or anti-anorexic? (David Epston and Rebecca).

Whenever possible, I use closer-to-home letters as examples to teach preferred letter-writing practices. I find excellent illustrations in students' own words. Introducing the preferred identity assignment (see Chapter 7), I read aloud letters of commitment from prior students. I provide ample opportunities for students to share their letters with one another – to read them aloud in class or post them online. I also share letters from my own practice as a family therapist.

I try to stay cognizant of some students' tendency to anxiously compare themselves to others, while striving to create an apprenticeship environment where everyone approaches the learning diligently and industriously. I have discovered that practice is the best antidote to feeling intimidated. I also notice students' relief when they find that their classmates share both similar performance anxieties and the tendency to compare themselves unfavorably to others. One class called this phenomenon "The Importance Police," which Ali aptly described as "going around policing my sense of importance, telling me that I am not important enough to share my thoughts." Her classmates chimed in online with posts about their own experiences with The Importance Police monitoring them, and telling them that their contributions were not up to par. They shared stories about holding back, worrying that what they had to contribute was not as worthy as those of the other students. Students continue to surprise me by the mutually supportive ways they exchange online once it is revealed that such concerns are commonplace.

I have chosen the following three examples to demonstrate some of the creative possibilities of letter-writing.

A Narrative Letter

Jane, who like Nicole, had struggled with anorexia and depression, was an outsider witness to the interview with Nicole, described in Chapter 10. About a month after the interview, I received the following letter, which I then shared with Nicole. I consider this letter an ideal illustration of an exemplary letter written in the narrative therapy tradition. Jane conveys how strongly Nicole's experience spoke to her, directly quotes Nicole, and keeps Nicole at the heart of the matter, while also reflecting on her own story within the letter.

Dear Nicole,

My name is Jane and I was one of the fortunate people who came to Peggy's class the day you visited. You shared parts of your life with us in a way that I will actively remember for the rest of my existence. I have been out of town for a month, so was unable to write this letter as promptly as I would have wished. However, since you spoke, I have solidly carried you with me. I hope this letter finds you well.

I want you to know the history of my listening and what connected me so deeply to your story. I not only listened from my position as a social worker trying to discover more helpful ways to work with people, but also as a woman who suffered from anorexia years ago and who continues to resist its misogynist voice today. During my life there have been times I needed to move underground; not able or willing to put up the "perfect fight." When I met you I was slightly below ground. However, when you spoke your truth that day, this life...this heart came rushing back and my body resurfaced. I felt you held me up and didn't let go. I remembered.

You have become part of a small yet loud and powerful orchestra of women I carry around with me. It reminds me of when you said "I have eighteen letters that keep me alive." When I think of having a collection of powerful women close by, a quote written by Audre Lord comes to mind: "The women who sustained me through that period were black and white, old and young, lesbian, bisexual, and heterosexual, and we all shared a war against the tyrannies of silence."

You told us how restriction, binging, purging, cutting, and depression (rbpdc-not to award them with upper case letters) had for many years tortured, brutalized, and attempted to seduce you into death. They became so dedicated to ending your life that you had 5 hospital experiences in one year. Cutting wanted you so much for itself that as you said, "I would have to match the cuts or do them worse every time." During the interview you said, "Sometimes I don't remember well and maybe I make things up or say they are worse then what they really are." Would you say rbpdc has had strong investments in you forgetting their viciousness? Especially when you may be breaking freer? What might they feel endangered by when you write? Speak? Or aspire for your own life?

Even as rbpdc tried shrinking you, throwing you out, abusing you, and choking you, you have managed to stand committed to "living your life with a capital L." Would you say living your life with a capital L is in opposition to rbpdc's wishes for you to live your life with a lower case l? You spoke of 5 major values that make up living a life with a capital "L." These included, "Speaking from my own truth," "caring for others," "staying connected to a collection of beautiful people," "pursuing interests in writing," and "living mindfully and gently." These capital "L" commitments caught my attention quite boldly and curiously.

When you said it was important for you to speak or write your own truth, it made me think of another quote by Audre Lord:

For those of us who write, it is necessary to scrutinize not only the truth of what we speak, but the truth of that language by which we speak it. For others, it is to share and spread also those words that are meaningful to us. But primarily for us all, it is necessary to teach by living and speaking those truths which we believe and know beyond understanding. Because in this way alone we can survive, by taking part in a process of life that is creative and continuing, that is growth.

I don't know if you have this experience, but when I tried speaking out for my own truth, anorexia's backlash would be so severe that many times I fell back silent. I can probably guess rbpdc also does not like when you refuse to be a puppet for its script. At the risk of experiencing backlash you walked into our classroom that day and spoke your truth. Where does rbpdc go when your voice is louder? When you hold your truth closer does their truth of you move further away? I thought of how strongly you must believe in "telling your own truth" given rbpdc has tried torturing it out of you countless times. When you spoke to our class and shared your writings it reminded me of a quote written by a woman from the Archives of Resistance (anti-anorexia/anti-bulimia league):

If you were to kill me, these Archives will survive. anorexia, you know as well as I do that anti-anorexia "truth" will survive you because it promises nothing more than a revolution, struggle, and eventually regaining of the freedoms of which you robbed so many women (and some men).

During the interview, you said "I really feel good when I can use my experiences to help others." I watched you do this in many ways, but especially when you told us as social workers ways you found "help" helpful. You said you appreciated being "seen in the moment and not have problems remedied right away." You said you liked "being seen through your preferences." And you said you appreciated "not having someone pathologize everything that comes out of your mouth."

I remember that when you said, "caring for others comes from a deep self-hatred" it reminded me of a traditional healer I recently met in Samoa. She spoke of ghosts and how they attempt to threaten people's lives through illness or spirit pain. When I heard her say ghosts, I thought of restriction, binging, purging, depression, and cutting. One of the members of the village said ghosts most violently want the traditional healer dead. I asked why. He said, "because she is their greatest threat – they know she helps people and it defeats their purposes." Similar to ghosts, would you say rbpdc has had a particular investment in convincing you of self-hate and death because they find your care for others particularly threatening/exposing?

I hope that as you have read this letter you picked out things which were helpful and left the rest. Thank you again Nicole for walking into the classroom that day. I will forever hold you close to my shore...

Yours in spirit for a meaningful life with a capital "L,"

> *Jane*

Jane's use of questions continually refocuses the attention on Nicole, showing both intention and skill in reaching out and connecting with her. These questions linger in the imagination. The letter evokes a sense of solidarity, emphasizing that Nicole is not alone. Imagine the potential impact of this approach to reaching out to another, with the recipient able to keep the letter, reading and reflecting on its content as often as she wishes.

To Everything about Me Queer

Sometimes students' understandings of course material shows up in unusual ways. Liz conveyed her understanding of externalization in the following letter, "To Everything about Me Queer." A 20 year-old student, she wrote this letter about her coming out experience. This is one of several extremely insightful letters written by students as they are learning about externalization by practicing it themselves.

Had you popped up years ago and told me you were here to stay, you would not have been welcome. I would probably still hate you; still resent you for existing and refusing to leave me alone. But you were slow to emerge, conscious to weave within my life a strong sense of self, an unbreakable foundation of open-minded, accepting values, so that when it was time for us to officially meet, we would get along and I would be thankful for you in my life.

I still have trouble liking you, feeling proud of you. So much of me wishes you did not exist at all – that I could roll you into a small ball and tuck it under my bed, hidden from anything real. But then I open my eyes and you are still there, sitting next to me, urging me to continue letting you in, urging me to trust you when you whisper that everything will work out in the end.

And it is. Working out in the end. For so long I breathed the air of the different, the secret different, the type of different where no one else can really tell. But instead of letting me close up you forced me outward, "Get out and learn," you said, over and over again. "Open your ears and extend your arms and allow yourself to listen." I listened; listened to your strange voice, for I knew not who you were, but still, something else inside of me knew that your advice was true.

And people talked. At first just friends in their daily happenings, then associates, family members, an older man whom I met on the plane. My ear liked their voices, my mind loved to search for that common ground between us. For so long it seemed that no matter how alienated or lonely or depressed someone seemed, I never shied away – I could not shy away, because again, your voice, raspy and unfamiliar, assured me that I understood their words.

And I did, inexplicably, understand their words. My parents could not fathom why I found such passion working with those inflicted with severe mental illness, but my energy did not falter. Stories; I wanted to hear the patients' stories, wanted to understand their evolutions, wanted to soak up their words and blink in their faces and vow to never stop listening. And I haven't. I won't. I simply can't.

I remember going through the routine steps of a Wyoming day and falling asleep with the stifling awareness that something drastic had changed. While she and I spent an afternoon sitting by Bomber Lake and laughed about a meaningless story, you crept up from behind and tapped me on the shoulder. I felt a chill at the nape of my neck and there you were, smiling, telling me that this was a special moment, that something was different, that I could retrace my steps through the years and understand just why you were here (of course she did not notice this, but continued to laugh, un-fazed by our sudden reunion).

Even when you and I finally met, I hid you for a long time. I hid you inside books, under desks, in my back pocket. You always seemed to creep out long enough for me to notice you, threatening to ruin the moment, threatening to ruin everything. "I won't ruin anything," you continued to tell me, but for so long I would not believe you. But now I know you have your own timetable too. Before I could fathom being open with anyone else I needed to grow stronger, grow more confident with who I am and who I want to be.

I am continually impressed with how hard you push me. Even after I finally sat down to tell my parents, you gave me a few moments of glory and then reminded me that I was not done. "There is a reason you spent so many years listening; it's not time to stop," you continue to say, reinforcing my passion to support those who wish they too could sometimes sneak beneath the floorboards. My father said it well: "Liz, you are something most people are not, and you have the ability to find common ground with any type of person. Use this strength." Perhaps it is, though two years ago I would have disagreed with tears dripping down my cheeks, burning my upper lip as the salt crept onto my tongue.

I let those same tears leak to my chin the night I told my parents. "Why are you crying?" They asked over and over again, I'm sure looking for you somewhere inside their daughter. How ironic that you did not appear when I needed you the most, when I needed the reassurance that this is for real, that

I could not simply go to bed dreaming you away and have you gone. And then I realize that without you I never would have had that instinct to listen, to put my ears close to the ground and watch for special movements. Thank you for that.

Intimate Strangers

I tell students stories of how I link my clients' lives while safeguarding confidentiality. For example, I read them a letter exchange between two clients recovering from depression, from which I quote below. As anonymous pen pals, these two women did not have any identifiable information about each other. Their correspondence conveys the support that intimate strangers can give each other.

I worked with Leah as she overcame a very difficult battle with depression. In her re-emergence back into life, she expressed a desire to be of service to others. Volunteering at the local homeless shelter, Head Start program, or senior center was not quite what she was looking for. Leah wanted to share her experience with others who might benefit from her hard-earned wisdom about overcoming depression. Living in a small community, she also wanted to protect her privacy. At the same time, I was working with Ruth, a woman feeling trapped in the depths of depression. Leah's face lit up when I mentioned the possibility of writing an anonymous letter to Ruth. The next time we met, Leah proudly handed me the following letter:

Dear Friend,

I am pretty sure that you feel hopeless right now; sad, dark, strange, scared and crazy. You feel you will never get better, that you will feel like this for the rest of your life, and that you'll never get relief. Hold on and hang on because you will. I was there, not long ago, and I have come out the other side. You will too.

You have to literally get through each day for a while, grit your teeth and let the miserable hours pass. It took time for you to get into this depression, and it will take time for you to get out. Take care of your self the best way you can. Try to sleep and eat. Some days the only thing I could swallow were those Ensure drinks; try these if you are having trouble with food.

During the worst of my experience, I had trouble getting out of bed, everything took too much energy. I stopped going out of the house, working, etc. I became a hermit for a while, unable to face the world. Nothing gave me pleasure. My eight year-old daughter would say to my husband, "What's wrong with Mommy, she doesn't look right"? She was used to a mommy with energy, who played and smiled and laughed. That mommy went away... I felt like that person was replaced by some miserable impostor. I felt worthless, ashamed, and terrified. I was sure I was losing my mind.

Here are some of the things I did to get out of my depression. Maybe some of them will help you. **You will get better, believe in that.** *I took medication, and slowly but surely it helped. I prayed a lot. I listened to beautiful music, and read spiritual and uplifting books that gave messages of hope. I spoke to my family often and held onto my husband in the middle of the night when I couldn't stand the darkness. I spoke with and cried with close friends. This whole experience felt personal and private, so I only let the extra special people in on what I was going through. I went to see my doctor and counselor a lot, and that always gave me a sense that I was being taken care of. With my family, friends, counselor and doctor surrounding me, and my faith, I felt like I had my team in place, and that all of that support would get me through. I told myself over and over (without always believing it) that not only was I going to get well, but that I was going to come out of this a better, stronger person. Guess what? That is what happened.*

You have to believe. You have to constantly remind yourself that this is temporary; it's horrible and scary, yes, but temporary. We live in an amazing time. For the vast majority of people, depression can be treated. With the right medication, and/or the right help and tools, you'll beat this. Millions of people suffer from depression at some point in their lives and millions of people recover.

It is an unforgettable experience. Getting out of it was slow for me, a glimmer of hope here, a moment of comfort there. Gradually my appetite came back, and food tasted good again. My sleep got better and my energy returned. After some time, I felt happy again, and things were funny, and hopeful and there was so much to look forward to.

It changed me, and for the better. That was the message I told myself over and over, and it was true. I believe we do learn and grow through suffering and coming out of that suffering was one of the greatest gifts I have ever received. Life is wonderful again, a true blessing and with time and patience you'll see exactly what I mean.

All the best to you,
Your friend

The next time I met with Ruth, I shared Leah's letter with her. This was during a very dark time. A few months later, Ruth brought the following letter she had written back to Leah to our session:

Dear friend,

I have been wanting to write you for a long time to thank you for the letter you wrote me and delivered via Peggy this winter.

It took me a LONG time to get out of the depression/anxiety black hole that I was in. And the midst of the worst of it, I wanted to write to you – but couldn't – a phenomenon I'm sure you understand, given your experience. I also knew even then that I wanted to someday write back to tell you that I had emerged, victorious, from that Dark Place. But it took longer than I ever expected and there were times that I feared it would never happen. It delights me to say that now I HAVE emerged victorious from the darkness (beginning in late April). Hooray!

During the times when I was suffering the most, I read your letter often. It meant a lot to me. I kept it in my top dresser drawer (where I tuck away many things that are precious to me).

There are some specific things that I want to thank you for in that letter. First, it was so helpful to hear your honest portrayal of how things felt for you. I experienced many of the same things. I couldn't eat. I couldn't sleep. I blamed myself a lot for what I was going through. I worried about the effect of my depression on my family and friends. I took a leave of absence from work and felt guilty and incompetent for doing so.

It helped SO much to hear your story. It made me feel less weird. It helped me to say (on a good day and more so in retrospect): "Depression is a mysterious Thing that happens to people – I'm not a flawed person who has caused this." Your words helped me feel less like a "bad" person and more like a normal person who was going through a very hard time.

The second thing about your letter that helped me so much was your hopefulness and faith that things would get better. Your letter along with conversations with some friends who had struggled with depression was a lifeline in this way. I would tell myself, "look how awful it was for her and she got through it – you will too." Of course, when things were really bad, I didn't always believe I would get better, but knowing that other people did helped me to hang on, to not give up.

So, you see, although you don't know me, you have given me a tremendous gift – and I'll bet you do that for many people.

I am much better now – though still quite freaked out about having gone through that whole experience. I feel not only that I am back to my "old self" in certain ways – but also that I have been "reborn" in some way. I feel that by having gone through this horrible experience and survived – that I am, in some ways – a new person. I have my energy and creativity back – but I also have changed my perspective on things. I have always loved life, but now I love it even more. I also feel a deep sense of compassion for myself, for others. And while I feel scared sometimes that the Depression will return, I mostly feel very excited about life and very curious about where it will lead me next.

One more thing I want to mention. I am so impressed that you endured this experience and got better while being a mother. I guess we just face what we have to – but I can't imagine trying to care for a daughter while going through such a hellish experience. You clearly have a tremendous amount of strength and courage.

Thank you so much for sharing your story with me. It means a LOT. In turn, I'm sharing a bit of my story back. I'm cheering you on (and us both, really) as we walk into new and exciting futures.

Warmly,
Your anonymous "pen pal" through the tough times

APPRENTICING TO THE CRAFT OF LETTER-WRITING

Posting by Alice

I was really nervous about writing a letter to someone I didn't know. I usually don't let my thoughts be known to strangers for fear of being judged. And I felt really exposed by the kind of specific questions I was encouraged to write in the letter. However, I then thought about how exposed Josie and Milo must feel, because their story is being told to complete strangers (see below). But then I told myself, "They don't feel that way; they are excited to have their stories told." I took that thought with me when I wrote to Kate and I found myself really enjoying that letter. Peggy, please thank them for letting us see a piece of themselves, and for letting us in their circle.

Often – and with permission – I begin class by giving a detailed account of a consultation experience where I highlight the actual words of the persons who have consulted with me. In the above quote, Alice referred to a couple who had graciously agreed for me to share some of their story with the class. Pregnant with twins while parenting an infant, Josie and Mylo were consulting with me during a highly stressful time of their lives. They had been recently told by Josie's obstetrician that there was a high probability that one of their expected twins would have developmental problems.

I ask my students to take notes as they listen to me share this story so they can include verbatim quotes before referring to anything else[38]. I then ask the students to take out pen and paper to write letters "from the heart." I remind them to reread the handout on letter-writing tips. After providing the class with time to write, I ask for a few volunteers to read their letters aloud. Each letter is unique, yet similarly filled with moving accounts of their writers having been personally impacted as witnesses.

Some students initially express discomfort being asked to spontaneously write a letter in class. They give me permission to pass their letters onto someone as long as I reassure them that I will first screen all of their letters. Linda felt the pressure of time, as well as expressing a sense of responsibility for the effect the letter could have. "Words are powerful. I am not an 'off the cuff' person. I felt the letter I wrote to be stilted because I preferred to err on the side of formality rather than inadvertently imply something disrespectful or write anything 'wrong.'"

In another class, responding to another story I shared, Michelle surprised herself by discovering how much she liked the letter-writing activity, since she generally doesn't like to write, thinking that "it takes too much time" – and had struggled with journaling throughout her classes. "I felt extremely unqualified when Peggy asked us to write a letter. But once I got a few lines down, I found that I did really connect with things that Meghan had said and I was curious to link these together with experiences. I love that we are repeating back in the client's own words."

Contribution of the Online Medium

After students have experienced the potency of letter-writing, I start a "practice" online discussion forum on "letters and therapeutic documents":

> *This is a space to share any lingering thoughts about this shared foray into letter-writing. Narrative therapy offers boundless opportunities for letter-writing and other therapeutic documents. What letter-writing skills would you like to further develop? What are your current thoughts about the possibilities for various kinds of therapeutic documents in your specific workplace? What are you reading about and/or hearing in class that you find yourself pondering? Can you think of a particular story to tell that would illustrate how these practices have or might contribute to "thickening the alternative story"?*

Students express their appreciation for the opportunity to write letters to someone real in need, rather than imagined; this urgency forces them to practice this skill knowing their letter could matter and certainly will not be inconsequential. The online forum offers space for students to candidly share their decidedly mixed reactions to such a prospect. To some extent, letter-writing "throws them in the deep end" of providing a service to another seeking service. This obliges them to take risks to articulate their challenges with one another. Laurie wrote, "Letter-writing seems to evoke thoughtfulness in people... I think this is why I had difficulty with the exercise; I felt pressure from the time limit. I think that practice with this would help."

Posting by Heidi

> *Upon hearing of this activity, I had a rush of thoughts that I eagerly wanted to put down onto paper, but then as I started writing I couldn't help but think, "Is it okay that I'm saying this? Would this somehow be considered unhelpful or even hurtful?" Then I decided that I needed to tuck those thoughts away, as they were interfering with what I wanted to convey. I went back to writing as if I were writing to a dear friend and tried hard not to let those questions of whether or not I was being therapeutic get in my way. I just tried to let my heart speak for me. That was difficult, however, because I felt as though my first and second voices were at war with each other. I'm sure that it will become easier for me once I've practiced this more. It will just take a little*

time. I like hearing that this wasn't necessarily easy for others as well because it makes me feel as thought this apprehension is natural and that it's not just me being a freak.

Sarah expressed amazement at how easily and gracefully so many of her classmates write both in class and on the discussion forum. "I continue to battle the inner critic that sometimes interferes when I am trying to express myself this way. At times, I am able to bypass this critic and connect with a more supportive and creative being. It seems as if (maybe through this class) people are having an easier time writing and sharing." Other students then joined the online conversation addressing Sarah's question, "Has anyone else had problems with this inner critic? Have you learned any strategies to lessen its influence"?

The process of writing their letters was difficult, though ultimately valuable, for Jessica as well:

Posting by Jessica

It was so challenging to bring myself into the letters. It was a struggle for me to share part of my story, even anonymously. It is such a shift to bring myself into the lives of the people we discuss in class. As mentioned, the usual format of "case presentations" allows us to distance ourselves from the person's experience. But in letter-writing we bring ourselves in, and I think gain a more clear and empathic understanding of the people and their stories.

Kerry1 also was moved by hearing her classmates read their letters aloud. She wants to improve her letter writing skills "to be more eloquent in my words and to figure out what is therapeutic or not. I wrote from the heart to someone I did not know. Would this change if it were my own client"? Working with children, she wondered about a client creating a therapeutic document as more of a picture. "How do we know when and in what form a therapeutic document can be helpful?" While she began the course with hesitancy, after the first day of class, Kerry1 was already eager to share her thoughts, pose earnest questions, and anticipate hearing more from her classmates.

The letter-writing experience extended Michelle's understanding of an emphasis in course reading:

Posting by Michelle

One of the things that I have been struggling with in the reading is the use of the word "redundancy." I immediately think, "Boring!" But it is all connecting with how we work with families; sometimes it takes many, many times for something to link for them and for a shift or change to happen. It is part of the slowing down that I am coming to believe is so essential in our work – making sure that we're not at the finish line waiting for the family to leave the starting gate... What are ways any of you have learned, discovered, or used to help you remember to slow it down? I need all the ideas I can get.

Breaking Through the Therapeutic Gaze

Conversing online gives space for students to apply deconstructive listening to their own experiences. I was riveted by their descriptions of the effects of an internalized "therapeutic gaze" – taking on the role of the helpful, wise therapist. Here is one example, written by Ginger, who situated her reflections in her own experience of depression:

> *As I was writing my letter, I struggled because my thoughts were being steered by this "therapeutic gaze" that wanted me to make this helpful for this woman who is struggling with the dark hole of depression. I noticed as I went in that direction that my ability to speak from my own source and my own truth of my experience was being stifled...As we are beginning, I am really in tune with the idea of being with people from a place of curiosity rather than trying to be therapeutic. I guess that is part of deconstructive listening, and the "slipperiness of meaning," listening and trying to explore and remain open to the many possible meanings that people give to their stories.*

Again, I am careful to join in while not elevating my online contribution as instructor. I am intrigued by the students' reflections on how to manage "the therapeutic gaze" while also being present and transparent. I ask:

> *Is it possible to speak from a place of resonance, while simultaneously making intentional choices about what feels appropriate to share? How can we speak with our heart while engaging the mind – using maps of practice to shape how we say what comes to mind without losing the connectedness of earnest conversation? I believe narrative practice can give us ways to link ourselves to the people who consult with us while decentering ourselves – staying focused on their story, not ours.*

Candidness

Students join in with their reflections and questions about how to be candid in letter-writing and still be careful not to overstep limits or do anything which might cause harm. Celia was conscious while writing of not being the therapist to this person and wondered how the letter would have been different had she been in the therapist role:

Posting by Celia

> *I don't really know what the limits are in the narrative world – they are so different from the regular therapy world – and mostly for the best in my opinion! But it still leaves me wondering sometimes exactly where others see this limit to rest. Could you speak to this a bit, Peggy, and anybody else that has opinions too. Peggy, would you possibly be willing to share any letters with the class that you have written to your actual clients, not as part of an outsider witness team or practice?*

I am still thinking about Celia's questions. Letter-writing in the narrative practice is indeed quite different from training in other therapeutic traditions, where professionals-in-training learn to prepare documentation from a more formal expert position. Hopefully, these practices make room for each person's unique letter-writing style to emerge. At the same time, I believe it is important for students to follow the letter-writing tips rather than simply writing whatever comes to mind. While there is space for the letter-writer to share personal stories, any sharing is in relation to the person whose life is at the center of the consultation. I tell students the best place to practice is with each other. I also seize any opportunity to read aloud letter exchanges – my own and others – to illustrate decentered personal sharing.

Heidi also struggled with not getting too wrapped up in her own experience when writing a letter. She wanted to show that while her experience was different, she shared many commonalities that enabled her to stand in solidarity with the person on her journey. As she listened to the account of the person's experience with depression and then wrote her letter, she came to realize something else about the process: "The outcome wasn't simply a therapeutic letter for this woman. In the process of writing it, I also felt validation and renewed strength from resonating with her experience and knowledge of her journey with depression."

Applications

Students frequently reflect on applications in their work contexts and beyond. Students pose many questions about how to use letters or other therapeutic documents at their internship sites and workplaces. Caroline wondered about her work with a community mental health crisis team. "I am wondering how these practices can be used within the parameters of crisis work with clients with whom I may only have short-term contact. It seems like most of what we are learning about narrative practice implies multiple meetings and longer-term contact." Her classmate, Bobbi, responded:

> *I am interested in what you wrote about using letter-writing in crisis work. What a great way to follow up on your work with someone. It has so many possibilities. And it's so needed, especially in a situation where you may meet with someone only once. You can summarize what happened and any resolutions or plans. You can also stay with the person as a support in the form of a letter and also bear witness to some significant event in their lives.*

Students often need to learn more about the letter-writing possibilities within their given agencies. For example, crisis services often follow protocols that place a premium on protecting the client's confidentiality and not sharing a person's contact information, because otherwise people might hesitate to come in for help. I encourage students to find allies without their organizations to explore what might be possible. Crisis workers could determine if there is someone in their agency who can explore the legal and ethical considerations for instituting letter-writing practices within the bounds of the protocols protecting privacy, at least for some clients.

Similarly, Foresta posed questions about barriers in applying letter-writing in her experiences working with people experiencing domestic and sexual violence, as well as refugees and asylum seekers. She questioned how an agency could guarantee that other people would not see the letter:

> *It might not be safe for certain people to keep the letter on their person. If the wrong person were to find out that person was working with me, it could have detrimental repercussions for them. Through these two areas of my work I also encounter people with lower literacy skills or people whose first language is not English and who are still struggling to learn it.*

Thinking about these groups of people made Foresta realize that there is a certain level of privilege that a service user must be able to attain in order for this strategy to be available to them. Like some other students, she would like to explore how using drawings or other mediums could be brought into the practice of letter-writing or even substitute for letter-writing.

Students exchange ideas online about future letter-writing possibilities. I ask questions to foster contemplation: "How might you incorporate letter-writing in your practice as social workers as a way to extend a reverberating conversation beyond face-to-face meetings? Where might it be helpful to create exchanges between intimate strangers to fortify solidarity and exchange hard-earned wisdom between people overcoming similar challenges? What else comes to mind?" Caroline responded that she liked thinking about letter-writing in her work with individuals, siblings, groups, and couples. Bobbi expressed appreciation for these applications and added her own ideas in working with children:

Posting by Bobbi

> *I also like the idea of having children write to their own temper or their loneliness and the therapist writing to the children to summarize their session, providing them something tangible to look at between meetings to remind them of what they are doing or working on. Pictures with non-readers would work; stickers are a nice way to do that as well. Giving homemade certificates and membership in leagues against problems also seem very strengthening. I have children write letters to themselves in the spring about goals for the next school year. Then I deliver these sometime after the start of the year.*

As teacher, I hope that these educational experiences will whet students' appetite for more. I also want to create an atmosphere where students can share their concerns about letter-writing in their particular work situations.

Students share some interesting discoveries when practicing letter-writing skills. Rachel found that letter-writing gave her a different perspective on online discussion: "Sometimes it feels as though I am writing a letter to the class, stating what I am noticing, relating it to my own life and practice, and then asking questions. Does anyone else feel this way?"

Danielle responded that she too experienced letter-writing practice as informing her way of responding to people's online posts, contributing to a heartier discussion.

Posting by Danielle

I think many people are reflecting more "narratively" within their posts than when we first started doing this. I see more questions posted after people making connections. I wonder if others are conscious of these richer posts as being connected to learning and practicing the skill of letter-writing, or perhaps it isn't that specific, but rather connected to the larger learning occurring in the whole class. Or is it from some other specific part of the class? Perhaps a better way to ask this is: are people finding parts of this class that have particularly resonated with them or informed how they are practicing these skills?

Rachel thought about possible applications in her internship working with children in an agency guided by protocols. Would her supervisors raise questions about confidentiality and boundaries, and if so, how might she respond to these concerns? She also wondered how letter-writing practice might affect the next letter or email that she writes to a friend.

Reflections

Letter-writing is a tangible way for students to experience some unique features of narrative practice. Letter-writing is not something apart from face-to-face meetings, but actually becomes part and parcel of the way we relate to people, of the back-and-forth that develops between us. It can become another way to deepen the conversation, enabling us to reflect back to people what we hear them saying, adding in some of our own experiences that resonate with theirs, and asking questions that engage the imagination and extend the conversation far beyond the bounds of our hour long meetings.

What might at first feel like an add-on technique, a "tool" to use as an adjunct to therapy, soon enough can become integral to our work with people. Contrary to my experience of report writing, I find letter-writing deeply satisfying and energizing. Composing a letter provides precious space to reflect on what I have heard, to share some of my thoughts and questions, and to give the reader a sense of my approach to my work.

I also recognize how time constraints pose a pragmatic limit to letter-writing. My students often raise this issue, asking me whether I write letters to all my clients. I let them know it takes both commitment and discipline to integrate letter-writing into the regular work-week. Like them, I can only write when I have time. I try to be realistic in my suggestion to set aside a regular time each week for writing letters.

Teaching letter-writing reminds me that I too wish to keep enhancing my own letter-writing practices, through the opportunities that each new client presents to extend my therapeutic skills. Throughout my teaching, I strive to drive home the concept that narrative practices are constructed with attention to particular details. Through practice, students develop their own voices, while also over time entering more artfully into other people's worlds. Students' concern about writing in a stilted manner or revealing too much lessens as they discover that they can lean on the letter-writing tips to guide them. In Chapter 13, "Apprenticing to a Craft," I show a "Take 2" letter-writing exercise that highlights how the process of skill development moves beyond pointing out positives. I offer an exchange with a student that shows a difference between email correspondences and letter-writing, both of which offer distinct possibilities. Together, we practice the delicate balance between students connecting with their own experience and their responsibility to keep their clients' experience the primary focus.

Though they share some similarities, writing a letter is quite a different practice from sending an email. While nothing can replace the feeling of holding a letter in your hand, in today's world, email is easier and far more commonplace. When using the more casual and immediate medium of email to write narrative letters, the writer needs to consciously slow down, become more reflective, and practice discipline.

Letter-writing can be a tight, two-way communication link; or it can be far more expansive, connecting many people, and creating energizing webs of relationships and mutual sharing and helping. Bringing in other witnesses as I do in my classes, both in person and online, is another way of creating a community of support for clients. We extend the way people can experience themselves as knowledged, able to reach others with their wisdom, outside of "designated" professional helpers. After all, remember how much Nicole in Chapter Nine got out of that packet of 18 letters – from people she never even met, all of them students.

CHAPTER 12

REMEMBER TO ASK

I worked in a small town where there is an inn that had been owned by the same family for 100 years. Every Sunday the long-time cook and her crew prepared a popular smorgasbord. New people bought the inn and put some money into it, renovating and rewiring the old structure. They hired experts to completely redo and modernize the kitchen from top to bottom. The Sunday the restaurant re-opened for smorgasbord, the cook came in and found it was a total disaster to work in. Her comment was, "They forgot to ask the cook!" The kitchen was state-of-the art everything, yet it was non-functioning. I work with day care providers. Sometimes I set up events that people don't attend and I wonder why. Ever since hearing this story, I am reminded, "Remember to ask the cook!"

Ellie, co-researcher, Finding Common Ground participatory action research project, (Sax, 2000)[39]

I believe it is important for a teacher of practitioners-in-training to structure ample opportunities for students to hear those in the client role share stories and recommendations about how human service providers have been most and least helpful to them. Students write letters and/or participate in reflecting teamwork in response to these teaching stories. In this chapter, I share insider accounts I use in my classes that include tips for practitioners from the following people: parents of children with special needs (Sax, 2000, 2007c); Alan, a teenager who experienced foster care and was then adopted as a young boy; and Meghan, a survivor of sexual abuse, family violence, psychopathologizing, and psychiatric maltreatment. I also give a glimpse into the vibrant online conversation that each of these classroom experiences has generated as people with insider knowledge graciously teach students invaluable lessons about what ethical, useful practice means to them.

PARENTS SPEAK OUT[40]

Students listen attentively to accounts by parents of children with special needs, who are overflowing with accrued knowledge about their children, parenting practices, and practicalities of life. Despite their years of parenting and seeking help for their children, they rarely presume to describe themselves as possessing valuable expertise and relevant experience. They share how difficult it can be to get anyone to hear their worries. Often parents seeking services describe their anger and tears in feeling discounted and patronized by professionals, as well as their growing confidence over time in their own good judgment regarding their children. Mothers highlight the centrality of friendship that can emerge when sharing their stories with other mothers, helping each other and their children.

I challenge students to hold themselves accountable to the people they aspire to serve and to develop accountability practices that acknowledges their professional privilege. I share a video clip in which Michael White queries in one research interview, "How can a group of service providers who are very well meaning, well intentioned, caring, and compassionate still find ways in those circumstances to set up contexts so that they are accountable in some way to their knowledge and acts of power?"

Students express appreciation when I read aloud recommendations from Pamela, a parent I met at a Vermont community gathering I organized. I brought together parents of children with emotional-behavioral difficulties, human service providers, and planners to actively explore what helps family members to speak up, feel supported, and be meaningfully involved in the planning, delivery and evaluation of human services. I also wanted to better understand the shifts required for professionals in attitude and practice to become accountable to those they serve and to build effective help-giving relationships based on parent-professional partnerships.

At one point, Pamela said she was too angry to speak, having lived through her own share of frustrating experiences with the provider system. When she did speak up, Pamela offered an exquisitely insightful perspective. I was especially affected by her choice of a positive approach to transform her anger into a language that professionals could hear. Her recommendations focused on professional attitudes that foster effective help-giving relationships:

– What you say and how you say it is very important.
– The main thing is to listen to the families. Really listen. A lot of times, parents dont't feel heard. A lot of these parents, by the time people are trying to help, are so frustrated because they have been ignored for so long. If there were more under-standing, there wouldn't be so much anger toward people that are trying to give services.
– The family might be going through situations that are very stressful to the parent, which the provider might not realize. It doesn't affect the provider like it does the parent. Something can trigger a situation from the parent's past. Show some compassion.
– It's okay to say, "I don't know the answer." Also, ask the parents what they think. They could come up with a lot of ideas. If you do it together, it's a great opportunity.
– Providers may be experts in their field of service but they need to understand that the parent knows the child better.
– Each family is at a different level, and may not have as much of an understanding as another parent. Share some of your experiences that you've grown through. This makes the parents feel that they are not alone. You are not just coming in there to tell them what to do, to change something. You are also coming there with your own experiences, and how you have grown from your experience.

I share with students parents' reflections on their relationships with different providers:

The relationship I had with the special education person who provides services for my 13 year-old is so adversarial that I don't go to meet with her unless I have a tape recorder. I don't go unless I have three or four people with me...because the person on the other side of the team is adversarial, and tells me I don't know anything.

And yet this same service seeker had very trusting relationships with other service providers who she knows "won't do anything sneaky, or tell me I don't know what I'm doing. We can work it out." The students and I explore specific professional practices identified by service seekers as contributing to effective help-giving relationships.

Lori, the mother of two young children diagnosed with autism, spoke about her love for her children, and how this informed her impatience with professionals:

When you want the best for your child, nothing is ever fast enough. No matter what you want, no matter how good it is or has already been, we want it – yesterday morning. When we go to a provider, we expect to hear...[something helpful] about our children. It's the way we feel about our children. I know my two children are two of many children in the system, but you get impatient when you've been to all these programs and you wait. My son is six, my daughter is four. It's going to take time to change services and to get things more positive. Meanwhile, my daughter's face looks like she always has the chickenpox because that's how her brother takes out his frustration on her. As a parent, you have a sense of urgency. Waiting 10 years is one thing, if you're not talking about children lives...We did have some services. But you always want more. You always want the missing link. Maybe this will help? We are always looking for something we don't know about as parents.

Feeling Devalued and Untitled

Many service seekers, especially low-income parents, describe feeling devalued and frustrated in their search for help for their children. I sometimes show a recording or read a transcript where Isabelle, a young mother of three, describes how she has struggled intensely in her relationships with professionals. She speaks about the isolation she experienced when services abruptly ended that were available during her pregnancies and the frustration she felt when she had to wait too long for services. Two of her children have been diagnosed with special needs; one was not diagnosed until she "let him go" into child protective services:

It took a lot to get anybody to listen to me. You wouldn't believe the phone calls I tried to make when I was in crisis and no one could help. Now that my children are older, I am getting services. But I really wish that someone could have been in my home when my children were three years old, and I was really having a hard time.

Straddling Multiple Roles

The lines separating service seeker, service provider, and service planner can be fluid. Mark, an early childhood consultant straddles several different roles: provider, planner, and parent. Despite all the professional expertise that he and his wife bring to the table, these are stripped away as soon as he is in the role as a parent. "When I go to a meeting, whether it's about therapy or services, our input is discounted, even with our experience. Now imagine putting in a parent who doesn't have our level of experience."

Mark cautioned providers to remember the differences in perspective as parent. Certainly, service providers and planners sometimes face difficult decisions and even get to the point of feeling quite frustrated at not knowing what to do about a challenging situation with a child they are seeing. Yet these experiences are nothing like what it is like for the parents, who cannot leave their situation behind when they go home from work. As one young mother put it, "The service provider is distracted by the paperwork in meetings, by the next family that comes up, and other things like that. But that common experience of frustration doesn't really compare with the fact that parents have a very different role that lasts 24 hours a day."

I sometimes show a video clip from my research project in which Joyce, an early childhood education provider, gives a poignant description of straddling the roles of service provider and service seeker. In response to hearing a mother's description of her frustrations in working with professionals, Joyce spoke from her personal experience of feeling intimidated and patronized by service providers. "People who know me can't imagine that I might be intimidated. But I remember as a parent going to school to meet with an educator, and feeling extreme apprehension. I felt I knew my child but that they were the experts. That was a real interesting thing for me to experience as a parent."

Joyce then gives a more recent illustration of her role as service seeker since her elderly parents have come to live with her. She describes the parallel between her experience as a home care provider with her parents and descriptions by parents of young children who feel like people do not listen:

> *I experience the same thing with agencies that come into my home – intrusion into my home, feeling that they come in with their agendas and are not listening to what I have to say, and that they are not really sensitive to stress that I am feeling. They kind of go forward with their agenda, with a total lack of awareness of the place I'm in, and the problems that I have in this situation.*

ALAN'S TIPS FOR SOCIAL WORKERS

Alan, a seventeen year-old who spent his first few years in foster care, allowed me to share with others his tips for social workers working with young children. His story illustrates how a public practice can provide multiple opportunities for students to learn from insider accounts and from each other. Alan and I had fun together creating a brief video recording and writing that I then presented to the class. Previously reticent about talking about his experience, Alan was forthcoming when he heard that his story might help others.

My name is Alan and I was in foster care for two and half years from the ages of three to five. I am now 17. When I was an infant, I was abused by my birth parents, who were teenagers. I ended up in the emergency room a lot of different times for countless injuries. I had stitches in my head from an accident once (though I can't recall what happened). I have a scar to prove it and know that my siblings that were in the household were abused as well. The oldest was my sister Kim. The youngest was my brother Joe. I was told that my parents got into a ton of fights, including one where my birth mother tried to stab my birth father in the hand with a kitchen knife.

I remember that one day three police officers came to the door and took us away from the house. Since then, I know nothing of my parents' whereabouts or my siblings either. They took us to different foster care homes. When I was taken from my parents at the age of three by the cops, my mother loved me and was doing what was best for me by taking me out of the home. She wanted to see me grow up in a safe environment where I would not get into bad situations like taking drugs…I am thankful for the fact that she did this not for herself, but for me. I still wish that I was with her today, but I have to understand that I would not be who I am now. I would not be a safe or an intelligent person who would be able to help my friends who need it or to get the advice I need from my friends to change myself.

When I was in foster care, I remember my social worker, Nonie, told me that she knew people that were interested in me. The next day she brought two men to the door of the house where I was staying. Their names were Brian and Bernie. When I saw them the first thing I said was "Daddy;" then I looked at Bernie and I said, "What do I call you"? I also remember them reading to me the first book I have ever heard or read. The book was called <u>One Dad, Two Dad, Brown Dad, Blue Dad</u>. *This book is about how families are different; some families have one dad and some have two. It also explains that diverse families are good families as well. I read the book every day until I was adopted. It still is one of my favorite books.*

It was only a matter of time before they adopted me. That day, August 1, 1992, was one of the best days of my life. I will always remember that day as a second birthday – a day where I could start a new and better life. My new parents threw a party for me that night. There were people and a lot of gifts as well. I got a green bike that said Giant on the side of it. I got a plaque with our family's picture on it. There was also a chocolate cake that read, "Welcome to the family A.J." I will never forget these things.

Another thought that comes and goes is that I want to know about my birth family. I have so many questions that it hurts inside me. I just don't know how to ask them. That is the main reason why I started to cut myself. I had this ache inside me that never seemed to go away. I had to get the pain out. But now I have a family who I know I can talk with. They won't abuse me if I ask questions that they don't want to talk about or if they don't know the answer. They will tell me the truth, but when they think I am old enough to hear it.

In addition to my two dads, Brian and Bernie, I also have an older brother who is 22 named Scott and a younger brother named Ned who is 14. They were both adopted as well which gave me a chance to have a say in their lives. I could help them and give them advice on things that have happened to me and they could help me with situations that I might have in the future. For example, when Ned was first adopted he needed to find people that he could hang out with and find a sport to play after school. I have been playing soccer for almost 11 years and asked him if he would be interested in coming to a practice with me to see what he thought of the game. He enjoyed it so much that he joined a local team for the school and was easily the best player.

Other things that I enjoy doing, and have been involved in are the VYCC (Vermont Youth Conservation Corps), VKAT (Vermont Kids Against Tobacco), and SWAT (Students Opposing Alcohol and Tobacco). I am involved in the youth group at the local Unitarian Universalist church and we recently went to New Orleans to help rebuild after Katrina. We raised the money to go there; some of the money came from people who heard this story from Peggy when she gave a workshop in December, 2006.

I have also been teaching some of my friends to break-dance, wrestle, and do gymnastics. I am also a yogi. I went to a three day yoga retreat with another yogi that travels the world with other yogis to help teach people around the world. Yoga is an exercise that builds muscle in your whole body and will strengthen your immune system. Just last week, I saw the Dalai Lama in Massachusetts.

I also make myself available to my friends who are going through a bad time. I have helped them stop cutting, get back together with their friends, and even get together with people that they end up loving. I help them out because of my experience, I have lost a lot of things that really matter to me and I don't want them to lose those things.

I had a rough early childhood; my parents support me and find ways for me to have a better future than what I could have been. By supporting me I mean that they respected the fact that I need help with some of the situations that I have been through. They were always telling me that I should talk to someone and find a way for me to stop or change my mind. This all came from the love that they have poured into this relationship they have with me and will always have for me and the rest of the family.

Alan's Guidelines

Alan offered the following suggestions for Child Protection and other social workers based on his experience from being in foster care from ages three to five.

– When you make your first connection with a child who is young and in the midst of a rough childhood, remember that he or she will be skeptical and shy. Play games. Talk to him or her. Tell him or her about yourself, what you do, and why you do it. Ask them their name, how old they are, and stuff like that.

– Start a connection and get to know each other. Build a strong bond. Find out what they like and do it. For example, if the kid likes to climb trees, take him tree-climbing. Bring along a picture of a bare tree with branches on it. Each time the kid climbs up a branch, pause and ask him or her something he or she likes or doesn't like that you can then fill in at the end the branch. Call this a special tree as a way of getting to know you. Give them a copy so they can have it.

– If possible, try to meet every day. This builds up a stronger connection, proving that the social worker likes the kid. If you can't meet every day, write letters saying something like "I'm coming back in two days, is there something I can bring you?" For example, if the kid likes books, bring him a few books.

– Any time you are going to bring a visitor who is interested in adopting, make sure you call ahead of time. That way the kid won't get nervous that he won't see the social worker again, thinking, "Who is this? Are you leaving me?"

– Don't use big words like "adoption" because a young child won't understand. Instead say, "Someone wants to see you."

I captured on videotape several reflections on Alan's story and tips from a workshop I held in New Zealand. Frances, a workshop participant, shared the following:

> *What amazed me was listening to your thoughts about how social workers can relate to the young people in their lives who are dealing with adoption issues. Your ideas...seemed to jump across this great ocean between us and seemed as relevant and powerful here as I imagine they are in their own country. In this moment through this video and your writing you were able to join us together. I am really glad to meet you and now be able to carry that wisdom with me and share it with others.*

MEGHAN

Students often respond powerfully to becoming witnesses to a recording in which a colleague, Mary, interviewed Meghan and me about our work together. Meghan grew up in a violent home with an alcoholic father who terrorized his wife and his children, while in another context using his intimidation skills to become a successful corporate lawyer. At age eleven, Meghan was raped by her father, the memory of which she questioned until her discovery of hospital records and journals that document how again and again she told mental health professionals about the sexual abuse. Instead of helping Meghan get help and safety, her hospital experiences contributed to her being pyschopathologized and to further alienation from her family. Meghan grew up feeling like she was crazy, rather than surviving within a crazy-making situation.

Nearly 20 years later, Meghan discovered a box of journals and hospital records in a storage unit she had rented. These materials give testimony to her childhood odyssey through multiple traumas, compounded by re-traumatization from professionals' treatment. In the years prior to reading these records, Meghan questioned her memory and blamed herself for not telling people that she had been raped by her father and sexually abused by her stepfather. Over and over again, the records document how Meghan did confide in professionals in outpatient and hospital settings, yet her disclosures did not impact her treatment.

In the interview, Meghan reflects on her lifelong learning about what has and has not contributed to her own healing, and how a collaborative approach to therapeutic work fortified her determination to live free from the suffocation of self-blame for what was clearly not her fault. Meghan's passion for ballet saved her as a growing child, yet until our work together, she had been separated from her beloved ballet world for nearly 20 years.

Meghan's first hospital experience was when she became depressed as a teenager.

> *I was tried on all sorts of drugs, which didn't get me better. My psychiatrist decided to do an experiment. It was around the time when Children of Alcoholics became a big deal in the 1980s. He decided that alcoholics and drug addicts and children of alcoholics and drug addicts are really quite similar and need to be treated the same way. He thought it was very clever to put me, a teenager who had never used alcohol or drugs, into an adult substance abuse treatment inpatient program for 30 days to be treated just like alcoholics and addicts... So I was in this unit for 30 days where at the time there was only one other woman. I had to follow the 12 steps, all of them.*

Documented in the records is a great moment of resistance and protest when Meghan could not readily complete the first step – admitting that she was powerless over alcohol. In our work together, Meghan realized she was not only traumatized but subjected to additional trauma, by professionals and their treatment of her.

> *If you look through my records, you'll see that the amount of drugs I was on was crazy. The doctor I was working with had a whole thing about thinking that maybe I had epilepsy. I had to go to a sleep clinic with all sorts of stuff on my head and at night. It was a little trying! The treatment for epilepsy meant taking a series of tests in which they would try to induce a seizure. There was a lot of experimental science going on. When I did a Google search on this doctor, I discovered that years later his medical license was revoked for doing the same kinds of things to other people over time that finally resulted in a death.*

In reviewing these records, I became a witness to some of the horrifying experiences that have shaped Meghan's life. Together, we re-engaged with her history including "the absent but implicit" (White, 2000a) ways that Meghan responded that were not evident to her. Throughout, she demonstrated incredible trust, the desire to help other people and a steadfast quality of going back over and over, always hoping that somebody would hear her throughout her multiple hospitalizations.

From reading the records and journals, it seems that what I continued wanting was to help people who were having difficulties, embracing the idea that life is hard. Maybe in the future, I could be somebody who could help other people. I eventually got my law degree and was a public interest lawyer representing kids in trouble. Now I've moved on to other things.

Meghan described her biggest discovery:

The absolutely most helpful thing in our work together was that we discovered that I'm not crazy. For most of my life, I have felt that there was something inherently wrong with me. The system pathologized me and categorized me into anything they could fit into the DSM and treated me in that way from that point on. They didn't see me. I thought I was crazy because of the power of a medical doctor saying that "Yes, in fact, you are seriously troubled..." Then my father used that as permission to say, "You really are crazy and so the disruption that happened in our family is all your fault." When I eventually did tell people that my father had sexually abused me, it could all be chalked up to be being crazy, as though I were making it up.

Meghan explained how this revelation has affected her life:

Realizing I'm not crazy has allowed for a wholeness, for the complete me to start emerging instead of a person who had a period of time she wants to dismiss. I had put up a wall. I didn't want to talk about it. I didn't want to think about it. I had forgotten most of it. In that process, I didn't allow ballet in my life. Ballet was my greatest passion. By needing to push away this whole period of my life, thinking that I was nuts, I also pushed away my greatest passion... Doing this work together, I can allow all of me back.

Letter-writing and Online Reflections

I have shown the recorded interview with Meghan in academic and workshop settings. I then ask people to take 15 minutes to write a "from the heart" letter to Meghan that will link their lives around shared themes. I remind them to stay as close as they can to the words and sentiments of the story that Meghan has shared, referring to their notes of anything that particularly caught their attention. I then request volunteers to read their letters aloud. Students listen attentively to each other's powerfully unique letters. An online forum offers an additional medium for students to reflect on letter-writing experiences. I include the following below: a few letters from students and workshop participants in New Zealand; Meghan's letter to students after reading their letters and students' online reflections.

Letters to Meghan

The impact of these experiences extends beyond the classroom. In her letter, Abby described the impact of Meghan's interview in changing how she will practice therapy:

Dear Meghan,

...I got so much out of watching the taped interview and was scribbling notes the whole way through. One thing I heard very clearly was how your work with Peggy allowed you to feel whole again. This stood out for me, as did many of the things you said: "In pushing away the pain, I also pushed away my passion" (referring to your love of ballet), and talking about your reaction to Peggy's description of your response to trauma "she does not like me in spite of my struggles, but because of them"

These words and how your work with Peggy has influenced you will affect the way I practice therapy. The honesty in which I allow myself to respond to others has often been stifled by traditional practice theory and ideas... I now see the benefit of allowing myself to be open and honest in response to a client.

This letter was written in a hurry but I want you to know how valuable this video viewing was for me. Thank you,

    Abby

Students express outrage at the treatment Meghan received in the hospital:

I am seething with anger over your hospital experience. I work as a school counselor and have gone out on a limb at times to prevent pathologizing practices in response to young people's difficulties. I am outraged! But abusive practices were used "experimentally" on you. I sometimes despair as a professional, wondering, "how many other Meghan's are out there"? Please know you are heard. My eyes and ears are wide open your story will forever inform my practice, my life, my ideas and understandings of what is truly ethical.

Meghan's story resonates with students and workshop participants across the globe. They are relieved to be reminded that I screen these letters. They share stories from their own lives, which I can then share with Meghan.

Dear Meghan,

Thank you for your courage and your generosity in giving Peggy permission to share the tape of your conversation with Mary and Peggy. I was very moved by how you were able to hold onto believing and acting with kindness in the face of oppressive and cruel experiences. A memory of my mother who was also labeled unhelpfully came to mind strongly. She too held onto her… dignity and belief in kindness through times of great suffering. I wish that she could've heard this tape as it would have, I believe, given her great comfort in knowing she was not alone. I think too, she would've cheered you on and seen in you what Peggy sees.

Watching the tape…has reinforced that in this crazy world acting with kindness is what connects us together. That's my belief anyway, and it has been wonderful to have you remind me of that.

With love,
   Aileen

I am amazed by what students can write in just a few minutes. Here, a student aptly turns the table to recognize Meghan as my teacher:

Dear Meghan,

Thank you for your generosity and courage in allowing us to meet you and hear some of your story. I feel quite tearful and have a lump in my throat to think of all the outrageous sufferings that have been inflicted upon you by people in positions of trust – first family members, then those professionals whose sacred duty it was to assist you to heal. Instead they added insult and injury to injury. I am reminded of a beautiful racehorse that has been starved and beaten but whose spirit miraculously was never broken. To hear your words "kindliness is a value I have" makes me marvel at your resilience and humaneness. Meghan, my principal professional contributions have been to raise awareness of the abuse of "clients" by "professionals," to assist persons to struggle against anorexia, perfectionism, despair. I feel enriched by the radiance of your warm character, your deep intellect, and your gift for connection with trustworthy people. I believe that your presence in anyone's life is and will be in the future, an experience of grace. Peggy is fortunate to have had you as a teacher.

Please accept my warmest wishes and heartfelt encouragement as you navigate "between worlds." Lovingly,
   Ann

Sometimes, several students decide to write a letter together:

Dear Meghan,

Thank you for allowing us to hear a part of your story. It was such a privilege to witness it. We are saddened that the abuses you experienced in your life started when you were young and continued over a long time.

Has knowing what it is like to be supported in a therapeutic relationship made it possible to "stretch the edges" and return to your home state? What are the things you take from your work with Peggy that help you through the difficult parts? Seeing yourself through Peggy's eyes – what is it you know about yourself that helps you? What knowledges and skills do you have to help you get through this hard time you're facing?

We enjoyed the laughter in the clip. As counselors, we really appreciate hearing you say that sharing laughter can play an important part in the therapeutic relationship. We also found it helpful to know that at times clients appreciate having us express our outrage when hearing their stories.

Thank you for the gift of your story. The courage we witnessed reminds us of the courage of our clients and encourages us to take up courage in our own lives.

Best wishes,
Averill & Jill & Ireni

After reading the first batch of students' letters, Meghan asked me to share the following letter with the class:

Dear Students,

Thank you for your heartfelt, kind, thought-provoking, and thoughtful letters. Many of you thanked me in your letters and now it is I who needs to thank you. For 20 years, I believed that anyone who knew the details regarding my hospitalizations would come to the same conclusions as the "professionals" – that there is something terribly wrong with me. Your letters show me something quite different. I cannot thank you enough for sharing with me your "gut" responses, all of which spoke of your outrage or sadness for what I experienced. It took a solid chunk out of the shame I have felt for so long.

In addition to combating my shame, you showed me that something terrific will come out of my horrific experiences. Each of your letters expressed a desire to examine how you want to work with clients and openness to a different way of being within the field of social work. Many of you seem eager to determine your professional identities, taking what is useful from your training, incorporating the skills you naturally have and creating the art of your work.

One of the joys I will carry with me is the knowledge that you witnessed the whole of what Peggy and I expressed on the DVD. Simply put, through your letters you demonstrated what you are learning. Rather than taking with you what you witnessed individually in Peggy or in me, you saw and heard that the true power is in what Peggy and I co-created, how we work together.

I also appreciate the vulnerability that many of you expressed. Hearing how you were personally impacted by our work created a shared experience that is deeply touching. Again, you displayed some of what Peggy and I were encouraging you to do, to be real and genuine in your interactions. Your personal stories are moving and created a feeling of connection with you even though we likely will never meet.

My words of appreciation seem inadequate for the depth of the gift you have all given me. I will always treasure your letters.

> *Best wishes,*
>   *Meghan*

This letter from Meghan meant far more to the students than anything I could have said or done. In situations like this, I act like a conduit or a honey bee, cross-pollinating between wild flowers. I believe the teacher's role is critically important in setting up the medium through which the electrical current flows, or the ecological environment for the transfer of pollen grains. Yet the most meaningful exchange takes place between the people themselves, who deeply touch each others' lives.

Online Reflections

After class, I start an online forum, inviting students to bring their reflections and questions online. Students give an array of responses. They often remark on how good it felt to respond directly to Meghan in a handwritten letter. Michelle describes what was "an amazing experience for me; I am not quite sure of its full impact on me, but it has been in my thoughts when I least expect it." Other students reflect online:

Posting by Mohammad

As the DVD began, watching the scene through my biased, prejudiced eyes, I saw Meghan, an obviously middle class, very healthy looking woman, with only a slight edge of anxiety about what was about to be revealed about her, expressed through her laughter. I thought she could not possibly have serious life difficulties. Meghan sat listening bravely, however, as Peggy recounted what she had learned about her life story of rape, trauma, and betrayal; all having been dismissed by the hotshot expert, the victim again victimized, all before she was even an adult. The account of what Meghan had experienced clobbered me. I felt the weight of it. I wondered if I would have survived an ordeal like that. Meghan's face, however, stayed healthy-looking. She looked adoringly at Peggy, for that is where she had seen the health first reflected back to her.

The problem is no longer her problem, it remains externalized. Meghan has told us all a story about life and the possibility to retell it as a celebration of life and not as it may be told in a case conference, where Meghan would have been treated as a "thing," devoid of her humanity; the clinicians shielded from her by their "white lab coats" and credentials. We are coming full circle, back to small groups of human beings taking turns holding the talking

stick, no ranks, all equal, and no subject excluded. Let us write a new story
for humanity.

The online forum gives students ample opportunity to build on each other's reflections. Having such genuine online conversation contributes to everyone's understanding of shared experiences.

Posting by Lauren

Thank you for that wonderful reflection I just read. I too wondered at first about who Meghan was – her knowledge, her appearance, I wondered, "What does she have to teach me?" But again a lesson in humility; she (as we all are) is marvelous and unique. What a powerful example of the need to hold open space for all possibilities when working with people. Thank you again for your words, Mohammad, as they mirror what Meghan and Peggy offered us through the sharing – as you said a story of "no subject excluded."

Cally appreciated the acknowledgement that Meghan and I gave to our special connection, and the loss that we would both feel in Meghan's leaving:

Posting by Cally

I found it really powerful that they were not defining exactly what their relationship will look like after Meghan's move, but continuing to let it evolve. Leaving room for the relationship to continue and not ending it completely honors the relationship, the work together, and Meghan as a person. For me that is a clear example and embodiment of some of the guiding principles of narrative therapy: the importance of being real, open, and genuine; that the work between client and therapist is a shared journey of unfolding the story together, and that the person is not the problem, the problem is the problem.

Students often reflect on the relevance to their own lives and work. Their online conversation addresses complexities that might otherwise go unnoticed in class. After hearing Meghan and me speak about our preparations for Meghan's impeding move, Amy reflected online about her own experiences as an intern in the middle of ending with a number of children as she changes jobs. She struggled with having gotten close to a number of them, imagining minimal contact in the future. "I'd like to leave my address so that if kids want to update me on how they are doing, they could write a letter to me, which I would then respond to. However, working for an agency, I find myself wondering whether this would be deemed 'acceptable and professional."

Amy shared a story about working closely with a mother during her internship who asked about keeping in touch after they ended. She took the request to her supervisor since the mother wanted more involvement than Amy could give her. Her supervisor told her she should not return a call after their work ended, but should instead tell the supervisor, who would be working with the mother after Amy left. Her words to Amy were: "When you end, you end." In fact, the mother did call her once – Amy called her supervisor, who told her not to return the call, that she would do it for her. After hearing Meghan's experience, Amy questioned an agency ending practice that now seemed inhospitable: "I felt as though I should have at least returned her phone call, especially since we had developed such a good relationship. I feel as though she may have taken offense to me not calling back, and I've wished that I'd handled it differently."

REFLECTIONS

I came of age as a human services practitioner in the 1970s, talking with parents at their kitchen tables and playing with babies among scattered toys on living room floors. As a therapist, I have always been drawn to collaborative ways of working, and repelled by professional preciousness. I learned to deeply value people's sovereignty over their own lives and to embrace a sense of solidarity with people whose lives touch mine. I am well aware that with a twist of fate, our roles could be reversed and I could become the person requesting services.

Current trends in the United States worry me. I hear alarming stories about training the next generation of mental health, psychiatric, and medical practitioners that risks putting paperwork ahead of people and restricting care to only those who can afford services. The fear of litigation and encroaching bureaucracy are formidable forces in everyone's lives. Yet the students I meet almost all share a belief in social justice and in the earnest desire to be of service to others.

When people bequest complete strangers with some of what they have faced and overcome - such as the accounts in this book documenting the experiences and insights of Pru, Pam, Kate, Nicole, Chava, Josie and Mylo, Ruth, Leah, Pamela, Isabelle, Lori, Alan, and Meghan – we become enlivened with a sense of humanity, a passion for our work, and for making a difference in others' lives. Learning directly from people rising to occasions of struggle teaches us far more than we could ever learn from any book or teacher. A hero(ine) is someone of distinguished courage or ability, admired for her or his brave deeds and noble qualities[41]. I am not being glib when I say this: These are my heroines and heroes. I am proud and honored that they grant me the privilege of bringing their hard-earned wisdom into my classroom and onto these pages.

APPRENTICING TO A CRAFT

Success is boring. Success is proving that you can do something that you already know you can do. Failure is how we learn.

John Carroll, "Watching a Daughter Fly By" From the series, *This I Believe.* National Public Radio, October 9, 2006

I have heard the co-founders of narrative therapy, David Epston and Michael White, each speak about their apprenticeship to the craft of narrative practice. After more than 30 years of practice, Michael White recently said, "I consider myself still in an early stage of apprenticeship, which I expect to be in for the rest of my life" (White, 2007d). Apprenticeship refers to a system for training a new generation of skilled practitioners in an art, trade, or craft[42]. Becoming an apprentice typically involves a combination of on-the-job training and related classroom instruction where people learn the practical and theoretical aspects of a skilled occupation. Apprenticing to narrative practice is a more informal process. I invite students to join me in a lifelong commitment to continually sharpen their therapeutic practices.

This chapter explores practices I use to encourage students to learn specific interviewing skills and outsider witness practices based on post-structural approaches in counseling while simultaneously making them their own (Behan, 2003). In each class, I try to provide students with the necessary time to hone the narrative skills I introduce; I want them to appreciate the features that are either unique to the narrative approach or at variance with other therapies they have been studying.

The chapter begins with dynamic online conversation about learning to ask questions that engage "the powerhouse of embodied curiosity." We revisit how the therapist can speak personally, bringing in her own stories, while still maintaining the focus on the other person. I show one way I set the stage for learning from trial and error in crafting letters so students can practice to "ask, don't tell." I illustrate with students' online reflections as they attend to questions asked by Michael White in the video-taped recording of the interview, "The Best of Friends" (White, 1994). I further excerpt students' reflections on two in-class exercises: 1) interviewing insider knowledge; and 2) co-constructing interview questions.

POWERHOUSE OF EMBODIED CURIOSITY

I give students opportunities to practice asking questions from what I have come to think of as speaking from "the powerhouse of embodied curiosity." I arrived at this metaphor from my love of Pilates. I want students to situate their responses from a stance of personal resonance as they listen attentively to people who consult with them. In an online class forum on letter-writing, I posted the following:

Recently, I discovered Pilates. Does anyone else practice Pilates? I love learning this discipline. One of my few regrets in life is that I did not start Pilates sooner. Now my mind often sees Pilates metaphors everywhere – so beware! I am being taught how to move from the abdominals – "the powerhouse." The effects are subtle yet profound. I am also learning how to work internally with forces in opposition with each other – to be scooping into my abdominals while simultaneously moving/pushing in an opposite direction. It's a bit like Taoism in action...or the dialectic of change referenced in Marxism or DBT (Dialectical Behavior Therapy)... I get small sensations that show me that I am actually learning (in small ways) to move while holding these tensions. It's hard work for me, fraught with nuances and mistakes – but I love doing a regular discipline that shows me how practice over time makes a difference.

I think narrative practice is similar. People who have not studied narrative therapy often think it is a superficial technique based on externalization. But this is so far from the truth. It is about finding a different kind of power-house – learning to listen from an embodied place of curiosity, holding the complexities to the best of your ability, often working with opposing forces such as being simultaneously transparent and decentered, developing comfort in one's own stories, yet intentional in putting the client's stories at the center of your conversations.

I want students to experience congruence in their approach to interviewing, reflecting teamwork, and letter-writing. I start a conversational forum with the following questions:

Narrative practice calls on us to be transparent about all sorts of things – power relations, the ideas informing our practices, and the stories that inform our lives. What skill development is needed in order to speak our own unique voice from an embodied place of candid curiosity while at the same time being clear about who is at the center of the conversation (not us!)?

When students hear that they don't need to leave themselves behind, they often express a great sense of relief. Carol worked as a hospice social worker. She reflected online after watching the interview in which Meghan describes her appreciation of honest responses that reflect service providers' emotions.

Posting by Carol

I was a little worried about my emotional responses to the great sadness that families were experiencing, especially since I am very apt to tear up or cry when I am deeply moved by a story I hear or when I experience some of people's pain. I was so relieved when a person with great experience said that the tears that "helpers" shed in empathy with the families were often remembered by families as the most significant gift that a helper could give. This information took away my worries, and I often did cry with families. I have rarely found that honest and caring expression of my humanity has been accepted as anything but just that.

Personal Sharing

In their online exchanges, students candidly struggle to unlearn some of their assumptions and inquire into what people in the designated role of service seeker prefer in those who intend to serve them. Ken posted about challenges in unlearning what he has known forever to be "right." Melissa added, "There is a fine line between revealing enough of oneself to be useful vs. going autobiographical. But, I also think we are not giving ourselves enough credit for our training and experience and curiosity. If anything, I am so preoccupied with how much to share, I think the important thing for me is unlearning the practice of not sharing. "

I marvel at the kind of open dialogue an online forum makes possible; people post different angles on a given question, without anyone needing to take the devil's advocate point of view. Celia wrote that she too generally thinks therapists in Western culture self-reveal too little. However, she added a caution:

A little personal information here and there from therapists has always seemed really helpful to me – it makes the person seem real. But I think any kind of advice or story that could be taken as advice has to be treated carefully. My friend in a Creativity Consulting master's program explained to me why facilitators of creativity sessions very rarely share any of their own ideas during a brainstorming session. She quoted some statistic noting that if the facilitator participates, 70-80% of the time after the brainstorming a group will choose to pursue an idea given by the facilitator. That was a powerful reminder for me of the weight and power we carry just be being the designated "leader!"

Adding my own questions to Celia's inquiry, I begin a forum with the following questions about personal sharing with clients:

What are some of the cautions that come to mind? If it is possible to draw from our own stories, what are other checks and balances that are important to put in place to ensure that we are acting ethically, keeping the focus on the other person, not on ourselves? What are useful ways to bring stories into our conversations with clients (written and in person), sharing what we have learned from our work with others we know as well as some of our own stories? Has anyone had experiences that you have learned from the hard way – such as telling a story about yourself that felt too personal to share, or being on the client end and experiencing the person in the therapist role taking up too much space talking about her/himself? How do you wish to put these learnings into practice in your own work?

Students agreed that in sharing one's own history, one needs to ask oneself, "Who is being served here?" Dorothy added: "Am I sharing to create trust, establish credibility, maintain some power differential"? She suggested that sharing of self can be helpful if it's done out of compassion, which is why support groups and communities of concern can be so powerful. "I don't think a therapist can be the last word on change and reclamation – nor should we try to be. Maybe the best we can hope for is to be part of an expanding team if that's what's called for." Dorothy further reflected after viewing the recorded interview with Meghan; she thought about Meghan's response to the question, "How is your relationship with Peggy different from a friendship?" While we might easily have been friends in another context, Meghan recognized the benefits of a protected relationship, where she did not have to take care of me as she might a friend. As much fun as it might be, she knew we wouldn't go bicycling together. Our focus is more specific.

Posting by Dorothy

Meghan's taped interview was particularly helpful for me around the question of dual relationships and the loss of a therapeutic relationship if you do introduce elements (activities) that might change the relationship. Clearly Meghan and Peggy care for and trust each other, but Meghan is relieved to know she doesn't have to worry about how any information she shares is affecting Peggy. How often do people censor themselves around friends or family if they think information may hurt or disturb that person? There's a non-judgmental quality to the therapeutic relationship that often cannot reside comfortably within family or friendship – the person seeking therapy needs to know they don't have to censor themselves for fear of damaging a relationship. I think Meghan and Peggy have worked out a thoughtful, caring way to continue their work that doesn't compromise what they've built together and still offers much support.

LEARNING FROM TRIAL AND ERROR

I often share with students a piece of wisdom my clinical supervisor passed on when I was just starting out as a family therapist. A seasoned therapist, Peter seemed to know something about everything. One day I asked him, "Peter, how do you know so much?" He responded, "The only difference between me and you is that I've been doing it longer." I tell students that through practice, reflection, and revision they too will become skilled and knowledgeable practitioners.

I tell my classes stories that exemplify my own ongoing learning from students. The following email exchange has served as an excellent demonstration of everyday learning about applause practices in letter-writing. Lauren gave me permission to share some of our email exchange with others to demonstrate how easy it is to fall into telling someone their story (a trap to which even the teacher isn't immune). Our exchange clearly illustrates the difference between my well-meaning, but not particularly helpful, reflective cheerleading stance and an interrogatory query from a place of earnest curiosity. I read this correspondence with Lauren to students as an introduction to "Take-Two Exercises" with letter-writing.

Lauren was the first to post in the course assignments forum in her cyber small-group. In my quick email, I thanked Lauren for finding the courage to be the first to post her letter and map. The tone of my communication was sweet yet embarrassingly predictable in pointing out positives. I was particularly drawn to one event on Lauren's map – the diagnosis of leukemia a few years prior. Rather than asking, I make assumptions in this letter excerpt:

Hi Lauren,

Just a quick email to thank you for finding the courage to be the first to post your map and letter. It is lovely to get to know you better... I was very touched by your letter and wonder if you will send this to Mom, Dad, and Marian. I imagine this would be so healing for them as well, to know that you hold gifts from all three in your heart, and how the totality of their love fills your veins and allows you to fly. What could any parent of separation/divorce want more for their child?

From our brief exchanges, I already knew that you had some kind of special knowledge – perhaps it is the experience of living with leukemia? I imagine you learned early (the hard way) life wisdom that most people don't learn till much older (if at all) – that life is precious, your pain is linked to my pain and your healing to my healing, to take risks, to play your unique role in creating social justice in this crazy world of ours, and to remember to DANCE throughout it all.

Lauren began her email by thanking me for my response.

It was lovely to wake up and turn on my computer and see a message from you waiting!...I do plan on giving the letter to my parents. This will be an interesting act of becoming more my own person and an adult, I feel. I wanted to respond to one of the things that you reflected in your email to me because it is familiar and I wonder if other people feel the same; if so, it might be a great thing for you to know from my perspective. :) You commented that I seemed to have a special knowledge and that this might come from my experience with leukemia...I feel like I did learn things through my illness, but that I have always had a special knowledge throughout my life based more on myself and upbringing. I sometimes bristle when people ask me how I was "changed" by the experience of being sick, because one interpretation is that there was something that needed to be changed. I know there was nothing in me that needed to be changed by leukemia. However, I can take all the growth that I get, including around my illness, and change. Does that make sense?

I was humbled by Lauren's email – the subject of my email response was "Take 2":

Good morning, Lauren! ...Thank you for your earnest and kind reply. Email has its limitations (as does time) but I still want to seize the moment to respond as best I can. First of all, for several reasons, I really appreciate what you shared with me from an insider's perspective on the origins of your "special knowledge," how this is based more on your understandings of yourself and your upbringing than on your experiences of illness. I am glad that you felt comfortable enough to speak up ("correct the teacher"), and you did this with such a clear and gentle voice. I think (hope!) I will always remember what you told me, especially since your words resonate with my own experience. I am often reflecting on (and telling others) how we are too quick to tell others their experiences – to weave stories based on fantasized and romanticized notions – without actually asking people to share their own unique experiences. Your email reminded me that this kind of "remember-to-ask-rather-than-to-tell" vigilance is a lifelong pursuit (maybe akin to resisting racism), to which I am far from immune.

I'd like to share a story with you. Two and a half years ago, my husband Shel was diagnosed with mouth cancer – an aggressive cancer that was caught early. He went through about two months of gruelling treatment and about a year of recovery. As a middle-aged man, this experience opened him up in ways that perhaps were already a part of your being, as a growing child. In June, Shel met his two year mark, post-treatment, which is real cause for celebration, since 90% of recurrence happens in the first two years...

It was/has been/still is rare to experience others' earnest curiosity about what my experience has been. Instead, I have experienced something perhaps similar to what you described as when people ask me how I was "changed" by the experience of being sick. I found that people (always with good intentions) would immediately either want to make my/our story into a tragedy or romanticize my/our/his experience ("You are so strong." "This must have brought you so much closer," and so on). As a result, I learned to hold my experiences close and to share them very selectively. How is this similar or different to the experience you describe?

Your email also drew me to re-read the email I wrote you and to critique how I might like to tweak this if I was sending it again, this time as "a letter" rather than as a quick email. With letter-writing, I ask students to practice writing and rewriting letters – so of course, I really should practice this myself. As an apprentice to the craft of letter-writing, I am reminded of how helpful it can be to ask questions, and not just with a reflective voice.

I then attached a "Take 2" of my original letter, requesting, "Can you let me know your response to the following letter? I'll also add the original to the bottom." My second draft included the following revision:

Hi Lauren,

Just a quick email to thank you for finding the courage to be the first to post your map & letter...One advantage of posting early is that I was able to sit with your story this morning over my morning coffee. It is lovely to get to know you better.

I was very touched by your letter and wonder if you will send this to Mom, Dad, and Marian? Do you think this might be healing for them as well, to know that you hold gifts from all three in your heart, and how the totality of their love fills your veins and allows you to fly? In what ways do you think parents of separation/divorce might want their child to take this unifying step?

Your map made me wish I could know more about so much – the risks you have taken, your commitment to social justice, your awareness of how your pain is linked to my pain and your healing to my healing, and what helps you to remember to DANCE through it all. Just from our brief exchanges, I already knew that you had some kind of special knowledge. Your map offers so many illustrations of life wisdom that most people don't learn till much older (if at all). In reading your map, I was drawn to the event of living with leukemia. Perhaps I was especially drawn to this event because my husband, Shel, is a cancer survivor. How do you think the experience of living with leukemia has contributed to your special knowledges about yourself and of living? In what ways do you feel connected to others who speak to the impact of life-threatening illness on their development of self-knowledge, in recognizing the preciousness of life and in our connection with each other? In what ways do you think your unique experiences set you apart from others who live through life-threatening illness? Do you think your upbringing somehow prepared you for the challenges posed by your illness, and if so, what would you want others to learn from your experiences?

Lauren responded:

Dear Peggy,

I read your re-letter yesterday at a cafe and started crying. You got it. You got it. You got it. In fact, writing this to you I am starting to cry again. What a gift for you to share yourself with me as you did and respond with your questions, validating my experience, making me the expert. Truly, I feel heard by you and honored by you. Thank you.

There is so much to respond to in your re-vision. Thank you for sharing your own story about your husband. I am so glad to hear that good health is continuing for him, as for me. I resonated with your description of feeling that others, with best intentions, would either "tragedize" or "romanticize" the experience, leaving you no room to share what was true and real for you. What you describe feels very akin to being told/or others assuming that I have grown. If I choose to reflect on my experience with someone in that way it is a true gift to them because it feels like a vulnerable, misunderstood, place. A place too that is so profound. Is this similar or different from what you shared?

Your rewording of the letter to me opened my heart and feels healing. When you ask rather than suggest, I feel so much more heard. I will remember this. How does it feel for you to hear this from me? When you included yourself in the end, joining with me in "dancing," I felt so recognized. Do you feel like the metaphor (and actual process) of dance is useful to you in your own journey? As you allude to, dance for me is profound, passion, life-giving, and affirming. What is profound, passionate, and life-giving for you?

I do not feel like I can give justice to your letter in this moment with final papers due and so on. I would love to explore the questions you pose more in the future. I wonder if we may continue a dialogue in space? I wonder what that would look like or feel like for me? What would it feel like for you?

Before I sign off today - I want to reiterate that this conversation is very healing, as is this course. I so appreciate your openness and loving kindness. This feels inadequate in some ways – but again, thank you for the conversation.

Best,
   Lauren

TAKE 2

I read aloud to my class excerpts from my email exchange with Lauren as an opportunity to teach the difference between telling and asking someone about their story, to invite students into the metaphor of apprenticing oneself to the craft of letter-writing (and reflecting), and to give opportunities to practice writing and rewriting letters from an interrogatory stance. I share part of my response to Lauren's letter back to me:

In your letter, you speak so clearly about how differently you feel when asked rather than having something suggested. In particular, you gently asserted how your special knowledge is based more on your upbringing and on yourself than from your experience with leukemia. In other words, you articulated a desire to story your own life instead of being told what it is, even by a person in a position of authority (teacher in this context, but could be therapist in another context).

I have discovered no better way to introduce the topic of revision than to show my own learning curve. I believe it is helpful for students to see their teachers make mistakes, "fess up," and correct them. Before hearing this exchange, I think quite a few of the students believed in "the strengths perspective" and "cheerleading" as their unequivocal preferred ways of being social workers. However, hearing Lauren's experience provoked their seeing the strengths perspective as a step forward from a pathologizing approach, yet still needing further refinement.

I have used this email exchange with Lauren as an introduction to the students' own "Take 2" letter-writing exercise. The prior week, they viewed the DVD of the interview with me and Meghan and then wrote letters to Meghan. While well-intentioned, their letters were filled with pointing out positives and too few questions or statements situated in their own experiences. I asked the students to do their own "Take 2" exercise, revising their letters much as I revised my own letter to Lauren. Sharing the example of my own cheerleading and applause and how I responded when Lauren pointed it out to me contributes to creating a more relaxed, less judgmental milieu for practice.

In preparation for this class, I typed out all the letters that students from several of my classes had written to Meghan, without any identifying information[43]. I then printed out a stack of letters. Each student chose a letter and worked on revising it in ways that would still honor the spirit of what was said, but making subtle changes from telling/suggesting to asking. I suspect it eased the way for students to attempt this with a randomly chosen letter so as not to get caught up in 'correcting' their own letters. They became more or less editors than authors in this 'Take 2." It really helped students to do this with someone else's letter first so as not to get caught in worries about not getting their own letters right.

Letters Revisions

Once they try it out themselves, students are almost uniformly convinced that letter writing can be an inspiring and powerful therapy tool. They express appreciation for more concrete application of the ideas they are learning and exploring in their graduate training. Rachel spoke candidly about her struggle with writing a letter to Meghan that appropriately states what she heard her say, how it related to her own life, and questions for the future. "However I think the questions were the hardest." She was thankful to be given a "Take 2" in class to further explore letter-writing.

To illustrate the Take 2 exercise, here are two letters – the original and a revision. A student revised the letter to experiment with adding her own reflections and questions to the above original letter as follows:

ORIGINAL	TAKE 2
Hi Meghan, Thank you for honoring us with your story, a piece of your story. I am sitting here thinking about how you said talking with us allows us to see you as a real person and not a disorder and	Hi Meghan, I feel honored to have seen the videotape you made with Peggy Sax of your last meeting together. Thank you for being willing to share your story with strangers and thank you for giving me the opportunity to witness this

how profound that was for you, how it allowed you to change. I heard this and first thought, "and what a person she is, what an amazingly brave, resilient person." I then thought of the time I felt really heard and understood. I remembered the struggle I had with feeling I'd be embarrassed, the person I was sharing with would see me as weak from what I shared. It felt similar to the feelings you describe. It made me wonder why we don't tell our stories more, hear our feelings more. I'm proud of you for sharing your story. I'm proud of you for creating a connection that helped you to be able to share it. I'm proud of all the story tellers, story sharers in this world. Thank you.
Warmly,

celebration and review of your work together. I wonder what this says about you that you are able to turn this experience into a learning tool for others.
What you said resonates with me about being cooperative throughout the trials and mistrials of providers and how it appears that you were able to heal, despite all of the "jaw dropping" behavior on the part of your step-father and then the professionals in your life. You mentioned being more than a disorder and the importance for helpers to recognize all of a person. When did you first realize this?
Hearing you speak made me wonder why we don't tell our stories more. I remember times when I have shared a story of struggle with another person, and then worried that the listener would think that I was weak because I had shared my story. When I realized that I had been heard, it was validating. I think that I understood you as having described similar feelings, that someone finally listened and you were understood, it helped you see that you are not "crazy" and you were able to start healing. Did I understand this correctly?

After the "Take 2" letter-writing exercise in class, I posted the following:

Today in class we spent some time crafting a "Take 2" of letters written to Meghan in response to having viewed the DVD of the conversation about our work together. Thank you to those of you who gave me these handwritten revisions. I really appreciate the specific ways you illustrate shifting from "telling" to "asking" in these letters. This is the forum for any of you to post any other newly crafted letters (Take 2 or even Take 3) and/or to share any reflections on letter-writing. What has been particularly interesting to you about our focus on letter-writing in this course? What do you find yourself pondering? How (if at all) do you think this practice might influence your work outside of this course?

Students shared their appreciation for practicing letter-writing using people's own words and incorporating questions. Ellen described how the "Take 2" exercise helped her put the art of asking questions into practice "rather than making sweeping judgments or platitudes." Danielle also emphasized how helpful the "Take 2" exercise was for her:

I definitely struggled with the first letter, [trying to] find a balance between appearing genuine and not appearing as though I was an "expert" of some sort. The Take 2 made me realize that one of the best ways to validate and appreciate someone's experience is to use their own words. I really enjoyed the questions as well. I was unsure of the effects of this at first, but it really sets the stage for reflection and intimate conversation.

Danielle further described how she hopes to use letter-writing in practice. She gave an illustration from her work with teenagers, demonstrating how letter-writing could be an excellent outlet for them to relate to each other and create bonds among one other.

To me, it is very powerful to see the words written down, and the ability to literally hold on to what someone has said, especially when you feel a connection of any sort. In many instances, especially for me, it is so easy to twist and over-analyze what someone has said; it's like you can't believe someone said something good about you or could understand you in any way, so you twist what was said in your mind so that you can tell yourself that they didn't really mean it or make up some excuse. However, in a letter, it's there on the page; you can't rewrite their words.

Amy articulated the ongoing challenge in narrative practice to speak in one's voice from a de-centered position:

I enjoyed writing the letter to Meghan, but I definitely found myself grappling with needing to say "the right thing" and then trying to get myself away from that thought. I was so personally struck by many of the things she talked about – I'm currently in the process of leaving my job. I also personally related to her comments about how after a period of change there is that chaotic period where everything seems "out of whack." I tried to incorporate that in my letter to her, but then found myself thinking, have I made this more about me than her?

REFLECTION ON IN-CLASS EXERCISES

Students consistently tell me they learn best from experiential learning. Structuring opportunities to practice listening and interviewing skills is an important aspect of teaching counseling skills. Constructing exercises is fun and additionally provides a way to connect with teaching colleagues, many of whom traditionally go about their teaching with limited opportunities for collegial support and co-invention. I have found a generosity of spirit in my fellow teachers sharing our exercise discoveries with each other[44].

The classroom becomes a learning lab for further refinement - I am always experimenting with interviewing exercises originated by others, using a hybrid of exercises for students to practice asking questions, think about problems, hold multiple listening positions, experience collaborative inquiry, and work with transcripts (Buckley & Decter, in press; Epston, 2003b; Epston, Lakusta, & Tomm, 2006; Lewis & Cheshire, 2007; Roth, 2007; White, 1992, 2003b).

In the online forum I create to reflect on in-class experiences, students share thoughtful reflections. They expand on our class sessions in ways that help deepen their own and classmates' learning, build connections with classmates, and give me valuable guidance regarding both course content and structure. I have chosen examples of reflections from two in-class exercises here: 1) "Interviewing Insider Knowledge" and 2) "Co-constructing Questions."

Interviewing Insider Knowledge[45]

I assign students to interview each other in dyads "as investigative reporters, not helpers" about a particular topic of personal enthusiasm, about which the interviewer knows very little. Students disclose an impressive range of knowledge on a wide range of topics, such as skiing, cooking, progressive politics, and parenting. Afterwards, I start the following thread:

> *My intention in creating classroom exercises such as the "Interviewing Insider Knowledge" exercise we did is to practice listening from a place of earnest curiosity in which we "Ask don't tell" the people who consult with us...What was it like for you to think of yourselves as investigative reporters rather than "helpers?" How do you experience learning to move from this "powerhouse of curiosity?" Do you have a sense of what further contributes to your repertoire of co-researching skills? What are some of the challenges along the way such as those posed by "therapeutic gaze?" What are you noticing along the way?*

Students responded in ways that let me know this was a vital learning experience for them. Dorothy wrote, "The 'ask don't tell' message can't be repeated enough for me – I have such a tendency to want to 'fix things.'" Ken added how hard it was to unlearn how to be a helper and relearn how to be an investigator. Heidi picked up this thread:

> *I liked investigating why another person felt passionate about something, instead of just assuming why they did, because it gives the other person (the client) more power in a relationship where the helper usually tends to be the one in the position of power. However, I couldn't help but wonder if my stance was somewhat condescending. Like in Michael's book, his client asked him, "Why are you asking me that question?... you should know." But, I guess that could be easily resolved by explaining, like Michael did, that one can only know about their own lives and experiences and that it isn't the social worker's place to put onto their clients what we believe they feel or know.*

I think that this experience will help me to become a better listener, which certainly is a tool needed for co-research. It also leaves me feeling somewhat uncomfortable, as I am not in control of where the conversation is heading. I think that co-research is about just that, not being in control of the direction the research takes. I think that with experience I will develop a toolbox full of questions that can be used to investigate rather than help. But, I'm not sure if I should have a toolbox, because if I am coming from a place of pure curiosity, shouldn't my questions be fresh, and not planned?

Interviewees in the dyads also take away a great deal from this exercise as well. Students notice their interviewer's difficulty taking the "investigative" rather than "helping" stance, yet comment on how refreshing it felt to be interviewed in this way. While the debriefing begins in class, after-thoughts are shared online; the dialogues goes well beyond what students could share in an in-class discussion undertaken immediately after the interview. As Donald Schon wrote, reflection-on-action takes time and shifts the source of satisfaction for the practitioner (Schon, 1983).

As the professional moves toward new competencies, he gives up some familiar sources of satisfaction and opens himself to the freedom to practice without challenge to his competence, the comfort of relative invulnerability, the gratifications of deference. The new satisfactions open to him are largely those of discovery – about the meanings of his advice to clients, about his knowledge-in-practice, and about himself. When a practitioner becomes a researcher into his own practice, he engages in a continuing process of self-education. When practice is a repetitive administration of techniques to the same kinds of problems, the practitioner may look to leisure as a source of relief, or to early retirement; but when he functions as a researcher-in-practice, the practice itself is a source of renewal. The recognition of discovery, with its resulting uncertainty, can become a source of discovery rather than an occasion for self-defense. (p. 299)

Co-Constructing Interview Questions

I adapt this exercise as a hybrid of several colleagues' innovative teaching practices: "Thinking about problems – multiple listening in groups" (Lewis & Cheshire, 2007) p 48; The Hot Seat Exercise; (Buckley & Decter, in press); Collaborative Inquiry (Roth, 2007); the Inner-view (Epston, 2003b); and the Failure Conversations Exercise (White, 2002). Each time I do it a bit differently, although some elements remain the same. The exercise includes student participation in various roles within a large group interview; personal reflection and small group collaboration on construction of questions; practice listening and asking questions from different positions with ongoing feedback from the interviewee, classmates, and instructor. This format works well for practicing interviewing skills according to specific narrative maps (White, 2007d) or that highlight different listening positions (see below). No one is ever really in "the hot seat" since the interviewer simply asks the questions constructed and chosen in collaboration with classmates.

I first ask for a volunteer to be interviewed about a problem he or she has overcome, "Why are you so proud of the problem from the past that either disappeared, dissolved or you overcame somehow or other?" (Epston, 2003b). Another student volunteers to take the role of the interviewer, asking questions that classmates first generate in small groups. Each small group listens, collaborates in small groups and then, in their small group, selects a question to ask the interviewee from one of the three following positions, borrowed from "the multiple listening exercise" (Lewis & Cheshire, 2007) p. 48:

– Skills, knowledge, and resilience;
– Possible exceptions to the problem; or
– Context and possible discourses contributing to the problem.

I ask each group member to take several minutes to jot down a question, then share their question with their small group. Each group then selects a favorite question. When the large group reconvenes, a volunteer from each small group takes a turn presenting the group's preferred question. As collaborative inquiry (Roth, 2007), the interviewee listens to the questions, and chooses which question to respond to. The interview then continues as the interviewee and interviewer proceed with the chosen question for a few minutes; soon, I give the "time-out' signal to pause, providing students with the chance to again switch positions for their inquiry in small groups.

Afterwards, I ask the following questions on the "Practice Forum":

What was it like for you to generate these questions? How much performance anxiety did you experience in generating these questions – and if it wasn't too stressful, what do you think contributed to making this exercise work? What did you notice about the questions that your classmate in the interviewee position chose? Jennifer, as the interviewee, what lingering thoughts about this experience would you be willing to share with us? What was it like for the rest of you to participate in this group exercise, and what are your lingering thoughts and questions? Would you recommend doing this exercise again and if so, are there any specific adaptations with which you would like to experiment? What would you like to practice next?

Heidi responds by describing what she appreciated about the different steps in this exercise: being given time to first reflect on her own question before sharing questions in her small group and then practicing question-asking as a class:

I like how we first got to sit in silence in the small groups by ourselves for a bit (to formulate an initial question). This helped me to digest the experience of witnessing the interview. I also liked how we then got together with our team, as it was nice to hear everyone's questions and to feel heard. It was also great to co-create questions with others. I feel as though our questions became more thoughtful, as everyone contributed to their formation (we didn't just choose the best one). For this reason, I had limited performance anxiety with developing and asking questions. It feels different to perform together as a group than to perform as a solo act. I also like that Jennifer was able to choose what suited her at the time. I, like Luke, think that this could really be a great practice in our work – offering choices of questions to those we work with. I feel like it would give them more power in the relationship. How did you feel about that, Jennifer?

Students remind me again and again about the pressure they feel to "get it right." After a bit of practice, they relax more with each other. They observe a multitude of possible questions with no one in particular having the perfect question up their sleeve. They join in, giving suggestions for continued practice. For example, Heidi suggested more one-on-one or small group work. "I am now up for failure. It is harder for me to volunteer for larger group work. Smaller group work will force me to just do it, and that is what I need to do now." Meanwhile, Andrew reflected online about why he liked working as a team to construct questions. At first, he felt the need for him and his group to come up with "brilliant" questions as if there was some competition or desire to get it "right." Yet he soon realized the impressive capacity of collaboration along with the many ways to respond to what the interviewee might be saying:

I couldn't help but think that I would love to have this class in my sessions, push "pause" with the client, and ask for questions from you. It was a huge reminder of how in any one conversation/statement there are many leads to pull on and directions to pursue. It also reminded me that if we could come up with four different ways to pursue a short conversation, then there is great fluctuation in individual interpretation, and thus the need for checking in with the client about the direction of the work to ensure that we are indeed being helpful. Good stuff!

Luke chimes in with his reflections on the in-class question-asking exercise:

This exercise really showed me the power of questions to move a conversation in certain directions. Of course, it also showed that a plethora of questions allowed Jennifer to choose the direction she was most interested in exploring. I think Kerry noted that we could do this in solo practice as well (or as Peggy said, consult with our question-forming team in our head to generate a choice).

In the second round I remember wanting to really just ask, "Jennifer, I'm struck by two ideas you've mentioned: your response to your father and the idea of 'escape.' Which would you like to pursue? Or is there something else burning for you?" And then formulate a question. In practice I think I'd ask a lot more questions like this. Any thoughts?

Foresta especially liked the idea of coming up with multiple questions from which the person being interviewed could then choose. This is something she would like to do more in her practice:

Sometimes I feel like I am asking questions about the areas of the person's story that stand out for me, but they are not really the most important for the service user, or the person isn't ready to answer that question yet. I like giving a choice so that the service user is still in charge of the direction of the conversation. I also felt that this exercise was helpful because it allowed us to think about what we wanted to ask separately and then join together in small groups to decide what to ask as a group... It was also very helpful for me to be reminded that it is okay to slow down and take a moment to figure out what and how we want to ask something. I think all too often I forget this and am left trying to listen and formulate questions at the same time, which doesn't always work so well. It takes some of the pressure off of the need to "get it right."

Attending to Questions

When I show a recorded interview, I often divide the class into sections, assigning each section a different task, such as practicing writing letters to people in the video, giving them opportunities to hone in on specific skills without worrying whether they are "doing it right." In the following exercise, I divide the class into thirds before watching the "Best of Friends" videotaped interview with a couple with concerns about their marriage (White, 1994).[46] Group One writes and posts online letters to the couple they saw interviewed, Shannon and Kenny; Group Two receives the letters as if they were Shannon or Kenny sharing reflections of their experience; and Group Three attends to the questions asked by the interviewer. I then set up three online forums for students to interact with each other in these different roles.

Narrative therapy views life as being multi-storied, with no such thing as neutrality. I want students to see the intentionality behind questions. Here is how I introduce the forum for Group Three:

What did you notice about Michael White's questions? Which questions stand out to you? Why? How open-ended and/or specific were his questions? Did you rate any of the questions from 1 to 5 stars, as we had discussed as a possibility, and if so, what did you discover? What do you find yourself contemplating? What else did you notice about this interview, in addition to the questions?

Students identify particular questions as shaping the interview. Katy wrote down many of the questions that Michael White asked. Looking them over, she became convinced that the conversation would have taken an entirely different shape if not for Michael's questions.

Posting by Katy

The questions in the beginning allowed M.W. to join with the couple; to show genuine curiosity in who they are, and a bit about what they bring to this meeting. He does not allow the conversation to begin with a focus on the "problems" the couple has been working on. Throughout the interview, M.W. asks many questions over again, in different ways – it seems that these shaping questions are instrumental in shaping the conversation as well: i.e., "Is this something you've always done"?

"So it contributes to honesty"?

"Is it something you've been able to do in sessions? How come? Has this been a valuable skill historically"?

"And that's an approach you've had your whole life"?

"Was that a skill when you were younger"?

This line of questioning to Kenny did not allow Kenny to fall back on his old habit of being a more passive participant. It allowed him to see other times when this skill worked/may not have worked and gave him a chance to discover alternate ways of being in this process. In my opinion, 5 stars! Another line of questioning followed the reclaiming of friendship... M.W. asks, "Is that part of your vision for a relationship"?

By asking about Shannon and Kenny's visions, M.W. is helping them to move forward, out of a potentially "stuck" place, and see their relationship as more fluid. It allows them to consider their dreams for the future of their relationship, as well as see what they used to find important to a romantic relationship.

Students are often struck by the intentionality of the interviewer's questions.

Posting by Amy

I tried to write down a lot of the questions. The first couple of questions seemed to just be to get to know Kenny and Shannon. At first I thought they would just be 1 star or 2, but then I was thinking that it is important to make some connections before delving into the externalizing conversation. I think all of the questions Michael asked were worth 5 stars.

Even when Shannon made the statement about couples fighting about religion, sex, or money and then Michael said something about "is that all they fight about?", I wasn't sure if he was just making a 2 star statement, but then he took them off on this whole conversation about how they managed to not fight about the intimate aspects of their relationship. It was amazing to see how he did that. I guess I do think that each question he asked did serve a purpose and was a 5 star question.

Danielle, reflecting on her reaction to Michael's questions, also rated many questions as 4 or 5 star.

Posting by Danielle

Most of the questions he asked were very specific. In the past I would have thought these questions were leading – but the way he asked them, especially

*using their words back, and following the threads they introduced, it felt
more like accompanying them in the discovery. And when he did seem to go
off in a certain direction different from where they had indicated (like
Shannon's agenda of religion, and he asked about other skills, which brought
them to intimacy) he was transparent with them about why he was asking –
what he was trying to get at. But this wasn't that he was trying to get at them
coming to some conclusion he wanted them to come to – but rather that he
was helping them to identify skills in their own lives that they may build on or
transfer to other areas – namely religion.*

Danielle could immediately see an exciting application in her work as an
employee of the State Department of Children and Families.

Posting by Danielle

*I have seen so many times when staff might lead a person to a conclusion.
The consumers often don't buy into the conclusion – yet that is the answer the
staff was "looking for." This method offers a way to help the consumer bring
out information through questions that are guiding without being controlling...
This is something I would like to have more practice with.*

Brenda noticed that the interviewer never told the clients how it appeared they felt.
Instead he would frame his reflection as a question to ensure that his understanding
was correct.

Posting by Brenda

*For example instead of, "That seems to be an important understanding for
you," he asked, "So is that an important understanding for you?" which was
usually followed up with, "Why is that an important understanding for you"?
I love how he dealt with Shannon's tears – "Could you tell me a little about
your tears"? instead of making an assumption about the tears or comforting
her, which might mask what is really going on for Shannon.*

*I noticed that most questions were narrow in focus and typically aimed at
clarifying his understanding of what they were trying to express. I also liked
how he would check in with them re: what was it like to hear or know this
about Shannon/Ken? We are so afraid of speaking what is truly in our hearts
for fear that we will be crushed by the response. How great for Shannon and
Ken to learn how that kind of information is received. This seems to me to be
a wonderful way to build trust.*

Bobbi further elaborated on the practice of asking questions rather than making
assumptions. She quotes from a course reading about the temptation for therapists
to fill in the gaps with our own knowledges and "subtly or not so subtly try to align
other people's lives and understandings with [our] own" (Hayward, 2006).

Apprenticeship to a Craft

When I first started teaching narrative practice, I felt intimidated by the responsibility to train students in interviewing skills. Comparing myself to my mentors Michael White and David Espton, I acutely felt my limitations. How could I adequately demonstrate questions that "scaffold conversations" from the known and familiar into a "zone of proximal development" (Hayward, 2006; Vygotsky, 1986; White, 2007f)? How could I possibly construct questions as cleverly as David Epston? At times, I was overwhelmed by the limitless possibilities for constructing exercises for practicing interviewing skills. I worried about whether I was creative enough to devise my own exercises, and if not, how my colleagues would feel about me relying heavily on their ideas. I knew the students would look toward me to set the tone, to give clear instructions and constructive feedback. How could I best offer useful pointers from a stance of respectful curiosity?

I expect that my anxiety as I began teaching is akin to many students' early reactions to experiential exercises. While we may feel reticent at first, it works best to jump in rather than dally around the edges. Once a course gets underway, I strive to structure practice time in every class. Students find that they love experiential exercises. And I love creating them! I think of each exercise as something of an experiment; during the debriefing that follows each one, I learn from students about what worked and what might work even better next time. I am constantly tweaking these exercises. Our process exemplifies the kind of "co-creating" that is possible between students and teacher-minimizing hierarchy without obscuring my responsibility as teacher.

As I continue my ongoing apprenticeship to the craft of narrative practice, I am also an apprentice to teaching narrative practice. I have come a long way, yet still have much to learn from seasoned teachers and to discover with students about effective teaching strategies. While building on each other's successes, we all need to find the teaching style that fits us best. My teaching improves greatly when I relax into my strengths while striving to keep my weak areas in check. I actually think one of my greatest strengths is the aspiration to a student state of mind – making it clear to students that I too am learning through trial and error, right alongside them.

PRACTICE, PRACTICE, PRACTICE

To be of use
by Marge Piercy

The people I love the best
jump into work head first
without dallying in the shallows
and swim off with sure strokes almost out of sight.
They seem to become natives of that element,
the black sleek heads of seals
bouncing like half submerged balls.
I love people who harness themselves, an ox to a heavy cart,
who pull like water buffalo, with massive patience,
who strain in the mud and the muck to move things forward,
who do what has to be done, again and again.
I want to be with people who submerge
in the task, who go into the fields to harvest
and work in a row and pass the bags along,
who stand in the line and haul in their places,
who are not parlor generals and field deserters
but move in a common rhythm
when the food must come in or the fire be put out.
The work of the world is common as mud.
Botched, it smears the hands, crumbles to dust.
But the thing worth doing well done
has a shape that satisfies, clean and evident.
Greek amphoras for wine or oil,
Hopi vases that held corn, are put in museums
but you know they were made to be used.
The pitcher cries for water to carry
and a person for work that is real.

I believe that my role as a teacher of narrative therapy is to expose people to the spirit and practices of narrative therapy so they can make informed choices about their own preferred therapeutic approach. As Marge Piercy captures in her poem, "To be of use," I want students to have robust experiences involving rigorous study and practice of specific narrative interviewing skills. I want the students to "jump into work head first without dallying in the shallows and swim off with sure strokes almost out of sight." While stressing ethical practice, I want students to get their hands dirty as they muck in the dirt of real work.

Throughout this book, I demonstrate how an interactive course website can enhance classroom teaching, bringing forth a richly textured web of reflections and questions congruent with the spirit and actual practices of narrative therapy. In this concluding chapter, I draw from online conversation to illustrate students' coming to terms with newly acquired knowledge and skills as they apply them to their work and lives. I illustrate exchanges where students consult not only with me but with each other about challenges in their work in the private and public sectors. I conclude with students' ponderings about their professional identities as they come to understand that narrative practice is more than just a "technique." Because it speaks to values and ethical behavior and working for change in the way professional help-givers relate to help-seekers, students face dilemmas about how to live these values and strive for change in their work – and indeed, in their lives.

IT'S THE COPYING THAT ORIGINATES

Michael White credits Lionel Trilling for having turned around the 18th Century aesthetician's lament: "How come it is that we all start out originals and end up copies"? into "How come it is that we all start out copies and end up originals"? (White, 1992). Clifford Geertz answered, "It is the copying that originates" (Geertz, 1986) p. 380. This saying has stayed in my mind ever since. In other words, it is through rigorous study of the ideas and practices of a particular discipline that a person can then be in a position to originate new possibilities. I encourage students to really dig into their studies – to learn, inquire and practice – and through the "copying" discover their unique style.

As I describe in Chapter Three, "Teaching Congruently," many ideas and mentors have influenced my particular epistemological stance toward collaborative approaches in working with families. The people who have consulted with me continually reaffirm my commitment to participatory practices that guide us to become partners in learning. I was drawn to study narrative therapy because the approach resonated with these accumulated beliefs, values, and practices. Despite my accrued knowledge and skills, my fifteen year long apprenticeship to narrative practice continues through my ongoing study of philosophical underpinnings and specific skill building in narrative interviewing practices.

Writing this book has challenged me again and again to speak in my own voice. After many years of practice and teaching, I still struggle to rewrite my mentors' language into words that more aptly describe my own experience. While there is no substitute for actual practice in the real world, I wonder if teaching and learning as I have described here can indeed provide something of a shortcut for students to take a rigorous approach to collaborative work with people from their own unique style of embodied curiosity.

APPLICATIONS

While studying narrative therapy, students are eager to apply the ideas and practices to their own work contexts. The "Applications" topic generates lively discussion, some of which is sprinkled throughout this book. I actively welcome students' inquiring into the many possibilities for narrative practice. I post the following questions:

> *In what ways do you imagine applying narrative practices to various work environments? What questions do you have about possibilities in working with people experiencing different life situations? What excites you about applications in your work? Do you envision specific dilemmas within your particular work setting, and if so, how would you like to approach them?*

Students have lots of questions about applications in diverse settings. What ways is narrative therapy currently being used? Are there groups or agencies focusing only on narrative practice? How do we manage if working in time sensitive ways? Rather than positioning myself as the expert answer-knower, I facilitate conversation that gives voice to the institutional complexities, goes to the heart of dilemmas, and provokes contemplation of new possibilities. Students ask each other astute questions as they ponder the ethical implications of taking on a more collaborative stance and experimenting with various narrative maps such as externalizing, re-authoring, and re-membering conversations.

Over the years, I have collected stories of my students' work with people ranging from young children to the elderly; community mental health, school and adventure-based programs, group homes and home-based services; families experiencing family violence; and those involved with child protection and other social services. Students reflect on applying letter-writing, interviewing and outsider witness practices to their unique work settings. As conveyed in the following section, many students share their passion for spanning both social justice and clinical practice, and for creating bridges between public and private sector work.

I like to remind students that they will make their own discoveries for narrative practice in their different work contexts:

> *In the past few months, I've been hearing a number of people inquiring into applications in child protection work. I don't know whether it is helpful or not to think of yourselves as the pioneers – but I think you are. So are the families with whom we work. Remember that narrative therapy has been around for less than 20 years. It began in therapeutic contexts and only recently has begun to be applied elsewhere.*

Working with Elderly People

I am heartened to discover students with deep commitments to working with elderly people. Lynn wondered about groups that are not specifically for "therapy" but primarily aim to validate elders' memories and identities. With fourteen years of experience as a veterinary technician/office manager, Lynn valued the importance of companion pets in her role leading groups at a senior center the previous year.

Posting by Lynn

During my internship last semester I developed a Pet Memory group which I facilitated for five meetings at a senior center. One week I asked the participants if they wanted to write about a special memory of a pet they had as a child, or their children had, or any special animal in their life and bring in the next week to share. I was honored that so many of them wanted to write stories, and poems, which we read and used as a group to ask more questions which stimulated discussions. It made a connection between the seniors as well and created a bond around this sharing that they did together.

Lynn further described learning the value in helping elderly people in therapeutic settings to recount memories, and in seeing how their life stories are shaped by not only by family, but by the external cultural and generational forces of their time. Working with older survivors of domestic and sexual violence, Lynn heard stories of how elderly women could not break free of the generational expectations of women's roles in our society and in a marriage. She felt moved listening to their stories of how they were torn by the loss of a spouse while also experiencing the relief of being freed from emotional and/or physical abuse for the first time in their lives. She realized, "I need to do more research on using narrative practices in the population of elders I will be serving. I think it is different than working with families and children when you take in the very specific cultural expectations that shaped our notions of femininity and masculinity 60-70 years ago."

Reaching out to Children

Often, students want to learn about potential strategies to use narrative practices in their work with children and families. Cally referred to her work as a school social work intern the previous year with a 10-year old girl who had recently moved into the school district. Struggling to find a sense of belonging and establish meaningful friendships, Mery often told Cally she felt like no one in her class liked her. She expressed frustration that her new classmates did not understand her because of her different culture, having moved from a community where she had many Bosnian friends and family members including cousins her age close by. Mery often talked about old friends and a particular teacher who supported her, celebrated her Bosnian culture, and with whom she felt a strong connection. Studying letter writing inspired Cally to recall Mery and realize that it might have been a positive experience for Mery to have written letters to her teacher and old friends recalling what she enjoyed most about their relationships and what she believed they valued about her and their relationships with her. "It would have helped her honor those connections and also highlight the qualities that her friends and the special teacher admired and valued in her." Mery also struggled a lot with English, expressing on several occasions that she felt like she was losing her Bosnian language and didn't like that she couldn't practice it in school. "Giving her the opportunity to write letters in Bosnian would have been a way for me to celebrate her language and culture with her, and would have given her the opportunity to build her confidence and 'thicken' her story by sharing her culture with me."

Stacey described beginning to slip little bits of the narrative practice into her work in a residential treatment program with children dealing with emotional and behavioral issues. She illustrated with a story about talking with "Todd" who had a strong identity as "angry kid." When Stacey referred to his anger as "the anger," Todd seemed really thrown, and asked what she meant. "When I responded that I wondered how he felt when "the anger" came around, he seemed to get more reflective and think in a different way about his actions." While we had only a short conversation around a specific event, the conversation seemed powerful. I loved seeing how this kid, for that moment at least, looked at things differently. It made me think of a part in the Freedman/Combs book where they mention that we say things or ask questions to clients that they may carry with them for hours/days/years."

Home Visiting

I have nearly 20 years of experience with home visiting – about twelve years visiting families with infants with special developmental needs, and seven years visiting with families experiencing other multi-stresses. While I was happy to join a student-initiated online forum on home-visiting, I was careful to not assert my expertise. Rather, my aim was to contribute to the conversation with understandings from my own experiences. I wrote, in part:

> *These experiences powerfully shaped who I am today, how I work, and what I hold dearest to my heart. Maybe home visiting "prepared the soil" for my sense of kinship for narrative therapy, which is rooted in the traditions of folk psychology (White, 2004a). It is hard to imagine where I might be otherwise or what human service work might be like without such experiences. I am gratified to hear that Meagan, Megan, Katy, Ivy, Sue, and Amy are following similar traditions.*

I then contributed some of my learnings, while inviting students to do the same:

> *Katy, I too learned to take the family's lead through home visiting – to respect, admire, and learn from the ways people deal with the complexities of their lives. Everyone's home is so uniquely personalized, filled with mementos of unique lives. I appreciate your expressed desire for tools "for giving back the power in any setting." I believe it is possible to bring this*

spirit with you wherever you go, including into child protection and office based work. I have heard this described as "an ethic of hospitality," something that I believe should guide all of our work with families.

I respond to a student's description of the challenges in gaining distance from the potency of visiting families in their own homes:

You meet person-to-person in ways that make it difficult to bullshit or put on airs. For example, it's an incredible experience being "up close and personal" with families living in fear of upcoming nighttime in the dead of winter, wondering how to stay warm, going through the intensity of the aftermath of an alcoholic binge (the children's struggle to carry on with normal life, the mother's determination to live with dignity). Often, I fell in love with the people I got to know behind the diagnoses, reports, and reputations and then grappled with how to deal with the dilemmas that emerged. I learned a lot of lessons the hard way, but mostly I learned respect and humility. I learned to follow families' priorities unless I had an agenda of my own that I could not ignore – and in such cases, I learned to be as straight-forward as possible.

Engaging with Challenging Situations

Online conversation often includes reflections and questions about responding to challenging situations. Chappell wondered how the narrative approach addresses resistance, a concept she has learned about in other courses:

There is something powerful to the narrative about resistance – especially in adolescents who may feel that it is the only way to have any power in their relationships with adults. Do you go ahead and start with the story of the resistance? Do you believe the story that the client may tell about there being no problem? Do you just focus on building rapport with the client, and if so, how does this differ from psychoanalytic therapy?

I responded:

Thanks for these ponderings – you ask great questions. Certainly, any therapeutic approach is challenged by work with individuals struggling with psychotic thought processes, mandated clients, and teens who don't want to be there. Working with people seeking healing from the effects of trauma can also be intense and powerful work. In no way do I want to minimize the complexity of these situations or to act as though narrative practice offers simple one-size-fits-all solutions to complex problems. However – coincidentally – I am currently working with people in each of these situations, and I would be happy to share some stories of my work: with a woman recovering from a psychotic depression, a mandated teen (substance abuse/court diversion), and a woman reclaiming her life from a history of incest.

I conclude my post by letting Chappell – and hence the class – know that I have now spoken to each of these people who seem pleased that I will share our work with the students. "I look forward to talking with you about the influence of narrative practice in each of these situations –maybe we can begin the class on Thursday with this conversation."

Melissa reflected on the use of narrative therapy with clients who are in some way "forced" into treatment. In particular, she recounted her experience working with adolescent girls in a residential facility. For most of these girls, "treatment" became a way in which they experienced adults as continually reenacting their early childhood experiences of dominance and control. In her online post, Melissa pondered the practitioner's responsibility to not place blame or responsibility for change squarely on the shoulders of the client. How could she expect these girls to understand and appreciate the control they had over their preferred ways of being in the world? She inquired:

Would that suggestion feel to them like another adult simply putting all of the responsibility for their behaviors on them? Although I understand, at least in theory if not in practice, how helping people draw connections to past experiences can help them see where their preferred identity may have been submerged by external forces - I still don't understand how to recognize that many factors continue to exert control over our identities and that it often doesn't feel like creating a preferred self is a matter of choice.

Working with an "Institution in the Room"

Often my students work in agencies where they must follow strict protocols and guidelines. Kathy described some of the challenges she faces in applying a narrative approach in her work with minors who are in state custody or in threat of being in state custody and their parents: "It's as if there is another being in a room meeting with people in these settings – the institution." She shared her dilemma online in bringing forth the departmental voice of child protection in interactions so that the "agent of social control" part of the work is understood as well as possible and out in the open. She has found setting the context helpful with both relationship building and also to remain focused on goals: "I guess this is how I use transparency as well as address the power dynamic."

Ellen resonated with the idea of working with "an institution in the room."

Posting by Ellen

The invisible third party is intense – even if you are an independent therapist, there must be this sense of the "power above," whether it is the notorious "third-party payer." society, history, etc...I actually think that when Danielle writes about "cheerleading" in the context of supporting a child who may be struggling against a dominant story (the "appropriate school behavior" story) by trying to point out his strengths to the teachers

257

and his team, she is doing exactly what Karen meant by acknowledging the other party in the room. For me, this ability to acknowledge these "invisible players" is one of those core ideas that makes narrative unique.

Sometimes students cautiously consult with each other about challenging work situations. After witnessing a session between Gwen and her client, Gwen's supervisor told her she didn't do anything at all and let the her client talk too much. However, the client told her that she appreciated the time she had to really talk, to have someone actually listen to her, while suspending judgment. Now as "a budding narrative apprentice," she recognized that she and her supervisor had philosophical practice differences. "What I didn't realize at the time was that I was doing something of my own with narrative, by asking my client where some of her beliefs, ideas, and perceptions about herself came from. They were not her own, but rather had been constructed by societal views about women, mothers, and wives, her husband's thoughts, and her in-laws' thoughts." Gwen wished she could go back into this situation with her new knowledge.

BEYOND THE THERAPY ROOM

The change in language from "narrative therapy" to "narrative practice" resonates with many students. This comes across in the vibrant dialogue that emerges when I post the following question:

As you too have been noticing, narrative practice has many applications beyond the therapy room. What do you think about building dialogue and creating bridges between practitioners doing private and public sector work? Can you readily envision more linking between the lives of people in independent practice and those who practice in agencies, and if so, how? Are there distinctions that seem too complex to bridge the gap?

Private and Public Sector

Sarah described her surprise on entering the social work world to find apparent divisions "between social workers and therapists, and clinical social workers and mental health providers." These professional and intra-professional jurisdictions created false dichotomies that didn't make sense to her: "I think narrative practice would be as useful in a staff meeting, community organizing, or private practice. I also have a hunch that a lot of this divisiveness has to do with economics – therapists probably make more money than a social worker working for the state, who in turn make more than a social worker working in a community organizer role."

Sarah started a discussion about the place of "private practice" in social work:

Since I've started the program I've had an underlying sense that within social work there is a tension between those working in private practice and those practicing in an agency. I've gotten the idea that going into private practice is often seen as "copping out." There was a short discussion of this somewhere else on the online forums, but it never really got going. I'm interested in hearing other's perspectives on this. Can we keep the "social" in social work in a private setting? Or, are private therapists "selling out" and putting aside their values for independence and more money (maybe?)? P.S. That's not really my point of view, but thought I might get the ball rolling....

Ellen described her reaction to the tension between the private and public arenas of social work. She was reminded of the tension she often felt as a member of the Christian church. "Most churches share so many core beliefs that I couldn't understand the need for so many denominations, competing for people, resources and viewpoints. Why is there this need for division when the Christian faith is supposed to promote unity?" She continued:

I feel frustrated that certain things (possibly self-righteousness, defensiveness and boundaries) prevent us from seeing that, for the most part, we are all doing the same "social" work, whether it is in public practice or in a more public arena – the work of trying to co-create positive transformation. Thinking that working with, for example, those in poverty is a more righteous cause than those in wealth seems like a terrible form of discrimination. Just as it is horrifying when people think that working with "those people" (people in poverty, jail, with disabilities, mental illness, etc.) is a useless waste of time and money. All of our work has value. Are there ways that private therapists can help those working in the public arena? What would those look like? What skills do you think would be needed in such a collaboration?

In another class, Mohammed wrote about his commitment to work with people living in poverty. He recounted participating as the only intern in a gathering of clinicians; most were middle-aged women with a handful of men, one Black, and then there was me, the only intern. The majority of clinicians he spoke with had their own private practices. "They looked healthy, with an aura of the elite about them." They wondered whether Mohammad would go into private practice once he got his degree. "Well, I certainly would not want to live through the painful agency politics, if I can help it. I have lived through it in the past and was getting a great dose of it at my placement. 'But,' I responded, "Can you reach the poor in private practice"?

Other students hope to bring their beliefs and values into their work as therapists in private practice. Lauren's posting drew from the shared class experience when knowledged veteran students, Beth and Stephen, visited their class. "Beth has shown us one model of possibility in a hospital setting, carrying the cloak of 'secret agent.' Can we do that too? Carry with us the spice, depth, difference of narrative into any context, especially as we are beginning our careers"?

Bridging Social Justice and Clinical Practice

When social work students first learn about narrative therapy, they often express relief in finding an approach that resonates with the social justice values that brought them to study social work in the first place. Abbie offered up the following metaphor: "I've been waiting for this class the whole time I've been in this MSW program. I feel like I've been walking around in shoes that were the wrong size for two years and I just got a pair of comfy sneakers that fit."

While Danielle had considered the ethics of therapeutic work with individuals or groups, she was newly considering the link to social justice. Danielle posed questions to her classmates about whether they view their work aspirations as promoting social justice. "If you feel your desired workplace doesn't promote social justice as it's currently organized, how could you promote social justice in the way you approach the work? If you feel the work inherently promotes social justice – what about the work makes this so?" Danielle pondered where she is headed and about her values. "I'm thinking that maybe social justice, like narrative practice, needs to be lived rather than simply 'practiced'...What do others think?"

Working within Organizations for Change

Studying narrative practice invites everyone to continually re-examine our participation in oppressive practices. Sometimes students link their heightened awareness to prior learnings. Kerry2 first realized her role in oppression when she was a Peace Corps volunteer. For a long time, she denied that she had a role in oppression, thinking her good intentions were sufficient. However, over time, something changed. While she wasn't proud to be part of an oppressive group – that group being North Americans – she realized she reaped benefits from her white American-ness, which made her inherently complicit. "I felt so sick in my skin." Kerry brings these sensitivities to her current work.

Posting by Kerry2

> *And now I work for the government – go figure! One of my tasks is to make community-based organizations fill out forms on their clients (no form = no money to the organization). The forms, at this point, provide no place for transgendered individuals to identify themselves as such and there are many other ways in which individuals are inappropriately lumped together. Some days I really struggle with my job/work and other days I just think to myself, "thank goodness I am the one here doing this job." I care about people and I will advocate for people, even in a bureaucratic setting. I know that if I were to leave my job, I could easily be replaced by someone who wouldn't advocate and who didn't care. And I have come to believe that, collectively, a positive difference can be made. The form I referred to above has been revised (though not yet released!) to be inclusive of transgendered individuals. I have to believe that my listening, and, most importantly, my sharing of what I heard, was part of the collective voice that brought about that change (this form is released under the Bush Administration, no less).*

Kerry remembered the National Association of Social Workers slogan "Work for Change" and the bumper sticker "Be the change you wish to see." Her online questions provoked further conversation about challenges in making a difference even in a bureaucratic, insensitive organization. Is it important to work in a place that resonates with one's own values and goals, or can someone be just as effective in trying to affect change in a place that does not? One student asked, "I wonder if we all only worked in environments that were already completely tailored to our beliefs, would we really be benefiting our communities?" Celia's posting wove in another thread of complexity. An experienced practitioner, she has worked in settings where she felt a great need to advocate for people and for needed changes in the system. She felt she was making a greater difference by working in systems that need to be changed and trying to nudge them in a new direction. "Sometimes I felt a lot of reward in this and sometimes I just felt very tired." The key for Celia is to find some kind of balance between the two horns of her dilemma – to get enough support elsewhere so that her commitments don't drain or overwhelm her. For example, she now privately engages a narrative supervisor to meet with her outside of work.

LIVING PRACTICE

Posting by Brenda

Maybe rather than thinking of narrative as a technique, such as applying a butterfly bandage to a certain type of wound, we might think of narrative practice as a way of being in the world together.

"Living practice" is a term I commonly use in my courses. By example, I encourage students to apply the concepts and practices to their own lives and relationships. Carol experienced something akin to a cultural awakening to understand this philosophy and begin incorporating it into her work. "I want to go in, find the problems, come up with solutions, and fix things. But this narrative philosophy demands we quiet our minds and open them and our hearts to the stories and experiences of others."

Online forums invite and then make room for candid conversation. Danielle's post conveys her struggle to integrate the current philosophies, values, and beliefs of social work studies with her past and current experiences. Having studied social constructionist principles and values that promote social justice in other social work courses, she was exploring what aspects and concepts to embrace in her own practice. "I would like to think that I am constantly upholding the values and beliefs of the social work field. Through practice and everyday life I am starting to realize that this is not as easy as it may first appear." Danielle found collaboration difficult with multiple organizations and individuals who may have opposing agendas, especially when it appeared that the client's goals or agenda were not a priority. She gave the concrete example of the paperwork required for clients to receive Medicaid, disability, or special education funding; certain diagnoses may need to be assigned or documents may have to be filled out that are in conflict with client desires. "How does a social worker work against the 'system' that holds the power and ultimately does have what seems to be the 'capital T Truth' of what needs to be done in order to serve clients when it seems there are not other ways to access services that our clients need?"

Katy reflected on a recent experience during a break from work and school when she finally had the opportunity to reflect on everything she had been reading and thinking about in the course. "During this time I thought about externalizing problems and about some of my own struggles and really saw them as separate from me. I could really grasp them as "the other" that would come and take over if I let them, or who were somehow let in and supported by other problems or people." Katy described an "ah hah!" moment in realizing firsthand that the "people are not their problems" concept truly resonated with her. In talking with other people, she realized that the course has really impacted her life, helping her to listen without just glossing over matters but instead, unpacking ideas and beliefs. "I think even my conversations and communication with others have improved." She illustrated with a story about a recent conversation. "My neighbor started telling me about a problem she is having with her partner and I kept thinking that I should ask her questions, and not succumb to the culture of applause by telling her how well she was handling things, or that things will get better."

I share with students my steadfast belief in "practicing what you preach." If I believe in guiding concepts such as "both/and," generous listening, and critical analysis of discourses, I must remember to continually apply these to myself and my own interactions in the world. Sometimes when I re-evaluate an interaction, I face my own shortcomings – such as when I let my enthusiasm for a given idea interfere with listening to another's contrasting idea. While this kind of self-reflection is never undertaken without some discomfort or unease, it helps guide me in exactly the direction I want to go – toward my own "preferred ways of being" in the world. I invite students to share how this process might be similar or different to what guides their approach to living their lives, including their work.

PRACTICE, PRACTICE, PRACTICE

With the course end in sight, I create an online forum for students to share hopes and possibilities for continued practice:

I continue to thoroughly enjoy this course and the opportunity to work with all of you. Really, it has been a pleasure. Of course, we all know that there is so much more to learn about narrative practice. Some of you hunger to continue in your studies of narrative practice. If you are one of these people, I strongly urge you to set up ways to continue your studies – otherwise as well all know, good intentions can easily get overtaken by the busyness of everyday life.

Throughout a course, I invite students to reflect on what they have learned. Often they articulate new understandings that significantly inform their lives and work. Amy responded by describing the implications in her work with domestic violence of realizing that "The belief that people are not their problems IS not a tool, it IS a way of viewing the world." She no longer viewed domestic violence as the woman's fault, looking to what contributed to the situation. Instead she saw domestic violence as a human rights and social justice issue. "What about the society that allows women to be abused?" Similarly, when she thought about depression, she thought about expectations, "The norms that people feel they must live up to and attain, and if they fall short, or realize that others' assumptions do not match their desires or goals, they might be viewed as being depressed." For Amy, making this shift felt like naming the elephant in the room.

Students teach me a great deal about their experiences with applying narrative practice to their work. Working with colleagues and supervisors within agency protocols poses unique challenges. For example, Foresta posted reflections on a discussion with one of her colleagues about some of her narrative studies such as letter-writing practices. What might be possible applications in their agency and where might there be limitations? Instead of replacing all of their old practices, Foresta's colleague suggested adding particular practices as tools to their tool box, so they could draw from a range of skills or methods. "I am not sure what others think of this, but for me this idea of adding tools seemed better for me because it did not mean that I had to give up old methods or convert to an entirely new method of practice." Foresta further described her concern about the tendency for her co-workers to talk about narrative therapy in relation to other therapies the agency used as a dichotomous relationship or an "us versus them" kind of mentality. In her post, she explored some of the complexities influencing embracing narrative practices in her work.

Posting by Foresta

My sense is that the notion of being perceived as legitimate goes against the "alternative stories" that narrative practices are working towards, because it is forcing it into a modernist structure of hierarchy. I wonder if part of the role of narrative practitioners is to call into question how we construct legitimacy within the social work/ psychology professions.

I really liked Ken's idea of Narrative being about "unlearning" certain taken-for-granted "truths" or ways of being. I really like this metaphor of unlearning but I think that this is what makes it so difficult to accept sometimes. It seems to me that there is an uncertainty and uneasiness that comes with unlearning and calling into question assumptions that makes it difficult for those who are not familiar with these ideas to join this kind of discourse.

Despite these and other obstacles, I have discovered that many people find ways to adapt aspects of narrative interviewing practices into their therapeutic repertoires. For example, Michelle works at a parent child center as an early educator and parent educator. She described online that she plans to discuss with her co-workers how they can develop and practice a more curious stance with their participants. "We need to let go of our judgments, or at least be aware of them and try to filter them out of our work."

Ripple Effects

As we near the end of the course, I set up a forum for students to reflect on the effects of the material on their own lives and relationships:

> *As we enter the final week of the course, so many conversations remain. If you find a few minutes, here is space for whatever remains unspoken. In what ways has this course contributed to your training as a practitioner? What are some of the ripple effects (if any) you are experiencing? What acknowledgments would you like to give to each other, such as ways you felt others inspired you, your hopes and dreams for the future (especially for those graduating this summer)? Are there any particular ways you would like to continue your studies of narrative practice? If you/we had more time, what would you like to explore? What feels most illuminating and what remains confusing? Which unanswered questions are most haunting? What have I forgotten to ask? No pressure intended – only if the spirit moves you.*

Often, narrative practice reconnects students with their most cherished values, as expressed by Jill, who was drawn to social because of the social justice component of the field. She commented on how comfortable she feels with the beliefs and values expressed through narrative practice – "not quite so comfortable with the application part yet, but that will come with time and practice." Throughout the prior year, she got bogged down trying to grasp the theoretical conversations and learn practice techniques, both of which she saw as worthwhile uses of her mental energy. "But I lost sight of the notion of social justice, which I suppose is really the foundation of this practice, but is rarely identified as such". As she began reading for this class, the concept of social justice came back into her focus.

Posting by Jill

> *In our first class Peggy said something to the effect of "live out and practice what you believe" and made it clear that you don't have to separate your values from your work, which was a relief for me to hear. I have thought about working as a therapist, but felt I would miss being "in the trenches" and the sense of being part of a larger social movement. Narrative practice has instilled in me a sense of hope that social justice work can be very much alive in therapy.*

Students often reflect online on the impact of course materials on their lives and relationships. Margot described a personal sentiment she has heard echoed by her classmates: "Our commitment to our social work practice is synonymous with our commitment to our personal growth. It seems to me that this combined commitment has a synergistic effect on both experiences. Our social work practice is enriched by our personal strivings, and our personal selves are enriched by our experience as social workers working with people, who are also part of this loop, giving and receiving!" Margot saw the narrative approach as opening the opportunity for this synergistic experience to unfold "in a graceful, honest, profound way that changes all of us." She ended her post with the question, "Does this fit with your experience?"

Catherine, an undergraduate psychology student in a highly competitive liberal arts college, described the bonds formed among classmates:

What stands out most is the relationships I developed with other class members. The way the class was structured encouraged students to feel more comfortable with fellow students, resulting in more of a sense of freedom to say what one wants. There was no sense of competition in class discussions or postings, which was refreshing. I learned a tremendous amount from others both academically and in terms of how I want to be in the world.

Writing this book, I reconnected with many students. I was moved again and again by their expressions of heartfelt enthusiasm about participating in this writing project. They shared stories about some of continued ripple effects of the course on them. They spoke about the impact of sharing their letters of commitment (see Chapter Seven) with family members, friends, and other influential persons in their lives. They told stories about sharing course experiences with other important people in their lives. For example, Ali wrote to tell me her plan to send her letter of commitment to Eileen, the therapist who had made a significant difference to her as a child. She shared this idea with her partner, Drew, who was very much in support of her taking this step.

Ali then told a story from two years ago when Drew was recovering in the hospital from a double hip replacement. A nurse walked in while he was crying out, feeling especially down in the dumps and helpless. The nurse was Tibetan and spoke very little English; he sat quietly with Drew while he cried. He then told Drew about a healing garden behind the hospital and suggested that he go there. Drew told Ali the healing garden was just what he needed at that time. While the other nurses took care of his physical needs, this man seemed to really understand his pain, both physical and emotional. Drew really appreciated the gentle way that this nurse sat with him while he experienced sadness and frustration. Then Ali continued with a story that took place at a video store the night before she emailed me, two years after this hospital experience.

While I was paying for our movies, Drew noticed that the nurse who had helped him two years ago was standing behind us in line. Drew turned to him and began to tell him how much he had helped him during his recovery. The man did not remember Drew, but as Drew described the comfort that this man's actions had brought him, the man began to cry. I was amazed that a moment of such sincere connection could take place between two men in line at a video store. I knew that if Drew could sincerely thank his nurse and if the nurse was moved to tears by hearing this thanks, that I could contact Eileen to thank her, and she would be happy to hear from me. Since the narrative class, I have been challenging my fear of going to that emotional place with others. I am learning that even though it can be uncomfortable or embarrassing to be in that place, it is worth dealing with the discomfort or embarrassment, because the moments of connection that are created by going there can be life changing.

These comments are always gratifying to me, and guide me in my planning for next time. Over the years, I notice that I place ever more value on building community between classmates and the bonds they create with each other. I consider the best classes as those where there is a sense of solidarity and shared purpose rather than a competition for marks that places every undertaking under the gaze of evaluation. It is common knowledge among teachers that some classes come together with greater ease than others. Sometimes I inherit dynamics among students who have shared prior classes. I strive to stay alert to a milieu that seems particularly divisive or, alternatively, one verging on "group think." Would students tell me if they felt left out, or belittled? Is there room for someone to express a different idea? I certainly hope so.

HAUNTING FROM A FRIENDLY GHOST FROM THE FUTURE

The online medium makes it possible for us to revisit exercises that I might not otherwise have classroom time to explore. In this case, I use a genre of inquiry created by David Epston (Epston et al., 2006) to invite students to playfully envision a visitation from a "friendly ghost of the future," as a way to express the significance to their work and their lives of attending this course.

Remember the first day of class when we were visited by a friendly ghost from the future? The ghost described the chance reconnection of many of the members of this class at a conference (was it in 2025?) – how among other things, you reminisced about the effects of that course on Narrative Approaches to Social Work on your lives, relationships and your identity as a reflective practitioner...(when exactly was that? Back in the year 2006 or 2007?). What was it that the ghost said that made that course a turning point experience in your lives? How do these reminiscences match or not match with your actual experience of this course? Now that you've (almost) completed this course, what would you want to add, delete or change about this visitation from the friendly ghosts from the future?

Danielle responded:

Remember that narrative class we took? Sometimes I wish I could go back to that with what I know now... I might get much more out of it and be that much further ahead now. I am grateful that it laid such a good foundation for my understanding the narrative approach. Since then I've taken several more trainings, including an intensive workshop on the subject. Over the years I have found ways to engage in narrative practice in therapeutic ways, but more realistically I've incorporated the approach into my everyday dealings with clients, peers and within supervision. I've found that decentering myself, remaining curious and inquisitive about others and myself and acknowledging problems in their "proper" place allows me to really focus on people and meet them where they are. I am really excited at how this approach has rounded out and made more substantive my preferred, family-centered way of working. I continue to attend trainings on the subject to improve my practice in this approach and I seek out supervision opportunities with peers who share this philosophical background – many of whom were in that initial class we took that summer at UVM!

Bobbi also reflected online on her conversation with a ghost from the future:

Dear Ghost,

That course I took in July 2006... had a profound impact on my practice.

It was kind of like I stopped taking my own reflections for granted and realized how much of my thinking needs to be shared to have meaning. It was right about then that I started walking with friends and resolved to have more meaningful relationships with people outside my own family.

I also made collaborative practice a focus. I spent the next year looking at collaborative relationships; this has influenced my practice with children and families and with communities. I started writing and consulting around this and worried less about what privileges me to be an expert but thinking more in terms of giving strength to others' voices and acknowledging that we are all theorizing on some level and making meaning of the experience or experiment of living. I have remained connected on some level with many of the people in the class professionally and personally by joining a supervision group and keeping up with what some are doing. We have collaborated on projects and influenced policy in Vermont, nationally and globally. Some have run successful political campaigns...

My online response joins in with the imaginative envisioning of future possibilities. Here is part of what I wrote back:

Thank you, Danielle and Bobbi for your tireless devotion to this course. I cannot imagine what this experience might have been without the two of you. Now I am enjoying imagining that I too am visited by the friendly ghost of 2026. I was so happy to catch up with you two at the International Conference on Narrative Practice. What joy for me to participate in each of your workshops! Thank you so much for sharing the photos of your children – what amazing adults they have become. Bobbi, Mazel Tov in becoming such a devoted grandmother!

What was it like to see so many of your UVM classmates at this conference and to have so many friendly faces smiling at you from the audience of your workshops? Danielle, seeing you up in front of that huge crowd reminded me of when I met you back in 2006. Do you remember the enthusiasm with which you committed yourself to your studies of social work and took charge of shaping your learning? I am amazed by the steadfast ways you kept your focus on what is important to you while also consistently honoring your primary commitment to your children. I recall that conversation 20 years ago when you talked of your commitment to shape your life to keep your spirit alive in your work. Can you imagine the joy I felt in feeling like in some small way I had contributed to this commitment and to all that arose out of it?

Bobbi, as I mentioned to you, I have read several of your pieces about collaborative approaches to working with children, families and communities. Do you think I was surprised when I first came across one of your articles, having remembered how much you contributed to that Narrative Approaches to Social Work course in the summer of 2006? I have so enjoyed both seeing and hearing how you have applied these practices to your political work in Vermont. I wish you all my best as you prepare for another year of political campaigning. I can only imagine how much this takes out of you, but I hope you realize the contribution you have been making to the citizens of Vermont.

When I look back to 2006, I remember that summer well as a time when my commitment to stretch myself in my work took me into new territory. Among other things, I decided to write a book about our teaching/learning experiences. I remember being amazed by all the fantastic people and opportunities that came my way. Somehow I managed through the personal challenges of feeling more "out there" and continued to use my voice to speak up for what I thought was most important in ways to work collaboratively with children, families and communities.

Now that I am in my mid 70s, I figure that, if I'm lucky, I've got another 20 years or so to keep my spirit alive in my work, and to thoroughly enjoy all that I reap from the connections with people that have continued to deepen and ripen over the years. I too love all of the joy and fun times that have come from hanging out with my grandchildren and other children of this new generation! And I am so happy that I have stuck with Pilates and cycling all these years. I don't know if I could have cycled across the country for the second time to celebrate my 70th birthday if I hadn't discovered the ways in which Pilates could strengthen my back!

There is so much more to say but it's time for my early morning bike ride. Just one question. Did you attend the workshop by Brenda and Kevin, "Social Work as Improvisational Dance?" I am still mulling over what they taught me and how I might use these ideas in my daily life and work as a family therapist.

PROFESSIONAL IDENTITY

Over the last decade, I have experienced a shift in thinking of myself as a narrative therapist. This has been gradual, more of a self-concept than something I need to advertise. Previously, I thought of myself as a "narratively- informed" therapist, as though this eclectic identity would give me some kind of protection from getting swept into "narrative fundamentalism" or "narrative correctness."

Students frequently ask me, "Do practitioners of narrative practice use only this approach"? "Do I need to become a narrative therapist in order to practice in these ways"? I know excellent therapists who practice in collaborative ways resonant with narrative therapy and yet have never studied it. I know others who have taken a narrative course, gone to a Michael White or David Epston workshop, or read a book or two, and have integrated a few concepts and techniques into their otherwise psychodynamic psychotherapeutic approach. I also know excellent students who study narrative therapy with me and yet choose to embrace another approach. We each need to find what fits best and where we shine.

I have found close colleagues who share similar interests, as well as other well respected colleagues who do not. I have had to work at this. I sense that this broad-based sense of community has paradoxically become more possible over time as I have developed a more solid confidence in my own preferences, beliefs, and values. I know what it feels like to be with someone who exudes fundamentalist evangelical beliefs – an experience I do not enjoy or learn from – and I try not to practice fundamentalism of any kind including "narrative fundamentalism." Spending time with like-minded people is truly invigorating; I also enjoy being in dialogue with those who have different beliefs, ideals, and ways of being, which offers another version of living with diversity. I aim to make room for differences, build dialogue, and create bridges.

NOTES

[1] A neologism is a recently coined word, phrase or expression that synthesizes existing concepts into a new cultural context. Neologizing is a common yet rarely commented on practice in narrative practice. Michael White uses the neologism "knowledged" as a reminder that we are knowledgeable in different ways. I first heard him use this term at a workshop in Portland, Maine (October, 2004), "Narrative practice with Michael White."

[2] I am extremely grateful to Betsy Buckley, Phil Decter, Steven Gilbert and Chris Behan. Together, we created a New England teaching group that for more than five years has been an ongoing source of inspiration, practical guidance and problem solving. Over the years, Betsy, Phil & Chris have all graciously donated their time to become in-class, at the University of Vermont, and Middlebury College and online guests to my courses. Sometimes that has involved significant travel time as well.

[3] "Knowledges" is another narrative neologism. Michael White and David Epston use plural to speak about "knowledges", "wisdoms" and "learnings" to accent the many ways of knowing.

[4] Contact me, Peggy Sax, at www.reauthoringteaching.com with any reflections, inquiry or acknowledgements regarding people's stories in this book. I will do my best to share constructive responses with the persons to whom they are addressed.

[5] "Being-Postmodern' in supervision and in the classroom" by Ann Hartman was presented at the International Narrative Therapy and Community Work Conference, Atlanta, Georgia, June, 2002.

[6] Preparing this manuscript, I have reviewed many email exchanges between members of my New England teaching support team. In addition, students and I learn a great deal from Betsy Buckley and Phil Decter as guest speakers on Ethics and Accountability (Buckley & Decter, 2006). I am also grateful to Chris Behan for sharing his preparation for "The Ethics of Multiple Relationships," a popular workshop in New England.

[7] For example, I teach intensive month long courses at the University of Vermont, and Middlebury College in which students focus on course materials for that period. However, Smith College social work students typically take four courses during a five-week semester within a primarily psychodynamic program. Sometimes these students are simultaneously preparing their theses. Hence Smith students are particularly squeezed for time, and often confused and unsettled as they discover that narrative practice contradicts much of what they have become committed to in their learning so far.

[8] Portions of this chapter originally appeared in Sax, P. (2003). It takes an audience to solve a problem: Teaching narrative therapy online. *New Zealand Social Work Review, XV*(4), 21-29.

[9] At The University of Vermont, I was assigned a competent course developer, Justin Henry, who like many good teachers, gave me the illusion of doing it myself while in fact he really took care of many of the more important details behind the scenes. Joseph Antonioli gave additional technical assistance. My husband, Shel, works with educational technology at Middlebury College, teaching faculty and staff how to use technology in their research and teaching. I am grateful for all he has taught me.

[10] I am especially grateful to David Epston for engaging with me around these ideas, and for encouraging to write about my teaching experiences.

[11] I was particularly interested to discover many pedagogical roles for online discussion (Funaro & Montell, 1999; Harasim, Hiltz, Teles, & Turoff, 1997; Program, nd). The literature reflects an enthusiasm for the learner-centered possibilities, and for designing learning environments that are "more authentic, situated, interactive, project-oriented, interdisciplinary, learner-centered, and which take into account the varieties of students' learning styles". (Berge, 1997), p.13. These principles are conducive to reflective thinking and creative problem-solving, and isomorphic to the guiding principles of narrative therapy.

[12] The Division of Continuing Education at The University of Vermont. For further interest contact Wendy Verrei-Berenback, Director of Instructional Technologies, wverreib@ced.uvm.edu.

[13] Thus far, I have utilized three course management tools in designing course websites: WebCT (The University of Vermont Social Work Department); Blackboard (Smith College School of Social

Work) and Seque (Middlebury College Psychology Department) The courses I have designed are entitled "Narrative Approaches to Social Work" and "Collaborative Approaches to Therapeutic Conversations."

[14] The recording of David Epston's interview with Sebastian entitled "Narrative therapy with a young boy: Hannah is in my heart now" is available through Master's Work, Andrews & Clark Explorations, 10650 Kinnard Ave. #109, Los Angeles, CA 90024, www.masterswork.com.

[15] Adapted from Michael White's "Re-authoring Conversations Map" handout, (White 2002), and "Your Personal Micro map" course assignment by Betsy Buckley & Phil Decter, Simmons College School of Social Work.

[16] The research conversations enlisted participants from a wide range of backgrounds including parents and professionals from child care services, parent/child centers, early childhood education, early intervention, mental health, social services, pediatrics and public health, education, substance abuse prevention, and community partnerships[16]. Co-researchers —whether parent or professional—put themselves in the shoes of service seekers, shared stories from their own lives, and reflected from the position of service seekers and upon their experiences of power relations. Their recommendations explored three aspects of family-centered practices: (1) effective help-giving, (2) meaningful parent involvement and (3) parent-to-parent support.

[17] Communicated in private email correspondence, March, 2005.

[18] Not all course websites readily give space for teacher reflection at such length and detail. I post "My Story" on Blackboard and Segue. I have not done so on WebCT.

[19] Chappell would like to honor her teacher, Dr. Mary Alice Delia who taught critical literary theory at Bethesda Chevy Chase High School in Bethesda, Maryland. Dr. Delia passed away in 1997 just two years after she mentored Chappell,; she was in the midst of writing a book about her experiences teaching critical literary theory to public high schoolers.

[20] Lynn would like to recognize her teacher by name. Sam Silverman, MSW teaches at Springfield College in St. Johnsbury, Vermont.

[21] An earlier version of this chapter originally appeared in Sax, Peggy (2006), "Developing stories of idenity as reflective practitioners," the Journal of Systemic Therapies, Vol 25, Issue 4, p 59-72. By permission of Guilford Press.

[22] This assignment is an adaptation of the "Personal Micro map" exercise that Betsy Buckley and Phil Decter (Simmons College of Social Work) adapted from the work of Michael White's (White, 1988) adaptation of Jerome Bruner (Bruner, 1986, 1990) work on the Landscape of Action and The Landscape of Meaning. Sarah, a Simmons social work student also graciously offered to share her computerized version of a personal micro map

[23] I am particularly grateful to Betsy Buckley and Phil Decter for their contributions to this exercise.

[24] Thus far, I have used this assignment with graduate students at The University of Vermont Social Work Department and Smith College School of Social Work as well as with undergraduates at The Middlebury College Psychology Department. The courses I have designed are entitled "Narrative Approaches to Social Work" and "Collaborative Approaches to Therapeutic Conversations."

[25] Because I primarily teach in social work programs, many of my illustrations draw upon social work identity. Whenever possible, I use the term "reflective practitioner" to make room for the reader to substitute a range of professional identities such as family therapist, psychologist, mental health counselor, early childhood mental health specialist, and so on.

[26] For purposes of brevity, I chose to use feminine pronouns to represent both men and women.

[27] I work with a "community consultation team" with four-part narrative interviews, including outsider witness practices. Through using this team I have recorded and then shown my classes illustrations of narrative interviews. Recording of interviews always requires clients' permission.

[28] In email correspondence (November 18, 2007), David Epston described "un-suffering yourself" as a neologism. "While we have considerable vocabulary around words that denote suffering, as far as I know, we have an impoverished vocabulary around actions of any kind taken to 'unsuffer' oneself. Unsuffering implies personal and moral agency." "Although the world is full of suffering, it is also full of the overcoming of it."

[29] In the United States, the focus on confidentiality in mental health field is even stronger since HIPAA regulations went into effect in 2004.

[30] Nicole's journey continues. We welcome reflections on this account of her perseverant efforts to "unsuffer" herself from self-harm, anorexia and suicidal depression.. Any correspondence for Nicole should be addressed to me, Peggy Sax, through the following website: www.reauthoringteaching.com

[31] Nicole was hopes someday to travel to Nepal to live in a monastery and work as a volunteer with young children.

[32] Circulating Local Wisdom While Safeguarding Confidentiality, Auckland, New Zealand, December 1, 2006.

[33] "Encountering the Spirit of Community in Narrative Therapy and in Cuban Social Programs," was a five-day program offered in Havana, Cuba by The World Psychiatric Association (Zone 3) in association with The International Federation of Social Workers and Leading Edge Seminars, was from January 15-19, 2007.

[34] Circulating Local Wisdom While Protecting Confidentiality, Family Institute of Cambridge, May 18, 2007

[35] Ellen Walnum coined the term "experience consultants" to describe people with insider knowledge who put their experiences with complex situations such as living with psychiatric difficulties to work for the benefit of others. A special issue of The International Journal of Narrative Therapy and Community Work (2007: Volume 2) focuses on the work of experience consultants, toward re-visioning mental health services that establish a partnership between experience and professional knowledge.

[36] David Epston, private communication.

[37] David Epston often requires anywhere from a third to 50 percent of the letter to be in the person's words, to encourage really listening to what is actually said.

[38] Ellie an early childhood provider, offered this story as an illustration of why practitioners need to listen to what is most important to family members – to remember to ask the cook – as they develop systems of care.

[39] Portions of this chapter section originally appeared in Sax, P. (2007). Finding common ground: Parents speak out about family centered practices. *Journal of Systemic Therapies, 26*(3), 72-90.

[40] Random House Unabridged Dictionary, © Random House, Inc. 2006.

[41] I gathered information about apprenticeship from online sources: A Dictionary of British History. Copyright © 2001, 2004 by Oxford University Press. All rights reserved. I used material from the Wikipedia article "Apprenticeship." Wikipedia information about apprenticeship is licensed under the GNU Free Documentation License

[42] I did this as a way to practice my new voice recognition software, which made for some peculiar shifts in language at times. I thought this practice was a good reminder to not take ourselves too seriously.

[43] Many colleagues have generously shared their teaching practices with me. This includes: Phil Decter, Betsy Buckley, Steven Gilbert, Chris Behan, Aileen Cheshire; Gene Combs, David Epston, Jill Freedman, Dorothea Lewis, Wally McKenzie, Bill Madsen, Marilyn O'Neill, Sallyann Roth and Gaye Stockell.

[44] The "Interviewing Insider Knowledge" exercise was co-constructed by David Epston and Joel Fay in Hamner Springs, New Zealand, December, 2006.

[45] I co-developed this exercise with Jennifer Andrews in the summer of 2004 when we discovered that we were simultaneously teaching similar courses. Our students joined up on the same website to write letters to each other.

REFERENCES

Adams, P., & Nelson, K. (Eds.). (1995). *Reinventing human services: Community- and family-centered practice.* New York: Aldine deGruyter.

Andersen, T. (1987). The reflecting team: Dialogue and meta-dialogue in clinical work. *Family Process, 26,* 415–428.

Andersen, T. (1991). *The reflecting team: Dialogues and dialogues about the dialogues.* New York, NY: Norton.

Anderson, H. (1997). *Conversation, language and possibilities.* New York, NY: Basic Books.

Anderson, H., & Goolishian, H. (1986). Systems consultation with agencies dealing with domestic violence. In L. C. Wynne, S. H. McDaniel, & T. T. Weber (Eds.), *Systems consultation: A new perspective for family therapy* (pp. 284–299). New York, NY: Guilford.

Apple, M. W. (2000, 2002). *Official knowledge: Democratic education in a conservative age.* New York, NY: Routledge.

Apple, M. W. (2003). *The state and the politics of knowledge.* New York, NY: Routledge.

Argyris, C. (1993). *Knowledge for action: A guide to overcoming barriers to organizational change.* San Francisco, CA: Jossey-Bass.

Argyris, C., & Schon, D. A. (1974). *Theory in practice: Increasing professional effectiveness.* San Francisco, CA: Jossey-Bass.

Argyris, C., & Schon, D. A. (1996). *Organizational learning II.* Reading, MA: Addison Wesley.

Bakhtin, M. M., Emerson, C., & Holquist, M. (1990). *The dialogic imagination.* Austin, TX: University of Texas Press.

Bateson, G. (1972). *Steps to an ecology of mind.* New York: Ballantine.

Beasley, C. (1999). *What is feminism? An introduction to feminist theory.* Thousand Oaks, CA: Sage.

Beels, C. C. (2001). *"A Different Story...:" The rise of narrative in psychotherapy.* Phoenix, AZ: Zeig, Tucker & Theisen.

Behan, C. (1999). Linking lives around shared themes: Narrative group therapy with gay men. *Gecko, 2,* 18–34.

Behan, C. (2003). Some ground to stand on: Supervision in narrative therapy. *Journal of Systemic Therapies, Volume 22*(4).

Belenky, M., Clinchy, B., & Goldberger, N., et al. (1986). *Women's ways of knowing.* New York, NY: Basic Books.

Berge, Z. (1997). Computer conferencing and the on-line classroom. *International Journal of Educational Telecommunications, 3*(1), 3–21.

Bird, J. (2001, September). *To do no harm.* Paper presented at the Inaugural Pan Pacific Family Therapy Congress.

Bonk, C. J., Graham, C. R., & Cross, J. (2005). *The handbook of blended learning: Global perspectives, local designs.* New York: Wiley.

Briar-Lawson, K., Lawson, H. A., & Hennon, C. B., et al. (2001). *Family-centered policies and practices: International implications.* New York: Columbia University Press.

Bromwich, R. (1981). *Working with parents of infants: An interactional approach.* Baltimore, MD: University Park Press.

Bronfenbrenner, U. (1979). *The ecology of human development: Experiments by nature and design.* Cambridge, MA: Harvard University Press.

REFERENCES

Brookfield, S. (1986). *Understanding and facilitating adult learning: A comprehensive analysis of principles and effective practices*. San Francisco, CA: Jossey-Bass.

Brookfield, S. (1990). *The skillful teacher: On technique, trust and responsiveness in the classroom*. San Franscico, CA: Jossey-Bass.

Brookfield, S. (1995). *Becoming a critically reflective teacher*. San Francisco: Jossey Bass.

Bruner, J. (1986). *Actual minds, possible worlds*. Cambridge, MA: Harvard University Press.

Bruner, J. (1990). *Acts of meaning*. Cambridge, MA: Harvard University Press.

Brynelsen, D., & Sax, P. (1980). Working together. In *A handbook for parents and professionals*. Vancouver, British Columbia: National Institute on Mental Retardation and British Columbians for Mentally Handicapped people.

Buckley, E., & Decter, P. (2006). *The three streams of ethics* (handout). Boston, MA.

Buckley, E., & Decter, P. (2008). The hot seat: An exercise in narrative practice. *The International Journal of Narrative Therapy and Community Work, 1*, 51–53.

Burr, V. (1995). *An introduction to social constructionism*. London: Routledge.

Caplan, P. (1998). "Mother blaming". In M. Ladd-Taylor & L. Umansky (Eds.), *"Bad" mothers: The politics of blame in twentieth-century America* (pp. 127–144). New York, NY: New York University Press.

Caplan, P. (2000). *The new "Don't blame mother"*. New York, NY: Routledge.

Carey, M., & Russell, S. (2003). Re-authoring: Some answers to commonly asked questions. *The International Journal of Narrative Therapy and Community Work, 3*, 60–71.

Chickering, W., & Ehrmann, S. C. (1996). Implementing the seven principles: Technology as lever. *American Association for Higher Education, October*, 3–6.

Cohee, G. (2004). Feminist teaching. *The Teaching Exchange*.

Collective, C. (1999). *Narrative therapy and community work*. Paper presented at the Dulwich Centre Publications' Narrative Therapy and Community Work Conference, Adelaide, South Australia.

Crocket, K., Kotzé, E., & Flintoff, V. (2007). Reflections on shaping the ethics of or teaching practices. *Journal of Systemic Therapies, 26*(3), 29–42.

Cushman, P. (1995). *Constructing the self, constructing America: A cultural history of psychotherapy. psychotherapy*. Reading, MA.: Addison-Wesley Pub. Co.

Davies, B., & Harré, R. (1990). Positioning: The discursive positioning of selves. *Journal for the Theory of Social Behaviour, 20*(1), 43–63.

Davies, C. (2000). Care and transformation of professionalism. In C. Davies, L. Finlay, & A. Bullman (Eds.), *Changing practice in health and social care*. London: Sage.

Dean, J. (1996). *Solidarity of strangers: Feminism after identity politics*. Berkeley, CA: University of California Press.

Del Piero, C. J. (1983). Un-covering the passion of dis-covery: Reflections on criteria for a feminist theology as applied to feminist pedagogy. Unpublished paper.

Denborough, D. (2004). Narrative therapy and research. *The International Journal of Narrative Therapy and Community Work, 2*, 29–36.

Derrida, J. (1978). *Writing and difference*. Chicago, Ill: University of Chicago Press.

Dunst, C. J., Trivette, C. M., & Cross, A. H. (1988). Social support networks of Appalachian and non-Appalachian families with handicapped children: Relationship to personal and family well-being. In S. Keefe (Ed.), *Mental health in Appalachia*. Lexington: University of Kentucky Press.

Dunst, C. J., Trivette, C. M., & Davis, M., et al. (1994). Characteristics of effective helpgiving practices. In C. Dunst & C. Trivette (Eds.), *Supporting and strengthening families: Methods strategies and practices* (Vol. 1, pp. 171–186).

Dunst, C., Trivette, C., & Deal, A. (1988). *Enabling and empowering families: Principles and guidelines for practice*. Cambridge, MA: Brookline Books.

Dunst, C., Trivette, C., & Deal, A. (Eds.). (1994). *Supporting & strengthening families. Volume 1: Methods, strategies and practices*. Cambridge, MA: Brookline Books.

Dunst, C., Trivette, C., & Thompson, R. (1991). Supporting and strengthening family functioning: Toward a congruence between principles and practice. In D. Unger & D. Powells (Eds.), *Families as nurturing systems: Support across the life span* (pp. 19–44). New York, NY: Hawthorn Press.

Ellinor, L., & Gerard, G. (1998). *Dialogue: Rediscover the transforming power of conversation.* New York, NY: John Wiley & Sons.

Epston, D. (1998). *"Catching up" with David Epston: A collection of narrative practice-based papers published between 1991 & 1996.* Adelaide, South. Australia: Dulwich Centre Publications.

Epston, D. (1998). *'Catching up' with David Epston: A collection of narrative practice-based papers published between 1991 & 1996.* Adelaide, S. Australia: Dulwich Centre Publications.

Epston, D. (1999). Co-research: The making of an alternative knowledge. In *Narrative therapy and community work?: A conference collection* (pp. 137–157). Adelaide, South. Australia: Dulwich Centre Publications.

Epston, D. (2003). Guest editorial. *New Zealand Social Work Review, XV15*(4), 1–3.

Epston, D. (2003, December 12). The Inner-view., *Workshop, December 12.* Family Institute of Cambridge.

Epston, D. (2003a). Guest editorial. *New Zealand Social Work Review, XV*(4), 1-3.

Epston, D. (2003b). The Inner-view, *Workshop, December 12.* Family Institute of Cambridge.

Epston, D. (2004). From empathy to ethnography: The origin of therapeutic co-research. *The International Journal of Narrative Therapy and Community Work, 2,* 31.

Epston, D. (2006). Email correspondence.

Epston, D., & White, M. (1992). Consulting your consultants: The documentation of alternative knowledge. In D. Epston & M. White (Eds.), *Experience, contradiction, narrative & imagination* (pp. 11–26). S. Adelaide, South. Australia: Dulwich Centre Publications.

Epston, D., Gavin, R., & Napan, K. (2004). On becoming a just practitioner: Experimenting with the final paper of an undergraduate programme as a rite of passage. *Social Work Review (New Zealand), summer,* 38–49.

Epston, D., Lakusta, C., & Tomm, K. (2006). Haunting from the future: A congenial approach to parent-child conflicts. *The International Journal of Narrative Therapy and Community Work, 2,* 61–70.

Epston, D., Rennie, G., & Napan, K. (2004). On becoming a just practitioner: Experimenting with the final paper of an undergraduate programme as a rite of passage. *Social Work Review (New Zealand), Summer,* 38-49.

Forgiveness and Reconciliation. . New York, NY: Routledge.

Foucault, M. (1973). *The order of things: An archaelogy of the human sciences.* New York, NY: Vintage Books.

Foucault, M. (1980). *Power/Knowledge: Selected interviews and other writings.* New York, NY: Pantheon Books.

Foucault, M. (Ed.). (1988). *The political technology of individuals.* Amherst, MA: The University of Massachusetts Press.

Fox, H. (2003). Using therapeutic documents - A review. *The International Journal of Narrative Therapy and Community Work, 4,* 26–36.

Freedman, E. B. (2002). *No turning back: The history of feminism and the future of women.* New York, NY: Ballantine Books (Random House).

Freedman, J., & Combs, G. (1996a). *Narrative therapy: The social construction of preferred realities.* New York, NY: W. W. Norton.

Freedman, J., & Combs, G. (1996b). Opening space for new stories. In *Narrative therapy: The social construction of preferred realities* (pp. 42-76). New York, NY: Norton.

Freeman, J., Epston, D., & Lobovits, D. (1997). *Playful approaches to serious problems: Narrative therapy with children and their families.* New York, NY: Norton.

Freeman, J., Epston, D., & Lobovits, D. (1997a). Building a narrative through letters. In *Playful approaches to serious problems* (pp. 112–124). New York, NY: Norton.

REFERENCES

Freire, P. (1973). *Pedagogy of the oppressed*. New York, NY: Continuum.

Freire, P. (1994). *Pedagogy of hope*. New York, NY: Continuum.

Freire, P. (1996). *Letters to Cristina: Reflections on my life and work*. New York, NY: Routledge.

Friedman, S. (Ed.). (1995). *The reflecting team in action*. New York, NY: Guilford.

Funaro, G. M., & Montell, F. (1999). Pedagogical roles and implementation guidelines for online communication tools. *ALN, 3*(2).

Gaddis, S. (2004). Re-positioning traditional research: Centring clients'' accounts in the construction of professional therapy knowledges. *The International Journal of Narrative Therapy and Community Work, 2*, 37–48.

Geertz, C. (1973). Thick description: Toward an interpretive theory of culture. In C. Geertz (Ed.), *The interpretation of cultures*. New York, NY: Basic Books.

Geertz, C. (1983). *Local knowledge: Further essays in interpretive anthropology*. New York, NY: Basic Books.

Geertz, C. (1986). Making experiences, authoring selves. In E. Bruner & V. Turner (Eds.), *The anthropology of experience*. Chicago: University of Illinois Press.

Gilligan, C. (1982). *In a different voice*. Cambridge, MA: Harvard University Press.

Hancock, F., & Epston, D. (2008). The craft and art of narrative inquiry in organization contexts. In D. Barry & H. Hansen (Eds.), The Sage handbook of new approaches to management and organization. London: Sage, p. 482–502.

Hancock, F., Chilcott, J., & Epston, D. (2007). Glen Innes visioning project: Documenting a tacit community vision. In L. Chile (Ed.), *Community development practice in New Zealand: Exploring good practice* (pp. 117–141). Auckland, New Zealand: AUT University.

Harasim, L., Hiltz, S. R., & Teles, L., et al. (1997). *Learning networks: A field guide to teaching and learning online*. Cambridge, MA: The MIT Press.

Hare-Mustin, R. T. (1994). Discourses in the mirrored room: A postmodern analysis of therapy. *Family Process, 33*, 9–35.

Hayward, M. (2006). Using a scaffolding distance map with a young man and his family. *The International Journal of Narrative Therapy and Community Work, 1*, 39–51.

Hedtke, L. (2003). Grief takes a holiday: Different kinds of conversations about bereavement and legacy. In *Andrews & Clark explorations*. Los Angeles: Master's Work.

Heinze, A., & Procter, C. (2004). *Reflections on the use of blended learning*. Paper presented at the Education in a changing environment conference proceedings. Education Development Unit.

Helgesen, S. (1995). *The web of inclusion*. New York: Bantam Doubleday.

Hoffman, L. (1992). A reflexive stance for family therapy. In S. McNamee & K. Gergen (Eds.), *Therapy as social construction* (pp. 7–24). London: Sage Publications.

Hoffman, L. (1993). *Exchanging voices: A collaborative approach to family therapy*. London: Karnac Books.

Hoffman, L. (2002). *Family therapy: An intimate history*. New York, NY: Norton.

Hooks, B. (1989). Toward a revolutionary feminist pedagogy. In *Talking back: Thinking feminist, thinking black* (pp. 49–54). Cambridge, MA: South End Press.

Janis, I. L. (1972). *Victims of groupthink*. Boston, MA: Houghton Mifflin Co.

Janis, I. L. (1982). *Groupthink: Psychological studies of policy decisions and fiascoes* (Second edition). New York, NY: Houghton Mifflin.

Jordan, J. V. (Ed.). (1997). *Women's growth in diversity: More writings from the Stone Center*. New York, NY: Guilford.

Jordan, J. V., Kaplan, A. G., & Miller, J. B., et al. (Eds.). (1991). *Women's growth in connection: Writings from the Stone Center*. New York, NY: Guilford.

Jorniak, E., & Paré, D. A. (2007). Teaching narrative therapy in Russia. *Journal of Systemic Therapies, 26*(3), 57–71.

Kagan, S. L., Powell, D. R., & Weissbourd, B., et al. (Eds.). (1987). *America's family support programs: The origins and development of a movement.* New Haven, CT: Yale University Press.

Keeney, B. (1983). *The aesthetics of change.* New York, NY: Guilford.

Kinney, J., Strand, K., & Hagerup, M., et al. (1994). *Beyond the buzzwords: Key principles in effective frontline practice.* Fall Church, VA: Jointly published by Tthe National Center for Service Integration and Tthe National Resource Center for Family Support Programs.

Kisthardt, W. E. (1992). A strengths model of case management: The principles and function of a helping partnership with persons with persistent mental illness. In D. Saleebey (Ed.), *The strengths perspective in social work practice* (pp. 59–83). White Plains:, NY: Longman.

Knowles, M. S. (1984). *Andragogy in action: Applying modern principles of adult education.* San Francisco: Jossey-Bass.

Knowles, M. S. (1989). *The making of an adult educator.* San Fransisco, CA: Jossey-Bass.

Lawrence-Lightfoot, S. (2000). *Respect: An exploration.* Cambridge, MA: Perseus Books.

Lax, W. D. (1995). Offering reflections: Some theoretical and practical considerations. In S. Friedman (Ed.), *The reflecting team in action: Collaborative practice in family therapy* (pp. 145–166). New York, NY: Guilford.

Lewis, D., & Cheshire, A. (2007). Te Whakaakona: Teaching and learning as one. *Journal of Systemic Therapies, 26*(3), 43–56.

Lobovits, D. (2007). Narrative Approaches.com: http://www.narrativeapproaches.com/

Lobovits, D. H., Maisel, R. L., & Freeman, J. C. (1995). Public practices: An ethic of circulation. In S. Friedman (Ed.), *The reflecting team in action: Collaborative practice in family therapy* (pp. 223–256). New York, NY: Guilford.

Lobovits, D., & Epston, D. (2007). *Archive of Rresistance: Anti-anorexia/anti-bulimia.* http://www.narrativeapproaches.com/

Lobovitz, D. H., Maisel, R. L., & Freeman, J. C. (1995). Public practices: An ethic of circulation. In S. Friedman (Ed.), *The reflecting team in action: Collaborative practice in family therapy* (pp. 223–256). New York, NY: Guiford.

Lussardi, D., & Miller, D. (1990). A reflecting team approach to adolescent substance abuse. In T. C. Todd & M. Selekman (Eds.), *Family therapy with adolescent substance abuse* (pp. 227–240). New York, NY: Norton.

Lysack, M. (2006). Developing one's own voice as a therapist: A dialogic approach to therapist education. *Journal of Systemic Therapies, 25*(4), 84–96.

Madigan, S. (1999). Inscription, description and deciphering chronic identities. In I. Parker (Ed.), *Deconstructing psychotherapy.* London: Sage.

Madigan, S. (2007). Anticipating hope within written and naming domains of despair. In C. Flaskas, I. McCarthy, & J. Sheehan (Eds.), *In Hope and despair in narrative and family therapy: Adversity, forgiveness and reconciliation.* New York, NY: Routledge.

Madsen, W. (2007a). *Collaborative therapy with multi-stressed families* (2nd ed.). New York, NY: Guildford.

Madsen, W. (2007b). Working with multi-stressed families: Recognizing the importance of relational stance. In W. Madsen (Ed.), *Collaborative therapy with multi-stressed families* (pp. 15–45). New York, NY: Guilford.

Madsen, W. (2007c). Working within traditional structures to support a collaborative clinical practice. *The International Journal of Narrative Therapy and Community Work, 2,* 51–61.

Maisel, R., Epston, D., & Borden, A. (2004). *Biting the hand that starves you: Inspiring resistance to anorexia/bulimia.* New York, NY: Norton.

Marsten, D., & Howard, G. (2006). Shared influence: A narrative approach to teaching narrative therapy. *Journal of Systemic Therapies, 25*(4), 97–110.

Maturana, H. R., & Varela, F. J. (1987). *The tree of knowledge: The biological roots of human understanding.* Boston, MA: Shambala.

REFERENCES

McGoldrick, M., Anderson, C. M., & Walsh, F. (Eds.). (1991). *Women in families: A framework for family therapy.* New York, NY: Norton.

McKeachie, W. J., & Svinicki (Eds.). (2006). *Teaching tips: Strategies, research, and theory for college and university teachers.* Boston, MA: Houghton Mifflin Co.

Mckenzie, W., & Monk, G. (1997). Learning and teaching narrative ideas. In G. Monk, J. Winslade, K. Crocket, & D. Epston (Eds.), *Narrative therapy in practice: The archaeology of hope* (pp. 82–120). 120). San Francisco, CA: Jossey-Bass.

McLeod, J. (1997, 2001). *Narrative and psychotherapy* Thousand Oaks, CA: Sage.

McNamee, S., & Gergen, K. (Eds.). (1992). *Therapy as social construction.* London: Sage.

Miller, J. B. (1986). *Toward a new psychology of women.* Boston: Beacon Press.

Monk, G., Winslade, J., Crocket, K., et al. (Eds.). (1997). *Narrative therapy in action: The archeology of hope.* San Francisco, CA: Jossey Bass.

Morgan, A. (2000a). Rituals and celebrations. In *What is narrative therapy?* (pp. 111–115). Adelaide, South. Australia: Dulwich Centre Publications.

Morgan, A. (2000b). *What is narrative therapy: An easy-to-read introduction.* Adelaide, South Australia: Dulwich Centre Publications.

Myerhoff, B. (1982). Life history among the elderly: Performance, visibility and remembering. In J. Ruby (Ed.), *A crack in the mirror: Reflexive perspectives in anthropology.* Chicago: University of Illinois Press.

Myerhoff, B. (1986). Life not death in Venice: Its second life. In V. W. Turner & E. M. Bruner (Eds.), *The anthropology of experience* (pp. 261–286). Chicago, Ill.: University of Illinois Press.

Paré, D. A. (1996). Culture and meaning: Expanding the metaphorical repertoire of family therapy. *Family Process, 35,* 21–42.

Paré, D. A. (2007). Taking a position: Therapist training and the politics of meaning. *Journal of Systemic Therapies, 26*(3), 11–14.

Paré, D., & Tarragona, M. (2006). Generous pedagogy: Teaching and learning postmodern therapies. *Journal of Systemic Therapies, 25*(4), 1–7.

Parton, N. (2003). Rethinking professional practice: The contributions of social constructionism and the feminist ethic of care. *British Journal of Social Work, 33*(1), 1–16.

Parton, N., & O'Byrne, P. (2000). *Constructive social work: Towards a new practice.* New York: St. Martin's Press.

Payne, M. (2000). *Narrative therapy: An introduction for counsellors.* Thousand Oaks, CA: Sage.

Poertner, J., & Ronnau, J. (1992). A strengths approach to children with emotional disabilities. In *A strengths perspective in social work practice* (pp. 111–121). White Plains, NY: Longman.

Program, A. F. D. T. (n.d). *Moving to the next level: The pedagogical role of discussion.*

Ragan, L. C. (1999). Good teaching is good teaching: An emerging set of guiding principles for the design and development of distance education. *Cause/Effect, 22*(1).

Reason, P. (1988). *Human inquiry in action.* Thousand Oaks, CA: Sage.

Reason, P. (1994a). Three approaches to participative inquiry. In N. Denzin & Y. Lincoln (Eds.), *Handbook of Qualitative Research* (pp. 324–339): Sage.

Reason, P. (Ed.). (1994b). *Participation in human inquiry.* Thousand Oaks:, CA: Sage.

Reason, P., & Rowan, J. (1994). *Human inquiry: A sourcebook of new paradigm research.* Chichester, UK: John Wiley & Sons.

Ritchie, D. C., & Hoffman, B. (1996, March 9, 1996). *Using instructional design principles to amplify learning on the World Wide Web.* Retrieved July 7, 2002, from http://edweb.sdsu.edu/clrit/WWWInstrdesign/WWWInstrDesign.html

Rombach, M. A. M. (2003). An inviation to therapeutic letter writing. *Journal of Systemic Therapies, 22*(1), 15–31.

Rosenberg, L. C. (1991). Update on National Science Foundation finding of the "collaboaratory". *Communications of the ACM, 34*(12), 83.

Roth, S. (2002). *The document as an extension and continuation of meetings.*Unpublished manuscript, Medford, MA.

Roth, S. (2007). From the theory to the practice of inquiring collaboratively: An exercise in and clinical example of an interviewee guided interview. In H. Anderson & D. Gehart (Eds.), *Collaborative therapy: Relationships and conversations that make a difference* (pp. 337–350). New York: Routledge [sallyannroth@comcast.net].

Roth, S., Epston, D., & Weingarten, K. (1998). *Creating a document to 'hold a fresh direction': the letter.* Unpublished manuscript, Watertown, MA.

Russell, S., & Carey, M. (2002). Re-membering: Responding to commonly asked questions. *The International Journal of Narrative Therapy and Community Work, 3,* 23–31.

Russell, S., & Carey, M. (2003). Outsider-witness practices: Some answers to commonly asked questions. *International Journal of Narrrative Therapy and Community Work, 1,* 3–16.

Russell, S., & Carey, M. (2004). *Narrative therapy: Responding to your questions.* Adelaide, South. Australia: Dulwich Centre Publications.

Saleebey, D. (2002). *The strengths perspective in social work practice.* Boston, MA: Longman/Allyn & Bacon.

Salter, C. (2001). Attention, class!!! 16 ways to be a smarter teacher. *FC, (53),* 114.

Sameroff, A. J., & Chandler, M. J. (1974). Reproductive risk and the continuum of caretaking casualty. In F. Horowitz, Hetherington, S. Scarr-Salapatek, & G. Siegel (Eds.), *Review of child development research* (Vol. 4). Chicago, IL: University of Chicago Press.

Sax, P. (1981). *Facilitating communication between mothers and infants with special needs: A rationale and guidelines for professionals.* Unpublished major paper submitted in partial fulfillment for Master of Education degree, University of British Columbia, Vancouver, British Columbia.

Sax, P. (2000). *Finding common ground between human service seekers, providers and planners: a reauthoring conversations approach.* Santa Barbara, CA: The Fielding Institute, Santa Barbara, CA.

Sax, P. (2003). It takes an audience to solve a problem: Teaching narrative therapy online. *New Zealand Social Work Review, XV*(4), 21–29.

Sax, P. (2006). Developing stories of identity as reflective practitioners. *Journal of Systemic Therapies, 25*(4), 59–72.

Sax, P. (2007). Finding common ground: Parents speak out about family centered practices. *The Journal of Systemic Therapies, 26*(3), 72–90.

Sax, P. (2007a). Constructing preferred identities as social workers. *Narrative Network News, March,* 42–50.

Schon, D. A. (1983). *The reflective practitioner: How professionals think in action.* New York: Basic Books.

Schon, D. A. (1987). *Educating the reflective practitioner: Towards a new design for teaching and learning in the professions.* New York: Basic Books.

Schorr, L. (1991). Attributes of effective services for young children: A brief survey of current knowledge and its implications for program and policy development. In L. Schorr, D. Both, & C. Copple (Eds.), *Effective services for young children* (pp. 23–47). Washington, D. C.: National Academy Press.

Schorr, L. B. (1997). *Common purpose: Strengthening families and neighborhoods to rebuild America.* New York: Doubleday.

Sevenhuijsen, S. (1998). *Citizenship and the ethics of care. Feminist consideration on justice, morality and politics.* London: Routledge.

Sheppard, M., Newstead, S., & DiCaccavo, A., et al. (2000). Reflexivity and the development of process knowledge in social work: A classification and empirical study. *British Journal of Social Worki, 30*(4), 465–488.

Simonson, M., Smaldino, S. E., & Albright, M., et al. (2006). *Teaching and learning at a distance: Foundations of distance education, 3/E.* Upper Saddle River, NJ: Merrill Prentice-Hall.

REFERENCES

Smith, C., & Nylund, D. (Eds.). (1997). *Narrative therapies with children and adolescents.* New York, NY: Guilford Press.

Stringer, E. (1996). *Action research: A handbook for practitioners:.* Thousand Oaks, CA: Sage.

Stroul, B. A. (Ed.). (1996). *Children's mental health: Creating systems of care in a changing society.* Baltimore, MD: Paul H. Brookes Publishing Co.

Stroul, B. A., & Friedman, R. M. (1988). Principles for a system of care. *Children Today, 17,* 11–15.

Tamasese, K., & Waldergrave, C. (1993). Cultural and gender accountability in the "Just Therapy" approach. *Journal of Feminist Family Therapy, 5,* 29–45.

Tamasese, K., Waldegrave, C., & Tuhaka, F., et al. (1998). Further conversation about partnerships of accountability. *Dulwich Centre Journal, 4,* 50–62.

Thomas, L. (2002). Poststructuralism and therapy - What's it all about? *Dulwich Centre Newsletter, 2,* 2, 76–84.

Tinker, R. (1997). Netcourses reform education using the power of the internet. *The Concord Consortium Newsletter, Spring.*

Tronto, J. C. (1993). *Moral boundaries: A political argument for an ethic of care.* New York, NY: Routledge.

Ungar, M. (2004). Surviving as a postmodern social worker: Two Ps and three Rs of direct practice. *National Association of Social Workers, 49*(3), 488–496.

Vella, J. (1995a). *Learning to listen, learning to teach: The power of dialogue in educating adults.* San Francisco, CA: Jossey-Bass.

Vella, J. (1995b). *Training through dialogue: Promoting effective learning and change with adults.* San Francisco, CA: Jossey-Bass.

Vodde, R., & Gallant, J. P. (2003). Bridging the gap between micro and macro practice: Large scale change and a unified model of narrative-deconstructive practice. *New Zealand Social Work Review, XV*(4), 4–13.

Vygotsky, L. (1986). *Thought and language* (A. Kozulin, Trans.). Cambridge, MA: MIT Press.

Waldergrave, C., Tamasese, K., & Tuhaka, T., et al. (2003). *Just therapy - A journey: A collection of papers from the Just Therapy Team, New Zealand.* Adelaide, South. Australia: Dulwich Centre Publications.

Walnum, E. (2007). Sharing stories: The work of an experience consultant. *The International Journal of Narrative Therapy and Community Work, 2,* 3–9.

Weimer, M. (2002). *Learner-centered teaching: Five key changes to practice.* San Francisco, CA: Jossey-Bass.

Weine, S. (2006). *Testimony after catastrophe: Narrating the traumas of political violence.* Evanston, IL: Northwestern University Press.

Welch, S. D. (1989). *A feminist ethic of risk.* Minneapolis, MN: Fortress Press.

Welch, S. D. (1999). *Sweet dreams in America: Making ethics and spirituality work.* New York, NY: Routledge.

White, C., & Denborough, D. (2005). Developing training courses which are congruent with narrative ideas. In C. White & D. Denborough (Eds.), *A community of ideas: Behind the scenes* (pp. 101–126). Adelaide, South. Australia: Dulwich Centre Publications.

White, M. (1988). The process of questioning: A therapy of literary merit? *Dulwich Centre Newsletter, Winter,* 8–14.

White, M. (1991). Deconstruction and therapy. *Dulwich Centre Newsletter, No. 3.*

White, M. (1992). Family therapy training and supervision in a world of experience and narrative. In D. Epston & M. White (Eds.), *Experience, contradiction, narrative & imagination* (pp. 75–96). Adelaide, South. Australia: Dulwich Centre Publications.

White, M. (1993). Commentary: The histories of the present. In S. Gilligan & R. Price (Eds.), *Therapeutic conversations* (Vol. 1, pp. 121–135). New York, NY: Norton.

White, M. (1994). *Best of friends*. Los Angeles: Masterswork. Retrieved from www.masterswork.com

White, M. (1995). Reflecting teamwork as definitional ceremony. In M. White (Ed.), *Re-authoring lives: Interviews & essays* (pp. 172–198). Adelaide:, South. Australia: Dulwich Centre Publications.

White, M. (1995). Therapeutic documents revisited. In *Re-authoring lives* (pp. 199–213). Adelaide, South. Australia: Dulwich Centre Publications.

White, M. (1995a). *Re-authoring lives: Interviews and essays* (Vol. 3). Adelaide, South Australia: Dulwich Centre Publications.

White, M. (1995b). Reflecting teamwork as definitional ceremony. In M. White (Ed.), *Re-Aauthoring lives: Interviews & essays* (pp. 172–198). Adelaide:, South. Australia: Dulwich Centre Publications.

White, M. (1997a). *Narratives of therapists' lives*. Adelaide, South. Australia: Dulwich Centre Publications.

White, M. (1997b). Training as 'co-research'. In M. White (Ed.), *Narratives of therapists' lives*. Adelaide, South Australia: Dulwich Centre Publications.

White, M. (1997c). Decentered practice. In *Narratives of therapists' lives* (pp. 200–214). Adelaide, South. Australia: Dulwich Centre Publications.

White, M. (1997d). Narrative therapy and poststructuralism. In *Narratives of therapists' lives* (pp. 220–231). Adelaide, South. Australia: Dulwich Centre Publications.

White, M. (1997e). *Narratives of therapists' lives*. Adelaide, South. Australia: Dulwich Centre Publications.

White, M. (1997f). The politics of practice. In M. White (Ed.), *Narratives of therapists' lives* (pp. 117–192). Adelaide, South. Australia: Dulwich Centre Publications.

White, M. (1997g). Training as 'co-research'. In M. White (Ed.), *Narratives of therapists' lives*. Adelaide, South Australia: Dulwich Centre Publications.

White, M. (2000a). Re-engaging with history: The absent but implicit. In M. White (Ed.), *Reflections on narrative practice* (pp. 35–58). Adelaide:, South Australia: Dulwich Centre Publications.

White, M. (2000b). *Reflections on narrative practice*. Adelaide, South. Australia: Dulwich Centre Publications.

White, M. (2001). Narrative practice and the unpacking of identity conclusions. *Gecko: A journal of deconstruction and narrative practice, 1*.

White, M. (2002). Addressing personal failure. *Dulwich Centre Newsletter, 3*, 33–76.

White, M. (2003a). Narrative practice and community assignments. *International Journal of Narrative Therapy and Community Work, 2*, 17–55.

White, M. (2003b). Workshop notes. Retrieved from www.dulwichcentre.com.au.

White, M. (2004a). Narrative practice, couple therapy and conflict dissolution. In M. White (Ed.), *Narrative practice and exotic lives: Resurrecting diversity in everyday life* (pp. 1–41). Adelaide, South. Australia: Dulwich Centre Publications.

White, M. (2004b). Folk psychology and narrative practice. In *Narrative practice and exotic lives: Resurrecting diversity in everyday life* (pp. 59–118). Adelaide:, South Australia: Dulwich Centre Publications.

White, M. (2004c). *Narrative practice and exotic lives: Resurrecting diversity in everyday life*. Adelaide, South. Australia: Dulwich Centre Publications.

White, M. (2004d, September 30–October 2). *Narrative practice with Michael White*. Second Annual Working Together Conference, Portland, Maine.

White, M. (2004e). *New modalities in narrative practice*. Workshop, Bridges, Halifax, Nova Scotia.

White, M. (2005). Children, trauma and subordinate storyline development. *The International Journal of Narrative Therapy and Community Work, 3 & 4*, 10–21.

White, M. (2007a). Conversations that highight unique outcomes. In M. White (Ed.), *Maps of narrative practice* (pp. 219–262). New York, NY: Norton.

REFERENCES

White, M. (2007b). Definitional ceremonies. In *Narrative maps of practice* (pp. 165–218). New York, NY: Norton.

White, M. (2007c). *Maps of narrative practice*. Colchester, Vermont: Family Therapy of Vermont (Conference).

White, M. (2007d). *Maps of narrative practice*. New York, NY: Norton.

White, M. (2007e). Re-authoring conversations. In M. White (Ed.), *Maps of narrative practice* (pp. 61–128). New York, NY: Norton.

White, M., & Epston, D. (1990a). *Narrative means to therapeutic ends*. New York, NY: Norton.

White, M., & Epston, D. (1990b). A storied therapy. In *Narrative means to therapeutic ends* (pp. 77–163). New York, NY: Norton.

White, W. (2007f). Scaffolding conversations. In *Maps of narrative practice* (pp. 263–290). New York, NY: Norton.

Wiliams, F. (1999). Good-enough principles for welfare. *Journal of Social Policy, 28*(4), 667–687.

Winslade, J. (2003). Storying professional identity. *International Journal of Narrative Therapy and Community Work, 3*.

Winslade, J., Crocket, K., & Monk, G., et al. (2000). The storying of professional development. In K. Eriksen & G. McAuliffe (Eds.), *Preparing counselors and therapists: Creating constructivist and developmental programs* (pp. 99–113.). Washington, DC: Association of Counselor Educators and Supervisors.

Wynne, L. C., McDaniel, S. H., & Weber, T. T. (Eds.). (1986). *Systems consultation: A new perspective for family therapy*. New York, NY: Guilford Press.